BRITAIN IN THE AGE OF THE
FRENCH REVOLUTION 1785-1820

Pearson
Education

We work with leading authors to develop the
strongest educational materials in history,
bringing cutting-edge thinking and best learning
practice to a global market.

Under a range of well-known imprints, including
Longman, we craft high quality print and
electronic publications which help readers to
understand and apply their content,
whether studying or at work.

To find out more about the complete range of our
publishing please visit us on the World Wide Web at:
www.pearsoneduc.com

BRITAIN IN THE AGE OF THE FRENCH REVOLUTION 1785–1820

JENNIFER MORI

An imprint of **Pearson Education**

Harlow, England · London · New York · Reading, Massachusetts · San Francisco
Toronto · Don Mills, Ontario · Sydney · Tokyo · Singapore · Hong Kong · Seoul
Taipei · Cape Town · Madrid · Mexico City · Amsterdam · Munich · Paris · Milan

Pearson Education Limited
Edinburgh Gate
Harlow
Essex CM20 2JE
United Kingdom

and Associated Companies throughout the world

Visit us on the World Wide Web at:
www.pearsoneduc.com

_____

First published in Great Britain in 2000

© Pearson Education Limited 2000

ISBN 0-582-23852-8 PPR
ISBN 0-582-23851-X CSD

British Library Cataloguing-in-Publication Data
A CIP catalogue record for this book can be obtained from the British
Library.

Transferred to digital print on demand, 2006
Printed and bound by CPI Antony Rowe, Eastbourne

CONTENTS

CONTENTS

PREFACE

The past two decades have witnessed a general revival of academic interest in all aspects of eighteenth-century British history, in which Britain's response to the French Revolution constitutes a discrete special subject with specialist historiographies of its own. The years from 1780 to 1830 have long occupied an uneasy place in the history of Britain: claimed simultaneously by advocates of a 'long eighteenth century' who emphasise the continuity of social, intellectual and political traditions from 1688 to 1832 and students of a 'modern' Britain presumed to start with the industrial revolution. The 'new' cultural history of the French Revolution pioneered during the past decade has, in its British incarnation, now created a 'long nineteenth century' stretching from 1790 to 1928 and Britain in the age of the French Revolution is now described both as an *ancien régime* confessional state and the cradle of a mass political culture. It is the aim of this book to introduce students to these debates and the research that fuels them through a survey of the politics, diplomacy, strategy, ideas, society and economy of Britain from 1785 to 1815. As this book has been written for an upper-year undergraduate audience, it is assumed that readers possess some rudimentary knowledge of significant names, dates and events of the period.

The French Revolution was loved and hated in Britain, the nation that mounted the most determined intellectual and military resistance to its effects in Europe during the 1790s. The impact of the revolution on British politics and intellectual life therefore constitutes one major theme of this book, explored in its first three chapters. Here Britain's loyalist opponents of the revolution, a long neglected group finally receiving the academic attention its strength and numbers warrant, are examined alongside more familiar radicals and reformers to elucidate the social and intellectual principles that motivated both. Both camps constructed compelling and popular cases in support of their claims: through a survey of these, this book aims to convey some sense of the subtlety, complexity and range of the arguments produced by loyalists and radicals.

Though the British debate on the French Revolution, waged in parliament, the press and public bodies of all descriptions shaped the minds and social cosmologies of a generation, equally important to the culture and politics of the period was the impact of a war waged for twenty-two years against revolutionary and Napoleonic France. The war was an important catalyst of change, accelerating state development in fiscal, military and legal spheres that touched the lives of all Britons. Chapter four deals with the reception of national directives respecting sedition and treason, the poor and religion by individuals and institutions at local levels to explain the paradox of growing metropolitan power in a decentralised state. Readers must jettison twentieth-century assumptions about the all-pervasive powers of parliament, the state and national bodies to understand a world where towns, counties and parishes interpreted central policies in their own ways and and cherished their freedom to do so as a fundamental liberty guaranteed by the constitution. State policies could, moreover, be appropriated by localities to serve specific social and political needs, as demonstrated by Chapter five.

The social and economic consequences of the war are treated in Chapters five and six in tandem with longer-term trends: most notably the 'industrial revolution' and class formation. Labour historians have long seen the origins of a working class in Britain's experience of war and first-stage industrialisation despite the fact that the socio-economic impact of each remains unclear. This book treats war and industrialisation as separate phenomena to assess their effects upon supply and demand patterns, the infrastructure of manufacturing, retail and finance, the wages and working conditions of labour and the re-negotiation of social relationships between rich and poor. The last two chapters of this book survey the military and diplomatic goals for which so much money and manpower were raised between 1793 and 1815.

I have accumulated numerous debts in the writing of this book: to the staff of the Bodleian and the British Library; to the editorial desk at Pearson, who have waited so patiently for this manuscript; to the University of Toronto, for funding this and other research projects; to John Stevenson, for unfailing moral support, and to Barbara Todd, who listened to so much of this book in conceptual form. I must also thank the many friends and colleagues who have saved me from egregious errors: any that remain are my own.

Jennifer Mori
Toronto

ABBREVIATIONS

AJ	*The Anti-Jacobin, or Weekly Political Register* (1799), 2 vols
AJR	*The Anti-Jacobin Review, or Monthly Magazine* (1798–1821)
APLP	Association for the Preservation of Liberty and Property against Republicans and Levellers
BC	*The British Critic* (1793–1828)
BL Add MS	British Library Additional Manuscripts
Canning MS	Harewood Estate Papers, West Yorkshire Record Office, Sheepscar, Leeds
Clements MS	Pitt Papers, W.L. Clements Library, Ann Arbor, Michigan
EIC	East India Company
FO	Foreign Office
FOP	Society of the Friends of the People
HO	Home Office
LCS	London Corresponding Society
LRS	London Revolution Society
MCM	Melville Castle Muniments, Scottish Record Office, West Register House, Edinburgh
MCS	Manchester Constitutional Society
MS	manuscripts
NLW	National Library of Wales, Aberystwyth
PD	*The Parliamentary Debates, from the Year 1803 to the Present Time: Forming a Continuation of the Work entitled 'The Parliamentary History of England from the Earliest Period to the Year 1803'*, ed. W. Cobbett (1804–20), 36 vols
PH	*The Parliamentary History of England, from the Earliest Period to the Year 1803*, ed. W. Cobbett (1806–20), 36 vols
PR	*The Parliamentary Register: or History, Debates and Proceedings of Both Houses of Parliament*, ed. J. Debrett, 2nd series (1781–96), 45 vols; 3rd series (1797–1802), 18 vols
PRO	Public Record Office, Ruskin Avenue, London
RO	Record Office
Rylands MS	Melville Papers, John Rylands University Library of Manchester, Deansgate

SBCP	Society for Bettering the Condition of the Poor
SCI	Society for Constitutional Information
SPCK	Society for Promoting Christian Knowledge
SRM	Society for the Reformation of Manners
SRO	Scottish Record Office, West Register House, Edinburgh
SSV	Society for the Suppression of Vice
UE	United Englishmen
UI	United Irishmen
US	United Scotsmen
WWM	Wentworth Woodhouse Muniments, Sheffield Central Library

CHAPTER ONE

Parties and Politics

Once upon a time, the political history of Britain during the French Revolutionary wars was simple and straightforward. Parliament, for much of the eighteenth century an assembly of independent MPs whose voting preferences were determined primarily by factional and family connections, reacted to the French Revolution by dividing into two groups. William Pitt the Younger, despite a liberal youth, had seemingly taken fright when confronted by the emergence of a militant French Revolution in Europe and democratic parliamentary reform at home. Having taken Britain to war against revolutionary France in 1793, supported by a corps of ministerial MPs who shared his fears, Pitt would superintend the emergence of a new Tory Party committed to the defence of the *status quo ante bellum* in Britain and Europe. A gallant band of liberal Opposition Whigs led by Charles James Fox, in sharp contrast, defended the civil liberties of Britons against the repressive policies of a reactionary government, finally coming to power in 1830 as a proto-Liberal Party.

Like all sharply delineated dichotomies, the division of British politicians into Whigs and Tories obscures the complexities of political theory and practice during the French wars. Although the French Revolution began to divide British high politics into groups that would become the Liberal and Conservative Parties of the nineteenth century, this bipolar split was superimposed over an older Commons comprised of Court, Country and independents that continued to exist up to 1832 (O'Gorman, 1982: 116–21). Pitt and Fox, the two great antagonists of the French wars, were canonised by the Victorians as the founding fathers of the Liberal and Conservative Parties, but these were apotheoses that ignored the many inconsistencies in the thoughts and actions of both men, not to mention the conduct of their contemporary and posthumous admirers. The aristocratic Whiggism of the

1

Foxites made them ambivalent about the wisdom of franchise and electoral reform, so much so that no party line could be laid down on the issue after Fox's death (Mitchell, 1967: 15–17; O'Gorman, 1982: 39–40, 68, 101–2; Smith, 1992: 210–11). The unity of the Pittites had been shattered by the resignation of their leader in 1801 in defence of Catholic Emancipation and they divided thereafter into pro- and anti-emancipation camps for the next three decades (O'Gorman, 1982; Sack, 1987; Harvey, 1978a,b). The nineteenth-century two-party system would be built upon myths of supposed strong leadership and intellectual consistency. The reality was different and much more complex.

Party Politics before the French Revolution, 1785–1789

In 1789 Prime Minister Younger Pitt was thirty years old, having taken office as First Lord of the Treasury in 1783. He was, like the vast majority of MPs, an enemy to the notion of party, believing that it divided a parliament that ought to function as a moderate and consensual body. His cold personality and refusal to curry support in the Commons ensured him a personal following of 52 MPs, only 20 of whom would support him out of office. His government majorities consequently depended upon two groups: the King's Friends, the 185–200 Court MPs who would support any government endorsed by the monarch; and the independent members, whose support could be unreliable but was nevertheless vital to the survival of any administration (O'Gorman, 1989a: 23–5). Anxious as Pitt had been during the 1780s to be a reforming minister, his reliance for survival upon the politics of consensus ensured his pursuit of a flexible and conciliatory conduct that, in the eyes of his critics, bordered upon hypocrisy. Pitt's famous 1785 Reform Bill was never seen again as a comprehensive package of reform measures following its first rejection by the House of Commons. The Irish Commercial Propositions met the same fate. An ambitious though poorly drafted Poor Law amendment bill was withdrawn from parliament in 1796 after widespread criticism of its provisions was expressed within and without doors and, in 1804, Pitt returned to office after promising George III that Catholic Emancipation would not be raised again during the king's lifetime. Pitt predeceased George III by fourteen years.

Pitt's willingness to trim or drop unpopular policies was evident by 1789, and has been blamed upon his subordination to George III, who had in 1783 made him the leader of a minority government to oust the Fox–North coalition (Barnes, 1939). While compromise with the crown was required on some issues of personal importance to the crown, most notably religious toleration, Pitt was not a royal cipher. His decision to oppose Test and Corporation Act repeal in 1787 was partially conditioned by the king's determination to oppose the measure and all who supported it. The premier nonetheless overrode the king's hatred of revolutionary France to make overtures of peace from 1795 to 1797 and, despite George III's open hostility to parliamentary reform, would continue to promote parts of his 1785 reform bill as an independent MP from 1785 to 1789. Before 1792, Pitt's freedom of action was limited by the presence in his Cabinet of several 'King's Friends', most notably Lord Chancellor Thurlow and Home Secretary Lord Sydney. In 1785 it was said that only two members of the Cabinet supported Pitt's reform bill, for the rest sided with the king. From 1789 to 1791, Pitt gained more control over executive decision-making by remodelling the Cabinet through the promotion of Henry Dundas and William Grenville to the posts of Home and Foreign Secretary respectively. In 1792, Pitt challenged George III by threatening to resign unless the obstreperous Thurlow was dismissed: following the king's compliance with the premier's request, Pitt, Grenville and Dundas made state policy with little direct interference from the crown. George III accepted their leadership without question during the 1790s to the extent that, by 1799, all three felt they could force Catholic Emancipation upon the king. In this they were mistaken (Mori, 1997b: 270–1; Mackesy, 1982: 197; Ehrman, 1996: 495–509).

Pitt's willingness to compromise was resented by his old mentor, Earl Shelburne, according to whom the 'economical' reform initiatives of the 1780s were pale shadows of Shelburne's original projects. To the 'Jesuit of Berkeley Square', piqued by his exclusion from Pitt's Cabinets, any deviation from the Shelburnite campaign to cut costs, increase bureaucratic accountability in the offices of state and conduct government in an efficient and rational manner was a betrayal of principle (Norris, 1963: 271–82; Brown, 1967: 101). The tale of Pitt's achievements from the East India Act of 1784 to the establishment of the Consolidated Fund for the redemption of the National Debt in 1786–1787 has been told many times. From it he emerges as a prudent and pragmatic administrative reformer (Ehrman, 1969: Chs 10–11). Seventeen years in power enabled Pitt to make a virtue of expediency, but the ground rules for this system of pragmatism had been laid down by 1789. Pitt's *modus operandi* of statesmanship was essentially Court Whig in conception, as he told a Commons Select Committee on dockyard reform in 1785. His professed subscription to traditional Blackstonian notions of executive power and responsibility and a reluctance to antagonise vested interests in the state bureaucracy militated against acting upon Public Accounts Commission recommendations to introduce

3

'economical reform' during the 1780s (Breihan, 1983: 80–1). These reservations did not prevent him from embarking upon moderate and consensual change in the interests of public welfare where possible. Pitt was no radical, original thinker or doctrinaire bureaucratic reformer, but he was determined in the aftermath of the American War to restore domestic public confidence in the structures and practices of Hanoverian government. This was restorative reform and, though interrupted by the French Revolution, did not stop in 1793 (Mori, 1997b: 39–43; Ehrman, 1969: 282–36, 308–11; Harling, 1996b: 58–63).

This begs the question what, if anything, Pitt learned from his father, the Elder Pitt, whose career appeared to embody the ideals of Country Whig radicalism (Brown, 1963; Robbins, 1959). When divested of the hagiography surrounding his name, Chatham appears as an intensely ambitious politician whose independent Whiggery was preordained by his lesser gentry social roots and exclusion from the circles of the Old Corps. His son's inheritance consisted of little more than a talent for public relations, a hatred of party politics, a spirit of conciliation towards the Thirteen Colonies and, come the war with France, a desire to emulate the swift and startling successes of the Seven Years War (Peters, 1998: 113–14, 238–42, 247–8). Pitt's political theory was shaped by a taste for Court Whig classical literature informed by Scottish Enlightenment theories of history and a critical desire to improve, if not revolutionise, existing structures and practices of government. Pitt's political economy was not that of Adam Smith: the so-called 'free trade' treaties of the 1780s with France and Portugal contain many anomalies while Pitt, during the bad harvest years of 1795–1796 and 1799–1800, authorised the statutory regulation of grain supplies, for which he was criticised by Grenville. 'I was not more convinced than you were of the soundness of Adam Smith's principles of political economy till Lord Liverpool lured you away from our arms into the mazes of the old system' (Stanhope, 1861–2: iii, 371; Ehrman, 1969: 47; 1983: 445–7; 1996: 278–82; Wells, 1988: 88–90). By the 1810s, Grenville would be demanding the repeal of the Corn Laws and an end to Pitt's own wartime funding system. A conceptual model of modernising state and society, rather than a strict code of *laissez-faire* principles, was what Pitt took from Scottish political economy. This vision of western European development functioned as the basis for limited bureaucratic reform, freer trade and a series of unsuccessful improving projects mooted over the 1780s and 1790s, including the commutation of tithes, the reform of the old poor law and moderate parliamentary reform. This *political* economy both drove and justified a series of state policies but was tempered by an awareness, visible from Pitt's earliest days in office, that compromise is the essence of statesmanship. Where Pitt learned this is not clear: possibly from Chatham though it is more likely, knowing Pitt's private fondness for systems of theory, that some system of expediency constituted a formal part of his political thought. The principle of utility had many advocates, amongst whom David Hume and William Paley (before 1800) were highly regarded by Pitt, though, in the absence of a felicific calculus, he cannot be described as a utilitarian (PH, 1792: xxix, 816–38; PR, 1792: xxxi, 216–17; Mori, 1997b: 39–43).

Both Pitt and his cousin Grenville have been described as conservative Whigs though neither was a disciple or friend of Edmund Burke. Grenville, a pious Anglican who believed in the divine ordination of social order, liked the *Reflections on the Revolution in France* from the day of its publication but Pitt, who cared little for religion and possessed a taste for cultural relativism, did not (Derry, 1981: 126–7; Jupp, 1985: 464; Wilberforce, 1838: i, 282, 315). All three men were, in general terms, Establishment Whigs. During the 1780s it mattered little: Pitt could claim to be leading a liberal administration, many of whose policies were more adventurous than those of the Opposition. The Foxite Whigs, who had rallied under the leadership of Fox following the death in 1782 of their old leader, the Marquis of Rockingham, never forgave Pitt or George III for ousting them from office in 1783. Because Pitt had taken office as the leader of a minority government, all Foxites concluded that he was a creature of the crown. The central tenet of Rockingham Whiggism – opposition to the royal prerogative – had made the Whigs ardent economical reformers but they had no other coherent policies to promote as alternatives to Pitt's government during the mid-1780s.

Economical reform for the Rockingham Whigs had always been fixated on real or perceived abuses of royal and ministerial power (Mitchell, 1971, 1992). Edmund Burke's Civil Establishment Act of 1782 abolished the Board of Trade and the Colonial Office whilst rooting out sinecures in the royal household and civil administration, but did not address questions of bureaucratic professionalism and accountability, even to the limited extent that they were dealt with by Pitt (Christie, 1970: 296–8). The Foxites expressed no interest in state finance except to bemoan the growth of the national debt, a case that was difficult to sustain following Pitt's establishment of the Consolidated Fund in 1786. For the Foxites, Parliamentary reform involved the reduction of ministerial influence in Treasury and Navy boroughs rather than an end to electoral corruption, much less any redistribution of parliamentary seats or widening of the franchise. As aristocratic Whigs, the Foxites relied upon the politics of oligarchy in town and country to maintain their party status. Starting in 1787, Fox would begin to move his party to the left by taking up the Dissenter cause for the repeal of the Test and Corporation Acts. This would begin to give the Whigs a new identity.

Foxite Whigs always saw Pitt as a Tory, by which they meant a supporter of a strong crown, and had used the same term of abuse against Lord North during the American War. The nomenclature of Toryism was a peculiarity of Foxite ideology. Finding self-professed Tories at Westminster before the 1800s is difficult because the term was still synonymous with Jacobite treason and therefore not willingly adopted by contemporaries. In 1924 Keith Feiling claimed that a 'new' Tory Party based on support for a strong crown and church had emerged amongst the King's Friends who formed the core of Lord North's parliamentary majorities during the 1700s, adopting a formal Tory identity under Pitt's leadership in 1792 (Feiling, 1924: 165–209). This claim had always been difficult to accept in the absence of any clear Tory identity, if not vestigial Tory principles, in Lords or Commons (Langford, 1980; Bradley, 1990). In 1804, the second Lord Kenyon described himself as an adherent to Tory principles 'on the subject of Emancipation and everything relating to the Church and State' and, in 1805, the future Lord Liverpool would call upon 'the Tories, the firm, steady and persevering supporters of the monarchy and the established church' to defeat an emancipation bill in the Commons (cited in Harvey, 1978a: 204; PD, 1805: iv, 691). By 1800 the partial rehabilitation of divine right and passive obedience, those original Tory principles of the seventeenth century, by loyalist authors during the 1790s had given some new respectability to old Tory ideas in the context of the war against revolutionary France. By 1815, Toryism would stand for the royal prerogative, traditional High Churchmanship, powerful executive government, militant hostility to radical reform and conservative patriotism (Harvey, 1978a,b: 2–4; Cookson, 1982: 12–16; Clark, 1985: 275–6; O'Gorman, 1989a: 7, 27–8; Sack, 1993: 49–50). Kenyon and the High Churchmen were unusual in openly calling themselves Tories during the 1800s, for the vast majority of politicians still defined themselves as Whigs.

The Foxites, bound by a heritage of aristocratic Whiggery, regarded themselves as the only true Whigs in parliament. They were unique amongst eighteenth-century politicians in their determination to view themselves as a party but, during the 1780s, commanded only 130–140 votes in the Commons. Without independent support, the Foxites could not defeat the ministry on any issue. Their one chance at government office came in 1789, when the possibly permanent madness of George III raised the prospect of a regency under the Prince of Wales. Fox, however, overplayed his hand by asserting the royal rights of an unpopular prince against a House of Commons that preferred to limit the powers of the crown, as stipulated by Pitt's Regency Bill, until the prince had proved himself in office (Derry, 1963; O'Gorman, 1967: 7–12, 32–7; Ehrman, 1969: 644–88; Mitchell, 1971: Ch. 4; Smith, 1975: 103–7). The recovery of the king in March 1789 scuppered the plans of the prince and the Whigs, in so doing exposing a rift that had been developing since 1787 amongst the Commons leaders of the party. The establishment of close relations between Richard Brinsley Sheridan and Carleton House, in addition to his growing influence over Fox, was alienating Burke from the Whig leadership and, when the Opposition Whigs began to differ in opinion over the meaning of the French Revolution, these personality conflicts would contribute to the splitting of the party between the disciples of Burke and the followers of Fox (O'Gorman, 1967: 40–69; Mitchell, 1971: 149–51).

Party Politics during the French Revolution, 1790–1799

On 18 April 1791, Fox and Burke would disagree during the Commons debates on Pitt's Canada Bill about the threat (or lack of it) that the French Revolution posed to western Europe and the British empire. Burke's opinions, no secret since the publication of the *Reflections* the previous November, saw in the ideas, actors and policies of the revolution a bourgeois Enlightenment conspiracy against all social order in its assaults upon the institutions of the *ancien régime* through which social order, both literal and metaphysical, was maintained in France. For Fox the revolution represented a welcome assault upon absolute monarchy and tyrannical government analogous to the 1688 Glorious Revolution. The dispute between the two men was exacerbated by the publication, in August 1791, of Burke's *Appeal from the Old to the New Whigs*, a tract which denounced Francophile Whiggery as a naïve and dangerous creed that stood to undermine Britain's political and social stability by encouraging criticism of the establishment. Backbench Whigs, asked to choose between Fox and Burke, would remain in a state of embarrassed and divided limbo until the end of 1792, when Burke and his chief disciple, William Windham, offered to support Pitt in the pursuit of 'vigorous Measures at Home and abroad' for the suppression of radicalism and the containment of French military expansion (Burke, 1958–78: vii, 291). When war broke out in February 1793, the Opposition was divided between radical Whig supporters of Fox, a Third Party of conservative Whigs headed by Burke, and the main body of the party led by the Duke of Portland. Over the course of 1793, the Portland group would join forces with the conservative Whigs, leaving Fox isolated with a rump of 60 Commons supporters and, in July 1794, the united 'Portland Whigs' would join the Pitt ministry in a coalition government, thus completing the disintegration of the Whig Party (O'Gorman, 1967; Mitchell, 1971; Smith, 1975; Derry, 1989).

Parliamentary reform was the issue that divided conservative from radical Whigs in 1792. On 11 April, the aristocratic Society of the Friends of the People (FOP) had been formed in London by Charles Grey, the Duke of Norfolk and other Whigs sympathetic to both parliamentary reform and the French Revolution. Grey's reform motion of 29 April split the party openly in the Commons, whereby Pitt moved to lure the conservative Whigs into the ranks of government with an invitation to join the Privy Council and participate in the concert of measures 'for checking any attempts dangerous to public order and tranquillity' (Windham, 1912: 249). Portland Whig participation in this venture would produce the 21 May royal proclamation against seditious writings and the movement of Whig MPs to the government lobby for the Commons vote of confidence for the measure. This set the precedent for future co-operation between the government and the Portland Whigs, who would begin to vote regularly with the ministry at the end of 1792 (O'Gorman, 1967: 84–6; Mitchell, 1971: 177–84; 1992: 120–1; Smith, 1992: 40–1).

Pitt's opposition to Grey's 1792 motion was preordained by its author's lack of specific proposals and his determination to act in concert with the popular reform societies forming in London and the provinces. The premier had abandoned his old allies but not, as far as we know, his attachment to moderate reform measures, and would say so during his 1797 speech against Grey's second reform bill (PH, 1797: 673–4). By this date, Grey and Fox had emerged as opponents of the war with France and defenders of radical civil rights against government and loyalist persecution. Although the Foxite or radical Whigs continued to support Test repeal and the abolition of the slave trade, they were not at heart democrats and Grey's 1797 bill advocated little more than Pitt's 1785 bill: the abolition of rotten boroughs, an increase of county MPs, the establishment of a household suffrage in the boroughs, and the replacement of two-member constituencies with single-member electoral districts. Neither Pitt nor Fox were innovators in the realm of parliamentary reform because both sought to repair – rather than rebuild – what they regarded as the best system of government on earth (Mitchell, 1992: 252–5, 258–61; Hampsher-Monk, 1978; Smith, 1992: 51–3, 66–7).

Foxite attitudes to radicalism and the French Revolution defy simple explanation. Fox, who loathed the writings of Thomas Paine, was saddened and horrified by the excesses of the revolution from late 1792 onwards, believing that constitutional reform had degenerated into anarchy. The evils of Bourbon absolutism were nonetheless of such magnitude that revolutionary experiments in government, however violent, were preferable to a restoration of the *ancien régime* monarchy. Fox was at heart a constitutional royalist but saw no merit in either of Louis XVI's brothers and consequently saw republican or Napoleonic government as preferable alternatives. He feared that British radicalism might metamorphose into violent Jacobinism, were not radical grievances given at least a fair hearing. For this reason the Foxites maintained social contact with metropolitan radical leaders throughout the 1790s, offered free legal defence services to radicals awaiting trial on sedition or treason charges, and defended radical rights of free speech in the Commons despite reservations about the wisdom of universal manhood suffrage. In so doing, the Foxites sought to act as mediators between an overmighty state and a potentially rebellious people (Fox, 1853–7: ii, 135–6, 149, 167; Derry, 1989: 43–4, 51–2; Mitchell, 1971: 233–6; 1980: 44–6; 1992: 130–3, 139–41; Mandler, 1990a: 19–21; Smith, 1992: 68).

The Foxites were suspected by Pitt of high treason at intervals throughout the 1790s, though no case could ever be proven against them. By this was meant actual collaboration with revolutionary France or, during the later 1790s, collusion with the London Corresponding Society (LCS) and United Irishmen (UI) in support of a British revolution. Following a public dinner held on 24 June 1798 by the Duke of Norfolk at which republican toasts were drunk, Fox and other leading Whigs were expelled from the Privy Council. Whig friendships with John and Benjamin Binns, John Gale Jones and other metropolitan radicals may have vindicated aristocratic Whiggism in the eyes of the LCS: the abolition of the House of Lords never appeared amongst its reform demands. In the eyes of the government, whose spies were collecting evidence of treason against the UI and LCS, the closeness of Whigs and radicals suggested possible Opposition involvement in United society plans for insurrection (given speculative consideration by Ann Hone, 1982: 41–7). Lord Edward Fitzgerald, leading member of the Dublin UI and first cousin to Fox, is, however, unlikely to have implicated members of his family in the Irish rebellion, while the Foxites' dread of violent revolution would have forestalled them from any active involvement in it. The character witness testimony of leading Whigs at the treason trials of Jones, the Binns brothers and Arthur O'Connor, thanks in part to which O'Connor and Jones were acquitted, formed part of the radical Whig campaign against state tyranny rather than sympathy for the British revolution (Derry, 1989: 43, 52–3; Mitchell, 1992: 150–6).

The radical Whigs employed the term Tory during the 1790s to describe Burke, Portland and their friends who were described in 1794 by Fox as 'worse Tories than those whom they have joined' (Fox, 1853–7: ii, 70). Such claims reflected the Foxite conviction that they alone represented the true traditions of Whiggery, a claim for which they were pilloried in

Canning's *Anti-Jacobin*: 'Is a Man *born* a Whig or is he *made* a Whig? and by what process? . . . Does it go in Families? . . . Can a Whig be divested of the name by other Whigs who are more numerous or better united, and give *the ton*? . . . Is it in the power of Clubs to monopolise it by a sort of Patent?' (AJR, 1799: i, 54–5). Here Pittites were mocking the culture of aristocratic Whiggery, based upon West End gentlemen's clubs, country houses and a cosmopolitan lifestyle that, in Foxite hands, flaunted existing moral and social conventions (Mandler, 1990a: 16–19, 45–55). Fox and some of his followers were atheists. All were sexual liberals and, in some cases, libertines. Grey fathered an illegitimate child upon Georgiana, Duchess of Devonshire; Fox lived with his mistress, the ex-prostitute Elizabeth Armistead; and Richard Brinsley Sheridan, who defected to the Prince of Wales's small Carlton House party in 1797, was a playwright whose connections to the 'seedy' world of the theatre raised eyebrows throughout his career. Such conduct was becoming increasingly unfashionable and presented a strong contrast to the incorruptible Pitt, who had no known vices except drink, and his partiality for port was not considered a great sin by the standards of the time (Brown, 1961: 21–4; Mitchell, 1971: 149; 1992: 96–100; Sack, 1993: 43–4; Harling, 1996b: 44–51).

Indefatigable as the Foxite Whigs were in their opposition to the war, their sixty votes could never outnumber Pitt's majorities and, by 1797, Fox had lost heart for the parliamentary conflict. He and his followers seceded from the House of Commons at the end of the session, although Fox laid no strict conditions upon their withdrawal from parliament, advising MPs to attend the House when affairs of personal interest to them were on the Commons agenda. All the Foxites returned to parliament during the debates on the 1797 naval mutinies, the 1798 Irish insurrection and the Act of Union, but they did not reappear in force until Pitt left office. Two-thirds of the party had gone with Portland, Burke and Windham to the ministry, an accession of strength that left Pitt less reliant upon the independent MPs, though he could by no means survive without them (Harvey, 1978a: 115; Derry, 1989: 51; O'Gorman, 1989a: 23; Mitchell, 1971: 236).

Beginning in the summer of 1792, Pitt had begun to entice the Portland Whigs away from their radical colleagues with offers of Cabinet posts. Fox too was offered the Foreign Office, which was possible in 1792 because his positions on popular radicalism and a war that had yet to be declared upon France had not yet developed. Repeated offers of government office would be made from November 1792 to July 1794. While Lord Loughborough succumbed early to these lures, becoming Lord Chancellor in January 1793, as did Sir Gilbert Elliot and James Harris, Lord Malmesbury, both joining the diplomatic corps, the rest of the conservative Whigs were reluctant to take Pitt's bait. This stemmed in part from old suspicions of Pitt that dated to the constitutional crisis of 1783 and the conditions under which he had first taken office. Having come to power as a cipher of the king and ousted the Rockingham Whigs from office, Pitt could only make amends by admitting them to government on a fair and equal footing (O'Gorman, 1967: 90–191; Mitchell, 1971: Ch. 6; Smith, 1975: 161–4; Mori, 1997b: 117–18, 187–8, 197). This he refused to do until 1794. The Portland Whigs also believed strongly in their identity as a party group, regarding this not as a faction but as a unit of social and political organisation. When the Portland Whigs began to separate in earnest from the Foxites, they retained their identity as a distinct party now acting in support of an anti-Jacobin ideological war against revolutionary France. When asked by Windham for advice about accepting the Home Office in June 1793, Portland warned the younger man against taking office, for doing so not only would damage the image of the party as the moral conscience of the nation, but would ruin it in the eyes of public opinion. Conservative Whig support for the government's war policy could not be taken for granted and, when parliament met in December 1793, Treasury MPs were worried that the Third Party 'might take the line of supporting the *War*, but impeaching the *Conduct* of it' (Windham, 1912: 199–208; Canning MS, 29dii: f. 28).

Threats of this behaviour did not end after the Portland Whigs joined the ministry. Burke who remained an independent MP, opposed the government's decision made in the autumn of 1795 to seek peace with the emerging Directory. The 1795–1796 *Letters on a Regicide Peace* recapitulated arguments made in private correspondence and Commons speeches to ministers and MPs by a man for whom the revolution and all its works in France were fit only for annihilation. Portland and his Cabinet colleagues could not speak openly against government policy in the Commons but protested in the Cabinet against the Pitt–Grenville–Dundas decision to make peace with France. The conservative Whigs had, nonetheless, been placed either in posts giving them no effective direction over the war effort, or in junior offices where they were answerable to Dundas or Pitt. Following the creation in 1794 of a third Secretary of Stateship for War and the Colonies especially for Dundas, Portland became a simple Home Secretary with no control over the conduct of the ministry's diplomatic and military policies. Spencer, at the Admiralty, answered to Dundas, as did Windham, relegated to the junior post of Secretary at War. Fitzwilliam disgraced himself in Ireland and by March 1795 was out of the government. Mansfield and Carlisle, as Lord President of the Council and Keeper of the Great Seal respectively, had few administrative responsibilities (O'Gorman: 1967: 201–10; Smith, 1975: 170–1; Ehrman, 1983: 408–14). Burke's counter-revolutionary agenda – the restoration of the Bourbon monarchy in co-operation with the *émigré* royalists – did not appeal much to the Pittites either before or after the outbreak of war with France: in fact all of Burke's projects and pleas fell on deaf ears (1981–97: viii, 47–51).

Portland Whig hostility to the French Revolution never entirely overcame old suspicions of Pitt. By 1796, a disillusioned Burke, who earlier in the war had described Pitt's life as 'precious' in the struggle against revolutionary France, was looking for a new national leader to set the war on an appropriately anti-Jacobin footing (Vincent, 1998: 27–8). Burke's friends had, however, joined the ministry to unite its enemies 'in one great family' (WWM F31(6)13). While the new coalition Cabinet was by no means free of disputes, these did not become open and irreconcilable until 1801. The King's Friends were horrified by Pitt's union with the Portland Whigs and, when five out of thirteen Cabinet seats went to them, many government career politicians with solid service records and promotion claims of longer standing were upset. On 25 January 1795, Solicitor-General Sir John Mitford, acting as a spokesman for these MPs, wrote to Pitt to complain about his reliance upon 'broken reeds', whose only merit lay in a conservative intellectual consistency that did not, to backbench eyes, entitle Portland and his friends to joint leadership of the government (PRO 30/8/170 (f. 158)). In coalescing with the conservative Whigs, Pitt had intended to claim an anti-Jacobin moral high ground for the government's foreign and domestic policies. This was a public relations strategy rather than a change of heart, for the government's war policies, whatever its leaders might say in parliament, remained firmly based upon pragmatic military and diplomatic considerations. By the beginning of 1795 the ministry's counter-revolutionary military policy was in tatters thanks to the revival of the first republic's military fortunes in Europe, and Pitt began in public to retreat from ideological warfare. Government MPs were told on 26 January 1795 that the premier cared nothing for the principles of or form taken by any French government: 'about Monarchy, or Republicanism, or Revolutionary Committees, or this or that set of men or set of principles, we have no care or consideration – *further* than as they go to promise of to make improbable, the secure maintenance of Peace, if on other grounds Peace should be desireable' (Canning MS, 29dii: ff. 90–1; Mori, 1997b: 206–31).

MPs operating in the unreformed parliament would not accept formal anti-Jacobinism as a basis for party political organisation during the 1790s. The official war platform, hastily cobbled together in 1793, was summed up in the slogan 'indemnification for the past and security for the future', a phrase with several possible interpretations. By indemnification might be meant no more than legitimate territorial and financial compensation for the expenses of the war, or anti-Jacobin revenge for the activities of a radical fifth column sympathetic to the first republic and all it stood for.

Security for the future might refer to the *ancien régime* restoration of the Bourbons, the establishment of a constitutional monarchy in France, or the making of a 'secure and lasting peace' with any stable French government willing to respect the rights of other states. Domestic security could lie in the simple containment of radicalism until the war's end or the repression of British Jacobinism wherever it might be found. 'Indemnification for the past and security for the future' was a platform flexible enough to command support from a broad cross-section of political opinion, and this it did, judging by Pitt's stable majorities, throughout the 1790s. The general election of 1796 gave Pitt a majority of over 250 votes and no government of the French wars enjoyed a majority of less than 150 (O'Gorman, 1989a: 24; Mori, 1997a). Loyalty to crown and constitution in general terms dictated the votes of the King's Friends. It did not necessarily commit independent MPs like 'the Saints', of whom Wilberforce was one, from voting against the government.

The Saints, or evangelical MPs of the French wars, were a group of conscientious objectors who felt the war was unjust and un-Christian. The group contained 20 core MPs but the total number of evangelical MPs was at least 100 and possibly higher (Bradley, 1974: 15–17). At the end of 1794, having concluded that no restoration of the Bourbon monarchy was possible in France, Wilberforce and six friends voted with Fox on the address of thanks to the crown, thereby opposing the continuation of the war. The Saints had accepted the war with reluctance in 1793 but had become disillusioned with Pitt. Their return to the government benches at the end of 1795, when the ministry declared its willingness to make peace with the Directory, was not permanent. They remained free agents in the Commons thereafter, voting as their consciences dictated on public issues. Some, like Wilberforce and Henry Thornton, remained supporters of moderate parliamentary reform and Christopher Wyvill's revived Yorkshire Association. All advocated the abolition of the slave trade (Bradley, 1974: Ch. 8, 1976: 165–78; Cookson, 1982; Hilton, 1988: 204–11; Harling, 1996b: 66–8). The Saints, nonetheless, cannot be described as true liberals, for they voted for both suspensions of *habeas corpus*, the Gagging Acts of 1795 and the Corresponding Societies Act of 1799. Pitt's grief at their original defection was partially attributable to the strength of his friendship with Wilberforce but also reflected concern about the moral leadership the Saints exercised in the House and the country at large. This group regarded itself as the political custodian of the nation's morals and critics of a government with whose aims they often disagreed. The presence of the Saints in the Commons ensured that independents continued to have a say in the public affairs of the 1790s in spite of Pitt's efforts to create a broadly based 'national' government.

What Pitt actually thought about the French Revolution became a contentious subject amongst his followers after his death. So ambiguous was the war platform of the 1790s that, assessed alongside his conduct on Catholic Emancipation and his reform record during the 1780s, he could be regarded as a liberal or a conservative, not that either term was used by contemporaries. The Foxites and some Saints, unable to find much uniformity in Pitt's speeches and policies, saw him as a hypocrite and a pragmatist (Cookson, 1982: 14–15). The conservative Whigs, for whom intellectual consistency mattered, stifled their doubts after joining the coalition ministry. Mitford's constituency of career politicians and many of the King's Friends did not much care. Pitt's own Cabinet, itself representing many shades of opinion from anti-Jacobinism to pragmatism, was content to endorse a war platform as subject to individual interpretation at ministerial rank as it was on the backbenches. Matters were complicated by the increasing conservatism of Pitt's war speeches as the war progressed: in 1793, he had been careful to keep Britain's diplomatic options open by remaining, in a manner of speaking, neutral to the French Revolution, but by 1797, Pitt was claiming that France ran 'a system of war most hideous, terrible and destructive that ever stained the pages of history, or debased the records of the world' (Pitt, 1797: 6).

The premier had welcomed the French Revolution in 1787, believing it to be a noble revolt likely to result in the establishment of a constitutional monarchy. This remained his ideal outcome to the revolution over the 1790s, though he was willing to make peace with a republican government, provided that it agreed to respect the conventions of pre-revolutionary international law and possessed enough domestic public support to remain stable. In the budget speech of 1792, Pitt had described the British constitution as an invisible hand directing the endeavours of citizens into economic, political and social channels productive of public benefit to the commonwealth. This 'union of law and liberty' was, in short, a complex mechanism for the regulation and reconciliation of self-interest that constituted the 'only true foundation and only rational object of all political societies'. As long as governments performed this duty, the principles on which they might be founded were irrelevant (PH, 1792: xxxviii, 834, 836; Mori, 1997b: 176–7, 283).

Pitt disliked the 1791 constitution because its strict separation of powers created conflicts between the executive and legislative branches of the French central government. He described the 1793 constitution as 'impracticable' because its provisions for regional devolution and direct democracy stripped executive government of all effective power. He did not, nonetheless, like absolute monarchy or dictatorship, either by individuals or by revolutionary committees (PR, 1793: xxxv, 676; Mori, 1997b: 281–3). Despite a personal longing for peace which became apparent to colleagues late in 1795, his public attitudes to the war hardened over the later 1790s. Pitt has never been regarded as a good military strategist. His reputation as a great wartime leader rests rather upon his conception of a progressive yet conservative vision of Britain's war aims and national identity. This war platform was constructed by drawing upon cultural traditions from old fashioned Anglican loyalism to Enlightenment social anthropology. At its core lay a commercial Whig political economy of the French Revolution, the mature version of which was in 1798 when this was first presented to the public in speech and print to justify the continuation of an unsuccessful war and new fiscal policies adopted to fund it. Here Britain represented 'rational' freedom and modern commercial civilisation pitted against a totalitarian Jacobin barbarism that, through a military system of conquest and exploitation, stood to plunge Europe from civilised wealth into primitive poverty. When soliciting voluntary contributions to the Triple Assessment in 1797, Pitt characterised the centralised command of French manpower and military resources thus: 'In *France*, this name [requisition] was applied to a System of Universal Plunder and Confiscation, which dissipated the whole Capital Wealth of the Country, in support of a new and intolerable Tyranny at home, and of unfounded Ambition abroad' (AJR, 1797: i, #3, 90–1). This differed markedly from Burke's 'culture and anarchy' reading of the French Revolution in its repudiation of feudal institutions and values for which Pitt had, as Grenville once noted, no respect whatsoever (Rogers, 1859: 177; Mori, 1998). While Pitt agreed with Burke that the principle of property was essential to the survival of social order, the premier did not regard the 'manners of a gentleman' as a pillar of western civilisation. Pitt, who viewed the trappings of monarchy and organised religion as useful instruments of social control, was much more sceptical in his assessment of their utility than Burke and did not care much what faith Britons professed as long as followers of it were exhorted to obey legally constituted authorities.

Pitt's commercial Whig defence of property and inequality was an important legacy for the Liberal Tories of the 1820s, enabling them to present themselves as modern and progressive conservative reformers. Though willing to sponsor the forces of vigilante conservative loyalism throughout the 1790s, Pitt remained aloof from its more reactionary manifestations and regarded it warily as a phenomenon possessing a life of its own. As an image-conscious minister he was determined to rally patriots and loyalists behind the government and, from 1798 onwards, did so with increasing vigour, culminating in an 1803 mobilisation of volunteers conceptualised as the sovereign will of the state (PH, 1803, xxxvi, 1644; Cookson, 1997: 187, 215–21). It is unlikely that this represented genuine conviction for, by 1801, the government knew the limitations of the volunteers as a home guard, however useful they might be for boosting civilian morale (Dickinson, 1989: 123). Pitt's willingness to appeal to British intellectual traditions, from quasi-Tory monarchism and High Church Anglicanism to utilitarianism and classical political economy, over a quarter of a century spent in the unreformed House of Commons has muddied the waters of scholarship for those seeking to ascertain his true thoughts on war, revolution, society and government. There is little evidence that he ever abandoned the ideals and objectives of his youth, tempered though these were by the realities of practical politics. His policies can be and have been explained as a product of pragmatism, but it should not be forgotten that this, like all human belief systems, is culturally constructed. His supporters interpreted his actions over time as evidence that he became more conservative as he aged. They received a severe shock when, in February 1801, he resigned over the issue of Catholic Emancipation.

The End of an Era, 1799–1806

On 18 November 1792, Pitt had written to Lord Lieutenant Westmoreland that the legislative union of Britain and Ireland was the only solution to a state of Anglo-Irish relations in which the British government was continually contesting a conservative Protestant Ascendancy determined to baulk all attempts to reconcile Ireland to English rule. After the failure of Pitt's 1785 Commercial Propositions, a project against which the Dublin Castle civil administration of Ireland had openly lobbied, Pitt's Lord Lieutenants had conceded temporary defeat and worked in partnership with a Castle and conservative Protestant Ascendancy they in truth disliked. When, however, in 1798 the Castle proved itself unable to contain the forces of Irish radicalism, Pitt and his Cabinet decided to abolish the Dublin parliament dominated by the conservative Ascendancy and introduce full Catholic Emancipation in Ireland (Rose, 1911: 73, 390; Elliott, 1982).

The 1793 Catholic Relief Act that gave votes to Irish 40s Catholic freeholders but left them unable to stand for parliament was an incomplete measure suggesting to the Irish that more ambitious measures were forthcoming from London. The 1792 and 1793 Catholic Relief Acts enabled Irish Catholics to practise law, become officers in the armed forces, bequeath property without penalty to their heirs, give their children a Catholic religious education, and occupy stipulated public offices under an amended oath of allegiance (McDowell, 1979: 399–421; Bartlett, 1992: Chs. 8–9; Smyth, 1990: Ch. 3). Mitford's 1791 Catholic Relief Act had given some of these civil liberties to British Catholics but the status of their Irish brethren was, after 1793, much higher than it was in England, Wales and Scotland. The 1792 and 1793 legislation had been intended to keep Catholic Ireland loyal to Britain and Catholics were permitted to join the militia also created for Ireland in 1793 (Cookson, 1997: 158–60). A union agenda, if it existed in fully fledged form in Pitt's mind at this time, would be foiled by the conduct of Lord Lieutenant Fitzwilliam in 1795. The new Lord Lieutenant, a follower of Burke and Portland, believed full emancipation necessary both to end the dominance of the conservative Ascendancy in Irish politics and to prevent a French-style Irish revolution. Starting in 1792, the Society of United Irishmen, a peaceful and genteel reform organisation, would find itself the victim of Castle repression, and Fitzwilliam's vocal professions of support for full Catholic emancipation led the society to expect relief from his Lord Lieutenancy. His dismissals of John and William Beresford, linchpins of conservative Ascendancy Castle power, within a month of his arrival in Dublin, however, antagonised the Ascendancy and led to demands for his dismissal that Pitt and Portland felt it unwise to ignore. Fitzwilliam was recalled to London late in February 1795. The grounds of his recall lay not so much in what he did as the way in which he did it. Reform in the government of Ireland was not to be launched through open antagonism of the Irish Protestant élite (Smith, 1975: Ch. 7; McDowell, 1979: 449–61; Ehrman, 1983: 421–38).

By 1798 it was clear that the Ascendancy could neither run a solvent government nor keep Ireland loyal, and the Pitt ministry saw its demands for English assistance as an opportunity to introduce the union and reform. Tithes for the episcopalian Church of Ireland were to be abolished and the Roman Catholic clergy placed on a partially state-funded footing. Rotten boroughs were to be swept away through the creation of new Irish urban constituencies for the United Kingdom parliament. The Act of Union passed the British parliament rapidly in 1799; in 1800 its Irish success was ensured in Ireland in part through the bribery of rotten borough owners but, in the final analysis, primarily through the Catholic voter conviction that the British government in London would be less hostile to its interests than the Ascendancy in Dublin. The union legislation was to be followed in 1801 by an Emancipation Bill qualifying Catholics for all public offices, including the 100 Westminster Commons seats set aside for Ireland, subject to swearing new oaths of allegiance against Jacobinism. Here Pitt ran into opposition from George III (McDowell, 1979: Ch. 19; Ehrman, 1996: 158–96, 495–533; Wilkinson, 1997).

Ministers had anticipated hostility from the crown but allowed Lord Lieutenant Cornwallis and Irish Secretary Castlereagh to advertise the emancipation project in Ireland to facilitate the passage of the union legislation. As late as October 1800 Pitt had not yet briefed the king on the measure nor, for that matter, on various aspects of military and diplomatic affairs. Having been informed by Lord Chancellor Loughborough that emancipation was in the offing, a horrified George III expressed his opposition to the measure in the same terms as he had rejected Fox's 1783 East India bill and the 1787 repeal of the Test and Corporation Acts. Pitt promptly resigned, accompanied by Grenville, Dundas, Spencer and Windham. Portland, Chatham and Eldon, who all opposed emancipation, remained in office while Spencer Perceval became the leader of the House of Commons. The premier may have wanted to go. His own health was poor and, following the decisive defeat of Austrian forces at Hohenlinden in November 1800, the Second Coalition was in tatters. Henry Addington, Speaker of the House of Commons, was recruited to lead an anti-emancipation government and Pitt, having helped Addington settle into office, retired to Walmer Castle, the official residence of the Lord Warden of the Cinque Ports (Mackesy, 1984: 168–77, 187–92; Harvey, 1978a: 119–21).

Addington, the son of the Pitt family doctor, had known the ex-prime minister since childhood and relied heavily on his advice up to the end of 1802. Despite the existence of good relations between the two men, most of Pitt's junior supporters refused to serve Addington while the premier's ex-Cabinet colleagues – Grenville, Windham and Dundas – were horrified by the terms of the Peace of Amiens by which Britain accepted France's domination of Europe and returned most of its colonial conquests. Pitt, aware that an exhausted Britain was in no position to strike hard bargains with Napoleon, accepted the peace without open complaint, but Grenville and Windham went into opposition, never to rejoin forces with Pitt. As a result of these reversals, the new administration was widely regarded as a second-rate government deficient in administrative and oratorical talent (Mackesy, 1984: 38–9, 139, 208–10; Jupp, 1985: 310–13). Catholic Emancipation had left the Pittites weak and divided. Grenville, now the leader of a 'New Opposition', hoped to entice Pitt away from Addington, but the ex-premier, bound to support his friend by a solemn promise 'not redeemable by any lapse of time', rejected Grenville's repeated pleas to join the new third party despite grave reservations about the wisdom of Addington's financial policies. Grenville, like Pitt, did not trust Napoleon to keep the peace and, by the end of 1802, it was apparent that France, having annexed Piedmont, refused to withdraw its troops from the Low Countries, and having barred British commerce from French-controlled Europe, was preparing for a resumption of hostilities. On 18 May 1803, Britain declared war on Napoleonic France (Grenville, 1853: ii, 212; Sack, 1979: 65–7; Ehrman, 1996: 575–87).

Addington, though not as incompetent a minister as was once assumed, did not possess the experience or strength to lead a wartime government. In his place Grenville hoped to form a strong administration 'comprehending as large a proportion of the weight, talents and character to be found in public men of all descriptions, and without any exception' (Stanhope, 1861: iii, 116). At the end of 1803, frustrated by Pitt's refusals to desert Addington, Grenville formed a partnership or 'co-operation' with Fox, a development facilitated by the fact that most of the one-time Portland Whigs, having joined the Grenvillite third party, welcomed a rapprochement with their old friends. The Grenville–Fox union, a marriage of convenience in the first instance, was as odious to contemporaries as the Fox–North coalition of 1783 but would endure until 1817 (Ziegler, 1965: Ch. 5; Mitchell, 1992: 203–11; Jupp, 1985: 317–36; Harvey, 1978a: 133–48; Sack, 1979: 73–5; Smith, 1975: 268–78, 1992: 89–93; Ehrman, 1996: 604–19).

In February 1804, Pitt finally went into opposition and Addington resigned on 30 April. Reunion with the Grenvillites was prevented by the king's refusal to give Fox a Cabinet seat, although Pitt had wished to include Fox in the new ministry that took office on 10 May (Ehrman, 1996: 628–62). Grenville remained with his new ally in opposition but Addington was given a peerage and an office, appearing in Pitt's second ministry as Viscount Sidmouth and Lord President of the Council. Pitt had promised the ailing George III not to revive Catholic Emancipation during the king's lifetime and the new government set about constructing a Third Coalition against Napoleonic France. In spite of appearances, the emancipation split in the ministerial camp had by no means been healed. It was no secret that Pitt remained personally sympathetic to emancipation and, while his leadership of the government was not contested, the Addingtonians now constituted a distinct faction demanding a fair share of office for themselves (Harvey, 1978b: 158–9; Sack, 1979: 89; Ehrman, 1996: 665–725). When this failed to materialise, Sidmouth resigned at the end of the 1805 parliamentary session. Independents too were less obedient and amenable to Pitt's powers of persuasion than they had been during the 1790s. Many new MPs had entered the House of Commons between 1801 and 1804 owing nothing to Pitt, although a younger generation of MPs, amongst them Canning, Palmerston and Castlereagh, had been recruited as followers during the 1790s and would be responsible for keeping their leader's 'liberal' memory alive during the opening decades of the nineteenth century.

On 23 January 1806, a 46-year-old Pitt died of suspected stomach cancer. On 13 September Fox too would die, a victim of possible cirrhosis of the liver. Their passing ended an era in British politics that witnessed the stirrings of a bipolarity in the House of Commons but not the firm foundation of a two-party system. Pitt's demise would finalise a tripartite division between Grenvillites, Addingtonians and 'mainstream' Pittites that would not be healed for fourteen years. Fox's passing deprived his party of its most liberal conscience and left the Whig Party without an effective leader in the Commons. The derisively named 'All Talents' government of 1806–1807 was a poor substitute for the strong and cohesive ministry envisaged by Grenville, and popular radicals disgusted by both the Fox–Grenville alliance and the ministry's lack of commitment to reform would desert the Opposition to place their faith instead in independent MPs.

The All Talents ministry, led by Grenville and no stronger than Pitt's second ministry in the Commons, achieved little beyond the abolition of the slave trade. Fox, now a supporter of war against the dictator Napoleon, finally entered the Foreign Office over the protests of George III but, despite his best efforts to resurrect the short-lived Third Coalition of 1805–1806, was soon contemplating compromise and peace with France. Only Windham displayed any decisive leadership with an army reform programme including the unpopular and unsuccessful bid to abolish the volunteer corps. The presence of the Addingtonians in the All Talents government gave it some protection against right-wing attacks, but the bulk of the Pittites, who looked to Grenville as their next natural leader, were excluded from the government, having agreed amongst themselves to support their one-time colleagues 'except on any measure brought forward by them either in derogation of Mr Pitt's system, or in discredit of his memory'; (quoted in Harvey, 1978a: 181). While the Talents were spared the prospect of excessive Pittite criticism, nothing could save the administration from the enmity of George III (Butterfield, 1962; Harvey, 1972, 1978b: Ch. 3; Ehrman, 1996: 126–9; Jupp, 1985: 355–73; Mitchell, 1992; Smith, 1992: 109–12).

On 4 February 1807, Lord Lieutenant the Duke of Bedford informed his masters in London that Catholic Ireland intended to petition the government for relief. Full emancipation was not, in light of the ministry's composition, viable, for Sidmouth, Ellenborough and Erskine opposed the grant of concessions to Ireland. Most of the Cabinet nonetheless wished to placate Ireland by opening selected public offices to English Catholics. The proposed admission of Catholics to the armed forces up to the ranks of admiral and colonel did no more than extend the liberties of the 1793 Irish Catholic Relief Act to the mainland, but an angry George III opposed it and demanded permanent ministerial silence on the subject of emancipation. The All Talents ministry promptly resigned *en masse* on 24 March and returned to opposition, in the case of the Whigs until 1830. Grenville resigned from active politics in 1817 but his followers, who took direction from the Marquis of Buckingham, the head of the family faction, would form a Third Party become reconciled to their old stablemates. In 1822, the Grenvillites would be welcomed back into the ministerial fold as long-lost disciples of Pitt. What this meant in intellectual and political terms by this date was very difficult to define (Sack, 1979: 113–16; Jupp, 1985: 399–410).

Unity and Disunity, 1807–1820

The resignations of Grenville and Grey over Catholic relief not only broke up the fragile All Talents coalition between the Opposition and the Sidmouthites, but ended all prospect of co-operation between those who had once been affiliated to Pitt. Three distinct groups of Sidmouthites (30–40 MPs), Grenvillites (20–30 MPs) and Canningites (10–15 MPs) coexisted alongside the 'mainstream' Pittites (50–60 MPs), all claiming direct political descent from Pitt. The governments of the later Napoleonic Wars, supported by 200–230 general Court–Treasury MPs and led by Portland (1807–1809), Perceval (1809–1812) and Liverpool (1812–1827), would claim to represent the personnel and principles of Pittism, though only the last would successfully reabsorb most of Pitt's old friends into their ranks (Sack, 1979: 92–4; O'Gorman, 1982: 53). In some respects the Whigs displayed more unity during the Napoleonic Wars, for the one lasting political achievement of the All Talents ministry was the partial reunification of the Whig Party. Windham, Fitzwilliam and even French Laurence, Burke's leading disciple and Professor of Civil Law at Oxford, had rejoined the Whig Party by 1806, although some of the one-time 'Portland' Whigs like Lords Carlisle, Spencer and Minto remained Grenvillites. Of the one-time leading conservative Whigs in Lords and Commons, only Portland, Malmesbury and Loughborough failed to return to the Whig Party. The Opposition in 1807 contained an interesting mix of Whigs and ex-Pittites, amongst them close personal friends of Pitt such as Lord Auckland and George Pretyman Tomline, Bishop of Lincoln. Although the Grenvillites were led in the Commons by Charles Wynn, nephew to Grenville and Buckingham, the formal Opposition was led by George Posonby, a genial nonentity whose elevation was sanctified by Grenvillite-Whig approval and his family's seniority in the Whig Party. The Whigs would not display much effective opposition in the Commons until Posonby died and was replaced in 1817 by George Tierney (Harvey, 1978a: 132; Sack, 1979: 92–4, 105, 135–6; O'Gorman, 1982: 34, 53; Smith, 1992: 151–2).

Portland's permanent estrangement from the Whigs was confirmed by his appointment in 1807 as the next premier to head a reconstruction of Pitt's second ministry. The duke's health was fast deteriorating and he served until his death in 1809 as an inoffensive figurehead under whom a motley crew of ministers, including Sidmouth, Canning and Castlereagh, could agree to serve. The Canningites and Addingtonians were the most prominent pro- and anti-emancipation groups in the government, but their disagreement on this issue was stifled by the ministry's collective promise not to agitate Catholic relief within George III's lifetime. This pledge did not prevent the king's servants from detesting each other and the chief culprit was Canning, who by 1809 had fought a duel with Castlereagh and refused to serve under Portland's successor. Perceval, an anti-emancipationist, had become prime minister only because the duke's death left the government without a senior leader acceptable to its Cabinet members. Perceval's attempts to reconstitute the government as a party of the crown were dictated by the belief that the magic of Pitt's name had lost its power to unite men in office: 'the principle on which we must rely to keep ourselves together, and to give us the assistance of floating strength, is the public sentiment of loyalty and attachment to the King. Amongst the independent part of the House', he added, 'the country gentlemen, the representatives of popular boroughs, we must find our saving strength or destruction' (Plumer Ward, 1850: i, 259). The independent vote was 70–80 MPs strong. This is not to say that Pitt's memory was no longer debated or appealed to by his followers: rather that its ability to divide had superseded its ability to unite. Perceval's assassination at the hands of the lunatic businessman John Bellingham in 1812 left the leadership and membership of the government once more open to all contenders. Charles Jenkinson, second Earl of Liverpool, took office at the head of a ministry so unstable that, in 1813, the Prince Regent asked Grey and Grenville to form an alternative government made impossible by the Opposition's determination to uphold Catholic Emancipation and introduce limited economical reform.

The Whig Opposition remained a lukewarm supporter of moderate parliamentary reform, a cause which Grenville by 1809 had come to accept on the grounds that moderate reform would contain the crown's secret influence in the Commons, reduce more insidious manifestations of government influence outside parliament and appease radical reformers who might otherwise advocate desperate measures. Despite the Whig conviction that corrupt and overbearing Pittites were undermining liberty and property, the Opposition's commitment to economic reform was limited, for all its leaders – Grenville, Grey and Holland – felt that places and pensions, in principle, were necessary perquisites of office. Aristocratic Whiggery, as it developed amongst the Rockingham Whigs during the 1760s and 1770s, had grafted Country critiques of the crown onto a Court Whig 'Old Corps' foundation of beliefs, a union of opposing political traditions inherited with all its contradictions by Fox and his successors. While this common past may have facilitated the *rapprochement* between Whigs and Grenvillites, the Court Whig background of both groups – however distant in the case of the Whigs – made both bad critics of old corruption, and the economic reform campaign of the 1800s and 1810s was led by the Saints and independent MPs (Roberts, 1939: 186–9, 197; Cannon, 1972: Ch. 8; Harvey, 1978a: 208–9; Harling, 1996b: 121–9). The Opposition was nonetheless split between the moderate, or pro-Grenville, Plain to which Grey and Holland belonged, and a more radical Mountain whose members – Stanhope, Lansdowne and Lauderdale in the Lords, with Samuel Whitbread and Samuel Romilly in the Commons – advocated the re-establishment of friendly relations with extraparliamentary reformers and a sustained assault upon executive power in all its forms. The fidelity of these men to an independent Country Whiggism kept this tradition alive on the Opposition benches while Holland House disseminated aristocratic Whiggery to junior MPs. Central to this was a hagiography of Fox and a liberal reading of the 1688 and 1789 revolutions as noble revolts against a tyrannical crown (Roberts, 1939: 234–5; Dinwiddy, 1970; Sack, 1979: 122–5; Smith, 1975: 315–16, 1992: 154–5; Rapp, 1982; Mandler, 1990a: 55–68).

The attraction of the Grenvilles for the Whigs lay partially in their identity as a family political unit, an institution in keeping with the principles and practices of aristocratic Whiggery. According to the Marquis of Buckingham, the family had been undervalued by Pitt, a conviction that eased the transfer of allegiance to opposition. Buckingham's repeated demands for family posts annoyed the Whigs and his own brother on the few occasions when the Opposition stood a chance at office, although the Whigs also found Grenville's retention of two sinecures embarrassing. During the 1813 negotiations with the Prince Regent, Grey demanded that his partner resign at least one of these before entering government (Sack, 1979: 20–41; Mitchell, 1992: 202–4, 206–16). Even Buckingham was persuaded on this occasion to give up one-third of his emoluments. More agreement could be found between the Whigs and Grenvillites on the war, which they supported in principle but opposed in policy. Grenville and Grey regarded the Peninsular campaign as a wasteful and unlikely route to victory, but the credibility of their opposition to the government's war policy was undermined by a lack of hard facts and an inconvenient hero-worship for Napoleon on the part of Holland, Whitbread and Byron. Grenville, soured by a decade in the Foreign Office, had abandoned all thought of grand alliances against France but still hankered after a post-war restoration of the French monarchy. The Whigs, who remained true to Fox's memory, remained suspicious of Bourbon absolutism (Davies, 1919; Sack, 1979: 159–63; Jupp, 1985: 421–3, 442–5; Derry, 1989: 56–7; Smith, 1975: 310–14, 1992: 166–70; Hall, 1992: 59–62).

Despite their disagreements, the Whigs and Grenvillites learned from each other during their thirteen-year partnership. By hiring Francis Horner as a tutor in political economy in 1809 and, in 1813, bringing him into parliament as a member for the pocket borough of St Mawes, Grenville played an important part in attaching the *Edinburgh Review* to the Opposition. By 1813, Grenville was the Opposition's chief economic affairs spokesman in the Lords, having rejected the 1797 paper pound, Pitt's income tax, the Orders in Council, the Corn Laws and the East India Company's monopoly. These and other principles of political economy were, despite the best efforts of Grenville and the *Edinburgh Review*, slow to be accepted by the leaders of the Whig Party, and the Liverpool ministry would have the better reputation for forward-looking economic thinking throughout the 1810s and 1820s (Sack, 1979: 33, 154–9; Jupp, 1985: 445–7, 457–8).

By 1812, Grenville was referring to ministerialists as 'the party of the Tories, & of the old Court, & High Church'. This was qualified by the statement that, in their blind support for crown and church, the said persons were no true heirs of Pitt, but Grenville's use of the term 'Tory' suggests that some intellectual cross-fertilisation had been taking place in Opposition ranks (BL Add 41853, ff. 255–60). At Holland House, the high temple of Foxite Whiggery, Pitt and Burke had been 'consigned to the lowest circles of Hell' (Mitchell, 1980: 40, 60–87, 72–3). Burke could not be forgiven for having split the Whig Party, a process that according to Foxite myth had been encouraged by the scheming Pitt. Party labels were increasingly used by politicians and the press after 1806. Although Fox had always been a party man, Pitt, in life, refused to lead a party. After death, however, his ghost presided over the transformation of Pittites into Tories. Demonologies and hagiographies were the stuff of which political theory and practice was made during the 1800s and 1810s. Within days of Pitt's death, Tomline and George Rose were describing the premier's demise to parliament as the passage of a saint martyred on the altar of public duty, complete with a fictitious taking of the sacrament symbolising Pitt's loyalty, whatever his views on Ireland, to the Established Church. The canonisation of Pitt as an Anglican saint continued into the 1810s with rumours spread by Rose that he had, upon careful reflection, abandoned both parliamentary reform and Catholic Emancipation, while the Pitt Clubs founded in 1809 venerated the memory of the pilot who weathered the storm. Fox, on the other hand, was apotheosised amongst the Whigs as a liberal defender of free speech, a free press and freedom of conscience. The Fox Clubs founded to commemorate the life of their leader acted as important *foci* for extraparliamentary Whig organisation and unity during the 1810s. The Pitt Clubs were sites of constant squabbling about the intellectual and political identity of Pitt. Both sets of clubs helped those inside and outside parliament identify themselves within a bipolar political system constructed around personalities. The extent to which principles mattered is more difficult to ascertain (Mitchell, 1980: 52–4; 1992: 262–4; O'Gorman, 1982: 61–70, 1989b: 331–2; Sack, 1987: 635–8, 1993: 89–90). Burke had no cult except amongst his friends, and the British right would not adopt him until the 1820s.

Pitt and Fox Clubs, allied to other extraparliamentary organisations such as the Orange Order and Dissenter bodies, were primarily responsible for making Britons think of politics in terms of party. The break-up of the Pittites in 1801 had increased the importance of independent MPs and floating voters in parliament: the 1806 general election returned no fewer than 208 'neutrals' as opposed to 349 committed ministerial and opposition supporters. The Namierite structure of politics characterised by a tripartite division between Court, Country and independents was alive and well. By 1812, however, the number of 'doubtfuls' had dropped to 37 while the independent component of the Commons had stabilised at 24. By 1818, the number of neutrals, 'doubtfuls', independents and Grenvillites, who had in 1817 broken with the Opposition, stood at only 49 (Thorn, 1986: 185, 235, 263). An increasing number of MPs were identifying with either the government or the opposition, and this could be seen at constituency levels in the conduct of elections and the affiliation of clubs and public bodies to Whigs or Tories (O'Gorman, 1989b, 1998). Having said this, no party discipline was imposed upon MPs in Commons divisions upon social and economic issues, nor could any real direction be given to members upon sensitive issues such as parliamentary reform for the Whigs and Catholic Emancipation for the Tories. Bipolarity was in increasing evidence at Westminster but a party system, as we would understand the term, was not. Personality cults were central to party politics in this period because they strove to unite dissident followers of the dead Pitt and Fox, and the hagiographies themselves must be assessed in the light of a changing political morality that set new standards for public duty and statesmanship in the opening decades of the nineteenth century (Hilton, 1977, 1988; Sack, 1979: 100; Jupp, 1985: 369–70).

In the 1805 impeachment of Dundas, now Lord Melville, for the embezzlement of funds in his capacity as Secretary of the Navy, Wilberforce's supporting vote had induced 40 independent MPs to endorse the measure. Evangelical constructions of political virtue, as exemplified by the conduct of the Saints, stipulated that personal piety and public conscience come before self-aggrandisement and party interest. For non-saints, a quasi-secular ethos of public life required that an individual's public conduct be justified by disinterested principles and that his private life conform to bourgeois domestic norms. By no means all politicians felt compelled to meet these standards of virtue. Older Foxite Whigs cared little for 'respectable' morality, though this could not be said for all the younger ones, while the Marquis Wellesley and his brother, the Duke of Wellington, remained unrepentant adulterers and sinecurists. The sainted Pitt combined the best of both virtue systems: a guardian of the *status quo* in church, state and society whose supposed enmity to the French Revolution and all its works had guided his lifelong endeavours in the service of king and country. Second-generation Pittites, who modelled their conduct upon that of their dead leader, employed these constructions of good statesmanship to combat Opposition and radical claims that the venality of the 'Pitt system' was sapping the public strength and morals of the nation (Harling, 1996b: 82–8).

Spencer Perceval, who succeeded Portland as Britain's first evangelical prime minister in 1809, owed his rise to a competent junior service record and reputation for independent integrity. If radical journalists were to be believed, Perceval had blackmailed his way into the Portland government by threatening to publish the findings of the 1806 'Delicate Investigation' into allegations that Queen Caroline had borne an illegitimate child, but, once in office, Perceval presented an image of Christian rectitude to the world, ending Monday sittings of the Commons to stop MPs from travelling on the Sabbath and embarking upon a programme of cautious reform at the Exchequer. Perceval, though unsympathetic to demands for economic reform, was determined to rationalise the structures and functions of the Exchequer to facilitate the prosecution of the war. The consolidation of stamp duties and the reformation of the assessed taxes was accompanied by the Bank of England's reduction, at Perceval's prodding, of interest charges on the national debt and a similar lowering of Treasury commissions on exchequer bills (Hilton, 1988: 218–20). Perceval was also determined to regain a modicum of moral authority for a ministry under attack from independent Saints like Henry Bankes, whose 1809 Superannuation Act forced the ministry to accept the principle that proper pensions, rather than sinecures, were the appropriate rewards for public service (Gray, 1963: 208–11, 311–16, 321, 355–8). The Mary Anne Clarke army commissions scandal of 1809, moreover, necessitated that the administration take a firm line on corruption at a time when radical journalists were taking up economic reform as a stick with which to beat the ministry. Independent MPs too were reforging their links to lobby groups without doors, a development eyed with suspicion and fear by supporters of the government (Harling, 1996b: 63–6, 149–50).

Perceval's assassination on 11 May 1812 ensured his placement within the Tory pantheon of saints with all his sins forgotten. His construction of a Regency along the exact 1789 lines laid down by Pitt when George III went irrevocably mad in 1810 earned him the respect of the Commons in which his commanding position had ensured him dominance within a Cabinet comprised largely of peers. The Prince Regent, who became George IV in 1820, was far less dominant in affairs of state than his father had been, and this decline of royal influence encouraged MPs to identify with a party rather than the crown. By 1812, the Perceval ministry was no longer the 'Government of Departments' it had been when Portland took office in 1807 but nevertheless remained a fragile coalition, rather than a true fusion, of the various Pittite groups (Walpole, 1874: ii, 16n.). This looked set to disintegrate when Liverpool took office and, within twelve months, the new premier had lost Marquis Wellesley, a one-time Grenvillite who had set up a faction on his own, and failed to acquire either Canning or Grenville (Harvey, 1978a: 273–5). Although the Pittites remained unhappy and divided, the Liverpool ministry faced no serious challenges to its authority from 1812 to 1815. Catholic Emancipation, which Liverpool had declared an issue of private conscience for his followers, was not a major embarrassment during the 1810s, and competent administration, combined with the turning of the military tide against Napoleon, ensured it the backing of independent MPs. The Liverpool administration had by 1822 successfully reabsorbed both Canning and the Grenvillites. Its history has often been divided into two phases: the Ultra Toryism of 1812–1822 characterised by the employment of legal and military repression against Luddites and popular radicals from 1812 to 1819; and the Liberal Toryism of 1822–1827, which saw the government's adoption of *laissez-faire* economic policies (Brock, 1941; Gordon, 1976). This distinction between the two phases of office is artificial, as is any attempt to attribute the liberalisation of 'Tory' policies primarily to the mending of ministerial fences with the progressive Grenvillites and Canningites. A premier determined to facilitate Britain's return to a peace-time economy was planning to dismantle the government's system of war-time finance as early as 1815, a process that was delayed by post-war depression. Liverpool was a good Pittite in theory and practice: a man committed to the encouragement of economic growth and the liberalisation of trade and a determined defender of the balanced constitution (O'Gorman, 1998: 262–3).

The motives underlying the Tory resurrection of economic reform were complex: part religious, economic and political. Ultras and Liberals both believed that their duty lay in the protection of a divinely ordained social and political order from reform and revolution. For Ultras this was to be achieved through old-fashioned elite paternalism, while Liberals placed their faith instead in a free market that, in their eyes, was ordered by God. The defence of the old order was to be achieved by cleaning up its image: to this end and the efficient running of the war effort were the economic reforms of Perceval and Liverpool directed before 1815 (Hilton, 1977: 313–14, 1988: 218–26; Harling, 1996b: 153–61). The government was in part compelled to introduce 'rigid sparing economy' after the war because a backbench revolt had abolished the property tax introduced in 1799 as a temporary wartime measure, consequently depriving the Exchequer of much-needed income at a time when the Cabinet was by no means sure, in the wake of the 100 Days, that the war with France was really over (Cookson, 1977:

116–29; Hilton, 1977: 32–3, 150–82; Harling, 1996b: 150–82; Fulcher, 1996: 54–8).

While the reduction of all government salaries by 10%, the pruning of sinecures from all departments of state and the demobilisation of the armed forces took place at a much faster pace than Liverpool and his colleagues had anticipated, it would be misleading to see the fiscal and administrative reforms of the post-war years as a simple public relations response to Whig, independent and radical demands for cheap and accountable government. The politicians of the later eighteenth and early nineteeenth centuries were as much participants in, as respondents to, the discourse through which a new morality of low-cost government, efficient administration and disinterested public service took shape from 1785 to 1820. The right-wing squabbling over the sainthood of Pitt, coupled with evangelical 'bourgeois' concepts of virtue as prevalent amongst government supporters as the friends of peace and a *noblesse oblige* code of public service that emerged from loyalist fears of the French Revolution during the 1790s, played important roles in the transformation of political ethics visible after 1800. British society did not convert *en masse* to evangelical Anglicanism, but the moral force of evangelical ideas during the 1790s and 1800s was partially attributable to a general elite sense of crisis about the threat of the French Revolution to the political and social structure of European society (Soloway, 1969: 28–9). Disinterested public service and low-cost efficient government were regarded as real ideals by Whigs and many Tories, while other politicians were prepared to heed evangelical calls for reform of their outward conduct, if not their inner morals. The government supporters of the 1810s and 1820s were, moreover, legatees of the public personas their dead saint had adopted during the 1780s and 1790s: as a great financier, as a bureaucratic reformer and as an enemy of revolutionary Jacobinism. The last conviction would begin to unite all the dissident Pittites in the aftermath of the Spa Fields meetings and the Peterloo Massacre, when ministers told each other that the French Revolution had come again. Both Wellesley and the Grenvillites suspended their sniping at the government's policies until domestic peace was restored to the country and both were to some extent reconciled with the Liverpool government: Wellesley would become Lord Lieutenant of Ireland in 1819 while the Grenvillites, after toying with the idea of becoming a third party, would return to the government under a patronage pact in 1822 (Sack, 1979: 165–7; Cookson, 1977: 178–99; Colley, 1992: Ch. 4).

Liverpool and his colleagues also inherited Pitt's political economy of the French Revolution: a conception of the revolution as a maelstrom of anti-commercial anarchy that, infused with an evangelical eschatology alien to Pitt, would inform Tory thought on a wide range of social and economic issues during the 1810s and 1820s. The European culture that Britain was defending against revolutionary and Napoleonic France was conceived by more liberal government supporters in terms of a natural theology that reconciled social science with religion, with the result that commercial Whiggism was for forward-looking Pittites the discourse of choice in the defence of the war and the British constitution. The ministerial belief that war was a militant arm of the revolution helped keep the military contest with France ideological in conception long after the demise of Jacobinism, and Napoleon was widely regarded as an agent of the French Revolution by Pittites during the 1800s. For Spencer Perceval, the emperor was a literal incarnation of the Whore of Babylon (Perceval, 1800; Gray, 1963: 46). Nicholas Vansittart, described by Bentham in 1818 as 'scarcely more distinguished by his situation as *Chancellor of the Exchequer*, than by the splendor of his piety according to the forms and rites of the Church of England' (xlvii), held Napoleon's Continental System responsible for the ruination of European trade, having 'in great measure thrown it back to the practices of barbarous and uncivilised nations' (PD, xix: 944). Classical political economy had been regarded with suspicion by many conservative loyalists during the 1790s as a product of the sterile and speculative Enlightenment logic that had presaged the rise of Jacobinism. From 1800 onwards, it was increasingly regarded by Anglicans as a divine instrument of pains and penalties, confrontation with whose sufferings and temptations was part of a divine plan for collective human progress in this world and salvation in the next. Liberal Tories sought to create in government what Boyd Hilton has called 'a Butlerian framework of moral harmony, truth and justice' (1988: 221): to strip away anomalies and corruptions to reveal a natural and self-regulating society (Hilton, 1988: 220–4). This was the Christian political economy that underlay the *laissez-faire* policies of the Canningite Chancellor William Huskisson during the 1820s. A surprising number of senior Pittites were either formal or informal evangelicals during the 1810s and 1820s. Liverpool, who came from a High Church family of King's Friends, was deeply pious, and the same could be said for Grenville, from 1817 the Chancellor of Oxford University, who had a strong interest in the revitalisation of the Church of England (Hilton, 1977: 39–40; Gray, 1963: 35–6; Pullen, 1986; Hilton, 1988: 226–33; Mandler, 1990a: 23–6).

Liverpool and his colleagues were slow to accept the Tory label and did not, in some respects, willingly do so. The distinguishing features of Toryism up to 1810 were support for a strong crown and a strong church: from 1810 onwards Tories replaced a strong crown with a strong government and the loyalist nationalist ideals of the 1790s. From here it was a short step to the acceptance of Burke as an ideological authority during the 1820s. The loyalism of the French wars had nevertheless refurbished eighteenth-century Court Whiggism with new constructions of moral, religious and political authority, a fact acknowledged by the insistence of most MPs and peers on a Whig identity of some description. Official Toryism could not be avowed until divine right and passive obedience had been transformed into more acceptable and less reactionary concepts: the worship of Pitt, a belief in an organic constitution based on history and prescription, and a vision of a protestant United Kingdom bound together by the common experience of sacrifice and struggle in an ultimately successful war against revolutionary and Napoleonic France. Opposition Whigs, demoralised and disorganised, clung to traditions of aristocratic Whiggery and memories of Fox to give them cohesion and purpose. It must not, moreover, be forgotten that MPs and peers also acted and reacted in response to a growing body of opinion outside parliament which, through the press and public interest groups, was gaining influence in a public sphere dominated by real social, economic and political problems. The French Revolution and French wars were important insofar as they required politicians to define the sort of society in which they wished to live and to conceive practical strategies by which their objectives might be achieved. The destinations of Whigs, Tories, Saints and independents might be similar, but the variety of routes they chose to get there was the stuff of which politics, if not strictly two-party politics, was made up to the death of George III.

CHAPTER TWO

Ideas and Influences

The French Revolution attracted much praise and blame in Britain, giving a new lease of life to old forms of traditional discourse while encouraging their fusion with newer forms of thought. Though it has been said many times, it is worth saying again that Britain's initial response to the French Revolution was positive across the intellectual spectrum from 1787 to 1791. Educated public opinion equated events in France with the 1688 Glorious Revolution and anticipated the establishment of constitutional monarchy across the Channel. While the outbreak of popular violence began to turn conservative opinion against the revolution, it was not until the outbreak of war in Europe, the emergence of popular radicalism in Britain and the overthrow of the monarchy in France that British opinion, in collective terms, would begin to reject the revolution. By the end of 1792, the nation would be polarised into two camps, whose members either admired France and its achievements or defended a British *status quo* now perceived to be threatened by French arms and principles.

The outbreak of war between France and Britain in February 1793 forced intellectuals to declare their allegiance to radicals or loyalists. Recantations were common throughout the 1790s and 1800s. When confronted with a climate of increasing official intolerance in Britain and, from 1795 onwards, with a revolution that had embarked upon the aggressive conquest and virtual annexation of neighbouring states in Europe, many moderates and radicals became disillusioned with a revolution that brought no lasting amelioration of the human condition. By 1798, William Wordsworth and Samuel Taylor Coleridge, the most famous of apostates from the cause of radicalism in Britain, had embraced romantic conservatism. Radicals and liberals were not the only persons to switch sides. Equally dramatic during the 1800s was the *volte-face* of William Cobbett, since 1795 one of the Pitt ministry's most loyal conservative journalists, who embraced the radical reform of parliament in 1805 despite the possession of a social cosmology inherently conservative and anti-Jacobin in outlook. Jeremy Bentham, whose identification with the forces of social order could be found in a 1792 defence of pocket boroughs entitled *Rottenness no Corruption* and the 1795 *Anarchical Fallacies*, would in 1809 become disillusioned with a British constitution whose defects outweighed its blessings and align himself alongside radicals and Whigs.

By 1796 many liberals had grave doubts about the course that the revolution had taken in Europe and, by 1800, native Jacobinism would be dead or in hiding. Radicals of the 1800s and 1810s, who saw little to like in Napoleonic France or Europe, had learned from the experience of the 1790s that any admiration for France would be equated with treason by Pittite governments. Although emblems of the revolution survived in the political culture of popular radicalism after 1800, reformers returned to native traditions of republican radical protest to criticise the *status quo* in state and society. The influence of international cosmopolitanism upon British thought had by 1820 become much weaker, thanks to radical reliance upon a long established discourse of British patriotism that constructed the good citizen as an independent critic of the establishment (Cunningham, 1981; Dinwiddy, 1986; Philp, 1991; Epstein, 1994: 5–11, 23–6). Patriotism, despite claims to the contrary, survived and took new forms throughout the French wars.

Loyalism, despite its general subscription to a traditional and conservative Judeo-Christian social cosmology, was a broad school containing reactionaries, moderates and some liberals. Loyalist hostility to the French Revolution did not extend to British social and moral reform, particularly on the part of evangelical Anglicans, nor did it repudiate the Enlightenment in its entirety. Utilitarians and classical political economists could be found in the loyalist camp alongside old-style Filmerian Tories and latitudinarians espousing critiques of radicalism and the revolution often hostile to *ancien régime* France and, in some cases, Hanoverian Britain (Clark, 1985: 247–76; Schofield, 1986; Hole, 1989; Claeys, 1990). The success of loyalism in appealing to Britons during the French wars was attributable as much to the survival of this critical consciousness as to the advocacy of patriarchal social doctrines (Christie, 1984, 1991: 169–87; Dickinson, 1992a,b). The minds of loyalists were not, moreover, closed to new literary, religious and economic ideas despite conservative fears of anarchy and revolution.

The Rights of Man

In January 1791, an indignant Thomas Paine, one-time Norfolk journey-man staymaker, published a reply to Burke's *Reflections on the Revolution in France*. Burke's book, published two months earlier, had in Paine's opinion grossly misrepresented the aims and character of recent events in Paris. Part I of the *Rights of Man* set out to set the record straight, in so doing presenting the American War of Independence as the inspiration and model for French reform. Part I received no official attention from the British government. Part II of the *Rights of Man*, published in February 1792, would invoke an indictment on a seditious libel charge, for which offence Paine was found guilty *in absentia* in December 1792.

Parts I and II, read either separately or together, comprise a working man's primer in Enlightenment theories of history and natural rights repub-lican political theory (Philp, 1986; Claeys, 1989; Dyck, 1992; Goodwin, 1979; Thompson, 1968). Many Britons did not read the book in its entirety, imbibing it instead in popularised and abridged forms, but its central mes-sage was clear: man, born with universal natural rights of life and liberty, was entitled to claim and assert the sovereignty of the people in the pursuit of just and rational government. Paine belongs to a republican tradition of English political thought, complete with its myths about the ancient Anglo-Saxon rights of the freeborn Englishman and the tyranny of the Norman Yoke (Paine, 1996: ii, 317, 411–12). Radical readings of history and liberty, once Puritan and Whig, had a long pedigree stretching back to the English civil wars of the seventeenth century (Pocock, 1975; Robbins, 1959). Their lasting influence upon English radicalism was attributable to the legitimacy, both historical and intellectual, that they gave to radical culture. To this traditional republicanism Paine married a beguiling vision of Enlighten-ment commercial progress, a pithy and lucid account of representative government as it should be, and critical censures of monarchy, war and organised religion (Claeys, 1989). Part II, written to arouse British popular interest in constitutional issues, was, with its attacks upon the Hanoverian crown, parliament, Established Church, national debt and old poor law, much more subversive in content than a Part I that had primarily disputed Burke's account of the revolution. This explains in part the swift movement of the Pitt ministry against Paine in 1792.

The government's caution was misplaced. Paine's appeal to popular rad-icals, for the most part peaceful and respectable constitutional monarchists, lay in his marriage of traditional English political theory to notions of responsible, rational and pro-active popular sovereignty. Of the two revolu-tions described by Paine, the example of America, still tied to Britain by

trade, religion, language, immigration and political theory, was more familiar and attractive to British and Irish radicals (Thompson, 1968: 84; Cone,
1968: 51-2; Goodwin, 1977: 175-7; Kramnick, 1982: 638-40; Claeys,
1989: 71-5). France gave British radicals hope but no blueprint for revolution, and the same could be said for Paine. His plans for an English welfare
state were widely admired but did not figure prominently in radical demands for constitutional reform, which were inherited largely from the
English radicals of the 1770s. British radicalism was strongly suspicious of
all state power and sought to see this reduced, rather than increased. Paine's
long-term utility to British reform lay in his ability to update and popularise
old radical critiques of government (LCS, 1983: 10-14, 18-19; Curtin,
1994: 22-5; O'Gorman, 1998: 272).

Paine has long been placed, alongside Richard Price and Joseph Priestley,
in a tradition of English deist revolutionary thought (Palmer, 1959; Goodwin, 1979; Clark, 1985). None of the three was, however, an advocate of
violent insurrections, while Price and Priestley are better regarded as children
of the cosmopolitan Enlightenment. Although Paine's deism, as expressed
in the 1794-1795 *Age of Reason*, would be a formative influence upon British
popular radicals, the impact of Price and Priestley was confined to genteel
intellectual circles. Anti-trinitarianism, of which Price's Arianism and
Priestley's Socinianism were the most visible English forms, produced unorthodox thinkers rather than revolutionaries (Bradley, 1990). Burke was right
to recognise Price's famous *Discourse on the Love of Our Country* (1789) as an
attempt to mobilise support for the 1787-1790 Dissenter campaign for the
repeal of the Test and Corporation Acts but wrongly attributed to it levelling sentiments that appeared nowhere in its pages (Fitzpatrick, 1990). The
Discourse in fact testified to general Dissenter satisfaction with a constitution
laid down in 1688 that enabled nonconformists, as loyal subjects, to criticise
and change governments if they chose. Anglican supporters of the Hanoverian
church–state nevertheless swallowed Burke's equation of deism and revolution
without question. This Priestley found to his cost in 1791: having organised
a Bastille Day dinner to be attended by Birmingham's Lunar Society of
amateur scientists, his party was broken up by an angry 'Church and King'
mob who attacked the homes and businesses of prominent local Dissenters
in addition to destroying Priestley's house, library and collection of scientific
instruments. He emigrated to America in 1794, disillusioned with England
(Rose, 1960; Money, 1977: 195-7, 219-23; Stevenson, 1992: 174-6).

Not all Dissenters were radicals, nor were all radicals Dissenters, but the
status of nonconformists as second-class citizens in a state that accorded full
civil and political rights only to practising members of the Established Church
ensured that some – if not all – Dissenters were active participants in every
reform campaign of the later eighteenth century (Bradley, 1975-6: 4, 14-15;

Seed, 1990; Watts, 1995: 394). Price, Priestley and the once-Calvinist turned atheist William Godwin, belonged to a cosmopolitan bourgeois milieu whose members regarded the French Revolution as a bold and ambitious experiment in social and political engineering: a quest to realise Enlightenment ideals of justice, truth, reason and liberty in new-modelled institutions of government and society. Their belief in the perfectibility of man and the human condition was best expressed in Godwin's 1793 *Political Justice*, a tract calling for the abolition of all private property and government in favour of small self-contained communities whose citizens lived in amicable and rational self-regulating harmony without any need for the cumbersome, expensive and repressive machinery of state to supervise their affairs. Godwin rejected natural rights, written constitutions and immutable standards of right and wrong to advocate an extreme individualism governed only by the absolute sovereignty of reason in a peaceful utopia. His 'perfectionist' anarchism, characterised by a total faith in the power of reason and benevolence to overcome evil and injustice, was best expressed in the 1794 Jacobin novel *Caleb Williams* (Philp, 1986: 80–98; Mee, 1992: 225).

Godwin's philosophy embraced both atheism and free love, but these beliefs did not prevent him from marrying Mary Wollstonecraft when she became pregnant with his daughter, the future Mary Shelley. Wollstonecraft's *Vindication of the Rights of Woman* (1793) had pilloried the domestication of women, castigating women for their complicity in the process, but still defined the primary social role of women as wives and mothers despite calling for their recognition as the intellectual equals of men. Her early death in childbirth ended a career as a journalist, novelist and travel writer shared by other female radicals of the 1790s, most notably Helen Maria Williams and Charlotte Smith (Jones, 1993). Their admiration for the French Revolution only contributed to a conservative loyalist backlash against the revolution that sought to label British women as the virtuous and domestic counterfoils to French *salon* bluestockings, whose attempts to invert the patriarchal social order were held responsible by more conservative loyalists, in part, for the outbreak of the revolution (Montluzin, 1988: 11–15, 67; Colley, 1992: Ch. 4).

In spite of their radical sensibilities and contempt for conventional morality, Wollstonecraft and her female colleagues were, in the final analysis, products of their genteel social and intellectual backgrounds. Genteel radicals regarded reason and reform as an affair of clubs, salons and an Enlightenment sociability that abhorred violence and enthusiasm. This distaste for vulgar radicalism and its potential violence could be seen in genteel radical responses to the Terror of 1793–1794. Some, like Godwin, Williams and the young Wordsworth, regarded it as a regrettable but necessary precondition to total social regeneration but, when no brave new order of reason and liberty emerged in France, radicals concluded that a French people unprepared in social, cultural and intellectual terms for a rational revolution had become victims of passion and prejudice. Enlightenment, be it in England or France, was to be achieved through polite and cultured routes: in 1794, Godwin broke with his admirer, the LCS activist John Thelwall, over the government's arrest and trial of leading LCS and SCI members on charges of high treason. No true understanding of liberty and reason, thought Godwin, could come from popular radical clubs where beer, tobacco and enthusiasm stood in for a solemn contemplation of truth and justice (Jones, 1993: 140–8; Chard II, 1975–6: 67; Rigby, 1989a, 1989b: 97–101; Marshall, 1984: 115–16; Philp, 1986: 117–19, 196–7; Mee, 1992: 50–1, 222–3). Attractive as the French Revolution had been in the first instance, most British radical and liberal intellectuals remained faithful to British ideals of polite and prescriptive liberty.

By 1796, genteel cosmopolitan radicalism was beginning to lose supporters. Wordsworth, Samuel Taylor Coleridge and Robert Southey, all enthusiastic admirers of the revolution up to 1793, were undergoing a change of heart towards France finalised in 1798 by the invasion of neutral and republican Switzerland by the first republic. In 1796 Coleridge wrote that he had 'hung up my baby squeaking trumpet of sedition' (Coleridge, 1956–71: i, 240). Whether or not he was a French spy, a claim he went to great lengths to repudiate in the 1817 *Biographia Litteraria*, by 1798 he and Wordsworth were on their way to a conservative poetic naturalism that would later be transformed into romantic radicalism. By 1800, there was little enthusiasm in genteel circles for events in France, be it in metropolitan Dissenter circles or provincial radical communities in Norwich, Manchester or south Wales (Jewson, 1975; Scott, 1989; Beer, 1977: 52–4; Corfield and Evans, 1996; Jenkins, 1983; Watson, 1976; Roe, 1988). Of the three liberal Dissenter-run literary periodicals of the 1790s, the *Analytical Review* had gone bankrupt in 1799 and the other two – the *Monthly Review* and *Critical Review* – fell into loyalist hands or irreversible decline. By this date genteel radicalism had nonetheless helped inspire a new breed of authors and printers to take up their pens against the old order in Britain. In their hands radical print culture would be transformed during the opening decades of the nineteenth century.

At the end of 1792, when the Pitt ministry began to crack down in earnest against radical publications, a series of London and provincial printers found themselves in court on charges of seditious libel. Thomas Spence and Daniel Isaac Eaton, editor–printers of the weekly London journals *Pig's Meat, or Lessons for the Swinish Multitude* and *Hog's Wash, or Politics for the People*, would nonetheless remain active throughout the decade despite repeated prosecution and imprisonment. Burke's description of the masses as 'the swinish multitude' had aroused the anger of radical authors, who responded with a rash of porcine publications from 1791 to 1793. Despite the best efforts of successive British governments to close down the radical press, readers had access to a rich body of radical literature that responded to government and loyalist persecution by experimentation with diverse forms of print media throughout the French wars.

Radical printers, who produced for a mass readership, relied upon the traditional vehicles of popular print culture: folk tales, ballads, penny pamphlets and handbills were all employed for the popularisation of radical doctrines, much to the chagrin of Home Office officials, who found these publications impossible to police (Mee, 1992: 216–20). Multiple conviction on seditious libel charges after 1795 could result in transportation to Australia with the result that many printers and journal editors fled the country to escape trial. The most famous of radical journalists to leave England is William Cobbett, who in 1817 followed a long series of newspapermen, including Eaton, Matthew Falkner and Simon Birch of the *Manchester Herald* and Joseph Gales of the *Sheffield Isis*, into temporary exile. Government attempts to raise the prices of newspapers by requiring them to be printed upon expensive stamped paper, beginning in 1798, only encouraged radical printers and authors to turn to the unstamped press, after 1800 diversifying into advertisements, chapbooks and children's literature – forms of media that had throughout the 1790s been the preserve of the loyalist press. In so doing, radical pressmen invented new media techniques: block headlines, inset illustrations and printed picture captions that belong as much to the history of the press as to the history of ideas. Radical printers were not, on the whole, original political thinkers and their significance lies rather in their inventiveness as satirists and media manipulators (McCalman, 1985; Wood, 1994).

Radical print culture, as it emerged during the 1790s, borrowed from several traditions: the 'high' or formal Enlightenment, neo-Harringtonian republicanism and millennialism. C.F. Volney's *Ruins of Empires*, published in English in 1792, represented the popularisation of a cosmopolitan Enlightenment that Spence, Eaton and the poet William Blake tried to disseminate to ordinary readers. Eaton's publishing activities included the translation and publication of works by Helvetius, d'Holbach, Volney, Condorcet and Robespierre *Pig's Meat* and *Hog's Wash* printed excerpts from 'canonical' Enlightenment texts in addition to selections from the works of classic English republicans such as James Harrington, Algernon Sidney and William Molyneux. For the illiterate, Thelwall's lectures provided oral instruction despite the attempts of the 1795 Treasonable Practices Act to ban radical professional lecturing. Blake combined popular antinomianism with Swedenborgian mysticism and millennialism in experimental poems and engravings that received little recognition in his own time, but, like other popular radical authors and printers, he was stretching the boundaries of print by experimentation with new modes of thought and expression (McCalman, 1988: 24, 63–7; Belchem, 1985: 87; Chase, 1988: 50–1, 61–2; Epstein, 1994: 75–7; Philp, 1991: 74–6; Mee, 1992: 1–19; Morley, 1993; Wood, 1994).

Millennialism, the belief in the second coming of Christ, took two eighteenth-century forms in Britain. Pre-millennialism, subscribed to by Price, Priestley and other high Enlightenment thinkers, saw the new society of the future as an outgrowth of the old, unlike an apocalyptic popular millennialism that foresaw drastic social upheaval: the world turned upside down (Mee, 1992: 36–8: Oliver, 1978: 20–3). When both forms of millennialism were fused with 'moral economy' notions of community justice common to the English crowd and a faith in the possibilities of human progress derived from the likes of Volney and Condorcet, they produced in the thought of Spence a republican revolutionary ideology of considerable appeal to London journeymen. For the prophet Spence, who believed that the meek would, literally speaking, inherit the earth, LCS-respectable radicalism, with its emphasis upon parliamentary reform within the framework of constitutional monarchy, was too tame (LCS, 1982: 1–5). The LCS division he left in 1794 may not in fact have been comprised of respectable radicals, for it was reported by London police spy Edward Gosling in April 1794 to be arming in preparation for an insurrection (Parsinnen, 1973b; LCS, 1983: 140).

At any rate, in 1795 Spence started his own society in London's East End where it survived, if not flourished, throughout the French wars. Although its founder died in 1814, the Spenceans would join the radical campaign for parliamentary reform during the 1810s and play major roles in the 1816 Spa Fields riots and 1820 Cato Street conspiracy. Spence's radicalism and interest in popular literacy long pre-dated the French Revolution. As a Newcastle schoolmaster, he had produced a phonetic alphabet he called the Cruzonian Method for the use of his pupils. In the 1775 *Real Rights of Man* he had first demanded the seizure and redistribution of all land in England and Wales to the common people. Spence was no Godwinian or socialist and in his demands for the total equalisation of property ownership, or agrarian justice, was akin to other land reformers of the 1790s, most notably William Ogilvie, whose *Essay on the Right of Property in Land* called for the abolition of all tenancy agreements. Through direct participation in agriculture and land ownership, felt Spence and Ogilvie, the people could finally exercise the rights to which they were entitled (Knox, 1977; Chase, 1988: 65–7; Cunliffe, 1994).

Spence's ideas were not as novel as the modes he adopted for their dissemination. The composition of drinking songs for the use of illiterate

Spenceans, the reworking of children's tales like *Jack the Giant Killer* with radical subtexts, the production of token coinage with subversive messages, and the scrawling of republican graffiti on London walls, testify to a life of active experimentation with the media devices of popular culture (Worrall, 1992: 26–9; Wood, 1991, 1994). Popular radical authors worked hard to make their ideas accessible to a mass audience by employing popular literary devices – folk tales, ballads and chapbooks – such as Thelwall's *Tale of Chaunticleer* (1793) in which Chaucer's barnyard game cock king, once beheaded, plucked and stewed, was no better than any other chicken in a feathered society with its own strict pecking order of ranks and stations. Eaton, in whose *Hog's Wash* journal the satire was printed, was prosecuted for the publication of this regicidal tract, although it did not stop him from publishing Paine's *Age of Reason*, for which too he was indicted on more than one seditious libel charge (Philp, 1991: 70–2).

Pig's Meat and *Hog's Wash* combined ballads, popular songs, fables, fake advertisements, dream visions and children's games with reprints of classical and Enlightenment texts on the themes of injustice, liberty and corruption. Popular literature had met formal theory, giving later and better known radical printers and journalists the language, modes of expression and literary devices to attack the establishment. The activities of Spence and Eaton in the production of journals, tokens, graffiti, trial reports and mock advertisements paved the way for William Cobbett, T.J. Wooler, William Hone and Richard Carlile a decade later (Wood, 1994: 186–214; Worrall, 1992: 48–50; Calhoun, 1982: 113; Gilmartin, 1996; Epstein, 1994: 32–6). By the 1800s, however, popular radical theorists were relying heavily upon native republican political theory, popular communitarianism and a post-millennialism inherently suspicious of formal book learning. *Axe Laid to the Root* (1817), the republican levelling tract written by the Spencean mulatto journeyman tailor and itinerant preacher Robert Wedderburn, displays little evidence of any acquaintance with the works of Volney and Rousseau. As radical print culture developed in Britain, it began to acquire a life of its own independent from international influences (McCalman, 1988: 43; Linebaugh, 1993).

Toryism Old and New

The *Reflections on the Revolution in France* was greeted with surprise upon its publication in November 1790. Most educated Britons were amused, not alarmed, by its prophecies of Armageddon and the book would not receive much respect outside Burke's circle of friends until late 1792, when his warnings began to bear fruit in France. High Churchmen nevertheless welcomed the *Reflections* in spite of the fact that the book told them nothing new. For the Reverend William Jones of Nayland, author of the 1776 *Reflections on the Growth of Heathenism among Modern Christians*, infidelity had long been undermining the foundations of social order throughout Europe, and many churchmen had been expressing private doubts about the course of the revolution in their diaries and correspondence since 1787. The Abbé Barruel's *Memoirs of the History of Jacobinism*, published and translated by John Robinson into English in 1797, only confirmed what English High Church Anglicans had long known, and Burke's *Reflections* were much more attractive and accessible to many readers than foreign Jacobin conspiracy theories (Hole, 1989: 153–4, 1991: 19–20; Sack, 1993: 32–3; Vincent, 1998: 142–3).

Burke's discovery of a sinister plot dreamt up by 'sophisters, oeconomists and calculators', who sought through systematic attacks on organised religion, the institution of monarchy and 'the manners of a gentleman' to destroy western civilisation, gave a new lease of life to Filmerian Tory concepts of divine right and passive obedience that had survived in Oxford University, the Established Church and Tory gentry families throughout the eighteenth century (Burke, 1981–97: viii, 53–293; Gunn, 1983; Clark, 1985; Colley, 1982). The formal revival of Tory ideas came at the end of 1792, when the loyalist pamphlet campaign against British radicalism reached maturity, spurred by the rise of native popular radicalism, the appearance of the loyal association movement and the looming prospect of British involvement in the war against France. Here churchmen were joined by 'alarmist' Britons who had regarded the revolution as an internal French problem until 1792. Having been awakened to the international dimensions of Jacobinism, they would turn decisively against radicalism and reform. John Reeves, founder of the loyalist association movement and himself a divine-right Tory, would publish the *Thoughts on English Government* in 1795, a tract claiming that the fount of all power in the state lay in the hands of a crown without which parliament had no legitimacy. This claim was tantamount to treason in an ostensibly Whig state (Gunn, 1983: 180–1; Beedell, 1993; Eastwood, 1994b).

Reeves' impeachment was demanded at the end of 1795 by a Foxite Whig opposition determined to defend what they called 'true Whiggery' against the revival of old Tory doctrines. Their first protest had been made against the 1793 state sermon, delivered on the anniversary of Charles I's execution on 30 January 1649, which normally dealt with the deliverance of England from the tyranny of Stuart absolutism. In the hands of the High Church Samuel Horsley, Bishop of St David's, it took as its text Romans 13.1: 'Let every soul be subject unto the higher powers' and became a homily on the evils of regicide. Neither Horsley nor Reeves, despite their Tory social and political views, were calling for a return to absolutism in Britain. If we accept that eighteenth-century Whiggism had retained elements of patriarchal social thought, thanks to the covert survival of Tory thought within its ranks, we must also accept that the Toryism of the 1790s and 1800s had become reconciled to representative government and some religious diversity (Clark, 1985: 182, 276, 408, 349–50; Browning, 1983: 90–6, 199; Gunn, 1983: 177–82, 188–9; Hole, 1989: 160–73). By 1796, when Reeves was tried and acquitted for seditious libel, his claim that the English constitution was a tree all of whose branches, not excepting parliament, derived their legitimacy and nourishment from a royal trunk, was not found contentious by an English jury (Beedell, 1993).

At the base of the Anglican loyalist case lay the conviction that all earthly government was ordained by God and that constitutional liberty was dependent upon the law (Hole, 1989, 1991: 31–4). Because the law protected private property, loyalist authors could justify liberty, property and the British constitution according to divine ordinance. Thus old Toryism acquired a new lease of life from the breakdown of order across the Channel: as Horsley put it during the House of Lords debates on the passage of the 1795 Seditious Meetings Act, 'he did not know what the bulk of the people in any country had to do with the laws but obey them' (PH, xxxii, 258; Gunn, 1983: 184–91; Hole, 1989, 1991; Morris, 1998: 62–3, 106). Loyalists produced propaganda in many forms, ranging from multi-volume histories of France to sermons, chapbooks and children's tracts: in fact the sheer volume and diversity of loyalist publishing acted as a stimulus to the radical press. Most stressed the divinely ordained nature of social inequality. The impact of these writings upon a popular audience is difficult to assess, but the material was widely distributed, having been bought in bulk by loyalist associations, clergymen and concerned gentlefolk for distribution to tenants, parishioners and employees. Here the doctrines of Burke and other conservative authors were popularised for mass readership (Dickinson, 1989: 104–13; Colley, 1984: 98; Vincent, 1993; Morris, 1998; Gunn, 1983: 301–6; Wood, 1994).

The *Reflections* can be read in several ways: as a Court Whig defence of the English constitution based on utility and prescription, as a conservative natural law attack on the revolution's attempt to realise sterile Enlightenment theories of government, or as a vindication of modern commercial civilisation (Courteney, 1974; Stanlis, 1958; O'Gorman, 1967: 107–41; Dinwiddy, 1974b, 1978; Macpherson, 1980; Browning, 1983; Pocock, 1985: 193–213; Claeys, 1989: 64–6). Contemporaries saw it as all of these things, and loyalist authors, following Burke's lead, denounced deism, the French Enlightenment and natural rights to argue that the true foundations of society and government lay in history and expediency (Burke, 1981–97: viii, 78–88, 108–12, 344–6; Hole, 1989: 67–72). Loyalist authors often returned to first principles in the loyalist crusade to discredit the concept of natural rights, a strategy motivated by British radical attacks on property and prescriptive liberty. 'Every civil right', wrote Paine in the *Rights of Man*, 'has for its foundation some natural right pre-existing in the individual, but to the enjoyment of which his individual power is not, in all cases, sufficiently competent' (Paine, 1996: ii, 306).

Amongst the most sophisticated of the tracts composed in reply were written by natural law and contract theorists. Such polite, as opposed to vulgar, loyalists claimed that all political and civil rights came not from nature, but from the societies and governments that emerged for specific purposes to serve the needs of their members (Philp, 1995b). Men could never be totally free and equal because some were stronger and more intelligent than others. Obedience was enjoined upon man either by the forming of a contract between the rulers and the ruled or by the natural law of God. Thus was man given moral and civil rights (Dickinson, 1989: 106–9). While loyalist contract theorists agreed with radicals that the contract could be dissolved in cases of tyranny and injustice, readers were warned that the disruption caused by rebellions to existing civil rights, particularly those of property, outweighed any gains that might be achieved by revolt against all but the most repressive of governments. For natural law theorists all governments conforming to the moral law of God were legitimate, regardless of the forms they took, and all enshrined the natural inequalities of man in the inequalities of property ownership and political power. Here natural law theorists reconciled their absolute standards of good and evil to the diversity of human social and political organisation. While equality before the law was absolutely necessary to safeguard the moral equality of man, other inequalities were to be tolerated because property was necessary to the security of government, government was necessary to the existence of society, and society, as Burke had stated, was formed to cater to human wants and needs (Dickinson, 1977: 290–318; Schofield, 1986: 609–22; Claeys, 1989: 160–4).

Any Christian church qualified as a representative of God's mercy and law on earth, but conservative loyalists remained reluctant to praise a Roman Catholic Church long regarded in Britain as a bulwark of popular superstition, idolatry and absolutism (Colley, 1992: 31–40). The French church was consequently presented in much the same terms as the pagan religions of ancient Greece and Rome: as necessary instruments of statecraft that kept the passions of the people in check whilst encouraging citizens in habits of obedience to all authority. Anglicanism was, of course, the rational Protestant religion best calculated to restrain human passions, and this latitudinarian Court Whiggism, as Sack points out, was much more attractive to loyalists than old Toryism (Sack, 1993: 70). The more sophisticated loyalist appeals to history, prescription, natural law and utility, as opposed to variations upon divine right, Christian morality and forms of passive obedience, began to construct a new Toryism that would become dominant in right-wing circles after 1800. Burke had attacked rational Dissent as part of an international Jacobin conspiracy against a civilisation part feudal and part modern, but the full elucidation of this case was left to churchmen like Jones and the Reverend Robert Nares, joint founders of the *British Critic*, a literary review launched in 1793 to contest the intellectual influence of the three liberal Dissenter reviews: the *Monthly*, *Analytical* and *Critical*. Most loyalist publications of the 1790s, with the exception of metropolitan newspapers and some pamphlets, were launched and funded under independent loyalist or High Church auspices, but a notable exception to this rule is the government-backed *Anti-Jacobin Review, or Monthly Magazine* that appeared in 1798 to succeed the more famous short-lived *Anti-Jacobin, or Weekly Political Magazine* produced by John Canning, William Gifford and J.H. Frere. In the pages of the *Anti-Jacobin Review*, Jacobinism was described by 1799 as a species of intellectual totalitarianism that represented the antithesis of all free speech and expression (AJR, 1798: i, 725–7; Sack, 1993: 12–27, 38–40).

Both the 'Tory' and radical reviews reached a wide audience of genteel readers with circulation figures of 3000 to 5000 throughout the 1790s. All these periodicals reviewed the latest books and, in many cases, pamphlets, thus ensuring the dissemination of contemporary publications to a wide audience of readers, many of whom shared copies or consulted them in lending libraries. The *Anti-Jacobin Review* and *British Critic* remained in print up to 1821 and 1828 respectively. All the radical and loyalist reviews were aimed at a genteel and prosperous audience. Although many clergymen and pamphleteers tried to write for a popular audience, they rarely rose above scurrilous abuse of Paine, popular radicals and the French Revolution (Hole, 1983; Claeys, 1989: 146–52). The famous John Bull tracts written by Jones display some familiarity with the culture, language and lifestyles of the people, but William Paley's *Reasons for Contentment, Addressed to the Journeymen, Mechanics and Labourers of Great Britain* (1792) emphatically did not, despite its ostensible composition for the masses (Hole, 1983: 53–63: Dinwiddy, 1991: 42–4).

Paley's *Principles of Moral and Political Philosophy*, published in 1785, was quarried by many a loyalist author for its pithy Court Whig defence of the British constitution (Christie, 1984: 160–4, 199). The *Moral and Political Philosophy*, much like Burke's *Reflections*, invoked history and expediency to explain the emergence and founding principles of Britain's governing institutions. Unlike the *Reflections*, the *Moral and Political Philosophy* articulated a form of conservative utilitarianism rarely espoused by loyalist authors, whose use of utility arguments often represented a form of common sense anti-intellectualism employed to discredit radical readings of history and rights (Paley, 1819: i, 398–443; Sack, 1993: 38–9; Claeys, 1989: 90–1).

Bentham's 1776 *Fragment on Government* had laid down the principle of utility as the 'greatest good of the greatest number', a quotation much abused over the past two centuries, and utilitarianism is more accurately described as a value system that assesses good and evil in relative terms according to the aggregate of pleasure or pain it promotes. 'Theological utilitarianism', a product of a Cambridge *via media* that sought to steer a middle path between Christianity and the Enlightenment during the last third of the eighteenth century, was the dominant form of the creed until Bentham's 'scientific' or secular utilitarianism emerged during the 1810s (Schofield, 1986: 605–9). According to Paley, Richard Hey and Adam Ferguson, the Professor of Moral Philosophy at the University of Glasgow, man was wrought by nature to seek pleasure, avoid pain and live in communities where his wants and needs generated rights and laws to protect his personal and corporate welfare. Liberty was defined by all loyalist utilitarians, contract and natural law theorists in negative terms as a responsibility conferring duties, rather than rights, upon citizens free only to pursue their desires insofar as their actions did not infringe upon the liberty and welfare of others. The 'felicific calculus' adopted by Bentham and Paley balanced the freedom of the individual against the good of the community by defining civil liberty as 'the not being restrained by any law, but what conduces in a greater degree to the public welfare' (Paley, 1819: i, 392–3).

Central to the principle of utility was the belief that definitions of the public welfare were subject to change over time and here some individuals were more tolerant than others. Burke, who accepted organic change over time nevertheless regarded a 'natural law' or set of immutable moral standards as the ultimate basis of utility (Stanlis, 1958: 73; Dinwiddy, 1974b, 1978). Paley, who questioned the relevance and justice of the game laws, poor laws and 'laws against Papists and Dissenters' to late eighteenth-century Britain, was at heart a Christian patriarchalist (1819: i, 393). All utilitarians rejected natural rights, described by Bentham as 'nonsense upon stilts', as the basis of citizenship because all rights were generated by social needs. The franchise, as Paley put it, could be regarded 'only as a right at all, as it conduces to public utility; that is, as it contributes to the establishment of good laws, or as it secures to the people the just administration of those laws . . . If the properest persons be elected, what matters it by whom they are elected?' (1819: i, 433–4; Gascoigne, 1989: 241–2; Claeys, 1989: 91–3,

150; Rosen, 1992: 26–39). Despite these views, Paley stood on the far left of the Anglican intellectual spectrum and, by 1802, the *Moral and Political Philosophy* would be receiving negative reviews from evangelical Anglicans, the *Anti-Jacobin Review* and Samuel Taylor Coleridge (Hole, 1989: 73–82; Hilton, 1988: 4–5, 170–9).

Contemporaries saw little difference between Bentham and Paley except, as Elie Halevy once put it, for the latter's belief in Hell (1928: 22–6). Despite admissions that Britain's constitution was not perfect, Paley maintained that it best realised God's stick-and-carrot system for promoting human happiness in this world and securing eternal salvation in the next. Bentham, who was moving towards atheism, preferred to construct elaborate systems of incentives and disincentives to mould human behaviour in this life. The vast 1789 *Introduction to the Principles and Morals of Legislation* laid out the principles upon which an ideal system of criminal law could maximise opportunities for the pursuit of happiness while protecting society from the ill-effects of malicious or careless self-interest. After a decade (1795–1805) spent in fruitless efforts to secure state funding for the Panopticon prison project and other pet schemes, a Bentham disillusioned with the British government and constitution would embrace radicalism and parliamentary reform, marking his change of heart by attaching himself to the Opposition Whigs and writing the 1809 *Parliamentary Reform Catechism*. This tract, finally published in 1817 as *The Plan of Parliamentary Reform*, laid out Bentham's mature system by which the interests of the governors and the governed were to be reconciled: this, the collective assembly of individual and corporate desires, was the greatest good of the greatest number to be best achieved through efficient and meritocratic institutions (Dinwiddy, 1986: 14–15; Crimmins, 1994). Bentham's *Church of England and Its Catechism Examined* (1818) and *Not Paul, but Jesus* (1823), both published under pseudonyms, would constitute withering attacks upon the doctrine and practices of the Church of England (Bentham, 1838: iii, 540, x, 451–9; Dinwiddy, 1975; Crimmins, 1990).

Loyalist utilitarians had no qualms about appealing to the enlightened self-interest of ordinary readers for, to their way of thinking, the human desire to pursue happiness was the engine that drove social development. Paley's *Equality, as Consistent with the British Constitution* (1793) pointed out that hard work and upward social mobility could give Britons both land and the political rights that accompanied it in Hanoverian Britain. 'Instead of working only five days a week, work six; and, in six years, you will have gained enough money to purchase a vote' (1793a: 5). Here Paley differed from other loyalist authors writing for a popular audience, who did not dress up self-interest in formal theoretical terms, much less admit that much economic and social elevation was an appropriate aim of the lower orders.

This principle, if carried to extremes, stood to subvert a society of rigidly demarcated ranks and orders. Arthur Young, who professed 'a constitutional abhorrence of theory, of all trust in abstract reasoning', simply told Britons to defend the highest living standards in Europe (Young, 1793: 3–4).

Self-improvement was proper for the lower orders only if conducted upon Christian principles and, for this reason, most loyalists were ambivalent about, or downright hostile to, a Scottish political economy that seemingly placed sordid acquisitiveness above all moral dictates. 'Dr. *Adam Smith*', wrote William Jones, 'seems to have reasoned wholly on a supposition, that national wealth is national happiness' (1793: 40). Classical political economy, part of the Enlightenment project to explain – and hopefully govern – social and political development, was rejected by many loyalists of the 1790s as a dismal science that sought to reduce all human relations to impersonal equations where happiness was measured in crude materialist terms (Hilton, 1988: 50; Sack, 1993: 180–3). Loyalists would be deeply suspicious of all market doctrines until they received a Christian justification from T.R. Malthus, whereupon political economy would bifurcate into two schools: the Scottish or classical system, and the English Christian tradition. Evangelical interpretations of enlightened self-interest would dominate much English thinking on self-love and possessive individualism, those once sacred cows of the Anglo-American liberal tradition (Burrow, 1988: 2–7) up to 1840 and ensure the descent of political economy through Whigs, Tories, liberals and moderates to inform a nineteenth-century British debate on wealth, commerce, free enterprise and industry long before Karl Marx sat down in north London to write *Das Kapital* (Mandler, 1990b: 84–5, 94–5).

Discourses of Commerce and Modernity

The survival of Enlightenment modes of thought during the wars against revolutionary and Napoleonic France can be most easily traced through the fortunes of political economy. This derives its name from its dual mission to explain the moral, political, cultural and economic conditions of life in commercial societies and to facilitate social progress through the adoption of appropriate state policies. Integral to both was an Enlightenment account of history explaining the rise and functions of western commercial civilisation from ancient to modern times (Hont and Ignatieff, 1983; Collini, Burrow and Winch, 1983; Pocock, 1985). This could be subscribed to by liberals, conservatives and moderates with the result that, by 1820, MPs and authors were facing each other in parliament and the press claiming common descent from Adam Smith.

Smith, having died in 1790, could not adjudicate between rival claimants to his intellectual inheritance. In writing the 1776 *Wealth of Nations* or the lesser known 1759 *Theory of Moral Sentiments*, Smith was not only conceptualising the interaction of supply and demand forces in the marketplace, but also the social mores that ought to regulate the world of truckle and barter. It was and remains possible to read Smith in several ways: as the father of free market economics, as a historian and social anthropologist, as a moral philosopher and as a Whig political theorist (Robertson, 1983a, 1983b). Smith's universe was not, as conservative critics claimed, an immoral place where greed reigned supreme, but rather one where benevolence and self-interest were mutually reinforcing (Winch, 1983a, 1992). Book V of the *Theory of Moral Sentiments* which contained Smith's 'science of a legislator', revised shortly before his death in 1790, has been read as a statement of disapproval for the French Revolution. Here the 'man of system', the slave to abstract doctrines who pursues them for their own sake regardless of their social cost, is derided in favour of the 'man of principle' whose measures were guided as much by expediency as by any theoretical set of convictions (Smith, 1976: i, 231–5, ii, 468). Pitt employed this argument in 1799 to explain the introduction of interventionist policies to conserve private and public sector grain reserves following an extremely bad harvest, for which he was criticised by Grenville, who was more wedded to strict *laissez-faire* (PR, 1799: xiii, 47–8).

Scottish political economy, as it emerged from the hands of Smith, identified commerce as the civilising and improving force in European history. For Paine, the American and French Revolutions had been made possible by the raising of popular expectations of all descriptions attendant upon the independent commercial progress of the modern era, and he predicted in Part II of the *Rights of Man* that the age of revolutions would engulf all of Europe within seven years because its societies had reached a state of intellectual, cultural and social development suitable for the widespread adoption of representative government (Paine, 1996: ii, 398). This vision of the French Revolution was shared by most British genteel radicals and James Mackintosh, whose 1791 *Vindiciae Gallicae* constituted a spirited defence of Paine, France and an Enlightenment four-stage model of anthropological evolution whereby humankind had moved from the primitive hunter-gatherer of antiquity to the modern commercial present (Mackintosh, 1791; McKenzie, 1986). This development paradigm was for much of the eighteenth century married to a critical radical Country Party consciousness complete with warnings against the corruption and moral enervation that accompanied the rise of rich and powerful societies. British Enlightenment thinkers were obsessed with the evils of decadence and complacence that had caused the downfall of ancient civilisations, and readers were reminded in the wake of the American Revolution by Edward Gibbon's timely *Decline and Fall of the Roman Empire* (1776–1785) that progress in all societies was finite (Hont and Ignatieff, 1983; Pocock, 1985: 486–7).

Subscription to the social and political theories of the Scottish Enlightenment during the 1790s was not confined to moderates, liberals and radicals, for which the assimilation of David Hume's ideas into mainstream Court Whig thought by 1780 was largely responsible. Burke and Paley reproduced Hume's classic defence of a conservative 1688 revolution without much of the critical scepticism that characterised its original author's musings on history, politics, society and government as expressed in the *History of Great Britain* (1754–1762), the *Essay Concerning Human Understanding* (1748) and the *Essays, Moral and Political* (1741–1742) (Forbes, 1970, 1976; Burrow, 1988: 54–6). Hume's cynicism and infidelity were in fact uncomfortable legacies for loyalists of the 1790s determined not to admit the existence of any deficiencies in the British constitution, with the result that only abridged or bowdlerised editions of his works were authorised by the *British Critic* as suitable for the education of the young and impressionable (BC, 1795: v, #4, 409–13). Loyalists tried to edit any potentially subversive text, not excepting the Bible, for which they foresaw a large audience during the 1790s and 1800s.

Loyalist political economists regarded the French Revolution as a reversal of *fortuna*'s wheel that, in the eyes of Gibbon and Burke, threatened to plunge Europe back into barbarism and poverty. By 1796 Mackintosh had joined the loyalist camp and apologised to Burke for the *Vindiciae Gallicae*, though he remained an Opposition Whig in political orientation, as did Francis Plowden, the natural law loyalist author of *Jura Anglorum: the Rights of Englishmen* (1794). Loyalist authors were defenders of constitution rather than the government: Burke had grown disillusioned with Pitt by 1796; Bentham, like his mentor Shelburne, distrusted the premier, while Paley often expressed contempt for 'that minister and his colleagues, *in private*' (Paley, 1819: i, xxxiv). For Burke, a modern civilisation and its notions of liberty and property was built upon the values of mediaeval feudalism as expressed in the institutions of monarchy, aristocracy and the Christian faith (Pocock, 1985: 199–210). Some commercial Whigs, not least Mackintosh, disagreed with this analysis, regarding the French Revolution as part of the historical process by which commercial modernity repudiated feudalism. The Pittite journalist William Playfair derided Burke's gothic fantasies and declared that a principal cause of the revolution had been the severe inequality in property ownership that had prevailed in *ancien régime* France (Playfair, 1796: 27, 1805: 182; McKenzie, 1986; Hampsher-Monk, 1991; Pocock, 1985; Walsh, 1995; Claeys, 1989: 153–7, 1990). Such authors identified an intellectual inconsistency in Paine's quest to restore the natural rights of the 'barbarian' hunter-gatherer past and, by implication, its accompanying poverty and anarchy, to a modern commercial civilisation that, whatever its defects, ensured all its citizens standards of living and civil liberty much higher than those enjoyed by primitive societies. This, the equation of natural rights with anarchy and the complete equalisation of property, was a misrepresentation of Paine's ideas common to all loyalist writing of the 1790s (Vincent, 1998: 74–5).

By claiming that some kind of aboriginal or Spartan total equality was the inevitable product of natural rights principles, commercial Whig loyalists were able to construct a positive defence of economic and social inequality. Rich societies were by definition inegalitarian, but the diversity of their trades, manufactures and arts ensured to all citizens the protection of their lives, liberties and livelihoods through institutions of law and government devised in the first instance for the protection of private property. America, as Paine's critics pointed out, was a state unsuitable for comparison to Europe, because its relative equality of property, low population density and lack of social distinctions created a society remarkably free, or so it seemed to Europeans, from crime, vice and poverty. Many commercial Whigs speculated that, as America grew and matured, its society would become as corrupt and enervated as any in *ancien régime* Europe (Claeys, 1989: 155–9, 1990: 62–3, 77, 1994; Hampsher-Monk, 1991: 8–9).

Radicals, wedded by history, discourse and inclination to aboriginal notions of universal natural rights, found it difficult to contest commercial Whig loyalist accusations that their ideal society repudiated the comforts of modern civilisation, much less commercial Whig claims that the revolution was destroying the French economy. This was a pillar of the Pittite case against revolutionary and Napoleonic France reiterated by many a loyalist pamphlet and every Chancellor of the Exchequer from 1793 to 1815 (AJR, 1797: i, #3, 85–6; Vincent, 1998: 77–8). Radical nostalgia envisaged a mythical golden age of peasant and artisan self-sufficiency that cast aside the mechanisms and moral conventions of a market economy, although some radical theorists, most notably Paine, Spence and Ogilvie, tried to incorporate some awareness of socio-commercial development into their projects. Spence and Ogilvie's land reform scheme gave labourers a free choice between land and manufacturing under conditions of total *laissez-faire* market equality in each sector, while Paine's welfare schemes, as laid out in the *Rights of Man* and 1796 *Agrarian Justice* (1996: ii, 393, iii, 328–44), came complete with provisions for universal education, old age pensions and compensation payments to the people for the existence of inequalities in property ownership. These projects constituted an attempt to reconcile natural rights and commercial development: in the case of *Agrarian Justice*, to protect the principle of property through a judicious redistribution of its benefits. The welfare state proposals in Part II of the *Rights of Man* constituted both an instrument of commercial Enlightenment and a safety net for its victims (Claeys, 1987: 23–4, 26, 1989: 96–101; Dinwiddy, 1976: 266–9, 1991b: 40–1; Horne, 1991: 237–8; Cunliffe, 1994: 544–7, 551–2).

Commercial civilisation nonetheless had enemies in radical theorists like Charles Hall, whose 1805 work, *The Effects of Civilization upon the People in European States*, advocated a division of land amongst the people, retaining only the coarsest of manufactures. 'The greatest phenomenon in a civilised nation is the inequality of property' claimed Hall (1805: 157–8). 'Good God!', exclaimed a horrified Spence: 'Would you have us to become again Goths and Vandals and give up every elegant Comfort of Life?' (Claeys, 1981: 317). Popular radicals found it difficult to reconcile radical concepts of liberty with the reality of inequality in developed market economies. Hall, often described as an early socialist who borrowed from Smithian and Malthusian *laissez-faire* to construct his own theory of labour exploitation (Dinwiddy, 1976), was in fact and essence an old-fashioned nostalgic radical repudiating the comforts of commercial civilisation. Only Thelwall adopted Smith's labour theory of value: as the property of workers lay in the labour that sustained the wealth of nations, they above all men were entitled to a say in the nation's affairs (Claeys, 1987: 29–30, 1994: 263–74; Hampsher-Monk, 1991: 12–18). Property-based arguments in defence of liberty were nevertheless anathema to most radicals, who preferred reason, justice and natural rights as justifications for citizenship. The fidelity of British popular radicals to visions of agrarian equality appeared in the Chartist Land Plan of 1848 and testifies to a rejection of commercial capitalism that by the mid-nineteenth century had become explicit amongst popular radicals. The *New View of Society* (1813), based by Robert Owen on twenty years' management of the famous New Lanark cotton mills, was unusual in identifying the interests of capitalists and workers as one and the same in a form of co-operative socialism that sought to distribute the fruits of manufacturing plenty to all those who participated in their production. History, for Owen, was not reversible, nor was such a reversal desirable (Claeys, 1981: 317, 1987: 34–48; Hont and Ignatieff, 1983: 1–43; Cunliffe, 1990, 1994).

In the 1803 edition of T.R. Malthus's *Essay on the Principle of Population*, theological utilitarianism met classical political economy to repudiate radical attacks on property and establish a school of Christian free market thought that would inform the Liberal Toryism of the 1820s. Malthus has often been described as a Tory because *Population*, written in part to refute Godwin's *Political Justice*, constituted a defence of land, private property and socio-economic inequality. Malthus, though an anti-utopian, was neither a reactionary nor a Tory. *Population* merely adumbrated that Godwinian perfection was unattainable because all societies, regardless of the principles on which they were constituted, grew in exponential terms, while agricultural output increased at an arithmetic rate and was subject to a law of diminishing marginal returns when less fertile lands were brought into cultivation to feed an increasing supply of mouths. When demand outran the food supply, suffering and death were bound to result (Malthus, 1992: 58–63).

The first (1798) edition of *Population* had attempted to refute Godwin's faith in the triumph of reason and benevolence over self-interest with a materialist psychology that described the creation of the human mind as an attempt to evade evil while presenting scarcity as a stimulant to hard work and social mobility. Radical unitarians were impressed by so unusual a heterodoxy from a Church of England clergyman, but liberal Anglicans were alarmed by a work that not only contradicted the teachings of the Christian faith but, in its predictions of mass starvation, denied the wisdom, mercy and omnipotence of God. The 1803 edition of *Population* that made Malthus's name appeared without the final two chapters, whose removal had been requested by 'some friends' who liked the economics, if not the theology, of the essay's contents (James, 1979: 116–21; Pullen, 1981; Hilton, 1988: 74–5; Waterman, 1991: 90–1).

Malthus differed from Smith and the commercial Whig loyalists in suggesting that increasing wealth did not automatically benefit the mass of humanity. If population rose without a corresponding increase in food supply, prices would creep upwards while both the wages and availability of employment would decline. If both grew in tandem, a competitive marketplace was the socio-economic mechanism that maximised the returns of land, labour and capital to arrive at an equilibrium between population, food and other resources. Human history was therefore characterised not by progress but rather by a state of constant oscillation between interrelated forms of supply and demand. The first edition of *Population* predicted that sexual passion, though likely to remain static amongst humans, would inevitably produce a population explosion that could be averted only by the adoption of preventive checks to procreation that Malthus felt were unlikely to appeal to many (Malthus, 1992: 25–9; Waterman, 1991: 51–7).

The second (1803) edition of *Population* was much less gloomy in outlook, having adopted a utilitarian perspective on psychology, theodicy and history derived from Paley's 1802 *Natural Theology*. God, having endowed man with passion and reason, intended the latter to overcome the former by confrontations with the temptations of vice and evil. As all life was a state of probation for the hereafter, moral struggles within a market economy that created poverty and inequality constituted a test of virtue to prepare the soul for the next life. The seemingly impersonal laws governing the operation of the free market had been placed in a Christian perspective, as had the relationship between self-love, reason and benevolence. Through late marriage and sexual restraint, population growth might be checked, which would produce greater wealth and security for the poor while safeguarding the future progress of humankind (Hilton, 1988: 220–3; Waterman, 1991: 137–50, 258; Winch, 1996; Heavner, 1996: 419–29).

Malthus completed the process by which commercial Whigs steered a middle road between Jacobinism and the mainstream loyalist conservatism so often dubbed Toryism in the writings of twentieth-century scholars. His fears of poverty and starvation were taken to heart by some radicals, amongst whom Francis Place emerged as an advocate of birth control during the 1810s (Miles, 1988). Liberal and evangelical Anglicans embraced a *laissez-faire* that not only placed poverty and suffering into a new eschatological dimension, but denied that any form of intervention in the economy could produce improvement in the human condition (Hilton, 1988: Ch. 2). Malthus called for the introduction of universal public education to inculcate virtuous self-interest amongst the people, but he also insisted upon the repeal of the old poor law to promote self-discipline. Only *ad hoc* private charity was an acceptable source of relief, for it would not encourage procreation by ensuring handouts to the poor in times of trouble. In 1815 Malthus would defend the Corn Laws on the grounds that the agricultural interest constituted the bedrock of Britain's wealth and future prosperity, for he feared that manufacturing and trade were more capable of attracting capital investment than land, a tendency that would encourage the decline of productive agriculture. He was appalled by the poverty of the industrial towns, which in part explains his hostility towards manufacturing, although he was no enemy to commercial progress, having defended wealth, luxury and trade in much the same terms as other commercial Whigs (Malthus, 1992: 133–50).

Population underwent continual refinement throughout the 1810s and 1820s, for Malthus felt compelled to respond to his many critics: radical, liberal and conservative. He is best described, in political terms, as some kind of Whig, for he gave no open support to any Pittite government of the day, reserving his defence of the *status quo* for the Hanoverian constitutional monarchy in general terms. In 1796 *The Crisis*, an anonymous Malthus pamphlet, had urged Britons to stand firm against corruption in the defence of liberty against arbitrary government, and he reflected in the 1817 edition of *Population* that the British government 'had shown no great love of peace and liberty during the last twenty-five years'. Malthus also deviated from mainstream loyalist party norms in his support for Catholic Emancipation and moderate constitutional reform (James, 1979: 50–1, 140–1, 153–4, 234, 422; Winch, 1983c: 75–7).

It is artificial to look for hard and fast distinctions between 'classical' and 'Christian' political economy during the first two decades of the nineteenth century (Hilton, 1988: 36–8). David Ricardo, who corresponded amicably with Malthus from 1811 to 1823, placed the theories of population and diminishing marginal returns at the centre of *The Principles of Political Economy and Taxation* (1817). Rent was deemed by Ricardo to increase as population grew, rising in proportion to the marginal costs of cultivation. If population grew too rapidly, wages would be driven down to subsistence levels while the increased costs of agricultural production would increase food prices and force down demand levels for fabricated goods, thereby reducing profits and depressing capital investment in both land and manufacturing. Ricardo defined the real domestic value of commodities not by short-term supply and demand as Smith had done, but by the cost of labour required for their production. Wages, however, were determined only by the cost of necessities and were unlikely to exceed them dramatically, whereas profits were inversely proportional to wages, rising as wages fell and falling as wages rose under conditions of static equilibrium between food and population (1951–3: i, 12–15, 74–7, 101–5, 117–27). Ricardo's prognosis for the future of British society was less gloomy than that of Malthus: the repeal of the Corn Laws and other restrictions on food imports, coupled with taxation policies that promoted capital accumulation and relieved the poor of unnecessary burdens, would, with the widespread adoption of family planning, enable Britain to support a rising population along with increasing standards of living, provided that the country abandoned expensive and inefficient agriculture in favour of industry and imported food from abroad. Malthus, who was alarmed by Ricardo's endorsements of capital accumulation that promoted manufacturing at the expense of agriculture, remonstrated with Ricardo on these subjects (Winch, 1983c: 73–5).

Despite their mutual engagement in debate on a series of topics common to political economy, Malthus and Ricardo represented different aspects of the Smithian inheritance reflected in their preoccupations and methodology. For Ricardo, the study of economics was only political insofar as it promoted healthy market growth and, despite his interest in currency management and taxation, he divorced economics from political theory, regarding it as 'a strict science, like mathematics' (1951–3: viii, 331). Ricardo's chief interest consequently lay in tracing the long-term tendencies of market trends, while Malthus, who still saw political economy in part as 'the science of a legislator', was rather inclined to concentrate upon short-term fluctuations and practical examples of economic principles; on occasion appealing not to logic nor science, but to the higher maxims of justice, virtue and happiness. The increasing specialisation of political economy as a social science of economics was deplored by many contemporaries, who felt that it was becoming impenetrable (Winch, 1996; Cremasci and Dascal, 1996).

The political science legacy of the Scottish Enlightenment was kept alive in the University of Edinburgh by Dugald Stewart, Professor of Moral Philosophy, ex-colleague and literary executor of Adam Smith. Stewart's lecture series on political economy, given from 1799 to 1809, exercised a formative influence upon Francis Horner, Francis Jeffrys, Henry Brougham and Sydney Smith, the founders of the most influential 'liberal' periodical of the early nineteenth century, *The Edinburgh Review* launched in 1802. Stewart was in part responsible for maintaining political economy as a broad school of study: undergraduates who thought political economy to consist of two subjects, wealth and population, were stunned to find themselves attending lectures on subjects from history to metaphysics (Clive, 1957: 25–6; Chitnis, 1976: 160–1, 175–6, 1986: 20–7; Winch, 1983a; Fontana, 1985: Ch. 1; Hilton, 1988: 38–40).

Stewart, like Mackintosh, turned against the French Revolution in 1792. Despite deploring the sterile, sceptical and infidel features of Enlightenment philosophy along with other loyalists of the 1790s, Stewart retained the conviction, derived from Condorcet rather than Godwin, that rational self-interest would triumph over vulgar passion. This belief in the perfectibility of human society was qualified by the recognition that pitfalls lay in the path of commercial progress, and Stewart was an early convert to the population theories of Malthus (Stewart, 1854–60: ii, 231–40, vii, 203–7). Stewart nevertheless maintained that universal enlightenment, in itself the motor and hallmark of commercial socio-economic development, was through the spread of consumerism and a free press producing a rational and informed body of public opinion to replace the civic virtue upon which Malthus still relied for responsible citizenship. The emergence of an enlightened public necessitated the investigation and adoption of 'those universal principles of justice and expediency which ought, under every form of government, to regulate the social order' (Stewart, 1854–60: ii, 309–13; Chitnis, 1976: 218–20; Burrow, 1988: 67–8).

The *Edinburgh Review* soared rapidly into the limelight to replace the old Dissenter-run *Monthly* and *Critical Reviews* as the liberal journal of educated readers: having started with only 750 subscribers, by 1814 the *Edinburgh* commanded 13,000. In 1807, the *Edinburgh* sided publicly with the Whig Opposition with which it would remain in partnership for the next three decades and, in 1809, the 'Tory' Canningite *Quarterly Review* would be founded to contest its influence (Chitnis, 1976: 213–26; Cookson, 1982: 84–114; Sack, 1987: 626). This marriage of liberal intellect with party politics was not brought about by any meeting of minds between the reviewers and the leaders of the Opposition, who with a few notable exceptions like the ex-Pittite Lord Grenville had no deep interest in political economy. The reviewers nevertheless believed that the chief practical object of the noble science – the peaceful integration of public opinion into the political nation – was most likely to be achieved in collaboration with moderate reform Whigs than reactionary Tories (Clive, 1957: 125, 127; Winch, 1983a: 44– 57; Fontana, 1985: 112–14, 117–18, 127–8, 135–7). The government did not lack devotees of political economy, but its invariable subordination to what Vansittart called 'higher truths of religion and morality', not to mention common subscription to a complacent Court Whig conviction that the unreformed British constitution gave the people, as Huskisson put it, 'more means of procuring to themselves the enjoyment of life than any of their predecessors', militated against the prospect of any reform coming from this quarter (PD, xiv, 1122–3, xix, 943–4, 960). Brougham and Horner, who entered parliament in 1806 and 1809 respectively, soon took seats on the Opposition benches as trenchant critics of government war spending, the income tax, the Corn Laws, the East India Company's monopoly and the paper pound as instruments of state tyranny employed against the liberties and property of the people.

The marriage of convenience between the *Edinburgh Review* and the Whigs required some compromises on the part of the editors; not least in the policing of articles critical of an Established Church seen by Stewart and his pupils as an agency of social control perpetuating vulgar prejudices fit only for eradication from the minds of the British people. The reviewers cared little for the natural theology of Malthus and Paley or, at the opposite end of the intellectual spectrum, the secular utilitarianism of Bentham. Neither theological nor secular utilitarians, however, opposed political economy or its history and vision of social progress. A free market, whether justified by Christian teachings or principles derived from empirical observation, ensured of all socio-economic systems the greatest freedom of choice to the greatest number of persons (Hilton, 1977, 1988: 32–3; Waterman, 1991). Radicals faithful to natural jurisprudence and loyalists moving towards romantic conservatism found both political economy and utilitarianism equally sterile, impersonal and objectionable, incorporating attacks against both into their critiques of a social order both old and new.

Radical Toryism and Romantic Conservatism

The radical print culture of the 1810s was distinctly different from that of the 1790s. Though both were indebted to the Country Party tradition of the eighteenth century, the strength of its intellectual influence over popular radicalism grew, rather than weakened, over the opening decades of the nineteenth century. As radical attacks upon the old order shifted from the general to the specific, namely the policies and personalities of the governments that ruled Britain during the revolutionary and Napoleonic Wars, the cosmopolitan Enlightenment was left behind in favour of borrowings from native or contemporary liberal schools of thought, amongst them the agrarian nostalgia of Spence, Protestant martyrology as it emerged from the radical press during the 1790s, and Benthamite utilitarianism.

Natural jurisprudence, in radical hands, turned decisively against political economy during the 1800s by adopting some of its own mid-eighteenth-century concerns. Hume had listed the growth of the national debt, imperial expansion and court corruption as sources of enervation that might reverse the process of growth and development experienced by European society since the Middle Ages; all were seized upon by radical journalists to contest government and commercial Whig claims that Britain's constitution and the prosperity it upheld would triumph over France. Paine's 1796 *Decline and Fall of the English System of Finance* was early to raise the spectre of imminent state bankruptcy, and its repeated reprints, one in the 1832 *Working Man's Political Companion*, testify to the strength of a radical conviction that Old Corruption carried within it the seeds of its own destruction: namely an uncontrollable debt that would eventually topple the old order and, with it, the financial, commercial and manufacturing interests with whom it constituted a cabal of corruption and exploitation. As cases went, it was exaggerated, for institutionalised government corruption was not, as far as we can tell, as extensive a cancer as radicals claimed and the case against it could not fully emerge until the 1810s, when a decade of unsuccessful warfare could be evinced in support of radical claims that a vast and sinister system of venery connecting the public debt, taxation, commercial expansion, paper currency and imperial expansion was at work in British politics and policy. To these concerns was added a pessimism about the finite limits of economic growth derived from Malthus, employed against the faith of successive Pittite governments and *Edinburgh Reviewers* in the possibilities of limitless progress.

The radical belief in the perfectibility of man had by 1816 given way to a strong sense of economic crisis that would intensify in the years after the war. In the hands of William Cobbett, T.J. Wooler, William Hone and Richard Carlile, the national debt and paper pound would become the tools with which the state manipulated the economy to produce illusions of profit and plenty belied by the realities of want and suffering amongst the poor. Inflation, rather than real economic growth, was held responsible by radicals for any seeming increase in the nation's wealth, and political economy in any form was therefore a 'zero-sum game' against which radical journalists employed their own calculus of deprivation. A spiralling national debt required punitive taxation to service it, authorised by MPs chosen by fraudulent elections that made a mockery of representation as a principle of government. The debt, in itself necessary to support a London money market where public and private sector credit was the literal stock-in-trade of bankers, merchants and brokers, bound the monied and commercial interests in partnership with a corrupt parliament and civil service. This interrelation of interests explained the commitment of all four to imperial and commercial expansion requiring high levels of military expenditure and, hence, more debt, for the defence of British colonies and British trade. The whole self-perpetuating system was nonetheless destined to collapse under its own weight when it outstripped the limited ability of land and labour to sustain the edifice (Gilmartin, 1996: 1–64; Cookson, 1982: 37–42, 53; Thompson, 1984: 191–3, 217; Claeys, 1987; Harling, 1996b: 15–21; Horne, 1991: 216–37; Cunliffe, 1994: 547–9; Spence, 1996: 182–7).

Agrarian justice and artisan independence consequently remained the ideals of radicals from the Country MP Sir Francis Burdett through Leigh Hunt, editor of the genteel *Examiner*, to Carlile, the infidel republican, and Cobbett, the radical Tory. Only T.J. Wooler and John Wade appealed to secular utilitarianism in a partial attempt to escape from the politics of nostalgia, but Wooler was as capable in *Black Dwarf* of quoting Paine as Bentham, and the mass platform of the 1810s was constructed as traditional foundations. Cobbett, who had spent the 1790s and early 1800s as an opponent of Paine, American democracy and the French Revolution, had joined the radical camp in 1805 after a dispute with his government press patron, William Windham (Prothero, 1979: 79–85; Smith, 1975: 267; Sack, 1979: 59–60, 1993: 87–8; Hone, 1982: 149–59; Emsley, 1979a: 129; Dinwiddy, 1986: 31–2). Notwithstanding a nominal conversion to natural rights and universal manhood suffrage, Cobbett remained an inveterate enemy of the French Revolution and its Jacobin assaults upon monarchy, aristocracy, property and organised religion until his death in 1835. To defend these institutions, a British constitution subverted by commercial corruption and the rights of the people, who were oppressed by a factory system that exposed the evils of so-called progress and modernity, Cobbett became a radical. He was anti-modern and anti-industrial: in the *Rural Rides*, he juxtaposed an idealised life of bucolic agricultural self-sufficiency against the poverty and squalor of the manufacturing towns (Dickinson, 1985: 64–5, 70–1; Dyck, 1992: 23–33; Natrass, 1995: 89–118; Gilmartin, 1996: 187–8; Green, 1985: 270).

The Enlightenment had nothing to teach Cobbett, whose radicalism sprang rather from an organic conservative nationalism that led him to venerate the monarchy, the gentry and the Church of England. The virulent bigotry displayed in his writings against the French, Jews, Catholics and Dissenters may well have increased the appeal of his work to a mass audience for whom his nationalist xenophobia accorded well with long-established popular prejudices (Colley, 1992; Dickinson, 1992a,b). Cobbett's talents as a radical journalist lay in pithy and abusive denunciations of the individuals and institutions he most loathed. Credit for the development of radical mock advertisements, trial accounts and children's books must go rather to Wooler, Carlile, Hone and John Wade, all of whom traced their radical nostalgia and descent directly from Country Party republicanism and the radical print culture of the 1790s, rather than Cobbett's sudden conversion to the cause of reform (Epstein, 1994: Ch. 2; Wood, 1994: 144–54, 186–263; Gilmartin, 1996: 70–157).

Equally hostile opponents of trade, capitalism and industry could be found amongst the first-generation romantic conservatives, whose renunciation of radicalism and the French Revolution had not destroyed their concern for the underprivileged. Wordsworth's autobiographical poem, the *Prelude* (1850), published posthumously after half a century of tinkering, explained its author's commitment to the ideals of the revolution as an outgrowth of a social conscience appalled by poverty and suffering (Roe, 1988; Scott, 1989; Morrow, 1990: 1–42; Eastwood, 1989b, 1992). By 1798, when Wordsworth started to compose the *Prelude*, he, Coleridge and Southey had adopted Burke's defence of the British constitution on the grounds of history and expediency, grafting onto it a vision of society as an organic and, ideally, harmonious entity of mutually interdependent orders bound by deference and duty (Roe, 1988; Jones, 1993: 189–218; Spence, 1996: 7). Having by 1800 turned against British popular radicalism – the French Terror of 1793–1794 having shown that violent anarchy was the product of uncontrolled experiments in mass political and cultural education – the romantics also rejected an Enlightenment science of human nature whose infidelity, irreverence and scepticism stood to destroy all social order and, in its apotheosis of pure reason, ignored the cultivation of the finer passions, namely sensibility and imagination, to be acquired through the contemplation of nature, be it in the Lake District or elsewhere. English pastoral poetry would never be the same again, and central to its celebration of England's green and pleasant land was a lament for a popular rural lifestyle whose organic harmony with the natural world was threatened by enclosure and industrialisation (Beer, 1977: 60–1; Robertson-Scott, 1989: 244–8; Eastwood, 1989b: 315–19).

Whatever the Lake Poets had repudiated since the 1790s – Jacobinism, Godwinian perfectionism and unitarianism – their social consciences remained alive to the emerging horrors of factories and slums. Wordsworth retired into Cumberland rusticity in 1809, but Southey and Coleridge remained trenchant public critics of Malthus, Bentham and Ricardo, not to mention a society they felt had abandoned the gentry paternalism and

Christian values of an earlier age to embrace the sensual and self-interested materialism of the present (Sack, 1993: 156, 160–6). The Lake Poets placed the blame for new – as opposed to old – corruption upon the manufacturing system rather than the National Debt beloved of radical reformers: as such, Wordsworth and Coleridge were devoted supporters of Pittite governments, the war against Napoleon and popular radicalism, the Church of England and the monarchy during the 1810s. Southey and Coleridge nevertheless advocated an adoption of extensive social welfare policies to redress the sufferings of the industrial and rural poor: here the romantic conservatives differed markedly from the governments they supported, whose members, convinced that in possessive individualism lay the future progress of British society, were moving towards *laissez-faire* over the 1810s. This was not the world sought by the Lake Poets, who were as attracted to golden age nostalgia as radicals: it satisfied their longings for a better society without requiring them to make the mental leap in the dark that the advocacy of a brave new world would bring. Having tried to do so and been disappointed in the example of France during the 1790s, Wordsworth, Coleridge and Southey now shrank away from radicalism and reform, fearing that its ignorant enthusiasm stood to destroy an old order already threatened by commerce and industry. They made unusual bedfellows for radicals in the quest for humanitarianism and social justice as Britain moved into the factory age.

CHAPTER THREE

Radicals and Loyalists

On 15 April 1811, Major John Cartwright, founder of the 1781 Society for Constitutional Information, wrote to fellow reform veteran Christopher Wyvill, leader of the Yorkshire Association, that fear alone would persuade parliament to reform itself. 'We are to remember that the despotism being legislative, it must be the very *agent of its own reformation*' (Cartwright, 1826: ii, 7). In 1776, Cartwright had outlined a six-point reform programme including the secret ballot, equal constituencies and the payment of MPs in *Take Your Choice!*, a pamphlet that would inform the demands of parliamentary reformers for the next century. The long struggle for the widening of the franchise has a deceptively united platform and appearance which should not blind students to the existence of serious social and political divisions amongst reformers (Philp, 1991). The trials and tribulations of popular radicalism from 1792 to 1820 moreover comprise but one part of the history of reform movements during this period. The abolition of the slave trade, repeal of the Test and Corporation Acts and reform of the old poor law were all mooted during these years, as were evangelical moral campaigns for the suppression of vice and the conversion of the heathen at home and abroad. Some of these causes, most notably the abolition of the slave trade, commanded far more public interest and support than the reform of parliament, while others, such as Catholic Emancipation, attracted little public support on the British mainland (Royle and Walvin, 1982).

Tireless as activists were in their efforts to mobilise public opinion behind their causes, the fact remained that the co-operation of parliament was instrumental to the success of reform. MPs and peers fearful of change or a loss of privilege were often reluctant to vote for reform measures: a conservatism that frustrated their supporters long before the outbreak of the

French Revolution. Successful reform bills also required a concert of aims and activities on the part of reformers both within parliament and outside its doors, for failure to reach agreement on tactical issues could do a cause considerable harm in the public eye. A Younger Pitt disillusioned by the failure of Wyvill's county associations to give adequate support to his 1785 reform bill decided thereafter never to rely exclusively upon extra-parliamentary lobby groups again. In 1793 Charles Grey, on behalf of the Society of the Friends of the People (FOP), warned the metropolitan re-form bodies, the London Corresponding Society (LCS) and the Society for Constitutional Information (SCI), that their radical objectives were inconsistent with the moderate reform bill he proposed to present to parlia-ment. The FOP was concerned about what it perceived as the extremism of popular radical groups who, in turn, were frustrated by the conservatism of the Foxite reform platform. Dissatisfaction with one's political allies cut both ways. MPs could, as Pitt and Grey did, choose to chastise and repudi-ate their followers. Extraparliamentary reform bodies did not find it so easy to disown their spokesmen. The London Committee for the Abolition of the Slave Trade spent the 1780s and 1790s in a state of acute dissatisfaction about the inefficiency of William Wilberforce and, despite repeated efforts on his part, no abolition bill passed both Houses until 1806 (Grey, 1861: 19; Anstey, 1975; Walvin, 1986).

Parliament's motives for accepting reform were often negative rather than positive. The loss of the American colonies in 1783 had delivered a severe shock to the British psyche, forcing peers and MPs to confront the shortcomings of their political system. Parliament during the 1780s was consequently sympathetic, if not always supportive, to reform initiatives ranging from Burke's Civil Establishment Act of 1782 to Mitford's Catholic Relief Act of 1791. This climate of relative tolerance would gradually dis-appear from 1789 onwards, to be replaced by 1793 with a general fear of the French Revolution and its possible repercussions in Britain (Dozier, 1983; Dickinson, 1977: 270–318, 1985: 25–9; Schofield, 1986: 601–3). Such ap-prehensions did not, however, shut down all reform activity in parliament. An evangelical consciousness strengthened by war and revolution ensured that reform causes presented in moral and Christian terms, most notably the abolition of the slave trade, could command considerable public sup-port. From 1792 onwards, the leadership of reform causes would shift to reformers outside parliament and the initiative would not return to the House of Commons until the later 1800s.

High and Low Politics, 1785–1792

Three reform causes of the 1780s – parliamentary reform, abolition of the slave trade and repeal of the Test and Corporation Acts – were successful in attracting support from leading MPs, thus ensuring high-profile attention from the media and House of Commons. In 1783 an alliance formed between William Pitt and Christopher Wyvill had led to county association participation outside parliament to raise support for Pitt's 1785 reform bill. Despite the general sympathy it evoked from the radical metropolitan reform organisations – Cartwright's SCI, the Westminster Association and the Middlesex Association – the bill failed to pass the House of Commons, never to be revived as a comprehensive package of legislation by Pitt. From the premier's perspective, the alliance with Wyvill had not been entirely satisfactory. Pitt, as an enemy to universal manhood suffrage or 'actual representation', disliked the Yorkshire Association's attempt to solicit supporting petitions from persons and reform bodies regardless of their political and intellectual backgrounds and, following the failure of the bill, decided to dispense with Wyvill's support in the future (Christie, 1962: 212–20, 1970: 261–83; Cannon, 1972: 86–95; Ehrman, 1983: 58–76, 223–8).

By the end of 1786, the SCI, the Yorkshire Association and the county association movement were moribund. Disillusionment with reform and its failure to make any headway in the House of Commons had overcome the reform societies and they faded away. Parliamentary reform was not yet dead in parliament, however, for radicals like London alderman Thomas Sawbridge continued, despite a lack of Commons interest, to present reform motions to the House on an annual basis, while Pitt and a coterie of young friends – Charles, third Earl Stanhope, William Wilberforce and Edward James Eliot – continued to advocate moderate reform. The young William Grenville, future Foreign Secretary and joint Leader of the Opposition, was a peripheral member of the group up to 1785. Pitt's bill, intended by its author to be the first and last reform of parliament, had proposed to abolish rotten boroughs and redistribute the 100 newly freed seats to manufacturing towns, outer London and the county constituencies while enfranchising tenant copyholders in the shires. Pitt's commitment to the creation of new urban constituencies and the creation of new voters was in fact lukewarm, for his chief interest lay in electoral reform and constituency boundary reform. After 1785 Pitt and his friends would concentrate on these objectives to the exclusion of the franchise (Stanhope and Gooch, 1914: 66–70; Jupp, 1985: 17, 30, 59; Mori, 1997b: 21–6).

By 1790 the young MPs, despite the repeated presentation of electoral registration and anti-bribery bills to the House (the latter carrying heavy penalties, including the temporary disenfranchisement of entire boroughs and the debarring from the Commons of guilty candidates), had scored only two victories: Grenville's 1785 Controverted Elections Act and a 1788 County Elections Act put together by Wilberforce and Stanhope. The first amended Commons procedures for the adjudication of disputed elections while the second strove to set up proper electoral registers. The County Elections Act was repealed in 1789 despite the valiant efforts of Pitt and Eliot. None of the Pittite projects had been popular in either House of Parliament, having been opposed by 'a formidable coalition of the King's Friends and the Whig Aristocracy' (Wyvill, 1794; iv, 29). Wyvill, who remained in correspondence with Pitt and Wilberforce, had hoped to revive their old alliance, but the failure of reform to appeal either to the public or to parliament made this prospect unlikely and, by 1790, all the young Pittites including Stanhope had given up parliamentary reform for the moment. Wilberforce, when agreeing in 1786 to act as the Commons spokesman for the abolition of the slave trade, a campaign of which Wyvill approved, hoped for the swift and successful passage of the measure before the public attention was caught by some other cause (Ditchfield, 1981: 227; Langford, 1991: 278–82; Mori, 1997b: 28–30; Wilberforce, 1838: i, 305–6).

The abolition campaign had been launched in 1787 by a non-denominational coalition of Quakers, Anglicans and philanthropists determined to end a traffic in human flesh that, in their opinion, degraded the name of British Christianity. Led by the London Committee for the Abolition of the Slave Trade the campaign had within twelve months received professions of support from Pitt and Fox. Despite these promising signs, the London Committee had been careful to define its aims before going public. Although the committee loathed slavery, it agreed that a demand for emancipation would be regarded as an attack on the British empire and therefore likely to damage their cause. Opposition could be foreseen from shipping firms, plantation owners, the City of London and other business interests with financial stakes in the highly lucrative West Indian sugar trade. The committee therefore decided to ask for nothing more than an end to the slave trade in the first instance, hoping through the distribution of abolition literature to raise public awareness and create a sense of moral outrage that would outweigh any economic arguments made by vested interests (Anstey, 1975: 224–74; Walvin, 1986: 149–53).

Before 1792 abolition was the cause with almost everything in its favour: government and opposition support, the blessing of the Established Church, and a body of sympathetic public opinion called into existence by a sophisticated public relations machine employing publicity devices from pamphlets and public meetings to consumer products carrying abolitionist messages (Royle and Walvin, 1982: 32–40; Oldfield, 1995: 155–63). The abolition movement owed its rapid spread in the provinces to Quaker networks mobilised in support of the measure: to this religious infrastructure was added a flood of abolition literature full of hard facts about mortality figures on the Middle Passage. A House of Commons presented with this mass of statistics would pass abolition twice in principle before Britain entered the French Revolutionary Wars. These Wilberforce initiatives of 1789 and 1792 would be foiled by the House of Lords, but MPs, in general, did not express hostility to the measure until they began to associate it with the French Revolution. In 1791 a rebellion of French slaves on the island of St Domingue (modern Haiti) led Britons to fear that English slaves would follow suit. Many supporters of abolition were enemies to emancipation and, when fear of the French Revolution began late in 1791 to replace complacence and admiration, many peers and MPs withdrew their support from the measure (Anstey, 1975: 276–7).

Equally damaging to the abolition cause was the Dissenter campaign for the repeal of the Test and Corporation Acts. The structure of the Test repeal lobby was similar to that of other reform causes, possessing a London co-ordinating committee, a network of provincial supporters and a Commons sponsor in the Unitarian MP Henry Beaufoy. The near success of Test repeal in 1787 by 124 to 104 votes encouraged the Dissenters to persist and, having acquired the support of Fox, it would be presented to parliament again in 1789, 1790 and 1794. Pitt, having sounded the Established Church and George III on the issue, had in 1787 spoken in opposition to Beaufoy's measure, thereby swaying many uncommitted MPs into rejecting the measure. The church and the king made powerful enemies and, after some private soul-searching, Pitt declared his support for the Tests on the grounds of expediency. Having taken up this position, he maintained it for the next decade (PR, xxi, 562–7; Goodwin, 1979: 82–95; Ehrman, 1983: 51–7). Test repeal would not be passed until 1828.

Despite the fact that Dissenters had long since shed their seventeenth-century Puritan enthusiasm, Test repeal was a public issue that revived old Anglican apprehensions about nonconformist radicalism in politics and religion. The dissolution of the erastian church–state partnership seemingly heralded by Test repeal suggested that the Dissenters sought more drastic root and branch constitutional reform. The campaign attracted the backing of leading Unitarians, and Price's *Discourse on the Love of Our Country* was only one shot fired in a Test repeal pamphlet war between Dissenters and Anglicans where 'liberal' political and religious ideas began to acquire a bad name. Sympathy for the French Revolution made Dissenters suspect in the eyes of many, and Wilberforce was told in the spring of 1792 that Anglican support for abolition was waning because it was widely believed that 'the

Dissenters wish for a French Revolution and the abolition of the slave trade is somehow connected with it' (Wilberforce, 1838: 89–90; Henriques, 1961: 62–3; Goodwin, 1977: 90–8; Clark, 1985: 91–3).

The emergence of British popular radicalism in 1792 would turn parliament against reform of many descriptions. Burke and his disciple, Windham, would oppose the independent MP Henry Flood's 1790 moderate parliamentary reform bill on the grounds that any change was unwise at a time when the French Revolution was threatening to destroy all social order. The defeat of the bill was attributable not to general agreement with Burke but to lack of Commons interest in Flood's plans to abolish 50 rotten boroughs, transfer the seats to other constituencies and create an urban householder franchise. By 29 April 1792, when Grey presented his first reform motion to the House, France would have declared war on Austria and, in organisations like the LCS, MPs were confronted with reformers from the 'lower orders' whose demands for universal manhood suffrage and annual parliaments were distressingly reminiscent of the American Revolution. 'Respectable' lobby groups like the abolition committees were by 1789 on their way to establishment as legitimate actors in national politics. Popular organisations would take the best part of the next century to do so. The reform initiative would nonetheless pass to reform bodies without-doors, there to be sustained until the end of the French wars.

Constitutional Radicalism and the Quest for Parliamentary Reform, 1792–1799

When Thomas Hardy and Francis Place met at the beginning of 1792 to draft the constitution of the LCS, the French Revolution had already attracted the attention of several grassroots bodies in Britain. The London and Norwich Revolution Societies, founded in 1788 to celebrate the centenary of the Glorious Revolution, regarded the outbreak of the revolution as a new dawn of liberty and reason in France. So did the Birmingham Lunar Society, a club of scientists and intellectuals that held its first Bastille Day dinner in 1790 and would try to stage another in 1791 despite the hostility of local church and king mobs. The Manchester Constitutional Society (MCS), formed in 1790, was reading Paine's *Rights of Man* and moving towards a position of support for universal manhood suffrage. The old SCI, quiescent since 1785, was reviving and its influence had led to the formation, in November 1791, of the Sheffield Society for Constitutional Information, the first working man's reform club in Britain (Jewson, 1975; Goodwin, 1979: 145–58; Dickinson, 1985: 10–13).

The present trend to redefine the Enlightenment as an urban cultural movement, rather than the lives and works of 'twenty dead white men', is to be welcomed because it gives an intellectual and social context to the English urban renaissance (Jacob, 1991; Habermas, 1989; Porter, 1990). The scientific, literary, philosophical and debating clubs of England's provincial towns were exemplars of bourgeois urban sociability that inspired town dwellers to form quasi-political societies as much in Britain as in France. By 1790 the Lunar Society was as much a political organisation as a scientific society, while the MCS recruited from the local Literary and Philosophical Society in addition to Manchester's business and professional communities. The genteel social background of such radicals predisposed them to identify with polite rather than popular Jacobinism but this did not protect them from loyalist reprisals. The Manchester Lit and Phil would be, in effect, closed down by the Society to Put Down Levellers during the 1790s (Gattrell, 1982: 32–4; Morris, 1990: 410).

The only radical society to move from intellectual cosmopolitanism to revolution was the United Irishmen, who in 1791 had rejected their country's history of sectarian religious violence in favour of a new secular national identity. By the end of 1792, the Belfast UI hnd committed itself to universal manhood suffrage and produced reform plans for Ireland heavily influenced by the 1791 French constitution. The UI did not seek independence from Britain in the first instance, but rather a sort of federal commercial and political independence within the empire. The social composition of the Belfast UI was largely middling-sort presbyterian and its members' exposure to the Enlightenment had come from Ulster religious, educational and kinship links to Scotland and America. English Country Party radicalism was nevertheless an important component of the UI's political theory and was the common element shared by all British radical societies of the French wars (Elliott, 1978: 405–28, 1982: 26–7; Boyce, 1982: 123–33; Curtin, 1985: 476–84; McBride, 1993: 51–60; McFarland, 1994: 3–25).

The LCS and UI modelled their divisions, cells and forms of address upon the Jacobin Club and National Convention. All radical clubs deplored the war with France, celebrated the overthrow of the Bourbon monarchy and welcomed the inauguration of the first republic. This did not automatically make them republicans. The UI did not embrace home rule until 1795 and, while the LCS flirted briefly with republicanism in 1792–1793, it never openly advocated the abolition of the British monarchy. Its official platform called for no more than universal manhood suffrage, the expulsion of placemen and pensioners from Lords and Commons, annual parliaments, lower taxes, and hints of penal and poor law reform picked up from the *Rights of Man* (Curtin, 1994: 25–7). Artisans, the skilled and literate component of labour, flocked to the LCS and Sheffield SCI, making these bodies more diverse in social composition than their genteel cousins. Paine had drawn attention to the civilising influence of commerce upon the understanding of men, and the *Rights of Man* can be read as a confirmation that the popular Enlightenment and consumer revolution had raised the aspirations of artisan labour to levels of self-recognition as bodies of formal public opinion (Paine, 1996: ii, 25, 62–3). Artisan membership of political clubs can be found as early as 1769, when the Wilkite Society for the Support of the Bill of Rights had embarked upon Britain's first campaign of mass political education through routes from the pamphlet and newspaper press to consumer products such as buttons and mugs bearing the slogans '45' or 'Wilkes and Liberty'. By September 1792, the *Rights of Man* was in such widespread circulation that its pages were employed to wrap children's sweets. A commodified mass media was raising the sights of British labour to new heights (Dickinson, 1990: 136–7).

Although mainstream popular radical clubs were seemingly obsessed with respectability, there is no hard evidence that the politicisation of artisan labour during the 1790s was a symptom of embourgeoisification. What we know of the LCS comes largely from Thomas Hardy, Francis Place, the spy reports of Home Office informers, and the papers of the society seized by the government in 1794 and 1798. Place, whose autobiography recorded in loving detail all the houses where he had lived during his rise to prosperity, was an ambitious man anxious to escape a world of Spencean popular culture whose sexual licence, rowdiness, criminality and alcoholism he deplored. The members of the Spencean societies, for the most part journeymen labourers, teetered on the knife edge between respectability and ruin, holding their 'speakeasies' in smoky pubs where anti-establishment drinking songs were sung (Place, 1972; Hardy, 1817; McCalman, 1988: 26–49, 182–95; Worrall, 1992: 35–41, 89–96, 165–86; Mee, 1992: 220–6; Epstein, 1994: 147–65). The LCS, as presented to us by Hardy and Place, was a club that eschewed riot and rebellion for the reading and discussion of political texts and reform manifestos, in weekly assemblies governed by strict regulations stressing order and decorum. Rules governing the conduct of public meetings were probably learned from London debating clubs that had met for fifty years to discuss a broad range of topical subjects (Thale, 1989: 32; Andrew, 1996: 421–3). Place sought to replace a traditional popular culture of drink, custom and community with a reformed artisan culture emphasising reason, the rights of the individual and a non-deferential plebian respectability: what has been called a 'new moral economy' of sobriety, self control, sexual restraint and respectability (Laqueur, 1976; Obelkevitch, 1990: 326). As such, he was probably typical of those who resigned from the society in 1794 and 1797.

At the end of 1792, government law officers closed down an Edinburgh Convention of British reform delegates hosted by the Scottish Friends of the People. Conventions or assemblies were nothing new in the theory or practice of British radicalism, having been advocated as early as 1776 in James Burgh's *Political Disquisitions* before adoption by American rebels, Irish volunteers of the 1770s and Wyvill's association movement (Parsinnen, 1973a; Royle and Walvin, 1982: 64; Dinwiddy, 1990: 545–6). Late in the summer of 1793, Judge Braxfield would sentence Thomas Muir and Thomas Fysshe Palmer, the Scottish organisers of the convention, to seven and fourteen years of transportation respectively. A second Edinburgh convention was closed down on its opening day in 1793. In England the courts moved instead against the authors and publishers of seditious libels. Despite this persecution, the message of respectable reform continued to be promoted by popular radicals through open-air meetings, parades, dinners, public lectures, petitions and the radical press. The LCS and SCI planned to stage their own British Convention in 1794 but this never met, for the leaders of both groups were arrested in April on charges of high treason, and *habeas corpus* was suspended in June. Although the Pitt ministry failed to prove at the October–November state trials that the staging of a British convention represented an attempt to supersede parliament in its legislative capacity and hence constituted an act of treason, radicals nonetheless found themselves widely regarded as subversives and incendiaries. All the radical leaders, amongst them Hardy, were either acquitted or released, but the SCI never recovered from the negative publicity of the state trials, while LCS membership figures dropped sharply over the winter of 1794; some LCS members were more concerned about keeping up appearances (Thompson, 1968; Cannon, 1972: 128–31; Goodwin, 1977: Ch. 9; Dinwiddy, 1990: 547–53; Wharam, 1992).

Discounting the more lurid reports of government spies, the publicity and proceedings of the LCS up to late 1795 conform to standards of polite civility and genteel decorum (LCS, 1983). The emergence of John and Benjamin Binns, ex-members of the UI, as leaders of the London society heralded a lurch to the left following the passage of the Two Acts. From the autumn of 1795, radicals were prevented from charging money for political lectures, staging meetings of over fifty without a licence from a magistrate, submitting 'unconstitutional' petitions disrespectful to the House of Commons to parliament, and expressing any contempt for the king or his ministers in speech or print. From 1796 to 1798 the LCS would face financial problems stemming from the bankruptcy of its *Political Magazine* and what

Place called a division in its ranks between moderate and militant radicals. In 1797, Place and other 'respectable' radicals would retire from the LCS, having voiced protests against the confrontational tactics employed by the society's leaders, in particular the staging of an open-air meeting in defiance of the Seditious Meetings Act on 31 July 1797 (Goodwin, 1979: 395–455; Hone, 1982: 96–117).

This meeting was called a 'riot' by Division 10, which seceded *en masse* soon afterwards. The rejection of Grey's second reform bill by the House of Commons on 26 May, followed by the breakup of the LCS mass meeting by government troops, drove the LCS leaders to embrace violent revolution, though, according to Division 10, the society had been dominated for some time by 'a factious spirit . . . damaging to public Civism and State Reformation' (LCS, 1983: 403–4). As early as 1795, the UI had begun to recruit on the mainland through Irish immigrant communities in London, north-west England and lowland Scotland and, by December 1796, Benjamin Binns had made contact with the Dublin UI. The hub of UE activity lay in the English north-west, where an independent Manchester Corresponding Society had been set up in 1796, and by the spring of 1798 an alliance between the militant wings of the UI and the LCS would be taking shape. Exact numbers for the United Britons are impossible to come by and it is not clear to what extent the society had really been radicalised by the Binns brothers (Place, 1972: 177–82). Father James Coigley, the UI's chief agent in England, would be arrested at Margate along with the Binns, Arthur O'Connor and John Gale Jones on 28 February 1798, carrying a letter inviting Napoleon Bonaparte to invade England. His arrest was part of a government campaign to close down radical societies throughout Britain and Ireland before their plans for revolution came to maturity: on 18 April, the UE leaders were arrested in London, followed by those of the LCS a day later (Elliott, 1982: 144–50, 174–5; Wells, 1983: 121–8). The 1799 Corresponding Societies Act would outlaw the LCS and UI by name, thereby forcing popular radicalism into hiding, from which it would not emerge for the next decade.

The United Societies and the French Revolution: 1795–1799

The genesis of the 1798 Irish insurrection lay in the disillusionment of the UI with the short lord lieutenancy of Earl Fitzwilliam, from whom Irish radicals had hoped for full Catholic Emancipation. Up to 1795 the UI had sought no separation from Britain for, despite the persecution it suffered at Castle hands from 1792 onwards, the passage of Catholic relief legislation in 1792 and 1793 at London's prodding had encouraged the UI to put faith in peaceful reform and British goodwill (Elliott, 1982). Fitzwilliam's recall and dismissal from the Pitt–Portland coalition ministry early in 1795 put an end to these illusions and, by the autumn, the UI would have dispatched agents to France in search of enemy support for an Irish revolution (Elliott, 1982: 69–71, 81–95, 1985; Curtin, 1994: 46–51, 61–2). Theobald Wolf Tone was welcomed in Paris by a Directory eager to distract Britain's attention from Europe and the Mediterranean, but French financial and military assistance could not overcome the religious and social fissures within the ranks of the UI. The Dublin UI regarded itself as a liberal and genteel society reluctant to embrace violence, as opposed to a more radical middling-sort Belfast UI that operated like a secret society. This social and, to some extent, cultural division would never be overcome with the result that, in 1798, Dublin UI leaders on trial for treason would try to disassociate themselves from the insurrection and their Belfast colleagues. The hitherto urban Ulster UI, having abandoned constitutional reform for republican home rule, began during the summer of 1795 to disseminate its revolutionary message to the Irish peasantry through alliance with the Catholic Defenders, the secret rural self-help groups that had emerged during the 1780s to pro-tect Catholics from Protestant bullying (Elliott, 1978: 416–21; Garvin, 1982; Cullen, 1990; Curtin, 1994: 149–52).

Despite its best efforts to incorporate agrarian peasant grievances into its manifesto, the UI never succeeded in converting the Irish countryside to cosmopolitan Jacobin republicanism. UI records listed 379,000 men enrolled in the society on the eve of the 1798 insurrection but the organisation remained led by Protestants, many of whom admitted in the aftermath of the rising that the Catholic peasantry understood neither emancipation nor parliamentary reform. Defender Catholic nationalism was based upon a Gaelic cultural history that the Protestant UI did not share, while the com-mercial Country Whiggism of the UI was alien to rural Ireland. UI leaders downplayed these internal divisions, placing their faith instead in the French Directory (Cullen, 1980, 1993; Garvin, 1982; Smyth, 1990; Whelan, 1993; Curtin, 1994: 28). Napoleon Bonaparte's decision to take the French army to Egypt deprived Ireland of its liberating army in 1798. A previous 12,000-man French expedition had been sent to the aid of the rebels in December 1796 but, scattered by bad weather at sea, never fulfilled its mission. In August 1798, a good two months after the insurrection was over, 1099 French troops landed at Killala in County Mayo on the north-west coast of Ireland, where it found the local peasantry ignorant of both the UI and the cause of revolution. The French, having been defeated and captured by government troops on 8 September, admitted that the expedition had been a terrible mistake (Pakenham, 1969: 304–21; Elliott, 1982: 111–15, 223–32).

The French would not help revolutionaries who did not help themselves and the Dublin UI, riddled with government spies and divided from within, was ill placed to do so (Pakenham, 1969: 44–6, 91; Curtin, 1993, 1994: 112–13). The Castle had been aware of its plans for insurrection from early 1796 onwards and, having tried to disarm Ulster by force in 1797, moved in tandem with the British government in London during the spring of 1798 to arrest the Dublin UI's leaders and thus forestall the rising. Martial law was proclaimed in Ireland on 30 March 1798 (Wells, 1983: 111–17, 128–30). The rebellion, which started in the south on 24 May and spread to Ulster on 8 June, consequently lacked organisation and discipline, although the same could be said for pro-government loyalist forces and many atrocities were committed by both sides. An estimated 30,000 people were killed in the Irish revolt (Pakenham, 1969: 17; Duffy, 1991: 136–40). The UI had, despite its best efforts, remained an organisation based firmly in urban English-speaking Ireland and, although the society had succeeded to a limited extent in penetrating the popular culture of ordinary Irish folk, its leaders had vastly overestimated the strength and influence of the UI in the countryside (Whelan, 1993). Belfast UI leaders fled to Scotland and America in the wake of the insurrection. Their Dublin colleagues took advantage of an amnesty issued by the new Lord Lieutenant Cornwallis to testify against their Ulster brethren and emigrate to France or America. The fragile alliance between Protestants, Catholics, gentry, middling sorts and peasants was at an end. Thomas Emmet's revolt of 1803 witnessed the last sparks of UI resistance to British rule but was easily put down by government forces (McDowell, 1940: 12–53; Elliott, 1982: 299–322; Curtin, 1994: 126–30).

Despite the failure of the UI to make liberal democrats out of the Irish Catholic peasantry, it succeeded in attracting some English and Scottish support for its mission. Perth, Dundee, Glasgow, Liverpool, Manchester and London, all towns with an established radical presence, welcomed UI agents during the 1790s. Scotland's interest in parliamentary reform dated back to the 1770s, the American War of Independence, the control of Scotland's burgh constituencies by local urban elites, and a 'Dundas despotism' by which the family of the Home Secretary maintained a stranglehold grip over Scottish state patronage (Fry, 1992: 159–72; Vincent, 1994; Brown, 1998). In 1792, Edinburgh, Perth and Dundee branches of the FOP were opened in imitation of the London society founded by the aristocratic Whigs. Like the Sheffield SCI, they shared little with their ostensible parent organisation but a name and a general commitment to reform: the Edinburgh branch responsible for staging the reform conventions of 1792 and 1793 was dominated by the liberal professional elite, while the Perth and Dundee societies contained many artisans and tradesmen. The Scottish FOP had nevertheless made contact with the UI as early as 1792 and, having lowered its subscription fees and widened its social base, had by 1796 left its genteel origins behind. The United Scotsmen (US), as they had become, were well placed to listen to calls to arms spread by UI agents. By July 1796 the Belfast UI had assurances of Scottish support for an armed rising and, by the autumn of 1797, the revolutionary message had taken root in Glasgow, Ayrshire, Renfrew, Lanark, Dumbarton, Fife and Perth (Meikle, 1912; Logue, 1979; Wells, 1983: 69–78; Dickinson, 1985; Brims, 1989, 1990, 1993; McFarland, 1994: 66–77, 152–8). By May 1797 George Mealmaker's US had 9653 members in the Perth–Dundee region. Thomas Muir, who had survived his experience of transportation, was by 1798 an embittered enemy of the British government resident in Paris and acted as the US link to the French Directory. Like his colleagues in the UI Paris embassy, he inflated the number of United society followers in Scotland and claimed that 50,000 Scots were prepared to rise in pursuit of freedom from British tyranny. While the UI could reasonably claim to have a mass movement in the making, the Highlanders were 'destined to remain something of a revolutionary elite in their own country' (McFarland, 1994: 32). The promised rising of 100,000 Scots in support of the Irish insurrection never materialised (Wells, 1983: 72–4, 124–5; Dickinson, 1985: 50–1; Brims, 1993: 165).

Although radicalism took root in north and south Wales, the Welsh, were not attracted to the UI. In 1792 the *Rights of Man* had been translated into Welsh with some effect, for nonconformist Brecon, Cardiff and Merthyr Tydfil had reform societies of their own, while branches of the LCS and SCI were established in north Wales (Jones, 1974: 32–3). The 'last invasion of Britain', the French landing at Fishguard on 22 February 1797, had been meant, in Directory and UI war plans, to support the 1796 Bantry Bay expedition headed for Ireland in conjunction with another French force bound for Newcastle by diverting the British government's attention away from the Irish insurrection. None of these plans succeeded, for the Newcastle and Bantry Bay forces were foiled by stormy seas and the 1400-strong Welsh expedition, largely manned by Irish exiles, prison convicts, *émigrés* on probation and other French social undesirables, was dispatched to Wales by General Lazare Hoche in order, one suspects, to get rid of it (Stuart-Jones, 1947; Horn, 1980b); rural Cardiganshire was destitute of Jacobins (Kinross, 1974).

Irish-inspired radicalism took root in parts of Britain possessing established trade, immigration or cultural contacts with Ireland. Although it is impossible to estimate the strength of the UI in Lancashire or Cheshire, food riot threat letters and handbills found in Bolton and Preston in 1800 indicate some popular acquaintance in the north-west with French ideas. The hand of the Belfast UI can also be seen in the religious oaths imposed upon Manchester UE millworkers taken from the book of Ezekiel: 'And thou profane wicked prince of Israel, whose day is come, whose iniquity shall have an end, thus saith the Lord God. Remove the diadem and take off the crown. This shall not be the same, exalt him that is low and abase him that is high. I will overturn, overturn, overturn it' (HO, 42/61, T. Coke to Portland, 19 March 1801). Oath swearing was a feature of Irish secret societies brought by impressed Irish seamen into the Royal Navy, where it served to unite the Nore mutineers in 1797. The Spithead mutiny of the Channel Fleet that started on 16 April 1797 was primarily a strike over low wages and bad working conditions easily resolved by the Admiralty's grant of a pay rise to the seamen. Frigate crews were excluded from the mutiny to give protection to British shipping, officers were treated with respect and, by 23 April, the Spithead mutiny was over. The Nore mutiny of the North Sea fleet, which broke out on 12 May, is less easily explained, for the North Sea fleet was aware of what had happened in the south. Richard Parker and his associates, the leaders of the protest, regarded the navy as a 'floating republic', ran their mutiny as a democracy and considered sailing their ships to France in search of asylum. Roger Wells has suggested that the UI and LCS sought to transform the mutinies into a political strike for peace but points out that neither organisation played a direct role in starting them (Wells, 1983: 95–6, 79–109; Benjamin, 1990). The government blamed the mutinies on the popular radicals and, having hanged Parker and his colleagues, promptly introduced legislation banning the administration of unlawful oaths to members of Britain's armed forces.

No historian would now deny that the mainland United societies proposed to rise in support of the UI to forestall the dispatch of British troops to Ireland, nor that they planned to establish separate republics in England, Scotland and Ireland. Both the numerical strength of the United Britons and the extent of the threat that they posed to public order are, nonetheless, unclear and, in the absence of hard evidence, unlikely to be elucidated in the near future. Scotland welcomed Ulster UI rebels in the aftermath of the '98, and secret societies formed on the UI model, many camouflaged as freemasons' lodges, continued to exist in Scotland up to 1820 (McFarland, 1994: 236–40). Claims have been made for the survival of 'Black Lamp' revolutionary radicals in the West Riding of Yorkshire into the 1800s, which the existence of York supporters for the 1802 Despard conspiracy would seem to confirm. Such radicals, if they existed in any significant numbers, remained hidden from the public eye, though they may have been involved in the Luddite and reform agitations of the 1810s (Thompson,

1968: 182–203; Dinwiddy, 1974a, 1979; Donnelly and Baxter, 1974; Elliott, 1977, 1982: 285–98; Emsley, 1979a: 87–8; Wells, 1983: 188–252). Colonel E.M. Despard, acting in concert with UE survivors, was supposed to attack key sites of government power in London to support an Irish rising sponsored by the French, but this plot too was foiled by government spies. After Despard and four co-conspirators were executed in England for treason at the beginning of 1803, Robert Emmet led a last revolt that was swiftly put down by the authorities (Emsley, 1979a: 95; Elliot, 1977, 1982). Mainstream Irish radicalism was channelled afterwards into the Catholic Association, which sought emancipation through legal routes. The irony of radical history during the 1790s is that the government, by its treatment of peaceful reformers as subversive revolutionaries, succeeded only in creating the very scenario it sought to avert: the commission of radical treason in the British Isles.

Quietus and Redivivus, 1800–1820

With the passage of the Corresponding Societies Act in 1799, the fortunes of reform hit a nadir. The UI and LCS had been outlawed by name, while the cause of parliamentary reform was now firmly associated in the British public mind with high treason. Catholic Emancipation had emerged in 1801 as a new cause calling for public support but received none from an English and Scottish people whose hatred and fear of Roman Catholics ran deep. The coming of peace with France in 1801 did, however, disassociate some reform causes from the French Revolution and improved the prospects for the abolition of the slave trade.

Abolitionists had been struggling throughout the 1790s to maintain public interest in the cause, and Wilberforce strove on an annual and unsuccessful basis to arouse parliament's compassion for the victims of the slave trade. The London committee did little after 1792 and the public's commitment to abolition was displayed through other routes, most notably a consumer boycott on West Indian sugar that began in 1791. When slavery was restored to the French colonies in 1803, having been abolished there in 1794, the ending of the slave trade could no longer be described as a Jacobin proposition and the London committee, accompanied by the provincial abolition committees, came out of retirement. In 1805 Pitt paved the way for the introduction of permanent abolition legislation by issuing an Order in Council prohibiting the supply of slaves to enemy states and their colonies, Britain having gone back to war with France in 1803 (Oldfield, 1995: 57–8; Bolt and Drescher, 1980).

Pitt, though sympathetic to abolition, had never made it a ministerial measure and could have done more to promote the cause during the 1790s (Anstey, 1975: 299–306). Wilberforce was by his own admission neither an efficient organiser nor a good Commons tactician. The appointment of the All Talents ministry, however, brought to power a man whose reputation was now solidly based upon the championship of libertarian reform causes, namely Fox. Grenville's record on abolition was less consistent but his departure from office in 1801 had left him a free agent and the All Talents Cabinet, with the exception of the Sidmouthites, approved of the measure. The old 1780s alliance between high and low politics having been reconstructed by Fox, Wilberforce and the London abolition committee in 1806, a petition campaign in London and the provinces was organised in support of the abolition bills presented to parliament by Fox and Whitbread. In 1806 the foreign slave trade was finally abolished; the domestic trade ended a year later but the high political leadership of reform causes would not long remain in Whig hands (Anstey, 1975: Chs. 14–15, 1980: 331–95; Jupp, 1985: 356–8, 389–91). Fox's death left his party without any strong commitment to reform and All Talents legislative inertia on other fronts convinced Cobbett, amongst others, that no real change would come from either the Whigs or the Tories. In 1807, parliamentary reform found itself another Commons spokesman in the independent MP Sir Francis Burdett, who made Fox's old constituency of Westminster a hive of metropolitan reform activity up to and beyond the conclusion to the Napoleonic Wars. Here veteran reformers like Place and Cartwright would be joined by a new generation of radicals and newspapermen to demand annual parliaments and the abolition of rotten boroughs once more (Hone, 1982: 133–219; Dinwiddy, 1980).

The radicalism of the 1800s bore little resemblance to that of the previous decade, for the vast majority of reformers, with the exception of infidel Spenceans, had renounced French-style Jacobinism in favour of English republicanism. Few radicals openly opposed the war with Napoleonic France while utopian schemes, such as those promoted by Charles Hall or Robert Owen, possessed no popular support (Dinwiddy, 1989: 44; Hone, 1982: 319–22). Country Party reform was espoused instead by moderates. Burdett was proud to call himself an independent gentry Queen Anne Tory but possessed no strong commitment to universal suffrage (Spence, 1996: 15–17). Cartwright was still fulminating against the ancient constitution and the Norman Yoke, while Wyvill continued to endorse what amounted to Pitt's 1785 reform bill (Dinwiddy, 1971, 1980). The enervating influence of Court corruption could be seen in the low standards of public virtue displayed by office-holders, who scrambled after places and patronage in Pittite governments (Harling, 1996a).

The potential mass appeal of Old Corruption had not been exploited prior to 1810 but its increasing association, by the radical and respectable press, with lower and middling sort interests, bore fruit in the participation of both groups in anti-war and anti-government demonstrations. The middling sort 'Friends of Peace' movement against the war and the 1807 Orders in Council, based largely in the North of England, had by 1812 begun to translate into grassroots demands for a House of Commons more representative of non-elite interests (Cookson, 1982). The original Hampden Club, with its property qualification of £300 p.a., was restricted to men from prosperous backgrounds but, following a union of reform leaders from Wyvill to Cobbett in the Society of the Friends of Parliamentary Reform founded in June 1811, reform clubs would begin to acquire a wider social base. The success of the 'Friends of Peace' campaign, led in parliament by Whig MP Henry Brougham, followed by the repeal of the property tax in 1815, had led the reformers to hope for Commons representation from the Opposition Whigs but their reluctance to endorse anything more than economical reform drove the reformers to eschew high political assistance and seek instead the support of true public opinion. Here, in 1816, lay the origins of the radical press campaign to mobilise a mass constituency of supporters (Belchem, 1978, 1985: Ch. 2; Fulcher, 1996). To the activities of Cartwright and Henry Hunt, now touring the provinces to popularise the Hampden Clubs and new Union Societies, was added a revival of the print war between radicals and loyalists on the true principles and meaning of the British constitution. A sharp divide nonetheless remained between respectable and non-respectable radicals. Burdett, Place and Hunt were concerned about the malleability of a mass movement they had called into existence. When the Spenceans started a London riot, breaking into gunshops, seizing arms and inciting the mob to violence following their departure from the Spa Fields open air reform meeting of 2 December 1816, they were repudiated by all the leading spokesmen for parliamentary reform.

Notwithstanding the clear divisions in the reform movement revealed by this episode, the Spa Fields meetings of 1816 helped create the 'mass platform' of the nineteenth century by creating a new public forum, complete with its own rituals and slogans, that would acquire a life of its own through print and pictorial representation in the radical press. Radicals of the 1810s were, on the whole, well disciplined lobbyists who responded to the revival of government repression with creative measures to maintain the momentum of the suffrage campaign but remain within the law. The most famous of these are the mass petition movement of 1817, in which 700 petitions from 350 localities were submitted to parliament in support of Burdett's 20 May motion for the appointment of a select committee on parliamentary reform, and the legislatorial attorney elections staged by unincorporated towns like Manchester and Birmingham during the summer of 1818 (Maccoby, 1955: 322–4, 355–7; Hone, 1982: 229–37; McCalman, 1988: 261–5, 267–9; Belchem, 1985: 54–64, 84–5, 100–1, 107–8; Chase, 1988: 89–103; Worrall, 1992: 97–113; Epstein, 1994: 14–17).

Despite this solidarity, social and political tensions continued to divide the reform movement. Respectable artisan radicals had always shunned the company of unskilled labour and the poor. Professional men disliked any association with tradesmen. Whigs of the 1810s were embarrassed, much as they had been two decades earlier, by the objectives of radical reformers whose aims differed so greatly from their own. These divisions were reflected in different forms of print culture. Smutty scandal was the stock-in-trade of 'gutter' press journalists like Davenport Sedley, Jacob Rey (alias 'Jew King') and Patrick Duffin, who combined blackmail and extortion with the authorship of anti-establishment articles in the *Independent Whig* and *British Guardian.* Their lurid exposes of the 1806 'Delicate Investigation' and the 1809 army commissions scandal in which Mary Anne Clarke, the Duke of York's mistress, was found to have sold military promotions with the duke's collaboration, are more reminiscent of Robert Darnton's forbidden best-sellers of pre-revolutionary France than the highbrow prose of the *Edinburgh Review* or Leigh Hunt's *Examiner.* While most pro-government journals did not even bother to acknowledge the existence of the gutter press during the 1800s, they could ill afford to neglect radical newspapers during the following decade and the wholesale revival of print loyalism shaped the form and content of much radical publishing from 1816 to 1820 (Prothero, 1979: 22–46, 86–92; McCalman, 1988: 43–5; Spence, 1996: Ch. 6; Fulcher, 1996: 64–5, 71–4).

The Spenceans, having been ostracised by other radicals, took matters into their own hands with the 1820 Cato Street conspiracy that was to have assassinated the Cabinet while it dined at Lord Harrowby's house. The conspirators were, however, caught and the plan came to naught (Thompson, 1968: 700–8; Stanhope, 1962; Johnson, 1974; Prothero, 1979: 120–31; Chase, 1988: 117–20; Worrall, 1992: 187–200). The Queen Caroline trial of 1820, with its accompanying marches, ballads, handbills, public dinners and blanket radical media coverage, was more representative of radical activity at the end of the 1810s for it united reformers of all stripes to martyr a wronged woman, pillory a hypocrite king and attack a Tory government whose veneration for the crown was symptomatic of its moral bankruptcy and political turpitude. Caroline had committed the multiple adulteries cited as grounds for her divorce but so too had her husband, the new George IV. The queen's apotheosis as saint and martyr was made possible by her image as the symbol of a helpless nation, itself pure and good, but soiled through union with a corrupt crown. Caroline's trial, the literal defence of her rights as queen and wife, became in radical hands an emblem of the struggle for freedom and justice and gave reformers an impeccably legal and loyal figurehead around which to rally. Her early death late in 1820, followed by the return of economic prosperity, sent parliamentary reformers once more into the shadows, not to emerge again until the passage of Catholic Emancipation in 1828 (Prothero, 1979: 132–55; Hone, 1982: 316–19; Hall and Davidoff, 1987: 150–5; Clark, 1990; Wahrman, 1996: 116–19).

Loyalists and the Old Order

Loyalism has often been equated with support for successive Tory governments and all their policies but in theory and practice it denoted little more than hostility to British radical reform and the French Revolution. Loyalists tendered allegiance first to the British constitution, not to William Pitt or his successors, and could espouse moderate parliamentary reform, the abolition of the slave trade, Catholic Emancipation and peace with either revolutionary or Napoleonic France. Eighteenth-century definitions of patriotism urged Britons to criticise their governments and societies so as to preserve the commonwealth from the threats of absolutism, corruption and complacence, a message taken to heart by loyalist authors from the High Church John Bowles to the commercial Whig Malthus. Emma Vincent has made a distinction between two types of loyalist authors: the war crusaders who embraced Burke's conception of the war as a counter-revolutionary conflict to exterminate Jacobinism and restore the French monarchy; and the more general loyalists, who were more flexible in their views (1998: 81–2). This is a useful way to assess degrees of commitment to the war. The earlier a Briton turned against the French Revolution, the more committed an enemy of its manifestations he or she was likely to be. Burke was early to condemn it as a public menace but others dated their conversion to specific events or developments: the forcing upon a recalcitrant Louis XVI of the 1791 constitution, the initial emergence of the popular radical societies in Britain, or the outbreak of war with France. For many Britons, the turning point came during the winter of 1792, when the enthusiasm displayed by native radicals for the abolition of the French monarchy and the success of French arms in Europe suggested that British reformers sought nothing less than a French-style revolution at home. Such 'alarmists' flocked to join the Association for the Preservation of Liberty and Property against Republicans and Levellers inaugurated by John Reeves on 20 November 1792 (Black, 1963; Dozier, 1983; Christie, 1984; Schofield, 1986).

Because Reeves was a London police magistrate with friends in the Home Office, scholars have always suspected some degree of government involvement in the genesis of the loyal associations. There is now no doubt that Reeves started the APLP by himself but, within five days of its creation, Pitt and Grenville had decided that Reeves had launched a movement 'very useful' to government purposes (Grenville, 1853: ii, 229; Mitchell, 1961; Black, 1963: 112–34; Dozier, 1983; Clements MS, 25 Nov. 1792, Pitt to Dundas). The government, then inundated with alarmist accounts of riots, demonstrations, strikes and sinister radical conspiracies, was intending to strengthen its hands against civil disobedience and possibly go to war with a new provisional French republican government seemingly intent on an invasion of the United Provinces. Pitt, having recognised that the presence of domestic radicals might very well weaken Britain's international image in the diplomatic arena, hoped that the Reevites would distribute anti-Jacobin pamphlets, collect funds for seditious libel prosecutions and send his government loyal petitions to give it the appearance of strong and popular leadership (Dickinson, 1989). The formation of 'armed associations' to assist magistrates in the suppression of riots was another possible function the Reevites might have served, but Pitt was unlikely to have sanctioned the arming of nominal loyalists without adequate safeguards, and another route, namely the creation of special constables by the London police bureaux under Reeves's supervision, seems to have been the preferred alternative (PRO 30/8/198, #4, ff. 109–10; HO 42/23, ff. 25–8, ff. 361–2; Stevenson, 1971a; Jupp, 1985: 143; Mori, 1996; Duffy, 1996). The issue of government involvement is an important one because some loyalist groups conducted vigilante warfare upon radicals in their localities, barring them from public houses and closing down their meetings. On 12 December 1792, a loyalist mob attacked the home of Thomas Walker, president of the Manchester Constitutional Society. As the Birmingham Riots of 1791 had demonstrated, angry 'church and king' crowds were capable of attacking local radicals without official instigation, but the extent of government direction, if any, exercised over the loyal associations would indicate the strength of its fear about popular radicalism and the lengths to which it would go to suppress civil disobedience (Dickinson, 1985; Thale, 1989; Rogers and Hay, 1997).

Reeves claimed to have been given a draft petition by Pitt for distribution to the loyalist clubs on 24 November, but whether he used it or not is unclear, and he went to great lengths to deny the existence of any links with the government (Association Papers, 1793: iv–vii; Duffy, 1996: 951–4). Many loyalist groups moreover drafted addresses of their own. All petitions, regardless of origin, swore their signatories to uphold the constitution as established by the 1688 Glorious Revolution against republicans and levellers, but such declarations did not necessarily commit their signatories to principles or acts of vigilante conservatism. Neither Pitt nor Grenville had been impressed by the 1791 Birmingham Riots, and the role envisaged by the premier for the loyalist clubs was one of limited activity. They were not to 'engage in much discussion at public meetings' nor to meet on a regular basis, but rather to disband 'for long intervals' until they were needed for public relations purposes (Ginter, 1966; Duffy, 1996; Mori, 1996; Clements MS, 25 and 27 Nov. 92, Pitt to Dundas). By June 1793, most of the provincial loyalist associations were seemingly dead and, as far as we know, no official or private directions were issued to Reeves about them by the government after November 1792. Harry Dickinson attributes the swift flowering and death of the loyalist associations to the ease with which they defeated the radical presence in their localities (Dickinson, 1985, 1989, 1992a,b). It is more likely, bearing in mind the lack of central direction – intellectual, organisational or directional – exerted over provincial loyalist associations, that many formed in a rush of patriotic enthusiasm and then faded away over the spring of 1793. The Pitt ministry never publicised its connection to the APLP, preferring the loyalist movement to look like a spontaneous rising of support for crown, church and constitution. Thousands of signatures were collected in London and all provincial towns for loyalist petitions, many unsolicited by the ministry (Dickinson, 1989: 113–14; Eastwood, 1991: 154–7).

Some loyalist organisations remained active into the mid-1790s, intent on harassing radicals in Manchester, Sheffield, Norwich and other provincial towns. The government subsidised the writings of some loyalist pamphleteers and newspapermen during the 1790s, having helped launch the *British Critic*, the *Anti-Jacobin, or Monthly Magazine*, the London morning daily *Sun* and evening *True Briton*. Most loyalist publishing activity was nevertheless independent of both the government and the Reevites: in 1798 a pamphlet written by John Gifford, Treasury writer and first editor of the *Anti-Jacobin Magazine*, called the loyalist associations out of retirement to contest the combined threats of invasion and insurrection. This call to arms was heeded by the volunteer corps but not the original Reevite groups (Aspinall, 1949: 78–9; Werkmeister, 1963: 317–80). Typical of the loyalist clubs active over the winter of 1792–1793 was the East Kent and Canterbury APLP, which distributed pamphlets such as Hannah More's *Village Politics* and Paley's *Reasons for Contentment* in vast quantities to the labouring poor (Dickinson, 1989: 110–11; Dinwiddy, 1991: 47–8; Philp, 1995b: 51–5; Cookson, 1997: 228). More active and sustained efforts were also made by some of the Anglican clergy as JPs and ministers of religion to instil proper notions of loyalism and deference into their parishioners. Another wave of loyalist pamphleteering would occur from 1815 to 1820 to avert, or so it was hoped, the spectre of revolution (Soloway, 1969: Ch. 1; Hole, 1989:

109–59; Eastwood, 1994a: 18–22). For those who attended church, sermons remained part of the nation's political culture; for those who did not, Anglican festivals, ceremonies and fast days ordered by the government to commemorate important events in the war still marked important dates in the calendar. Loyalists were aware of the power that rituals exercised over the popular mind and staged burnings-in-effigy of Paine over the winter of 1792–1793 to drive home the message that radicalism was synonymous with treason (Claeys, 1989: 144–5; Dickinson, 1989: 118–19; Hole, 1989; Stevenson, 1992: 177–9; Epstein, 1994: 101–2, 153). Attempts were also made by loyalist organisations to collect funds by subscription for seditious libel prosecutions, but Treasury Solicitor instructions to provincial firms of solicitors often advised the dropping of charges on the grounds of insufficient or inconclusive evidence (Emsley, 1979a, 1981, 1985). Much of the active loyalist campaign against popular radicalism was informal. Although the Reevites were useful to a government lacking both money and manpower to monitor popular radicalism, the loyalists did not act as an extra-official police force throughout the 1790s.

Loyalists came in all sizes, shapes and political colours. In December 1792, Fox joined his local Reevite association in Westminster, while the mission statement produced by a Merchant Taylor Hall inaugural meeting of City loyalists on 5 December pledged its members to a commercial Whig constitution that 'has on former occasions been, and we trust will be in future, found competent to correct its errors, and reform its abuses' (Tomline, 1821: ii, 557–61). Loyalism in practice represented little more than a statement of commitment to the principal features of the old Hanoverian order. As Wilberforce, who called himself a loyalist and detested radicals, put it in 1793: 'I look upon all moderate reformers, who are sincerely attached to our present constitution of King, Lords and Commons, with a very different eye, and should think it right to pay great regard to them, and to the object of bringing them to act cordially for the constitution and against the republicans'. Much the same motives underlay the revival of Wyvill's interest in moderate parliamentary reform during the 1790s and 1800s (Wilberforce, 1838: ii, 8–9; Dinwiddy, 1979). Not enough is known about loyalist associations in the provinces to draw hard and fast conclusions about the intellectual complexion of the movement on a national basis. If the diversity of opinion expressed in the loyalist pamphlet press is any accurate indicator of British right-wing responses to the French Revolution, loyalism was a school of thought flexible enough to contain many moderates (Ginter, 1966).

We know much more about the volunteers, the militia corps whose formation was authorised in England and Wales in 1794 to defend Britain, or so the government claimed, against the twin threats of French invasion and domestic radicalism. The volunteer corps have traditionally been depicted as successors to the loyalist associations, as a paramilitary conservative force embodied to assist magistrates in the suppression of riots and radicalism (Black, 1963; Western, 1965; Dozier, 1983). Attitudes to the corps are, however, changing, and they have more recently been portrayed as a military institution through which a conservative national consciousness developed amongst the thousands of Britons who served in volunteer ranks from 1794 to 1815 (Colley, 1992), or as provincial bodies superficially subscribing to a 'national defence' patriotic agenda set by the Pitt government, but in truth representative of little more than local identities, concerns and rivalries (Cookson, 1989, 1997).

The invasion scare of 1794 in response to which the volunteers were first embodied was real in the eyes of the government, if not twentieth-century historians (Dozier, 1983). The Pitt ministry was also afraid of the public relations that would ensue if no special measures were taken for national defence at a time when the British army was hard pressed to meet all its overseas military commitments. The popular radical presence in Britain was problematic for two reasons: domestic loyalist concern about its strength, which manifested itself in repeated demands for action, and foreign doubt about the government's strength and stability. Fears of both, in addition to the actual threat of French invasion, could be seen in the Cabinet during the autumn of 1793. When the decision was made to permit the sailing of the 1793 West India expedition on the grounds that the retention of the troops in England would exacerbate public concern about the French and radical threats, George Rose was horrified: '*No considerations* should induce me to sacrifice the *existence* of the country to appearances!' (Bath and Wells, 1861: iii, 162). Throughout the 1790s the government tried to acknowledge, yet contain, public fears of radicalism while employing those fears as a justification for its public order policies. The 1794 French invasion never took place, nor did the radical rising which the Home Office thought would accompany any attempted enemy landing. The creation of volunteer corps for large manufacturing towns and small coastal communities indicates that both were envisaged as probable centres of unrest in the event of an invasion. Coastal defence nevertheless remained the primary purpose of the volunteers, and one that they would serve again in 1798 and 1803–1804 (Cookson, 1989, 1997).

By 1803, there were 380,000 volunteers under arms (Cookson, 1997: 80). Although invasion scares were experienced in all those years, the volunteers were never called upon to drive the French from Britain's shores. The volunteers were primarily a morale-boosting device rather than a home guard or experiment in mass conscription and, by the 1800s, they were depicted by Pitt as an armed nation: the sovereign will of the state (Cookson,

1997: 34–7, 71–2). The motives of men for joining the corps were nonetheless complex, for employer or peer group pressure, not to mention automatic exemption from regular military service, drew men to a movement they served as members of their local communities (Emsley, 1979a: 73–4). The gorgeous uniforms and military exercises of the volunteers no doubt gave many men an escapist route for their military fantasies whilst fostering a sense of comradeship and local identity. As self-forming, self-financing and self-governing units, the corps were difficult to submit to central government control. The corps remained parochial, rather than national, in outlook and many rank and file volunteers regarded themselves as citizens first and soldiers second (Cookson, 1997: 26–8). There were numerous instances during the food riots of 1795–1796 and 1799–1800 when they either refused to fight or joined food rioters protesting against high grain prices (Bohstedt, 1983: 49–51; Wells, 1988: 268–73). While regarding themselves as defenders of the constitution, volunteers were capable of distinguishing between real and bogus threats to the stability of the social and political order (Dickinson, 1989; Cookson, 1989, 1997: 189–93; Colley, 1992).

By 1798 the British government was aware that the volunteers were no real substitute for the regular army. Their appeal lay in their low cost, their performance of home duties normally assigned to the army, and the image of a nation in arms they presented at home and abroad (Eastwood, 1991: 158–61). The volunteers had not been conceived by Pitt in 1794 as a British *levée en masse*, and late that year he had voiced his contempt for the French concept of an armed nation – of a sovereign will expressed through, and embodied in, a citizen army (PR, 1794: xxxvii, 276–7). By 1798 he was becoming increasingly concerned about what he called 'the spirit of the country' in the face of a lengthening and unsuccessful war, and the public relations purpose of the volunteers was outweighing their military utility. Despite the deficiencies of the volunteers, a fresh 1798 mobilisation would be undertaken in part to unify the country against two real threats: French invasion and Irish-inspired radical insurrection. In 1803, when Britain returned to war with Napoleonic France, extensive plans would be drawn up in which the volunteers, an Army of Reserve and a Supplementary Militia were added to the nation's defences (Emsley, 1979a: 101–2).

In 1798 the corps were extended to Scotland by Dundas, who sought through it to foster the Highlands martial spirit that had rejuvenated the British army of the mid-eighteenth century. This may have been part of a ministerial campaign to invent the illusion of a united Britain. Precedents for doing so existed in the past, for a similar public relations campaign had been employed by the Elder Pitt during the 1750s and 1760s to create a vision of an empire behind which all Britons could subsume their internal differences, a major consideration at a time when memories of Scottish

Jacobite treachery were strong. Although the volunteer corps were welcomed in the Highlands clans as a source of employment and revenue, much as the British army had been during the days of the Elder Pitt, the experiment did not create a community of militant conservative Highland Scots loyal either to his son or to the 'Dundas despotism' (Colley, 1992; Cookson, 1997: 34–6, 136–50). The consolidation of Dundas power in Scotland was facilitated rahter by the extension of English local government institutions to Scotland during the 1790s. This exercise in administrative empire building, of which the volunteers formed a part, did not automatically entail a growth of vigilante loyalist sentiment in Scotland. The Kirk appears to have been the chief institution through which loyalism operated in Scotland despite an attempt on the part of Henry and Robert Dundas to introduce loyalist associations there (Whetstone, 1981: 95–111; Vincent, 1994). Scottish loyalism remains an under-researched subject deserving of investigation, and almost nothing is known of Welsh loyalism during the 1790s and 1800s. Wales did not have the Dundas family but it did have the one-time old Tory Williams-Wynns, in-laws of the Grenvilles, who performed for their English cousins in north Wales some of the same political services undertaken by the Dundas family in Scotland. Four Welsh county MPs belonged to the Williams-Wynn family and, having like their Grenville relatives deserted Pitt in 1801, would form the core of the Grenvillite Opposition in the House of Commons during the Napoleonic Wars (Sack, 1979: 116–17, 133).

Irish loyalism is notorious on two counts: the emergence of the Orange Lodges in 1795 and the paranoia of an episcopalian Protestant Ascendancy whose refusal to accept UI involvement in an insurrection it preferred to regard as a sectarian Catholic conspiracy against Irish Protestantism resulted in its desertion by Pitt. The Ulster Orange Lodges, most conservative of all loyalist groups in the British Isles, took their name from William of Orange, whose defeat of James II's Catholic forces at the Battle of the Boyne in 1690 had preserved Protestant Ireland from a Catholic Stuart restoration. The lodges, formed to defend the lives, property and interests of Ulster presbyterians, were no new development in the history of Irish sectarianism, for secret societies, of which the Catholic Defenders were one, had practised agrarian terrorism for decades. Orange Boys, similar to Whiteboys, Peep O'Day Boys and other gangs of Irish vigilantes, had turned into lodges in response to UI recruiting activity in Ulster. By 1798, the Orangemen were 100,000 members strong (Senior, 1966: 2–14). The lodges were unique in the openness with which they antagonised Catholics, a defiance that made Ascendancy landlords fearful for the maintenance of public order on their estates. Here lay a truly popular loyalist movement comprised of men from the lower to middle ranks of Ulster society, but the parades through which the Orangemen tried to stake a literal claim to the 'ownership' of contested territory resulted in frequent clashes between the lodges and resentful Catholics.

The Orangemen were staunch supporters of crown, church and constitution, a commitment demonstrated by the strength of their numbers in the Yeomanry, the Irish equivalent of the British volunteers, whose formation had been demanded from the Irish government in 1796 by Ulster magistrates fearful of the UI and the Defenders in their localities (Senior, 1966: 58–60, 100–1; Morton, 1967; Blackstock, 1993). The Yeomanry was joined by loyalists of many descriptions, amongst them moderate reformers who left the UI following the Bantry Bay episode of 1797 (Curtin, 1994: 76–7). So inflammatory and disruptive were the activities of the Orangemen that, despite the tacit gentry and government support they received in Ulster, they alarmed Castle personnel already fearful about the strength of Catholic hostility to Protestant rule. John Beresford would blame the 1798 insurrection upon successful UI exploitation of the Orange Order's unpopularity (Bath and Wells, 1861: iii, 392–3). The failure of Catholic Emancipation ensured the Orange Lodges a voice in post-Union politics, for their loyalty to a Protestant Ireland, distasteful though it might be to many Irishmen, was acknowledged to have its uses in defence of Protestant Ireland against the Catholic majority (Whelan, 1996: 115–26). In 1798 the lodges had begun to spread to the English north-west, brought over from Ireland by army and militia units. Manchester – with its high population of Irish immigrants – soon became the centre of English Orangism. Opposition to Catholic Emancipation would define the history of the movement up to 1829 (Senior, 1966: 140, 151, 156–7).

Recent historians of conservatism are right to claim that loyalism won the hearts and minds of Britons during the French wars provided that the terms and nature of the 'debate' between radicals and loyalists is understood (Philp, 1991, 1995a,b). Loyalism should not be defined solely as 'church and king' conservatism but should rather denote allegiance to Britain's constitutional monarchy as established by the 1688 Glorious Revolution, a set of national and local institutions ranging from parliament to the poor law and a set of rights and liberties guaranteed by statute or tradition. Central to these struggles was the definition of true patriotism and the various meanings of virtue, civilisation, rights and liberty discussed by both radicals and loyalists at length in the press. By 1800 loyalists could claim a victory of sorts in the intellectual debate over the meaning of a revolution that had failed to bring lasting liberty, prosperity or stability to France and Europe. This battle had been won by the passage of events rather than superior force of argument: not that loyalists were lacking in ingenuity, having updated their image by redefining the monarchy as a bourgeois soap opera and employing Enlightenment discourses in defence of modern society and government (O'Gorman, 1989a: 28–30; Colley, 1984; Sack, 1993: 129–45; Morris, 1998). By 1800 all loyalists, active and passive, had concluded for various reasons that Britain represented a bastion of rational and practical liberty opposed to the anarchic principles and policies of revolutionary France. When Britain returned to war with Napoleon in 1803, loyalists once more took up arms against a French aggressor now defined primarily in terms of military ambition and conquest. Loyalists could be traditionalists and reactionaries but even the most conservative of them were capable of believing that British society was in need of improvement. Their desire to ameliorate the human condition often took humanitarian and philanthropic forms, as the educational, welfare and temperance campaigns of evangelicals were to demonstrate in the opening decades of the nineteenth century.

The Wages of Sin

Vigilante loyalism throughout the British Isles was seemingly quiescent by 1800, if only because there was no longer a public radical presence to be contested. Anglican loyalists of the 1790s, be they High Church, evangelical or, in some cases, latitudinarian in orientation, were convinced that the French Revolution was an awful warning of divine punishment to come, a fate that could be averted through a reformation of manners in this life to prepare for spiritual redemption in the next (Hole, 1989, 1991). This was the Anglican equivalent of Dissenter or popular millennialism, though the deliverance of British society from vice was an evangelical crusade that had taken many practical forms before 1789: the campaign by the Society for the Promotion of Christian Knowledge (SPCK) against gay prostitution from 1707 to 1730; the Sunday School movement to promote popular literacy during the 1780s; and the reconstitution, in 1785, of the Society for the Reformation of Manners (SRM) to teach the rich the error of their frivolous ways. The French Revolution only brought a new spirit of urgency to the quest for salvation: during the 1790s, thirty new medical, religious, educational and moral charities were founded in London alone, during the following decade that figure would rise to thirty-six and, from 1811 to 1820, to fifty-five (Brown, 1961: 329–37; Laqueur, 1976: 2; Trumbach, 1991). The new British and Foreign Bible Society (BFBS) responded to the 1804 French invasion scare by distributing religious literature to the nation.

More practical campaigns for the moral regeneration of British society were launched by the innumerable societies devoted to the aid of the poor founded throughout the French wars. Christian fervour was not a necessary precondition for membership: Brougham and Bentham, members of the Society for Bettering the Condition of the Poor (SBCP), possessed no religious beliefs to speak of; but levels of evangelical interest in such organisations were high – too high for Bentham, whose National Charity Company project, a joint-stock poorhouse scheme, was promoted as a secular and commercial alternative to the old poor law (Brown, 1961; Soloway, 1969; Bahmueller, 1981; Andrew, 1989: 174–8). Some moral reform societies possessed a strong vigilante loyalist identity, most notably the Proclamation Society, founded in 1787, and the Society for the Suppression of Vice (SSV), inaugurated in 1802. Both were enemies of licentiousness, immoral stage plays, smoky alehouses and infidelity in all their printed forms. Staunch as the SSV was in its support for the abolition of slavery, it worked closely with the government in the preparation of prosecution briefs against blasphemous books such as Paine's *Age of Reason* (Place, 1972: 160–5). The society's reputation as a crusading champion of orthodox Christianity against the forces of Jacobinism attracted two of the Pitt ministry's most prolific journalists, John Gifford, editor of the *Anti-Jacobin Magazine*, and John Bowles, into SSV ranks during the 1790s (Vincent, 1993). In 1812, the SSV lost both Bowles and Reeves, after which it became less overtly anti-Jacobin and more evangelical in focus (Brown, 1961: 15, 84–7, 428–36; Soloway, 1969: 110–28; Jones, 1983; Innes, 1990; Turley, 1991: 109–10).

All evangelicals accepted that a patriarchal, deferential and ordered society was ordained by God, which made them natural conservatives despite the willingness of the Saints to oppose war on the grounds of sin, injustice and cruelty. Although evangelicals made good propagators of loyalist nationalism (Newman, 1987: 235), they did not make uncritical conservatives. Evangelicals believed that the moral and spiritual regeneration of *all* Britons was imperative to the salvation of the nation from eternal damnation and Jacobin anarchy (Bebbington, 1989; Vincent, 1998). Wilberforce and his friends eschewed dancing, gambling, sports and all such frivolous occupations on the grounds that they corrupted the soul, and the *Cheap Repository Tracts*, a series of penny pamphlets aimed at the rural poor, were launched by Hannah More in 1795 to inculcate Christian virtue in the lower orders. More, who ran her own Sunday schools in the Mendip Hills, was well qualified to write for a popular audience and had made a careful study of popular chapbooks before embarking upon the project. Although the series was later taken over by an evangelical clerical consortium, More wrote some of the *Cheap Repository*'s best known and most popular pamphlets (Jones, 1983; Laqueur, 1976: 25–8, 34–5; Turley, 1991: 108–12).

Although all of More's tracts were infused with conservative values, few of them were overtly political in content. Jack Anvil, the loyalist blacksmith, and Tom Hod, the radical mason, were the two stock characters of her anti-Jacobin loyalist tracts introduced to readers in the 1793 *Village Politics*. This placed a paternalist Establishment Whig defence of the crown, church and constitution into Jack's mouth that won Tom, who had been reading Paine's *Rights of Man*, over to the cause of loyalism. Most of her tracts, however, dwelt on moral themes and attempted 'to vindicate the justice of God in the apparently unequal distribution of goodness in this world, by pointing to another.' Beilby Porteous, Bishop of London, told More that in the ballad *Turn the Carpet*, 'Here you have Bishop [Samuel] Butler's *Analogy* for a halfpenny' (More, 1835: ii, 457–8; Hole, 1983). More's *Hymn for an Abundant Harvest*, published in 1796, described the poor crop yields of the prior two years as punishments upon a sinful people sent by a sorrowful deity.

The *Cheap Repository*'s morality tales were bestsellers of the 1790s and helped loyalists corner the market in didactic pamphlets and children's literature. This spurred radical authors and printers to retaliate during the next two decades with mock children's rhymes and tales culminating in John Wade's 1820 *Man in the Moon* and *The Political House that Jack Built*. The interest of More and other loyalist evangelicals in the inculcation of popular literacy had predated the French Revolution by a good two decades and explains their rush to publish popular tracts for a semi-literate audience during the 1790s. In 1792, William Jones published not only the first of the famous John Bull pamphlets, but also *The Book of Nature, or the True Sense of Things, explained and made easy for the Capacities of Children, in Two Parts*. This alphabetical primer employed some of the chapbook typographical and illustrational conventions that would be adopted by More and the *Cheap Repository* (Jones, 1952: 140–1, 148; Hone, 1982: 345–7; Claeys, 1989: 60–2; Crimmins, 1990: 169–79; Jackson, 1989: 169–223; Wood, 1994: 220–1).

Susan Pedersen (1986) has suggested that the *Cheap Repository* represented part of an evangelical assault upon popular culture, and it is difficult for the modern reader to see much appeal in the moralising tracts of the later 1790s and 1800s: a far cry from the sensationalist tales of highwaymen and murderers that had been chapbook bestsellers during the eighteenth century. More's own work up to 1800 nonetheless repays examination, for she wrote with a genuine love and knowledge of her audience, churning out ballads, recipes, prayers, narratives, dialogues and catechisms for the *Cheap Repository*. Two million copies of the tracts had been sold by 1796, though as More herself pointed out, many were bought by the gentry for the instruction of their own children (1835: ii, 460–1). She began the *Cheap Repository* with no intention of blending entertainment and instruction but, by 1798, godly paternalism and pure didacticism were taking over (Ford, 1996: 134–71).

Neither the work ethic nor the religiosity More promoted in her pamphlets was nonetheless alien to artisans, for whom honesty, hard work and pride in one's labour had long been familiar values. The 'working class' experience of Sunday schools, from which on estimated 3m children acquired literacy skills between 1780 and 1830, suggests that the schools were employed by artisans to reinforce those values and, in the case of manufacturing labourers, to acquire and appropriate them (Laqueur, 1975: 214–18). More herself tried to make respectability attractive, rewarding her chapbook heroes and heroines with material comforts and security in this life, thereby endorsing the loyalist claim that Britain's social and political order was the world's best guarantor of happiness in this world and, in all likelihood, the next. Despite More's retirement from the *Cheap Repository* project in 1798, the tracts continued to be bestsellers and carried the war against radicals, infidels and the immoral into the 1800s (Philp, 1991: 8, n. 20; Pendleton, 1976; Cookson, 1997: 213).

Self-help was a doctrine to which utilitarians, evangelicals and commercial Whigs could subscribe, which explains the diverse membership of the SBCP founded in 1796 to circulate '*useful* and *practical* information, derived from experience' on the subject of poverty and the old poor law (SBCP, 1797–1817: i, 265). Wilberforce was a founding member of this organisation, the Proclamation Society and the SSV. Thomas Bernard, the SBCP's evangelical president, was convinced that the poor were as eager as the rich to indulge 'the desire implanted in the human breast of bettering its condition'. Throughout its first decade of existence the SBCP endorsed a range of self-sufficiency poor relief projects, from allotment gardens and contributory unemployment insurance schemes to Lord Winchelsea's 1796 proposal that parishes lend money to the poor for the purchase of livestock. Self-improvement would, in Bernard's opinion, teach the poor 'the true value of those gradations of rank which our Creator has thought fit to establish'. The SBCP was not alone in its advocacy of property ownership, be it ever so humble, as an antidote to riot and revolution (SBCP, 1797–1817: ii, 282–5, iv, 1–60; Barnett, 1967; Hilton, 1988: 98–100; Eastwood, 1991: 164–6). The Land Plan of the agriculturalist Arthur Young proposed to give land to the poor in return for their voluntary disqualification from poor relief, in so doing ensuring their loyalty to state and society. The acquisition of a literal stake in the nation would, according to loyalists, give the poor an interest to defend and identify with in a wider nexus of British legal, political and constitutional conventions based upon property ownership (Young, 1800).

Under Bernard's leadership the SBCP was an enemy to workhouses, unregulated child labour, poor hygiene in hospitals, night work in the textile mills and short-term parochial employment schemes. In 1799 the establishment of a Clapham SBCP by the Reverend Henry Venn denoted the arrival of private poor relief as an 'official' evangelical campaign, and the Saints' example would be followed by other communities. By 1802 Bernard's interests had shifted from the promotion of scientific private charity and the exposure of deficiencies in the old poor law and the moral education of the poor. Notwithstanding the interest of More, Jones and others in the Sunday school movement, the Church of England emerged from the 1790s divided on the wisdom of promoting popular literacy, thanks to ultra-conservative claims that reading skills of any description would only encourage the lower order to forget their social station and become infected with Jacobin ideas (Hole, 1989: 187–95). Bernard would defend the cause of primary education as a mode of proper politico-religious indoctrination, a route to spiritual salvation and a sacred right of the people. The British and Foreign Bible Society, which emerged in 1804 under such crusading evangelical auspices, is best known for its sponsorship of missionary work amongst 'the heathen' overseas. The society's chief domestic objective was, however, the production of a sanitised loyalist Bible for native consumption, and it was active in the publication of schoolbooks, tracts, prayerbooks and creeds for use in evangelical schools (Best, 1964: 185–7; Poynter, 1969: 195–200; Jackson, 1989).

In the Lancaster–Bell primary schools debate of the early nineteenth century, Bernard and the SBCP sided with the Anglican Andrew Bell and his call for a national elementary school system superintended by the national church. The real innovator in primary schooling for the poor was Joseph Lancaster, in whose schools no text but the Bible was used, had been running since 1789. There was little to choose between the Lancaster and Bell systems, in which older children were appointed as 'monitors' to supervise and pass lessons on to their fellow students. Very large classes could be taught in this manner but, despite the open support of George III, Lancaster's identity as a Quaker ensured his methods the hostility of evangelicals and High Churchmen alike, a state of affairs far removed from the non-denominational co-operation visible in the Sunday school movement from 1780 to 1800. In 1784 Manchester Anglicans, Dissenters and Roman Catholics all contributed money to Sunday schools launched in that year (Henriques, 1961: 203–7, 200–1; Hempton, 1984: 89).

The founding of the Royal Lancaster Society in 1809 was quickly followed by the appearance of the National Society for Promoting the Education of the Poor in the Principles of the Established Church and had been preceded by a flurry of evangelical activity on the education front. By 1811 only a few parishes in England and Wales would be lacking a school and, though standards of education left much to be desired, the schools ensured that some basic educational provision existed throughout the country (Mitch,

1993: 268–72). Whigs and radicals, partially to spite the Tory Anglican government, took up Lancaster's system as a cheap and non-denominational alternative model by which to construct an infrastructure of national public education (Hone, 1982: 238–48). Bernard had been early to sponsor primary education as a worthy cause and, as evangelicals went, was less partisan in his support of it than others, supporting some of Samuel Whitbread's 1807 proposals, part of an unsuccessful poor law reform bill, to create a national network of parish schools governed by a state board of education (Poynter, 1969: 214–21). Although the education project was rejected by the House of Lords, Bernard had hoped that Whitbread's board of education could conduct scientific experiments in teaching and learning and set national guidelines for all existing schools (SBCP, 1807: 21–30; Laqueur, 1975: 128–31).

Neither evangelical Dissenters nor Anglicans succeeded in converting souls through the Sunday schools which, though widely attended by the poor, were used primarily for the acquisition of literacy skills and the values of self-improvement. Very few of the pupils later became full church or chapel members (Ward, 1972: 13; Hempton, 1984: 86–92). Evangelical loyalist reform sought to defend and, where necessary, to strengthen the social order, and the conservative subtext of their endeavours should not be forgotten, in spite of the fact that, by 1815, they were not alone in their quest to improve the manners, morals, lifestyles and living standards of their fellow Britons. The involvement of philanthropists and social theorists such as Bentham and Owen in prison, legal, poor law and factory reform during the 1810s and 1820s represented only one aspect of an age of improvement that remained, for many, an age of atonement capable of attracting loyalists, moderates, liberals and, indeed, radicals to many reform causes during the French wars.

CHAPTER FOUR

Individuals and Institutions

If the memoirs of Thomas Hardy (1817: 111–16) and Francis Place (1972: 196–7) are to be taken at face value, Pitt imposed an English 'reign of terror' upon the British public during the 1790s. Not content with creating a climate of intense hostility to the popular radicalism, Pitt's Home Office embarked in 1792 upon a policy of active persecution in parliament and the law courts. The radicals, hounded through the courts on sedition, libel and treason charges, faced continual harassment and, from 1795 onwards, prohibitions on their freedom of public assembly, right to petition parliament and ability to criticise the government in writing or speech. Having been made outlaws by the Corresponding Societies Act of 1799, radicals retired to their workshops to dream of reform, having been denied all routes of 'legitimate' access to the political realm.

While radicals and liberals suffered much formal and informal persecution during the French wars, the opportunities for any British government to impose its will upon the country were restricted by the structures and practices of the eighteenth-century constitution. This, a blend of customary law and statute legislation that had emerged since the Middle Ages, possessed few formal statements of principle besides landmark documents like the 1215 Magna Carta and the 1689 Bill of Rights, neither of which possessed any status as legal enactments. The constitution was therefore in theory whatever Britons chose to make it. Most educated persons subscribed to the theory of a balanced constitution where the power of parliament balanced the prerogatives of the crown and executive government (Dickinson, 1977; Gash, 1986: 1–15). In practice, Britain possessed a decentralised government where all real power in the provinces was exercised by rural and urban elites who, as voluntary officials, comprised the personnel of local government. Much of parliament's legislation was consequently permissive by necessity (Eastwood, 1994a, 1997).

Despite its impressive ability to mobilise manpower and resources for the French wars, the British government was subject to the same restrictions upon the use – or abuse – of executive power as any early modern European state. Britons were staunch defenders of their liberties, having long resented and resisted all centralising attempts on the part of the core to control the nation's peripheries. Had Pitt tried to enforce national standards upon the provinces, he would have been accused of absolutism and tyranny by even the most conservative of MPs. The House of Commons was, in fact, to reject his 1796 proposals for reform of the old poor law, in part because they subjected the provinces to a degree of external scrutiny considered inappropriate for an autonomous parochial institution. Many MPs and peers nevertheless felt that sedition, poverty and irreligion were national evils to which both the state and local government were inadequately responsive, and new legislation to police all three would be presented to parliament at regular intervals throughout the French wars. Some of these enactments originated with the governments of the day but the rest, a not inconsiderable amount, took the form of private members' bills. Much of this legislative activity was directed, not towards the strengthening of central government *per se*, but to the establishment of new standards for the guidance of local communities. This was a purpose that parliament would continue to serve well into the nineteenth century.

Sedition and Treason

The presence of native popular radicals sympathetic to the French Revolution posed peculiar public order problems for successive governments throughout the revolutionary and Napoleonic Wars. Public order had to be maintained without infringing upon the civil rights of Britons, a dilemma that determined the shape and timing of state policy throughout the period. Official perceptions of radicals and reformers changed little from 1792 to 1820, for Pittite attitudes towards both radicals and the constitution were inherited largely intact by the Liverpool ministry, which consciously resurrected the entire Pittite programme of repressive measures from 1817 to 1819.

Before going any further, it is necessary to define what the British constitution represented for Pitt and his successors. In 1792 the premier had described the constitution as a vast and complex device that preserved a delicate balance between freedom and constraint: 'It is this union of law and liberty, which, by raising a barrier equally firm against the encroachments of power, and the violence of popular commotion, affords to property its just security, produces the exertion of genius and labour, the extent and solidity of credit, the circulation and increase of capital, which forms and upholds the national character, and sets in motion all the springs which actuate the great mass of the community through all its various descriptions' (PH, xxviii, 835–6).

While it would seem from the public order legislation of the 1790s that Pitt worried more about the popular commotions than the encroachments of power, any study of government documents and private correspondence reveals that the Cabinets of the French wars were determined to preserve a balance between law and liberty: the former could not be allowed to erode the latter, no matter how frightening popular radicalism might seem (Derry, 1981: 128–32; O'Gorman, 1989a). Pittites did not believe that Britons, for the most part happy and loyal subjects, made natural radicals. The people and, in particular, the crowd were nevertheless potentially amenable to manipulation by a small number of 'mischievous' incendiaries employing the cause of peaceful parliamentary reform as a shield for more sinister designs. What these might be was subject to interpretation. Perceval told the Commons frankly in his 1796 maiden speech that 'the spirit of democracy' frightened him more than 'the growing influence of the Crown' and, from 1817 to 1820, Liverpool and his colleagues were convinced that radicals, driven by their Jacobin principles and post-war social hardship, sought nothing less than a French Revolution (Gray, 1963: 36; Cone, 1968: 202; Cookson, 1975: 180–2, 1997: 182; Hilton, 1977: 74–5, 79–87). Home Secretary Sidmouth saw the revolutionary menace everywhere from the sermons of itinerant Dissenter preachers to Luddite disturbances. Pitt and his colleagues tended to be less intolerant in their attitudes. Having watched the rise of popular reform in Britain accompany the radicalisation of the revolution in France and the outbreak of war in Europe, they maintained throughout the 1790s that domestic Jacobinism was a direct offshoot of its French parent: for Pitt, Grenville and Dundas radicalism constituted an enemy weapon of diplomacy and war deployed to distract and harass the British government rather than a native popular movement in its own right (PR, 1793: xxxiv, 384–92). The Pitt Cabinet therefore expected the radical problem to disappear with the advent of peace, confined themselves to the passage of short-term legislation, and sought Jacobins in radical clubs, the metropolitan press and treasonable conspiracies rather than trade unions, Methodist chapels or the vast majority of riots (Mori, 1997b).

This official case against British radicalism took shape over the course of 1792. The 21 May royal proclamation against seditious writings has often been regarded as a simple response to the rise of popular radicalism and the publication of Paine's *Rights of Man* (Part II). Matters were more complex. While the proclamation claimed that wicked and seditious publications were disposing the people to riot and rebellion, there was no evidence that radicals had caused any public disturbances with the exception of the 1791 Birmingham church and king riots staged by loyalists. These had puzzled the ministry in their extent and ferocity, spreading quickly from Birmingham to other Midlands towns. Home Office enquiries as to their causes conducted during the autumn of 1791 produced disturbing reports of Paine's popularity amongst artisans and soldiers in the north of England. Copies of Part II had been read by the Cabinet three weeks before its publication and, within a week of the book's appearance, it was declared a seditious libel by the government. A review of troops and barracks in the south of England undertaken during the spring of 1792 indicates that the government was expecting trouble that summer but from whom is not clear. What made a libel seditious was its ability to incite civil disobedience, and Part II, with its denunciations of the Hanoverian monarchy, the old poor law and the British fiscal–military state, was seen as an inflammatory text at a time when, as Dundas told the Commons, Manchester manufacturers and Sheffield cutlers were forming associations to promote parliamentary reform. Although this insinuates that the government was afraid of radicals, the official sources reveal more concern about loyalist troublemakers (PR, 1793: xxxiii, 130–2, 175–8; Emsley, 1985: 805–6; Mori, 1996, 1997b: 114–16).

The Portland Whigs, alarmed by the launch of the FOP in London, agreed at Pitt's invitation both to endorse the proclamation and to help organise loyalist petitions in its defence. They had been told that the government had 'undoubted information of many foreigners who are employed to raise sedition in England' and the attention paid by the Home Office to the surveillance of French embassy personnel in 1792 suggests that these fears were real (Elliot, 1874: ii, 23–4; Bath and Wells, 1861: ii, 436). The government was nevertheless scaremongering about the radical threat. Lord Auckland, through whom Pitt's initial approach to Portland had been made, wrote to a colleague that 'the government does not feel any serious uneasiness' on account of the radicals because 'nineteen-twentieths' of the nation was loyal to the constitution (Keith, 1849: ii, 518–20). The proclamation nevertheless served as a precautionary statement of official concern – it had no status as an enactment – and a loyalty test for the provinces incorporating an appeal for information about the radical presence, if any, in the localities (O'Gorman, 1989a: 31). It is possible that the May Proclamation represented an intellectual *cordon sanitaire* against revolutionary France: on 19 September, Dundas wrote that government policy consisted of vigilance at home and neutrality to the war abroad declared by France against

Austria on 20 April (SRO GD 224/30/9/9/2–3). Two months later, Dundas was demanding decisive action, for widespread food and wage riots, combined with the recovery of French arms in the Low Countries, had seemingly combined to produce a revival of popular radicalism now overtly sympathetic to a revolution that had deposed Louis XVI and inaugurated the first republic (PRO 30/8/157). By 7 November, a prime minister and Home Office inundated with panic accounts of radical pro-French demonstrations, riots, strikes and the arrival of suspicious French refugees in flight from the September massacres felt compelled to take decisive action.

From 8 to 14 November, Pitt and Grenville drew up a programme of extraordinary measures including the compulsory registration of all printing presses, the increasing of legal penalties for sedition, the suspension of *habeas corpus*, the introduction of volunteer corps, the launch of a nationwide seditious libel prosecution campaign, and the passage of an Aliens Act requiring foreigners – by this was meant French refugees – to register their addresses and movements in Britain. Had this entire programme been adopted in 1792, it would have significantly strengthened the hands of government. By 18 November, however, Pitt and Grenville had concluded that provincial accounts of the radical threat were wildly exaggerated, and had abandoned all but the Aliens Act and the libel campaign. The Lord Mayor of London was nevertheless advised to start moving against the city's debating societies and, on 6 December, Thomas Spence was arrested for selling copies of Paine's *Rights of Man* (Thale, 1989: 65). Provincial solicitors were instructed by circular letter on 7 December to launch legal proceedings against radical authors. Before that date, however, the government's public order programme had undergone further modification following the receipt of fresh news from Europe (Mori, 1996).

From Auckland, British ambassador at the Hague, the Cabinet learned of a rumoured Dutch radical rising in support of the French, whose army was fast advancing through the Austrian Netherlands. This news reached London on 22 November and did not concern the government until, on 25 November, it received both the 16 November decree by which the revolutionary army justified its forced entry of the River Scheldt, sovereignty over which lay with the Dutch, and the 19 November First Fraternal decree offering liberty and equality to the peoples of Europe. Armed with this information, ministers now suspected that the radical demonstrations of the autumn were linked to the movements of the revolutionary armies in the Low Countries and these apprehensions were seemingly confirmed by French *émigré* refugees who warned the Home Office about a 'London insurrection' supposedly scheduled by artisans and radicals for early December (Emsley, 1978; HO 42/22, fo. 319; PRO 30/8/198, #4, ff. 113–16). As the 1 December royal proclamation embodying the militias of England's eastern counties put it: 'The utmost industry is still employed by evil-disposed persons within this kingdom, acting in concert with persons in foreign parts, with a view to subvert the laws and constitution of this realm, and to destroy all order and government therein'. A second 5 December militia proclamation would reinforce the government case for imminent insurrection (Grenville, 1853: ii, 230–2; Bath and Wells, 1861: ii, 472–3; Murley, 1959: 205–17; Emsley, 1979b, 1981, 1985: 806).

The fifth-column case had been born. Pitt now believed that French-backed popular radicals sought, at the least, to prevent Britain from assisting its ally, the United Provinces, or at worst to depose Britain's government and overthrow its constitution. He, Grenville and Dundas were confident of the government's ability to thwart any rising that might occur but were now determined to recruit public support both for the containment of popular radicalism and for possible war with France. In the loyalist association movement founded by Reeves, Pitt saw a body of public opinion that could be mobilised in what was becoming a public relations war with France. The seeming strength of cosmopolitan Jacobin radicalism was to be contested with a display of British loyalism that, in the words of Grenville, had by 13 December boosted levels of public morale 'in a manner little short of miraculous' (Grenville, 1853: ii, 233). How afraid the government was of actual insurrection is unknown, but the confidence expressed by Pitt on 1 December that a vote of confidence from parliament, due to meet on 13 December, 'added to the proper exertions of our Party, and aided by the spirit which shows itself in the capital and which will probably soon spread, will, I flatter myself, fully ensure the security of the country', suggests that he and the Cabinet had succumbed to a temporary fit of panic about the radical menace (Granville, 1916: i, 61). The government's failure to revive its anti-Jacobin programme of repressive measures testifies to its determination not to overreact (Stanhope, 1861–2: ii, 176–7; Duffy, 1996; Mori, 1996).

The events of 1792 set the government on a path of harassment rather than outright persecution. Only 200 seditious libel prosecutions were brought against radicals during the 1790s, most of these during the first six months of 1793. The Treasury Solicitors were in fact reluctant to authorise such trials unless prospects of conviction were high, while English juries refused to convict suspects for publishing their opinions unless they vilified the monarchy and constitution. Despite the use of special juries and *ex officio* informations by the crown, most suspects were released without conviction. Over the 1790s, the Treasury Solicitors found juries more prepared to punish radical authors and printers for blasphemy but still found it difficult to get convictions for seditious words (Emsley, 1979b, 1981, 1985). Although Pitt had hoped that loyalist associations would collect funds to subsidise libel prosecutions, the quick disappearance of the Reevites soon put an end to this source of income, and the limited resources of the state for legal work ensured that rank and file radicals were not threatened with the vengeance of the law. They suffered instead from informal harassment: exclusion from pubs or meeting houses and intimidation from church and king mobs. The Alien Office set up in 1793 served as a registration and surveillance centre for French refugees, of whom suspected spies and incendiary agents were the primary targets for deportation (Dinwiddy, 1968: 195–6). Under William Wickham's leadership from 1798 onwards, it would become a 'secret service' headquarters for foreign and domestic espionage (Sparrow, 1990, 1998). Reeves later became Superintendent of Aliens but his APLP was never formally revived despite his voluntary offer to resurrect the loyalists in 1795 (Emsley, 1981: 176–84; Thale, 1989: 65–85; Lobban, 1990: 309; Wood, 1994: 96–154).

Suspensions of *habeas corpus* were requested from parliament in 1794 and 1798 to facilitate the conduct of special investigations by the Home Office. On both occasions the government suspected that the metropolitan radical societies were planning to rise in support of French invasion projects and moved to arrest leading radicals before any rebellion could take place. In 1794 radical plans to stage a British Convention were interpreted as a pretext for an armed insurrection and officers of both the LCS and SCI were arrested in April. When Home Office enquiries conducted over the summer of 1794 failed to establish any connection between British radicals and the French government, Attorney-General Sir John Scott was left with a difficult case for high treason to prosecute in the Court of King's Bench. In a series of highly publicised state trials Scott attempted to establish a doctrine of constructive treason that equated the projected British Convention with the supercession of parliament in its legislative capacity, but the case was thin and the evidence scanty (Wharam, 1992). After John Thelwall, Thomas Hardy and John Horne Tooke were acquitted, the government released the rest of its suspects without trial and *habeas corpus* was restored in June 1795. In 1798 the threats of invasion and insurrection were real, although the number of revolutionaries was small, and in a series of arrests over the spring of 1798 the Home Office rounded up UE, UI and LCS suspects in London and Manchester on suspicion of high treason (Ehrman, 1996: 117–20, 303–6). At the state trials of 1798–1799 the government could finally claim that British radicals, in collusion with French paymasters, had sought to subvert the constitution, overthrow the government and establish a democratic republic in Britain. Despite the existence of a genuine conspiracy only James O'Coigley was convicted. While Arthur O'Connor, John Binns, John Allen and Jeremy Leary were freed, the remaining suspects remained in prison until 1801 (Prochaska, 1973; Elliott, 1982: 181–9).

The significance of the 1794 state trials lies in their attempt to establish a new interpretation of treason law without recourse to new legislation. The original 1351 statute of treasons protected the king's person but not his government from designs against the state and, despite its deficiencies, no attempt was made to update the law of treason by statute until 1795 because ministers were uncertain about the constitutionality of such new legislation. Statute law was absolute while the common law was not, and guilty verdicts in 1794 would have strengthened the government's hand against radicals by establishing that plots against the state, rather than the crown, represented a form of treason without recourse to an act of parliament. Research had been done in the Home Office on the treason and sedition legislation of the past at the end of 1792, but none of it appealed to any MP brought up on myths of Tudor and Stuart absolutism. In 1795, following the London mob's attack upon the king's coach as it bore George III to the state opening of parliament, the government finally used 1571 and 1661 statutes as precedents for the introduction of the Two Acts (Mori, 1997b: 278–9). The Seditious Meetings Act required all meetings of over 50 persons in size to be licensed by a magistrate, while the Seditious and Treasonable Practices Act made any verbal or written attack on either the king or his ministers a treasonable offence. A second consecutive bad harvest, extremely high grain prices, nationwide rioting and the militancy of the LCS had aroused the genuine alarm of the Cabinet: at no other point in the 1790s was the government in such fear of an English insurrection. Even under these circumstances, the Seditious and Treasonable Practices Act was due to expire at the end of the first parliament following George III's death, while the Seditious Meetings Act had a lifespan of only three years (O'Gorman, 1989a: 32–3; Emsley, 1985: 811–13).

The passage of the Newspaper Stamp Duty Act in 1798 and the Corresponding Societies Act in 1799 seemingly completed the enactment of repressive measures conceived by Pitt in 1792. Two acts to prevent the seduction of seamen and the administering of unlawful oaths to members of the armed forces had been passed in the aftermath of the 1797 naval mutinies. These minor planks in the government's public order strategy were set to expire one month after the beginning of the next parliamentary session; more far reaching in conception and impact were the regulations introduced by the Newspaper Stamp Duty Act which, bolstered by clauses of the Corresponding Societies Act, required printers to give recognisances for good behaviour and acknowledge their publications by printing their names and addresses on the title pages of books, pamphlets and periodicals. The 1798 act, passed in response to the discovery of radical papers and books on vessels bound for France, must be seen as part of the government's campaign to avert the prospect of enemy-backed insurrection. Here lies the driving principle behind the repressive measures of the 1790s but questions must be asked about the timing of their introduction (Aspinall, 1949: 38–9; Emsley, 1985: 814–19). Six years was a long time to wait for the outlawing of the LCS by name, especially for those supposedly convinced that it represented a force of anarchy and terror.

Three reasons can be given for the delayed implementation of Pitt's 1792 programme: lack of fear, lack of incentive and lack of enthusiasm. The private and official correspondence of the king's servants displays little apprehension about the actual or potential activities of radicals except at crisis points during the 1790s. Ministers knew popular radicalism was a minority movement and, for the most part, regarded it as a peculiar by-product of the revolutionary wars rather than a long-term threat to British society. The government could not, moreover, move against radical societies without hard evidence of sedition and treason nor extend the government's powers of surveillance over radicals without manpower resources they did not possess: 'Our laws suppose magistrates and Grand Juries to do their duty, and if they do it not, I have little faith in its being done by a Government such as the Constitution has made ours' (Grenville, 1853: ii, 227). The independence of JPs was a time-honoured tradition in the provinces and no government of the French wars could exercise any real control over the shape of the active magistracy, only one-third of which was active at any given time during the eighteenth century. The numbers of active JPs increased from 2656 in 1796 to 4000 in 1808, but this had little to do with government prompting and everything to do with their own apprehensions for the safety of their communities (Eastwood, 1991: 167, 1994a: 22, 76–8).

More control could be exercised over London magistrates, thanks to the passage of the 1792 Middlesex Justices Act that established police bureaux of stipendiary magistrates answering to Reeves. The government also employed spies throughout the 1790s to infiltrate the radical clubs, by whom it was not well served, for many informers told the Home Office what they thought it wanted to hear (Emsley, 1979b; Eastwood, 1989a; McFarland, 1994: 120–1). Ministers spent little of their time during the 1790s worrying about popular radicalism. In 1800 Pitt wrote to Granville that 'by some unaccountable negligence, the Bill passed in 1795 respecting meetings has been suffered to expire' (Fortescue, 1892–1927: vi, 373). When the Seditious Meetings Act had been passed, both men had anticipated, at most, another two years of war and neither enjoyed the introduction of repressive legislation, aware that in doing so the government set dangerous precedents for the suppression of civil liberties that might be resorted to in the future. The landmark legislation of the 1790s would indeed be only too well recalled by the Liverpool ministry, but amongst the things that Pittites inherited from their master was a regard for the constitutional proprieties and a disinclination to hasty action that governed the conception and introduction of the Six Acts from 1817 to 1819.

From the Two Acts to the Six Acts

When London radicals began once more to demand reform from 1807 onwards, Pitt's successors did not panic. Not only had the 1790s proved that most Britons were loyal to the constitution but even the Opposition, of which Grenville was now a leader, admitted that the war had lost much of its ideological character. In the absence of a professional police force, no government could pursue and prosecute all members of radical clubs, with the result that they concentrated upon the arrest of easily identifiable radicals, be they authors, publishers or spokesmen for the movement. In 1810 Sir Francis Burdett would be sent to the Tower for contempt of the Commons while journalists and printers were hauled before the courts on sedition and blasphemy charges. Mass membership of the radical movement was not an issue during the 1800s but, despite the employment of a small army to put down the Luddites, ministers did not confuse industrial protest and food rioting with incipient revolution (Sack, 1979; Cookson, 1975; Gilmartin, 1996: 115–20, 141–3).

The rise of the Hampden Clubs, the return of peace in 1815 and the economic distress of the post-war years created conditions in which radicalism flourished. The Spa Fields mass meetings that took place during the winter of 1816–1817 were reminiscent of 1795, when the Copenhagen House open-air rally of the LCS had drawn a crowd of listeners reportedly 100,000 strong to listen to radical demands for parliamentary reform. The involvement of the Spenceans in the Spa Fields riots allowed the government to claim that the mass meetings were a dress rehearsal for a British revolution (Chase, 1988: 102–3). When the Prince Regent's coach was attacked on 28 January 1817 the government revisited the legislation of the 1790s: a Habeas Corpus Suspension Act, an Act for Punishing Traitorous Practices, Seditious Assemblies and Publications, and a Seduction of Soldiers from their Duties Act; the Spencean Society was also outlawed by name. The distress of the people, claimed Liverpool, had been shamefully exploited by so-called reformers, who sought nothing less than the establishment of a new order in state and society. With Britain at peace with France, this zeal could only be attributable to the long-term effects of Jacobin poison upon English radical minds. Despite the strength of the government's convictions, *habeas corpus* was suspended temporarily once more, while the Seditious and Treasonable Practices Act was changed only by the insertion of the Prince Regent's name in the place of the now mad George III's. The new Seditious Meetings Act not only revived the 1795 licensing regulations for public meetings over 50 persons, but forbade any political assemblies, be they in fields, houses or public rooms (Cookson, 1977: 108–15).

The Home Office, in keeping with the official belief that a deluded people were the dupes of popular demagogues, chose its targets of attack with care. Henry Hunt, Francis Burdett, T.J. Wooler and the leading Spenceans: Dr James Watson, Arthur Thistlewood, cobbler Thomas Preston and cordwainer John Hooper were arrested and held for trial on suspicion of high treason in the hope that their trials would either produce convictions or, at least, discredit the reform movement. This had been part of Pitt's rationale for staging the 1794 state trials. The speedy acquittal of the suspects by English juries put an end to this strategy, while the March of the Blanketeers and continuing reports of reform meetings convinced the Liverpool government that a process of mass politicisation was taking place under their noses. This belief began to reunify the old Pittites. The Grenvillites, convinced that reform meetings served 'under the pretence of discussing Parliamentary Reform', to train persons in the use of arms 'to frame a new order of society through the same bloody practices which have attended the French Revolution', returned to the government benches in 1817 to vote for the new legislation, and it could be said that the introduction of the Six Acts represented a bid to reunite the friends and followers of Pittism behind the government (NLW Coed-y-Maen MS, T. Grenville to C. Williams-Wynn, 1 Oct. 1819; Cookson, 1977: 181–2).

In spite of this seeming unanimity, Liverpool and Home Secretary Sidmouth did not agree on the timing for the introduction of new repressive legislation. Sidmouth, convinced that the country was swarming with radical conspirators, sought to take immediate and decisive action, but Liverpool, convinced that radicalism was a product of socio-economic distress rather than popular conviction, wanted more evidence of plots and arms before enacting new measures. The employment of *agents provocateurs* by the Home Office during the 1790s and 1810s is consistent with the Pittite belief that some radicals were amenable to levelling persuasion: while the Pop Gun Plot of June 1794, by which George III was purportedly to be shot by an airgun whilst attending the theatre, was an informer fabrication, the Pentrich Rising of June 1817 was a more serious attempted rising of Derbyshire nailers and stockingers led by Jeremiah Brandreth betrayed to the government by 'Oliver the Spy'. The true identity of the former carpenter and surveyor, William Oliver, was exposed by the *Leeds Mercury* a week after the abortive attempt of Pentrich and Ripley villagers to march upon

Nottingham, and another spy, George Edwards, was involved in the Cato Street conspiracy (Hammond and Hammond, 1912: 288; Maccoby, 1955: 334–5; Ziegler, 1965: 322–3, 348–54, 360–6; Thompson, 1968: 433, 731–3; Cookson, 1977: 183–4; Belchem, 1985: 75–7; Watts, 1995: 400–2).

When the government introduced the Six Acts following the Peterloo 'massacre' of 1819, it revived the Pittite public order programme in its entirety. The Seditious Meetings Act, the Military Training Prevention Act and the Seizure of Arms Act gave magistrates extensive powers to seize arms whilst preventing their use by 'unauthorised' personnel and confining public meetings of all descriptions to individual parishes except for those convened by 'properly constituted authorities'. The Misdemeanours Act prevented radical suspects from manipulating the due process of law to postpone trial while released on bail, a response to the legal evasions conducted by Hunt and Burdett in 1817–1818. The Newspaper Stamp Duties Act levied a steep £200 surety upon London printers, slapped a 4d duty on cheap weekly newspapers and set a minimum price of 6d on all other periodicals. The Blasphemous and Seditious Libels Act made fourteen years' banishment or transportation the maximum penalty for a second conviction (Maccoby, 1955: 363–5; Cookson, 1975: 191–8; Gilmartin, 1996: 32–3, 97–8).

Draconian though this legislation appears, it was framed to punish radicals while preserving the rights of other Britons intact. The institutionalised censorship of the press, a blanket ban on all public meetings and the formation of a professional police force were all regarded as inappropriately harsh solutions to the problems of disorder and distress. The Six Acts moreover relied, as the Two Acts had done, upon the willingness of magistrates to enforce the legislation. This JPs failed to do, for they had many duties above and beyond the chasing of radicals or, in many cases, sent the government frightened accounts of radical plots in their localities that were dismissed by the Home Office as incidents of alarmist panic (Emsley, 1979b; Eastwood, 1989a: 278, 1994a: 47–8). The construction of the government case against sedition had changed in some respects since 1794. Eager though the crown's attorneys were to find radical plots and conspiracies that would permit them to adhere to the spirit of Pittite seditious and treasonable practices legislation, the inability of the crown to do so resulted either in prosecutions for simple calumnious libels or in the making of fine distinctions between verbal expressions of private opinions at meetings and verbal attempts to incite hatred or contempt of the king and constitution. John Binns's 1797 trial for seditious words had established that the former was a civil liberty while the latter was sedition. Henry Hunt's 1819–1820 state trial further laid down that meetings were not in themselves seditious although the acts committed in them might be illegal (Lobban, 1990).

Some of the government's new legislation was deployed against Queen Caroline rioters and Cato Street conspirators in 1820, but the threat of popular radicalism faded away over the early 1820s as post-war economic recovery brought prosperity back to the country (Ziegler, 1965: 382–5). Liverpool's assessment of popular radicalism had seemingly been vindicated by events. Condescending though Pittite attitudes to popular radicalism were, they gave restraint to the public order policies of the 1790s and 1810s and confirmed statesmen in a determination not to endanger liberties of Britons if possible. Much of Liverpool's repression was, like Pitt's, temporary in conception and execution. No MP or peer could forget that the British constitution had acquired its eighteenth-century form because seventeenth-century attempts to augment the central executive powers of the state had threatened the rights and privileges that Britons enjoyed. The exercise of true leadership required the defence of that constitution against both state and people during the French wars.

Pauperism and Poverty

The old poor law, like the machinery of justice, operated within a framework of decentralised local government, remaining dependent upon unpaid parish officials for its administration throughout the French wars. Calls for the reform of the poor law, though heard throughout the later 1790s and 1810s, were not new, having been aired in the House of Commons from 1770 onwards. The old poor law was an expensive burden, by 1776 costing ratepayers £1.5m per annum and widely perceived to be inefficient in town and country. MPs little understood the forces behind increasing under- and unemployment but were aware that poverty was on the rise. Enclosure in the countryside from 1760 onwards was creating a rural proletariat while the rapid growth of towns, whether industrial or not, was overpopulating urban parishes whose numbers of eligible ratepayers were, in many cases, dropping in proportion to claimants of poor relief. From 1760 onwards, 10% of the population was on poor relief at any given time, while during crisis years of the French wars such as 1801 that proportion rose to 40% (Hay, 1982: 131–3).

The first half of the eighteenth century saw many urban parishes experimenting with workhouses as employment centres for the able-bodied poor and residential homes for the elderly, disabled, infirm or very young. Although Gilbert's Act of 1782 permitted adjoining parishes to join without formal incorporation for the purposes of workhouse construction, by this date workhouses were under increasing criticism as harsh and ineffective solutions to the problems of crime and poverty, while few parishes had the money to build them. Little workhouse building or disbursal of 'indoor relief' took pace during the French wars (Snell, 1985: 106–9; Rule, 1992a: 127). Rural parishes, by far more numerous, relied upon 'outdoor relief': pensions, relief in kind and income supplements – the cheapest and most effective forms of assistance. A series of bad harvests during the 1790s and 1810s, with crisis points reached in 1794–1795, 1800–1801, 1811–1812 and 1817–1818 relieved by only three abundant harvests between 1793 and 1815, ensured that poor relief remained a major public concern throughout the period. The famous Speenhamland system inaugurated by Berkshire magistrates on 6 May 1795 gave the able-bodied poor income supplements regulated by two criteria: family size and the market price of bread. This mode of relief was not new, having been employed previously by rural parishes during bad harvest years, and never became, as has often been claimed, a national system. Each parish chose its own modes of poor relief and levied its own rates to pay for them, which made the parishes independent kingdoms in their own right. The allowance system was adopted primarily in southern agricultural counties with social and economic conditions similar to those that prevailed in Berkshire (Neuman, 1982: 75–80; Pollard, 1978: 142–3; Henriques, 1979: 18–19; Boyer, 1990; Eastwood, 1994a: 110–14). Other forms of poor relief adopted in town and country included the raising of county funds by subscription, the establishment of parochial soup kitchens, the sale of subsidised food, the provision of allotment gardens, and the suspension of the settlement laws governing the acquisition of claim rights on the part of new residents (Horn, 1980a: 102–3). Manchester's Soup Charity distributed 12,000 quarts of soup per week in 1800 alone and, in the same year, a Union of Friendly Societies bought food for resale at subsidised prices (Bohstedt, 1983: 91–9).

On 8 December 1795, the Foxite MP Samuel Whitbread presented a minimum wage bill to the House that, if successful, would have permitted magistrates to fix wages in their localities. Whitbread's bill represented an attempt to remind JPs of their duties to the poor, for the regulation of wages and prices, which lay within the legal powers of magistrates, had been quietly abandoned after 1660. Whitbread's initiative was symptomatic of a humanitarianism towards the poor prevalent in the later eighteenth century (Coats, 1960–1; Poynter, 1969: Chs. 1–2; Eastwood, 1994a: 101–7). The bill was nevertheless defeated by a chorus of *laissez-faire* claims that wages set at levels above the market price of bread would only increase consumption, drive up prices and hasten the depletion of existing grain stocks. According to Edmund Burke's *Thoughts on Scarcity* (1795), an unfettered marketplace would, in time, bring grain prices back to reasonable levels, and scarcity could only be relieved by reducing the consumption of scarce foodstuffs and private charity.

Burke, who maintained that redistributive justice was a form of Jacobinism, was attached to *laissez-faire* because he believed that the laws of commerce were laws of nature and, consequently, of God (1981–97: ix, 119–45). By November 1795, fearing that hunger and sedition might go hand in hand, Pitt announced in a speech opposing Whitbread's bill that he would introduce poor law reform proposals of his own during the next year. Despite claiming that 'wages and prices should be left to find their own level' (PR, 1795: xlii, 1689), Pitt had spent the autumn of 1795 contemplating the introduction of import bounties to increase the nation's corn stocks, and this policy would be adopted in 1796 and 1799–1801. Throughout the later 1790s the government was divided on the wisdom of market intervention and here Grenville and Portland, the free traders, sided against Hawkesbury, President of the Board of Trade, and in the final analysis Pitt (Wells, 1988: 191–201, 243–4). The premier, though reluctant in the first instance to subsidise the price or supply of grain, had by June 1795 concluded that short-term extraordinary measures were required to relieve the distress of soaring prices. In the long term, he thought that more efficient and humane administration of the poor law would prevent the recurrence of such subsistence crises.

The 1796 Bill for Bettering the Condition of the Poor was not regarded in this light by MPs and disappeared from the agenda of the House of Commons at the beginning of 1797. Though comprehensive in scope, the bill was badly drafted and contained a mish-mash of contemporary schemes for poor relief cobbled together without any assessment of their financial or administrative implications. A partial adherence to market principles could be seen in Pitt's attempt to base all outdoor relief on parish-set sliding scales of cash payments determined by the relative difference between local average wages and the market price of grain. This mechanism, as Pitt told the Commons, 'imposed no arbitrary regulation upon the price of labour, which would very prudently be left to find its own level' (PH, xxxii, 1405–6). Pitt had also endowed the old poor law with a cumbersome governing structure of wardens and guardians obliged to report and submit accounts to ecclesiastical visitors. Workhouses were to become 'Houses of Industry' for the vocational training of the young. Pitt, who considered reviving the project again in 1799–1800, did not believe that raising wages alone would solve the problem of scarcity and, as a result, the able-bodied adult poor had been endowed with extensive relief rights: to employment from the parish at a fair wage, to wage supplements calculated according to the price of corn, to child support payments, and to parish loans for the purchase of cows. Old-age pensions would be paid from a Parochial Fund financed by parish rates and worker contributions. Most contentious was the compulsory relief of the non-settled poor, for which reimbursement was to be sought from their home parishes (PRO 30/8/307, ff. 159–96, 298–331; Fortescue, 1892–1927: vi, 357–8; Derry, 1981: 132–3; Poynter, 1969: 62–76; Henriques, 1979: 19–21; Ehrman, 1983: 471–6, 1996: 277–97; Mori, 1997b: 258–60).

Pitt's scheme combined humanitarianism with an assault upon the worst features of the old poor law: the evils of workhouse management and the relief of the unsettled poor. The promotion of commercial Whig loyalism amongst the lower orders was an important subtext of the bill visible in the parochial fund and loan proposals. Contributory pension schemes had been mooted since the 1780s, and George Rose's 1793 Friendly Societies Act had encouraged the formation of worker clubs with an offer of exemption from the removal of unsettled society members unless they tried to claim relief. Between 1793 and 1802, 9672 friendly societies, whose membership represented 8% of the English population, had registered under Rose's act (Gosden, 1961, 1973; Rule, 1986: 165–6). The parochial fund was intended to encourage saving habits amongst the poor, and Pitt further stipulated that owners of real property up to £30 were not to be disqualified from relief. Social and economic inequality might be an inescapable fact of life in a commercial society, but those without property might be encouraged to acquire some via the cow money loan scheme (PRO 30/8/207, f. 299). Self-help was very much in vogue and the chief objections to Pitt's project lay in its cost, in the principle of parochial accountability to visitors, which was resented as an extension of government power, and in the perceived impracticability of the proposals – most notably the cow money, old-age pensions and vocational schools. Despite the bill's withdrawal from the Commons, MPs were not hostile to the Speenhamland-style outdoor relief it advocated, for many were active in their home parishes as magistrates setting bread and family allowance scales.

A parliament unwilling to experiment with radical and expensive changes to the old poor law was nevertheless prepared to force change upon the dietary habits of Britons. The Brown Bread Act of 1800, otherwise known as the 'Act for the Better Provision of the Poor and for Diminishing the Consumption of Bread Corn', compelled Britons to consume wheat substitutes, ranging from oats and barley to dried fish, in place of the white bread that functioned as a status symbol of 'working class' respectability in much of the south and Midlands. In 1795 magistrates had begun to employ the Assize of Bread, the legal device that stipulated the production and sale of standard wheat bread at a fixed quality and price, to regulate bread prices and corn supplies, and JPs would do so again in 1799–1800. Such market regulating powers were, however, unpopular with bakers and millers, with the result that voluntary food substitution was enjoined in the first instance

(Stern, 1964; Wells, 1988: 62–3; Eastwood, 1994a: 45–6). On 9 December 1795, both Houses of Parliament had pledged their members' households to the consumption of bread comprised of at least one-third of non-wheaten flour. Oats, barley, maize, rice and potatoes made viable substitutes for wheat enjoined upon the common people by parish vestries, the SBCP and charitable organisations. The poor in the north, as F.M. Eden noted approvingly in the *State of the Poor* (1797), were less enslaved to fashion than their southern compatriots in terms of diet and food. Eden contrasted their hardy frugality with what he described as the wasteful habits of the southern poor, addicted to white bread and tea (1797: i, 496–7, 526–7, 533). 'Brown George' was in fact loathed by the poor, whose cultural prejudices extended also to potatoes, the food of the Irish. In 1800 parliament abandoned the compulsory use of mixed bread, having become aware of the aversion in which it was held by the populace (Wells, 1988: Ch. 13).

The old poor law and allowance system were much criticised after 1800, and the 1834 Poor Law Commissioners' Report would demand the replacement of both with the harsh principle of 'less eligibility'. Wage supplements have often been blamed for depressing agricultural wages and making the poor dependent upon the parish, but the allowance system was not in itself responsible for these evils. In parishes of arable cornland where the allowance system was adopted, enclosure, the decline of labour in husbandry, the associated decline of an independent cottager lifestyle and the creation of a wage labour workforce had been taking place since 1760. Rural families by 1790 were therefore suffering from under- rather than unemployment, and wage supplements constituted an effective way of topping up the household income. Agricultural wages in London and the south of England had been on the decline since 1760 and the introduction of allowances in some respects halted this trend: wages did not improve in real terms but nor did they worsen (Blaug, 1963: 148, 1964: 243).

The allowance system did not, moreover, replace older forms of poor relief but worked alongside them: make-work schemes, occasional cash payments, roundsman billet systems and labour rates were resorted to between 1795 and 1820 (Boyer, 1990; Eastwood, 1994a: 172–4). Occasional handouts in money or kind – shoes, burials, clothes, etc. – were nevertheless reduced in 1795 and 1800–1801; by 1815, such payments had altogether disappeared (Snell, 1985: 109). The labour rate amounted to a minimum wage for the poor while the billet system that set the poor to work for parish consortia of local employers, usually farmers, only encouraged the standardisation of wages at low rates throughout the parish. Both systems assumed that any shortfall in minimum or roundsman wages would be made up by parish allowances. Money was also collected by county and charitable subscription for distribution to the poor, while organisations like the SBCP and other charitable bodies spent much time and energy on agricultural self-sufficiency projects of all descriptions (Barnett, 1967: 169–70). Vestries were committed in theory to the concept of a self-sufficient labouring poor but, in many parishes, the poor became in part dependent upon the parish for a living wage, if only through the claiming of occasional relief, for the index-linked allowance system habituated the poor to receiving regular relief at stipulated rates. In certain agricultural counties, relief dependency was very high, affecting a quarter to a half of village populations (Snell, 1985: 28). With the return of normal if not abundant harvests in the autumn of 1802, the old poor law declined in importance as a political issue but would return with a vengeance in 1814, when it became inextricable from post-war debates about the reconstruction of the economy and the future of British agriculture.

By the end of the war, the poor were widely regarded as a problem rather than an object of compassion and the old poor law had few defenders (Poynter, 1969: Ch. 6; Eastwood, 1994a: 114–17, 121, 133–40). Malthus had been the first to denounce the entire poor law as an incentive to wanton procreation in the 1803 edition of *Population*, a text whose impact, tone and appeal cannot be understood without reference to the real fears of mass starvation that gripped educated Britons during the 1790s and early 1800s. Throughout the later 1790s, parochial and general enclosure had been advocated by authorities from Arthur Young to Sir John Sinclair, President of the Board of Agriculture, as the solution to the nation's grain shortages, and Britain's first general enclosure bill would be passed in 1801. Although Malthus demanded British investment in agriculture, he regarded enclosure as an object lesson in the law of diminishing marginal returns, for improvements in farming were not enough in themselves to maintain a balance between supply and demand. Moral restraint, of which self-help was a variant, would encourage the development of enlightened self-love in the national community. For this reason, Malthus was an enthusiastic advocate of savings banks, friendly societies and other voluntary self-sufficiency projects. Compulsory unemployment insurance schemes or other communitarian assistance projects would not, in his opinion, encourage the independence of the poor. In his opinion, the old poor law had created a dependency culture, depressed wages, raised food prices and failed to provide gainful employment to those who needed it (Malthus, 1992: 75–80, 98–110).

Although Malthus was often cited by abolitionists and moral reformers, his position on poverty and the old poor law, was not theirs. Malthus did not believe that the poor were naturally immoral, nor that institutionalised poor relief served no purpose. He entirely approved of many short-term expedients, with the exception of relief in aid of wages, adopted in 1795–1796 and 1799–1801, writing in the 1806 edition of *Population* that 'both humanity and true policy seriously require that we should give every assistance to the poor on those occasions that the nature of the case will admit'. By this Malthus meant harvest failures (Wrigley, 1988: 821; Malthus, 1992: 99). Malthus received support from the *Edinburgh Review* up to 1815 and, thereafter, the *Quarterly Review*, the vast majority of churchwardens, overseers of the poor, vestrymen and JPs were neither classical nor Christian political economists. All four sets of officials have been cleared of the blame heaped upon their heads for callous, selfish or inefficient management of the old poor law. Churchwardens, overseers and vestrymen were tenant farmers, employers and ratepayers but not wealthy men. They understood the needs of the poor and gave careful consideration to the validity and justice of relief claims. We know less about the direct contact of magistrates with the poor, but evidence suggests that they administered the Settlement and Vagrancy Laws regulating claim rights with humanity and compassion, in many counties suspending the former voluntarily during the 1790s (Snell, 1985: 104–7; Landau, 1990, 1991; Rule, 1992b: 119–20; Eastwood, 1994a: 26, 34). In 1793, the old poor law cost England and Wales £2.6m. By 1812, that figure had risen to £12m and ratepayers were finding the old poor law an onerous financial burden. Cost does not, however, seem to have been a major issue during the 1800s, for the government's publication of a national poor law census in 1804 was attended with no spate of pamphlets calling for reform despite the fact that £6m had been spent in 1803 alone. When Whitbread took up the poor law again in 1807, he admitted that his fellow MPs were not much interested in the subject (Poynter, 1969: 187–95; Rule, 1992b: 128; Eastwood, 1994a: 155–60).

Whitbread's poor law proposals were presented to parliament in three separate bills. The Poor Fund Bill proposed to establish a national insurance fund and national savings bank for the poor, the former to be funded from the poor rates and individual contributions. The Settlement and Relief Bill aimed at concentrating vestry votes in the hands of wealthier ratepayers and relaxing the settlement laws to permit the reimbursement of relief to the unsettled poor, while the Education Bill gave parishes the duty of building primary schools. This, the only bill to pass the Commons, fell foul of the Lancaster–Bell schools controversy in the House of Lords and the reluctance of peers to make education a public responsibility. Although Whitbread's attempt to reform the old poor law had failed, it indicated the beginning of a sea change in attitudes towards the poor law and county government. Demands for vestry reform and a national supervisory authority would be increasingly heard during the 1810s and represented a recognition that local government was becoming too complex for amateur administration. Pitt's 1796 bill had been thrown out, in part because it proposed to make parishes accountable for their actions to external authorities; from 1800 onwards, the establishment of 'national' institutions to fulfil research, advisory and supervisory functions was increasingly advocated by men from Thomas Bernard of the SBCP to Patrick Colquhoun, author of *A Treatise on Indigence* (1806). This, the most important work on poverty published between 1798 and 1815, claimed that crime was produced by indigence, defined simply by Colquhoun as the inability to make an adequate living through employment. As the prevention of both was regarded by Colquhoun as a natural duty of government, his treatise advocated the establishment of a 'Board of Pauper and General Police' to collect information on crime and poverty before advising parliament and parishes on suitable reforms. Colquhoun, who was heavily influenced by Bentham, also advocated the establishment of a national board of education, a national deposit bank and a system for licensing alehouses. He is best remembered as an early advocate of a professional police force and his treatise contributed to a shift in public attitudes away from decentralised local government to professional public administration (Poynter, 1969: 200–7; Eastwood, 1994a: 125–6).

Although severe bad harvests were experienced in 1811–1812, few demands for poor law reform, let alone its abolition, were to be heard. These came in 1817–1818 when demobilisation had glutted a rural workforce already suffering from structural underemployment, and poor rates soared by £7.87m, a 40% increase from 1814–1815 (Eastwood, 1994a: 127–32). With the partial opening of European ports in 1814, grain prices had tumbled throughout the country and Britain would remain in a state of agricultural depression up to 1822. The connection between recession and poverty was not lost upon MPs, evangelicals and landowners, who now regarded the allowance system as a charge upon rents and profits, an incentive to pauper procreation and a spur to popular immorality. In 1817 a Commons Select Committee on the Poor Laws chaired by the Canningite MP William Sturges Bourne delivered a report scathingly critical of relief in aid of wages and the entire system of parochial poor law administration. While the report, said to have been written by fellow Canningite Frankland Lewis, stopped short of demanding a new poor law, it buttressed a case for abolition that, given theoretical justification by Malthus, was based primarily on the sheer cost and complexity of poor relief. Wage subsidies had been a humane answer to the problem of indigence, but the fiscal and administrative burdens of the old poor law had taxed parochial government to its limits.

By 1815, the old poor law was no longer a safety net to assist the poor in hard times, for the allowance system had, as critics claimed, become embedded in the rural economy. Relief in aid of wages had translated the high grain prices of 1793–1815 into pay rises for workers at the cost of subsidising what had become endemic rural underemployment. We know less about the impact of wage subsidies upon towns, but the witnesses summoned by the 1816 Sturges Bourne committee blamed increases in urban poor rates and expenditure upon short-term factors, namely the war and trade fluctuations. This suggests that the allowance system, if adopted by towns, gave occasional rather than regular relief to residents (Horn, 1980a: 49–50). Two national problems affecting town and country had nevertheless become acute by 1815: a vast increase in the numbers of occasional relief claimants and an absence of bureaucratic and legal mechanisms for shifting resources from rich to poor parishes (Poynter, 1969: 223–37, 245–8). MPs were disposed to do something about the old poor law, for the return of widespread poverty, coupled with the revival of parliamentary reform, the rise of Luddism and post-war depression, convinced many that mass rebellion was a very real possibility (Thompson, 1968: Ch. 15; Stevenson, 1992: 33–74; Gash, 1978).

A Mendicity Committee had been appointed by the Commons in 1815 and a separate Lords committee would investigate the poor laws in 1817 at the prime minister's request. Liverpool was alarmed by the critical stance taken by the Sturges Bourne committee and, by suspending its enquiries, raised backbench hopes that ministerial leadership would result in decisive action. The Lords' committee report of 1818, however, recommended that no change be made to the old poor law and predicted that a return to prosperity would follow the teething pains of transition to a peacetime economy. Some government aid went to the parishes via the 1817 Poor Employment Act that authorised the grant of £1.75m in Exchequer Bills for local public works projects, although the government's interventionist, paternalistic ultra-Tory stance clashed in policy, if not principle, with the Canningite Liberal Tory desire for *laissez-faire* and efficient local government. Official approval for self-help was expressed via support for Rose's Savings Bank Act of 1817, a private member's bill that reflected its author's Pittite obsession with debt reduction and the inculcation of commercial Whig loyalism. Radicals were appalled to find that the deposits made to local banks founded under the bill were destined for the Consolidated Fund at an interest rate 1.5% higher than that given to ordinary investors. Cobbett was right to claim that 'Old George Rose's Savings Bank Bubble' was trying to turn the poor into fundholders loyal to crown, church and constitution (Poynter, 1969: 290–4; Eastwood, 1994a: 199–204).

When faced by the ministry's lack of action, Sturges Bourne tried as a private member to get his reforms onto the statute book. While his attempts to transfer authority over pauper children from parents to the parish failed in the Lords, three other bills culminating in the Poor Law Amendment Act of 1819 empowered parishes to form select vestries and appoint salaried assistant overseers. Whitbread's 1807 bill had also sought to increase the voting power of wealthier ratepayers at the expense of their poorer colleagues, for the vestries, dominated by the latter, were reluctant both to increase rates and to experiment with new modes of poor relief. Along with salaried overseers went regulations for the keeping of minutes and accounts to professionalise the administration of the poor law. The Sturges Bourne reforms represented a major and radical overhaul of local government for which contemporaries were ready: although the 1819 Act was permissive, by 1822 over 2000 parishes had availed themselves of its provisions to re-establish themselves on a semi-professional footing (Eastwood, 1994a: 35, 38, 128–32). Few people, even Sturges Bourne, wanted to do away entirely with the old poor law, for the independent parish remained an English ideal of local government. An older ethos of paternalistic decentralised government was nevertheless giving way to new visions of utilitarian efficiency and unbridled *laissez-faire*. The old order was not dead but it was passing.

Religion and Society

When confronted with the twin spectres of French atheism and anarchy during the 1790s, all of Britain's religious groups would eventually turn against the French Revolution, though many Dissenters reserved judgement on the justice of the war, the perfections of the constitution and the wisdom of Pitt's policies. These reservations, coupled with High Church Anglican and evangelical convictions that international infidelity was in part responsible for the rise of Jacobinism, ensured that inter-denominational strife remained rife throughout the revolutionary and Napoleonic Wars. The French Revolution gave the Church of England a golden opportunity to reassert its legitimacy as the natural partner of the state, and central to the case for Anglican supremacy touted by loyalists throughout the 1790s was the denigration of Old Dissent as an engine of sedition and irreligion. Having spent the 1790s venting its spleen upon Socinianism and Arianism, the church would turn during the 1800s and 1810s to Methodism and New Dissent, fast becoming the religion of the English people.

The Church of England emerged from the French wars with its formal status intact but had lost its grip on the hearts and minds of the nation. The 1818 Additional Churches Act authorised the grant of £1m for the building of sorely needed churches in town and country but came too late to revive the fortunes of English and Welsh Anglicanism. The 152 new churches constructed between 1810 and 1820 would remain half empty while 15,601 Dissenter chapels were built throughout England and Wales. Methodists, Particular Baptists and Congregationalists deployed an emotional religion that spoke to the hopes and fears of the poor in ways that 'rational' Christianity, be it Anglican, Unitarian, General Baptist or Quaker, could not. Rational Dissenters, having eschewed the theology and recruitment tactics of evangelical Dissent, marked time and lost worshippers throughout the French wars.

The deficiencies of the eighteenth-century Established Church are numerous and well attested (Best, 1964; Gilbert, 1976; Evans, 1976; Rupp, 1986; Virgin, 1989). Pluralism and non-residence, which went hand in hand, did not begin to decline until the 1820s, but in 1809 Queen Anne's Bounty, the fund established in 1704 to augment the incomes of the poorer clergy, was revived by parliament to inject much-needed cash into poorer livings. Further legislation in 1813 tried to enforce residency and to fix the salaries of curates, the slave labour of the parishes, at a minimum of £80 p.a. By 1810 clerics had realised that change was sorely needed and began to call in public for ecclesiastical reform. *The Church in Danger* and *The Basis of National Welfare*, published in 1815 and 1817 respectively by Richard Yates, Chaplain of Chelsea Hospital, demanded that long-standing problems like the lack of church accommodation in towns and the dilapidated condition of urban and rural parsonages be redressed. The Whig reforms of the 1830s nevertheless came too late to rehabilitate the church in the eyes of its people (Best, 1964: 147–9, 195–231).

The reform initiatives of the 1810s had begun to redress a serious evil: the inequitable distribution of immobile resources within the church. The vast gulf between the rich and poor clergy can be blamed upon differences in the sizes and resources of livings. Vicarages and rectories in regions of established arable agriculture, if well endowed with glebe lands, could give their incumbents a comfortable gentry existence. Curacies, on the other hand, often supplied little more than a tithe income to their holders, while incumbents of urban parishes were primarily dependent for a living upon surplice fees and pew rents. The 1835 Ecclesiastical Commissioners' Report revealed that 15.6% of the English clergy earned less than £100 p.a. and the proportion was much higher before wartime enclosure and bounty reform improved the position of the poorer clergy (Evans, 1976: 9–12; Virgin, 1989: 34–7).

The obsessive interest of eighteenth-century bishops in the commutation of tithes through enclosure indicates their importance as a source of income to the clergy. Their conversion into land, cash payments or a corn rent was eagerly sought by clerics for whom the collection of tithes was a major burden. Enclosure, which transformed tithe collection rights into real estate, accounted for 85–90% of all commutations before 1810 (Virgin, 1989: 36–9, 54–9). The commutation of tithes was a complex and contentious legal process, thanks to a sixteenth-century Reformation that had sold monastic land and its tithes to laymen. Lay and clerical improprietors were nevertheless well placed to strike hard bargains during the enclosure boom of the French wars because their refusal to co-operate in an enclosure could stop it from taking place. Poorer arable livings rose 675% in value over the French wars (Evans, 1976: Ch. 3, 94–110; Gilbert, 1976: 5–6; Ditchfield, 1985).

Rural church attendance had been declining since the late seventeenth century but the extent of non-attendance at the end of the eighteenth century is difficult to calculate with any certainty. In 1800 Tomline commissioned a survey of church attendance in 79 Lincoln parishes, according to which congregations were believed to number 33% of the adult population (Virgin, 1989: 5). Half of all Anglican benefices had no resident priest and non-residence was as much a problem on the episcopal bench. In 1799 Tomline lobbied Pitt via Grenville for government support of a project to enforce 'a constant superintendance and control over the clergy' (Fortescue, 1892–1927: vi, 5–8; Hempton, 1984: 77–9; Virgin, 1989: 258). To what extent the bishops succeeded in doing so is questionable. Nancy Uhler Murray has suggested that the militant conservative loyalism of the Anglican clergy during the French wars alienated the English people and hastened their flight from the church. This could well be true, for High Church Anglicanism was quasi–Tory, Latitudinarian Anglicanism had never appealed to the people, and Evangelical Anglicanism, despite all its charitable good works, was a religion of the gentry and better-off middling sort (Murray, 1975; Hole, 1989; Morris, 1998). One thing to be said for the French wars was their unifying influence upon the Established Church, for all Anglican clergymen agreed on the need to suppress infidel levelling atheism for the protection of Christianity and organised religion (Soloway, 1969: 26–54; Hole, 1989: 109–44, 160–73; Eastwood, 1991: 151–3).

The Anglican church remained strong in the arable lands of southern and eastern England, specifically in compact nucleated villages where the dominant landlord was sympathetic to the church. There was a direct correlation between parish size, population, land ownership patterns and church attendance. In the 1851 religious census, attendance at Anglican services was highest in parishes with fewer than 200 inhabitants where one landlord owned more than half the land. It was lowest in parishes of over 600 in which land ownership was split amongst freeholders possessing less than 40 acres apiece. Here all forms of rural nonconformity flourished and the same could be said for market towns, boundary settlements and industrial villages (Hempton, 1984: 15–16). These facts were equally true half a century earlier, when the church and great house operated as the *foci* of parish life and, despite changes in the socio-economy of rural England, the church remained for some the centre of the village community (Watts, 1995: 113–19). The Church of England was nonetheless drawing less than half the population of England and Wales on census Sunday 1851 and the situation was worse in Scotland, where only one-third of all residents were attending church.

Urban social identities, particularly in the industrial towns, were forged in other churches. The Church of England, lacking transferable resources, could not seat three-quarters of the residents in London and the major provincial towns. Evangelical Dissent – Methodism, Particular Baptism and Congregationalism – would during the nineteenth century become the religion, of the people, the latter two rising to success by adopting the Methodist systems of itinerancy and connexional organisation (Lovegrove, 1988: 31–2). The Congregationalists and Particular Baptists, both numbering less than 20,000 in 1750, had by 1800 increased their numbers to 35,000 and 24,000 respectively (Gilbert, 1976: 36). Rational Dissent was, however, losing adherents. The General Baptists, torn between the old and new Connexion, had by 1800 only 24 churches associated with the old General Assembly. The Quakers, whose message of salvation through 'inner light' and spiritual meditation no longer appealed to the people, was becoming an increasingly inbred group of merchants and professionals (Seed, 1990; Watts, 1995: 81–99). The Swedenborgians, the new deists of the later eighteenth century, were a sect rather than a church, taking their name from the Swedish scientist and visionary, Emmanuel Swedenborg, who claimed that Christ had returned to earth in 1757 to found a new church. Upon his death in London in 1772, his disciples diverged into two groups, one based in London and the other in Manchester. The Swedenborgians, who rejected the Trinity and the doctrine of Christ's atonement, were regarded as eccentric mystics by most Britons, but easily the most unorthodox in theology by 1820 were the Unitarians (Morley, 1993).

The Unitarians and the Quakers were the most worldly of Dissenter groups old and new, for they sanctioned sports, card playing, dancing and novel reading in moderation: to this acceptance of the good life, joined to the Protestant work ethic, has been attributed much of their business success during the eighteenth century. No hard proof can be adduced to support this theory, though it can be said that Unitarianism, of all Dissenting religions, was the most attractive to entrepreneurs and attracted a steady trickle of converts from all churches. While its worldliness, tolerance and relaxed attitude to worship made it attractive to upwardly mobile liberal professionals and businessmen, its theology never appealed to the people and by 1851 there would be only 50,000 Unitarians in Britain. In 1800, there were only 20,000 Quakers in the country. By 1790, Unitarians no longer believed in the immortality of the soul, predestination or the atonement, replacing these with universal salvation and reincarnation. No benevolent God, they thought, could condemn a significant proportion of mankind to eternal damnation (Ward, 1972: 63–9; Gilbert, 1976: 36–42; Bradley, 1990; Watts, 1995: 83–90, 329–45).

Quakers and Unitarians, despite their small numbers, led the rational Dissenter opposition to the wars with France. Their political allegiance had been split between Fox and Pitt up to 1787, but the premier's stand on Test repeal during the later 1780s tilted the balance in favour of the Opposition and most Dissenters held Pitt responsible for the outbreak of a war that could, in their opinion, have been averted by negotiation with France. Unitarians and Swedenborgians thought the war was irrational while other Dissenters bemoaned the loss of life that sent unconverted souls to Hell. Quakers expelled from their congregations any member making any business contribution to the war effort and, along with Unitarians, soon joined the Friends of Peace movement. These conscientious objectors to the revolutionary and Napoleonic Wars, led in the House of Commons by Wilberforce and the Saints, regularly petitioned the government for an end to the conflict from the mid-1790s onwards. Although the Friends of Peace movement would not gather steam until the later 1800s, attracting support from northern business communities hard hit by Napoleon's Continental System and the 1807 Orders in Council, the friends were active throughout the French wars in the distribution of anti-war propaganda. Many Dissenters gravitated towards the Foxites, receiving their reward in the repeated and unsuccessful presentation of Test repeal motions to the House of Commons (Cookson, 1982: 214–37; Watts, 1995: 206, 349–57).

Unitarians, the chief organisers of the 1811–1812 Friends of Peace petition movement, were easily the most politically active of all Dissenters. Their mastery of extra-parliamentary public relations and lobbying bore fruit in the 1812 Little Toleration Act and their absolution, a year later, from the Blasphemy Laws. By 1810, Anglicans had lost their fears of Rational Dissent, for the popular loyalism of the 1790s had demonstrated that old Dissent did not appeal to ordinary men and women. Anglicans therefore concluded that the real danger to the Established Church lay elsewhere: in evangelical Methodism, Baptism and Congregationalism, fast making converts in town and country (Cookson, 1982; Lovegrove, 1988: 124; Watts, 1995: 367–72, 385–7; Morris, 1998). In 1799, senior churchmen had begun to campaign for restrictions on itinerant preaching and, in February 1800, Michael Angelo Taylor presented the Commons with a bill to amend the Toleration Act and require the licensing of circuit preachers. To Dissenter lobbying against the bill was added the influence of Wilberforce over Pitt, and the premier's opposition to the legislation denied the bill the government's support (Murray, 1975: Ch. 2; Ward, 1972: 52).

In 1810, Sidmouth tried unsuccessfully to solicit old Dissenter support for a bill to strengthen the 1689 Toleration Act against all itinerant preachers. By this he really meant Methodists, who to Anglican bishops were akin to ecclesiastical Jacobins. For many loyalists, Methodists too closely resembled the Levellers of the Civil Wars with their criticisms of their social superiors and the parish clergy. Methodists, much like old Dissenters, were often the targets of mob violence in Britain and Ireland and the 1790s witnessed a decade of chapel wrecking in Birmingham, Manchester and Sheffield (Walsh, 1972; Morris, 1990: 407; Hempton, 1996: 149). The Unitarians and Quakers rejected Sidmouth's overtures and forged a tactical alliance instead with Methodists to oppose the proposed legislation (Watts, 1995: 367–71, 378–87). Although the bill failed to pass the Commons, the attempts of magistrates to deny licences to circuit preachers led to complaints from Methodists and Unitarians in 1811 and, thanks to continued negotiation with the government by Unitarians, Quakers and Methodists, the passage of the Little Toleration Act in 1812. By repealing the Five Mile Act and Conventicles Act, the 1812 legislation legalised all Dissenter religious meetings and the construction of new urban chapels (Hempton, 1984: 98–104).

Although Rational Dissenters have always been regarded as proto-liberals and, in the case of Unitarians, children of the Enlightenment, more controversy surrounds the Methodists (Hempton, 1984: 11–18). The Methodist Connexion was fraught with tensions during the decade following John Wesley's death in 1791. Its 74,000 worshippers, who belonged to a connexional network of self-sustaining communities bound by an itinerant ministry and representative church government, struggled with the problems of survival without their leader. By 1816, Methodism would have 180,000 followers. The majority of the Methodist clergy were Wesleyans in their theology, authoritarianism and self-identity as Anglicans. Many worshippers were not, and here lay the root of the divisions in the Methodist Church. By declaring themselves Dissenters, Methodists were legally entitled to build chapels and obtain licences for their preachers but, sensitive to the political and intellectual climate of the times, Conference – the governing body of the Methodist Church – made repeated declarations of loyalty to crown and constitution (Ziegler, 1965: 297–9). These offended lay preachers, who feared that Conference loyalism would alienate worshippers and resented Conference attempts to prevent the administration of the sacrament by lay preachers. Under the 1795 Plan of Pacification devised by Conference, they were only permitted to do so if sanctioned by a chapel's trustees and stewards. Methodist congregations unwilling to attend Anglican services battled within their chapels for the right to take communion throughout the later 1790s (Hempton, 1984: 56–80).

The sacramentalist controversy highlights three chief problems faced by Methodists during the 1790s: the position of the Methodist Connexion relative to the Established Church the true seat of power and authority within the movement, and the continued recruitment of popular worshippers without antagonising church and state. Methodism and other forms of evangelical Dissent, with their connexional systems, lay preachers, message of salvation and participatory forms of chapel organisation, were well placed to exploit the deficiencies of the Established Church in the industrial towns. Methodism, which did not appeal to unskilled labour or the poor, nevertheless grew at 5% p.a. during the 1790s. It was very attractive to artisans in London, the north, the north-east, the north Midlands and parts of the west and south-west of England (Hempton, 1984: 74; Bebbington, 1989: 25). While many Methodists continued to take communion in the local Anglican church well into the nineteenth century (Walsh, 1965: 288), preachers and worshippers unwilling to accept Conference discipline followed Alexander Kilham, the most vocal sacramentalist preacher on the Methodist left, out of the Wesleyan Methodist movement.

In the *Progress of Liberty amongst the People called Methodists* (1795), Kilham demanded freedom of worship and self-government for all Methodist chapels. The appearance of this pamphlet coincided with the passage of the Seditious Meetings Act that made Methodists, along with others wishing to stage mass meetings, apply to magistrates for the appropriate licences. A horrified Conference fearing possible church or state reprisals rushed to discipline Kilham, who was formally expelled from the Connexion in 1797 (Hempton, 1984: 59–73). The New Connexion he founded was slow to recruit both preachers and followers. Nearly half of the 84 preachers admitted between 1797 and 1814 resigned from the New Connexion after an average service of six years and the number of its adherents did not surpass 10,000 until 1821 (Watts, 1995: 30–5, 358–66). Kilham's radicalism was nevertheless frightening enough to unite moderate sacramentalists and Conference on the need for unity. Samuel Bradburn, who had written in 1792 that '*vox populi* should be our motto', was claiming by 1796 that 'in general, we are not enemies to the King, nor have we a wish to alter the Government of our Country' (cited in Hempton, 1984: 61, 69). With Kilham's expulsion and the closing of ranks amongst Methodist preachers, the Connexion was set on a course of defensive loyalism for the rest of the French wars.

Conference condemned both popular radicalism and infidelity during the French wars, but reserved its greatest abuse for Methodist splinter groups during the 1800s. In 1806 the Independent Methodists too left the Wesleyan Connexion, to be followed in 1811–1812 by the Primitive Methodists. Magic

Methodists and Tent Methodists were independent rural groups of worshippers led by men possessing some literacy and more spiritual conviction. Wesley knew – though his later followers seem to have forgotten – that popular superstition and millenarianism had much in common with an evangelical providentialism that laid emphasis upon the active intervention of an omnipotent God to reward virtue and punish vice. The Primitive Methodists, Bible Christians and Magic Methodists, with their trances, visions, exorcisms and divine interventions, both appealed to and reinforced popular superstitions that had co-existed alongside Christianity for centuries (Obelkevitch, 1976; Hempton, 1980: 182–6). An appalled Conference responded to the emergence of revivalist Methodism by expelling its leaders, Hugh Bourne and William Clowes, in 1810. While 'cottage religion' remained independent of any church, Primitive Methodism organised itself into separate chapels and a connexional network (Hempton, 1984: 93–6; Valenze, 1978; Watts, 1995: 39–52, 72–6, 103–9).

Whether rank and file Methodists shared the views of their preachers is, for the most part, unknown. Marxist historians have not been kind to the movement: Eric Hobsbawm suggested that Methodism, radicalism and trade unionism grew together but represented different responses to a common working-class experience of industrialisation. E.P. Thompson, disappointed by the official loyalism of Methodists, concluded that the movement represented a form of popular counter-revolution or 'psychic masturbation' for the masses (Hobsbawm, 1964: 28–32; Thompson, 1968: 49–50, 375, 428–9). Hobsbawm and Thompson were reacting to Elie Halevy's 1928 claims that Methodism contained industrial unrest, prevented a French Revolution and eased Britain's transition to a modern society. The Halevy thesis nevertheless survived the onslaught in modified form, thanks to reworking by Bernard Semmel and Alan Gilbert to suggest that Methodism gave its worshippers a religious route for the expression of social and political dissent, thus acting as a 'safety valve' in early industrial politics. For Gilbert, rank and file Methodists were liberals, if not radicals (Halevy, 1928: 334–5, 371, 839; Semmel, 1973: 152, 171; Gilbert, 1979: 381–99, 1993).

Conference could not control the activities and beliefs of all Methodists (Wells, 1991: 200–3). Although it urged the rank and file in 1812 to 'Fear the Lord and King, and meddle not with them that are given to change', this injunction was ignored for the next five years by Luddites, Friends of Peace and artisans who joined reform societies in Manchester, South Shields, Rochdale, Bury, Bolton, Derby, Belper and Nottingham. In 1819, the central Committee of Privileges issued a statement to all Methodist societies reiterating that their members owed allegiance to the government 'for the undisturbed enjoyment of their Religious Liberties'. Industrial workers, given a choice between loyalist Wesleyan Methodism and radical independent

Congregationalism, opted in many cases for the latter (Hempton, 1984: 104–10). Having said this, Methodists were still difficult to police, for chapel communities were self-governing entities over which Conference and itinerant preachers could exercise little real control (Gilbert, 1993: 88–9, 91–3). Many Methodists were, moreover, not political activists of any description. The success of new Dissenter recruitment from 1790 to 1820 is attributable to economic insecurity and hardships of the French wars rather than the politics and principles of the French Revolution, about which most countryfolk, the chief targets of evangelical recruitment from 1785 to 1820, knew little (Lovegrove, 1988: 153). Evangelical religion spoke to their immediate hopes and fears, giving comfort, drama, music and fellowship to artisan and labourer communities. The growth rate of Methodism closely corresponded to ebbs and surges in costs of living and picked up after 1796 (Watts, 1995: 68–73).

For evangelical Dissenters, worldly affairs were irrelevant to the saving of souls except to illustrate the workings of divine providence. For many, the French Revolution either betokened the Last Judgement or represented an awful manifestation of God's wrath, and all Dissenter churches old and new, when faced with conservative loyalist hostility, withdrew from the world during the later 1790s. Church and king mobs attacked Unitarians and Baptists in Manchester, Nottingham and Loughborough in 1792 and too many such incidents occurred during the 1790s for them all to have been orchestrated by the gentry and Anglican clergy (Dickinson, 1989: 118–19). The appeal of loyalism to the British people may have had less to do with the sophistication of conservative ideology than to its compatibility with the norms of community justice and popular culture: not that these should be seen as static or backwards-looking, for millenarian revolution was quite as attractive to some Britons as providentialist obedience (Wells, 1991: 199–201). Britons had nonetheless feared and distrusted Dissenters for over a century and in some localities were all too prepared to believe that non-Anglicans were enemies of the people. The caution of Conference is understandable in light of the formal and informal persecution faced by all Dissenters throughout the French wars, and other Dissenting denominations followed the Methodist lead. Even Unitarians and Quakers could withdraw from the world to conclude, much like Anglicans, that the French Revolution was an apocalyptic manifestation of scepticism and modern infidelity. The Committee of the Dissenting Deputies and the General Body of Protestant Dissenting Ministers of the Three Denominations followed the Methodist lead in submitting declarations of loyal support for king and constitution (Lovegrove, 1983; Dickinson, 1989: 112; Watts, 1995: 353–6).

Methodism is best regarded as an apolitical religious movement (Walsh, 1965: 304). Its appeal to a constituency of artisans should not be misinterpreted as mass radical politicisation any more than the primary interest of its leadership from 1780 to 1815 in rural missionary work should be mistaken for reactionary Toryism. The real importance of evangelical Dissent lies not in its political complexion, but in the comfort, faith and sense of community that it gave to its followers and, as David Hempton has put it: 'The manifold process of cultural brokerage between popular evangelicalism and the communities in which it took root offer more possibilities than the search for a single narrative which is, by definition, unnecessarily reductionist' (Hempton, 1996: 178). Many factors went into Britain's avoidance of revolution during the French wars enumerated by Ian Christie in 1984: the generosity of the old poor law; the contentment of Britons with the highest living standards in Europe; the existence of a fluid and socially mobile society more inherently meritocratic than that of France; and, more recently, the appeal of conservative loyalism to the British people (Dickinson, 1989, 1992a,b). The issues of living standards and social mobility will be addressed in the next chapter: on the poor law, Christie has been vindicated by statistical proof that the old poor law redistributed more of the national product from rich to poor between 1780 and 1834 than was seen at any time in any European country before 1914 (Lindert, 1994: 359). While there is no doubt that many members of the middling and lower orders found loyalism attractive, the reasons for this have yet to receive full social, cultural and political elucidation. Pittite repression, though by no means a reign of terror, played an important role in criminalising radicalism in the public mind, but here it is worth remembering the practical autonomy enjoyed by local communities in local government and religion. This functional freedom, so much a part of public life and thought at all social levels in the eighteenth century, was what Britons regarded as part of their national birthright. Liberty was for the British a living thing and they exercised it in many ways far beyond the control or regulation of any supervisory authority.

CHAPTER FIVE

From Orders to Class?

Twenty-two years of war against revolutionary and Napoleonic France coincided with the onset of an industrial revolution that, according to an economic and social history orthodoxy, created the social and economic relationships of modern British society. Industrialisation, having according to traditional accounts launched a 'takeoff into sustained economic growth' (Rostow, 1960), created a new world of industrial towns and industrial relations that transformed Britain's middle and lower classes from amorphous groups into articulate, unified and self-aware social entities with specific interests, cultures and aspirations (Briggs, 1959; Perkin, 1969; Thompson, 1968; Hobsbawm, 1964). Industrialisation was not, however, as revolutionary as it once seemed. We are now told that it was slow and gradual rather than fast and disruptive, taking, according to some scholars, 100 years to run its course (Crafts, 1985). It did not drive rural labour into dark satanic mills from 1760 to 1830 nor subject all artisan craftsmen and women to a unilinear process of deskilling and pauperisation (Sabel and Zeitlin, 1985; Berg, 1994a, 1994b). The industrial revolution was not made by professional scientists or engineers, much less by 'big business' or the 'factory system'. Much of the potential for social and economic conflict between land, labour and capital central to Marxist notions of class creation had therefore disappeared from British history in the century between 1750 and 1850.

The French wars used to occupy a central role in the history of modern class formation. E.P. Thompson's *Making of the English Working Class* was the seminal text that saw in the radical movement of the 1790s the stirrings of self-awareness that would launch the proletariat into class warfare against the old order. The origins of working-class formation, however, predated the rise of modern industry, for in a series of path-breaking articles reprinted in the 1991 volume *Customs in Common*, Thompson sited it in an eighteenth-century patrician–plebeian conflict that arose in part from the development of a commercial market economy and the adoption of its social and moral values by the landed elite: here lay class conflict without class. Industrialisation would only exacerbate already apparent social tensions. The middle class, left out of Thompson's analysis, was dealt with by Harold Perkin's *Origins of Modern English Society*, according to which three articulate classes of Britons bound by income and interest emerged alongside industrialisation to conduct political, cultural and economic struggles of separate class ideals that culminated in the triumph of *laissez-faire*, gradualist parliamentary reform, the rise of the middle class and an 'entrepreneurial society' of late Victorian Britain in which big business had virtually replaced land at the top of the social ladder.

No social historian ever claimed that a modern three-part class system was in place by 1820 but, despite the flood of revisionist scholarship in economic, social, cultural and gender history that is remapping the contours of late Hanoverian England, many still implicitly assume that some process of tripartite class formation was well underway before 1800. The concept of class is itself problematic for it was not in general use amongst contemporaries, who at the end of the eighteenth century referred to three general groups of Britons, each with its place in a hierarchical and multi-tier Great Chain of Being. The many subdivisions in the chain were reflected in the use of plural terms of which 'class' was only one: ranks, orders, stations and sorts were also common. By 1815 the terms 'middle' and 'working classes' had entered Britain's social and political vocabulary and, while this suggests that a three-class model was now in use, so too was a 'two nations' model dating from the 1790s that pitted the rich in general terms against the poor. The great chain and its terminology remained in use up to 1850 (Seed, 1992; Corfield, 1991: 122–30; Wahrman, 1995: 83–90; Cannadine, 1999: 12–17). A three-class system was only one of the social cosmologies by which Britons oriented themselves in the world and was not the dominant one during the French Revolutionary and Napoleonic Wars.

The Upper Ten Thousand

The aristocracy and gentry succeeded, despite the criticism of radicals and liberals, in maintaining their leadership of British politics and society throughout the French wars. Throughout the early modern period, the culture and values of landed life had resided in the gentry, that group of untitled but armigerous families whose status and wealth lay in the ownership of broad acres. The gentry were split into two general but overlapping groups: the parish or lesser gentry, whose estates were modest in size and whose influence extended, at most, to two or three villages; and the more educated and cosmopolitan county gentry, whose lands and corresponding socio-political clout were much greater. The parish gentry, or village squirearchy, rarely rose further than the county commissions of the peace but as such, and in association with the greater gentry, *were* local government in the counties. The county gentry dominated the House of Commons from 1625 to 1800, where their suspicions of royal government had defined Puritan and Whig ideals of liberty throughout the reigns of the Stuarts. By 1800, there were 273 English and British peers with seats in the House of Lords, an additional 231 Scots and Irish peers entitled to elect members of their order to the upper house, and 651 baronets (Burke, 1803: 963–83). Gerald Mingay has calculated that there were 400 great landlords with an average income of over £1000 p.a. who owned between 20 and 25% of the cultivated land in England and Wales. Below them were 14,000 to 25,000 members of the gentry enjoying incomes of £300–£500 p.a. who owned 50–60% of the land (Mingay, 1963: 3–26; Thompson, 1966: 507; Cannon, 1982: 121–2; Beckett, 1985: 35).

Neither the parish nor the county gentry can be called simple defenders of the landed interest, for they had long been sending their younger sons into trade and the professions, a trend that accelerated after 1660 when hard times drove increasing numbers of gentry families to adopt the legal device of strict settlement to safeguard the estate for their eldest sons. By 1720 they had colonised the upper reaches of commerce, the church, law, trade and government service: indeed, this last branch of employment had been their saviour during England's long wars against Louis XIV's France (Holmes, 1981, 1986). Despite these successes, the failure of many Tudor and Stuart landed families to produce sons from 1700 to 1750 would constitute a demographic crisis that placed gentry heiresses on the Hanoverian marriage market and consolidated land ownership in a smaller core of families (Roebuck, 1981: 276–316; Jenkins, 1983: 38–9; Beckett, 1985: 96–7; Howell, 1986: 16–19). This set the stage for what David Cannadine (1994: 11–12) has called the birth of the British upper classes between 1780 and 1830: by this is meant the emergence of a new supra-national and predominantly aristocratic elite whose dominance in parliament, state service and the church would not be broken until the twentieth century.

Cannadine's upper class, formed from the survivors of the old aristocracy and gentry, supplemented by some new money entrants, consists of British nobles and their extended families, whose wealth, acres and social prestige were enhanced from 1793 to 1815 through estate improvement, state employment, intermarriage, coal mining, canal building and urban property ownership (1994: 13–18). This upper class included those gentryfolk fortunate enough to be related or connected to true peers. Under Pitt's direction George III created 113 peers from 1780 to 1800, most of whom already belonged to the landed elite (McCahill, 1981; Cannon, 1982: 10, 21–3). Only seven men with no prior connections to the peerage were elevated to the Lords, while 55 already possessed some blood ties to the aristocracy. Pitt was particularly generous to borough-mongers and service peers: the diplomats, generals, admirals and civil servants who received titles as good conduct prizes (Cannon, 1982: 22). By 1820 the aristocracy, as a collective group, had become much wealthier than it was a century earlier but could be described as new in only two respects: it had received a new infusion of gentry blood and was now truly British in composition and outlook. A century of intermarriage between Scottish, Irish, Welsh and English elite families had created truly British supra-national noble estates encouraging the integration of once separate ethnic elite groups, while the incorporation of the Irish and Scottish peerages into the Westminster House of Lords had given the Celtic fringe a share of political power.

It is questionable to what extent this was a *new* ruling class. Pitt's peerage creations might better be described as the gentrification of the aristocracy, and perhaps consciously so, for Pitt, the second son of a first-generation peer, disliked the politics and culture of aristocratic Whiggery (Mandler, 1990a: 17–18, 24–6). The number of aristocrats in the House of Commons certainly increased over the eighteenth century, rising from 8% in 1713 to 25% in 1825, but aristocratic patronage in the lower house reached a peak of 236 seats in 1807, thereafter to decline (Sack, 1980; Cannon, 1982: 104–15). The country gentry were losing their dominance in the Commons, both to the aristocracy and to what Ian Christie calls 'non-elite' MPs, who had taken 103 seats at the 1784 general election and would return 136 MPs to the 1818 parliament (Christie, 1996: 206). The elite parasitism denounced by Cobbett and Wade during the 1810s extended from aristocratic dominance of the Cabinet and Commons to the clientage networks through which military, ecclesiastical and civil service appointments were made in the service of church and state (Cannon, 1982: 115–20; Cannadine, 1994: 17–21).

The fate of the gentry is not clear from Cannadine's work. One infers that they clung to the coat tails of their aristocratic relatives – if fortunate enough to possess any – and continued to exist as a sub-group of the upper class or, possibly, joined the middling sorts. Between the aristocracy and great majority of the gentry 'there yawned always a measurable social gulf' (Mingay, 1976: 4). Both groups regarded themselves – and were regarded by others – as the leaders of the national community. The aristocracy is described instead by John Beckett as that social group encompassing everyone 'from the peerage assembled in the House of Lords, through the titled non-peers, to the gentry landowners acting as justices of the peace' (1986: 21). This begs the question what it took to make the gentry: a vexed question in English social history. Any income from £100 to £3000 p.a. qualified a landed family for lesser gentry status during the eighteenth century. In south Wales, birth was more important than money and there was little cultural or social separation of the county and parish gentry. Over £3000 p.a. was required from an English estate for membership of the greater or county gentry and this status took two to three generations to acquire (Mingay, 1976: 15; Howell, 1986: 10). By 1830, Burke's *Peerage, Baronetage and Knightage* noted that only 400 families of any significant wealth without heritable honours existed in the United Kingdom, a statistic that leaves unclear the fate of those families possessing moderate landed wealth, for half the land in England was still owned by the lesser gentry (Thompson, 1966: 510–14). Mingay points out that the gentry as a group gave up contesting elections during the early nineteenth century because they had become prohibitively expensive, but employment was still needed for their younger sons and could be found in the army, navy and church (1976: 173).

While the army's elite regiments – the Life Guards, Blues, First Foot Guards and Scots Guards – had by 1830 become finishing schools for young men from aristocratic families, the navy was a far less aristocratic institution; of the 53% of army officers and 40% of naval officers who came from landed backgrounds between 1791 and 1823, the majority came from the gentry. The influence of the nobility in the Established Church had grown during the French wars – no less than 60% of its bishops coming from noble families (Cannon, 1982: 61–5; Cannadine, 1994: 22) 'Squiresons' or clerical magistrates by 1800 also comprised 25% of some county benches, though, on a national basis, the clergy never made more than 10% of the county commissions of the peace. The rising incomes of clerical livings deriving from enclosure over the French wars had made the church increasingly attractive to the nobility, but aristocrats were not the only landowners with livings in their gift, and their flight, alongside the greater gentry, from the county commissions of the peace since 1750 is not likely to have been reversed by the 'squireson' route (Rule, 1992a: 41). The number of prelates related to the peerage also fell heavily after 1830 (Soloway, 1969: 11). Landed paternalism survived on the county bench throughout the French wars: the compassion and sensitivity with which magistrates handled poor law claims, food riots and other social problems in fact reinforced the status of the landed classes as social and political leaders of the nation.

Although gradations in wealth and conspicuous consumption clearly marked off gentry from the aristocracy, after 1660 virtue, sensibility and manners were as important as birth, money, field sports, and country house life to gentle status. Much wealthier than many of the parish gentry, as a collective group, were the overseas traders of London and major port towns, who indulged a taste for country villas, farms, landscape gardening, foreign travel and art collecting throughout the eighteenth century. Nicholas Rogers has given the 'big bourgeoisie' of Hanoverian London a social status parallel to that of the gentry, with whom they often intermarried, and metropolitan businessmen were seemingly happy with this social position for they rarely left their counting houses for a country seat (Rogers, 1979: 439–41; Hancock, 1995; Rule, 1992a: 46–7; Beckett, 1985). Lawrence and Jeanne Stone found only 137 *nouveau riche* families buying their way into the county elite from 1540 to 1880 (1984: 403), but by this the Stones meant the county gentry and a country house of over 5000 square feet, a residence beyond the means of all but the very rich. Many professional and commercial men with less social confidence or more ambition than Rogers's big bourgeoisie aimed first at parish gentry status and left further social climbing to the next generation.

The lack of formal legal barriers to social mobility in England meant that entire families were always moving up or down the social ladder, and the descent of younger sons to trade and the professions ensured that social mixing between the worlds of land and trade remained a fact of gentry life throughout the eighteenth century. The upper 10,000 was not totally open to newcomers but, over time, was accessible to the upwardly mobile. This was true of all of Britain's social ranks (Christie, 1991: 170–3). By 1750, let alone 1800, London, Bristol, Liverpool, Manchester and Leeds all had elite communities of 'gentlemen merchants', some of whom came from landed backgrounds and many of whom had acquired land as a token of success. 'Gentlemanly capitalism' had long sent younger sons of the gentry, and on occasion aristocracy, into great chartered companies, import–export houses and prestige trade guilds. To do so was not cheap: in 1700 it cost £400 to purchase an apprenticeship in the elite wholesale trades or with an overseas merchant, and by 1750 anywhere from £1500 to £5000 was required to set oneself up in foreign trade (Wilson, 1971: 66–9; Cain and Hopkins, 1980; Brooks, 1994: 70; Chapman, 1992: 24–7; Bowen, 1996: 56–7). Lesser gentry families contented themselves with apprenticeships to provincial firms from 1680 onwards (Holmes, 1981, 1986).

Other employment opportunities existed in government service and the professions, whose infiltration by the gentry had increased their social cachet, making them a magnet for the socially ambitious or risk-averse sons of mercantile and manufacturing families. A second to third generation flight from trade to the church, the law and medicine was established by 1800. The professions were a suitably genteel employment smacking neither of trade nor of manual labour and all three had grown at a spectacular rate during the eighteenth century (Aylmer, 1980; Miles, 1986; Rule, 1992a: 60–6; Corfield, 1995). Overseas trade was, however, becoming less attractive to the aristocracy and gentry, in part because the French wars of 1793–1815 had dealt death blows to the gentlemen general merchants of the eighteenth century. Foreign trade from 1805 onwards was increasingly conducted by the new agency houses and their representatives, who made fortunes in distant and uncertain markets on small capitals at high risk (Chapman, 1992). Such enterprises were not for the gentry and aristocracy, who never turned up their noses at commercial investment in the pursuit of estate improvement – be it in mines, canals, roads or urban development – but preferred to gamble at race meetings and West End clubs.

Blood made the aristocracy but what made the gentry was more difficult to fathom, for lesser gentry status could be obtained in one generation with a small estate and a good income. Albion Urdank found in a study of Gloucestershire between 1780 and 1850 that 'wealth had become a more obvious criterion for defining status than in the past, so much so that men with the humblest occupations might call themselves "gentlemen" if the size of their personal estates seemed to warrant the title' (1990: 52). The urban gentry could get by with a respectable job, a decent income and appropriate blood connections though, without an estate, no return to rural gentry status was possible and, by 1800, this group constituted a provincial urban elite. The pseudo-gentry or urban patriciate, who had money and manners but no blood ties to the old elite, belonged to the middling sorts (Stone and Stone, 1984; Brooks, 1994: 71–2; Heal and Holmes, 1994: 19; Hancock, 1995: 280). The decline of the gentry did not come until the last quarter of the nineteenth century, when falling rental incomes from land and Britain's increasing reliance upon cheap food from the empire reduced the economic and social status of landownership (Mingay, 1976: 165–70).

However one wishes to define the composition of the elite, it is clear that the aristocracy and gentry of the British Isles became more socially and culturally homogeneous between 1780 and 1830. The cultural impetus for this came from the American and French Revolutions, both coming as a severe shock to an aristocracy and gentry not accustomed to having its authority, be it political, social or cultural, challenged in any way. Criticisms of aristocratic government and elite parasitism were the stuff of which radical politics were made during the 1810s. Texts like Thomas Oldfield's 1816 *Representative History of Great Britain and Ireland* and John Wade's *The Black Book; or Corruption Unmasked* (1819) explained in detail the monopoly of political power and state patronage possessed by the aristocracy. While

Linda Colley points out that no *conscious* effort was made by the aristocracy and gentry to remodel *noblesse oblige* in response to these external threats, by 1830 a new ethos of landed nobility based upon military prowess, imperialism, professionalism and patriotic state service had emerged in Britain (1992: Ch. 4).

The 'new' ethics of the upper 10,000 were inculcated in the public schools, the universities, art, blood sports and a new quasi-military dress code that put soldiers and sailors into gorgeous and impractical uniforms while outfitting civilians in subdued and expensive tailoring. From the 1770s onwards, an increasing proportion of the elite sent their sons to the public schools and universities, where they imbibed a classical curriculum of Roman literature that celebrated the glories of British imperialism and its achievements (Cannon, 1982: 45–54). Not for nothing did the Duke of Wellington claim that the Battle of Waterloo was won on the playing fields of Eton, for sport and its manly virtues were becoming characteristics of public school culture (Girouard, 1981: 269–70; Cannon, 1982: 34–49; Colley, 1992: 167–93; Cannadine, 1994: 21). Ideals of classical patriotism could, nonetheless, produce interesting results in the minds of the young, such as the 1792 Jacobin revolt of Eton schoolboys, and the exact timing by which a conservative Ciceronian imperialism replaced older classical republican traditions of study is unclear, particularly in the Scottish universities. The suspension of the classic Grand Tour in 1793 following the outbreak of war with France sent an increasing proportion of English youth to the Universities of Edinburgh and Glasgow, where a critical liberal arts education was to be had throughout the French wars (Chitnis, 1986: 48–52, Chs. 3–4; Mandler, 1990a: 52).

Having said this, most of the upper 10,000 were horrified by the process of social cleansing taking place in France from 1792 to 1794 and, as a collective group, felt bound to resist French ideas and British reform. Reconfiguring *noblesse oblige* as an ethos of patriotic state service was but one way of legitimating landed rule and it took several forms during the French wars. The British honours system, from service peerages to knighthoods and medals, gave the landed orders an appearance of utilitarian meritocracy of considerable social and cultural value to the state. The government nevertheless preferred to promote patriotism through veneration of church, crown and constitution because, in the hands of radicals and liberals, meritocracy became a potentially dangerous weapon for use against the establishment (Cannon, 1982: 164–6; Colley, 1984, 1986). State-sponsored patriotism, often conservative loyalist in tone, relied upon the voluntary exertions of local notables to give it the appearance of widespread popular support. In practice, private sector patriotism was dominant in Britain (Eastwood, 1991). No official cults of heroism existed in Britain during the

French wars but unofficial cults grew around the figures of Pitt, Nelson and Wellington. Heroism could be constructed in several ways: for elite youth, state service seemingly embodied the values of true nobility (Girouard, 1981), but for the masses the popularity of Nelson was attributable to a reputation for outspoken independence and compassionate paternalism (Rogers and Jordan, 1989: 215–24). Both military heroes were lionised by the people and, literally, fought over in theatre and victory riots, the former serving as sites of contest between varying interpretations of patriotism and heroism between radicals, moderates and loyalists (Russell, 1995).

The ideal of the English gentleman, which also emerged during the war years, was adopted from the noble values supposedly embodied in the heroes of the age. The lives of Pitt, Nelson, Wellington and Fox did not, however, epitomise the sexual propriety coming into fashion. Nelson, Wellington and Fox had well-publicised mistresses while Pitt, who never married, was suspected of homosexuality, despite one well-publicised heterosexual love episode in 1797. Pitt and Wellington were respected primarily for their modesty, reserve, *sang-froid* and efficient professionalism, while Fox and Nelson, more flamboyant and outspoken characters, were idolised instead for their independence and egotism. Suspicions that Pitt was gay, though there is no evidence to prove it, were suppressed after his death for they accorded ill with the macho, sporting and heterosexual elite culture in which genteel domesticity was promoted as the female counterpart to male militarism (Harvey, 1992: 136–40, 155; Colley, 1992: 189–91).

Bourgeois domesticity in wartime Britain was subscribed to as much by the aristocracy and gentry as by the middling sort. Colley suggests that British women were willing participants in this process of gender role definition: certainly the number of female supporters for the wronged Queen Caroline in 1820 suggests that notions of female passivity and male chivalry were sinking into the British psyche. The executions of Marie Antoinette and French noblewomen horrified a British public becoming accustomed to regarding women as sheltered inhabitants of a domestic private sphere, and many elite women felt a genuine vested interest in defending their social order against French anarchy and atheism. By raising money and supplies for the war effort, elite women presented themselves as the helpmeets of their warrior men. British elite women may also have felt compelled to assert their modesty and virtue against domestic social critics who had begun to attack aristocratic vice long before the French Revolution. Bourgeois domesticity deserves its defining adjective when applied to press critiques of the 1784 Westminster general election campaign in which Georgiana, Duchess of Devonshire, was pilloried for her canvassing activities in support of Fox's candidacy. Here the duchess was depicted as a strumpet who had inverted the patriarchal social order and betrayed the delicacy of her rank and sex to trade kisses for votes, leaving the duke at home to mind the children in her absence (Colley, 1992: Ch. 6; Deutsch, 1996).

Aristocratic immorality, which the duchess and her activities represented, had since 1750 been targets of novelists and travel writers, for whom noble vice was exemplified in a Grand Tour that posed an enervating threat to the virtue and manhood of Britain's landed youth. In Tobias Smollett's *Travels through France and Italy* (1766) lay early 'middle class' condemnations of aristocratic luxury and dissipation, all associated with exposure to the emasculating effects of foreign, and in particular French, culture that pointed the way to future claims to 'middle class' virtue on the part of radical and liberal journalists during the 1790s and 1800s (Turner, 1993). By 1800 the evils of French *ancien régime* culture had been supplanted by the infidelity and irreverence of a Jacobinism that, according to Treasury writer John Bowles, stood to corrupt the virtue of British man and womanhood with the dreadful freethinking of the French salons (Montluzin, 1988: 67). Female liberal intellectuals, most notably Mary Wollstonecraft and Catherine Macauley, were favourite targets of abuse for the *Anti-Jacobin Magazine* and *British Critic*: against them was posited a model of British femininity stressing modesty, morality, piety and delicacy as ideal attributes of the fair sex (Barker-Benfield, 1987: 368–95).

This model of British womanhood was certainly genteel but not wholly domestic. In the hands of an evangelical activist like Hannah More, such values could be empowering, for the age of atonement not only gave elite and middling-sort women opportunities to venture outside the home, but enabled them to employ semi-private domestic social networks to mobilise support for good causes, most notably the abolition of the slave trade. War and charity work were double-edged swords for women for, while allowing them to foster their caring, nurturing or religious instincts in respectable ways, reinforcing their image and identity as domestic females, their activities outside the home also gave them moral power and authority (Hall and Davidoff, 1987: 115–16, 137–8, 167–72). Notions of a rigid and separate domestic sphere for women moreover break down when contemplating the involvement of wealthy women in the charities, philanthropic societies and patriotic campaigns of the late eighteenth and early nineteenth centuries. More's Sunday schools and Elizabeth Fry's prison reform campaign testify to the zealous public activities of women often resented but tolerated by men. The loyalist prescriptive literature of the 1790s and 1800s told elite women that their chief duties to state and society lay as wives and mothers within the home but, as creatures with the economic security, leisure and social status to leave the home, dynamic women could turn their domestic, caring and supportive instincts into public activities whilst keeping a wary eye upon the social standards supposed to govern their lives (Colley, 1992: 261–2; Vickery, 1993b; Oldfield, 1995: 135–42; Vincent, 1998: 159–61).

Conflict and Cohesion in Urban Communities

If the social history of western Europe written in the twentieth century is to be believed, the middle class has been rising in wealth and self-awareness ever since the twelfth century. Most scholars used to agree that the English middle class emerged somewhere between 1780 and 1830 but, in the wake of need and revisionist scholarship dealing with the rise of consumerism, the urban renaissance, the modest pace of industrialisation and the development of modern gender distinctions, no clear consensus exists on dates for the self-conscious appearance of this social group. Journalists and political economists, those self-appointed spokesmen for the 'middle classes', are, as Dror Wahrman states, responsible for much of the confusion surrounding the chronology of class formation. The middle class, according to classic accounts of British politics and society in the French wars, came of age during the 1810s, thanks to its exposure to the liberal ideas of the French Revolution, the negative experience of high wartime taxation, and a sense of outrage at the injustice of the 1815 Corn Law (Briggs, 1956, 1959, 1967; Perkin, 1969: 165, 192, 214; Rubinstein, 1983). The middle class then joined the parliamentary reform movement of the later 1810s and would continue to agitate for the vote up to 1832. According to Wahrman (1996), by asserting the claims and interests of a fictitious unitary middle class between 1790 and 1832, liberal journalists not only created the illusion of class struggle between the upper and middle classes, but defined a middle class identity that, though employed in politics to legitimate the claims of the middling sort, would not be widely adopted on a social scale until the 1830s and 1840s. Historians of consumerism, urban civic culture and eighteenth-century literature are determined to assert a distinct cultural, if not political, identity for the middling sorts before 1820, siting it in a set of cultural, social and economic values separate and consciously opposed to the landed elites, in which they include the gentry, and the lower orders. In such accounts, middle-class formation is dated anywhere from 1730 to 1850 and based upon the novels, prescriptive literature, newspapers, magazines, consumer choices and urban civic culture of London and provincial towns (Hall and Davidoff, 1987; Earle, 1987; Langford, 1991; Smail, 1993; Hunt, 1995).

Attempts to define the eighteenth-century middling sorts by birth and occupation have never been satisfactory, thanks to the existence of the urban gentry and pseudo-gentry. By 1800, the former were well established in many provincial towns, not least Manchester and Liverpool, where they constituted what John Walton has called a dynastic, Tory Anglican middle class connected closely by blood and social ties to the rural gentry (Walton, 1987: 128–30). Here lay the Manchester loyalists of the revolutionary and Napoleonic Wars. While David Hancock has tried to prove that estate-buying Atlantic merchants before 1785 remained partially separate from the gentry in their subscription to 'polite, industrious and moral' values (1995: 16, 20, 346–7, 357–75), this does not explain what happened to the Leeds general merchants who retired altogether into rural gentility from 1793 to 1815, the harsh conditions of wartime trade having forced them out of business (Wilson, 1971: 105–7). By 1800, the Peels and Arkwrights, those first-generation industrial entrepreneurs, had climbed into the estate-owning ranks and this process would continue throughout the nineteenth century (Rapp, 1974; Jones, 1967; Raybould, 1973). Any definition of proto-industrial or 'modern' industry as the preserve of the self-made middling sort is moreover false, for the gentlemen clothiers of the West Country, some worth £40,000, had long been involved in manufacturing while the Lancashire and West Riding gentry were heavy investors and employers in coal mining, wool and iron production to maximise the profits from their estates (Lacy, 1971: 116–20; Koditschek, 1990: 45–51).

At the lower end of the middling-sort social scale, artisans were always difficult to place. While masters often belonged to the middle ranks of society, their journeymen and apprentices did not, and mass consumerism created entirely new categories of employment such as shopkeeping that evade easy definition. While artisans belong, like mechanics and artificers, to the world of skilled labour that made up perhaps 20% of the British population, poorer shopkeepers, who required only £10 of capital to set up shop, were technically middling-sort merchants who possessed socio-cultural values more akin to the lower orders. Journalists, another new eighteenth-century occupational group, often teetered – much like journey-men – on the economic brink between respectability and ruin (Walvin, 1990; Rule, 1992a: 6–7). Most of the middling sort lived in towns where social historians have tried to locate the origins of their specific culture. While it is safe, if hardly illuminating, to say that a middle-class work ethic grew out of the culture of the guilds, values such as hard work, pride in one's job, thrift and occupational solidarity were as characteristic of skilled labour as of trade or the professions (Brooks, 1994: 76–81).

Historians of consumerism and material culture have tried to identify class-specific cultural values in the tastes and buying patterns of middle-income households. Peter Earle's claims to a London middle-class identity, established by 1730 and based upon modest domestic consumption, capital accumulation and prudent reinvestment in one's business, are based on a database of only 375 domestic inventories (1987: Ch. 10). This source of evidence unfortunately peters out after 1720 and, while research from private diaries and correspondence is revealing more about the material culture of eighteenth-century society, this is still a new field of research. Consumer historians are right to question the validity of the emulation thesis that bases market trends upon taste patterns laid down by the rich, but it is clear that new standards of general gentility were determining the book, clothing, food and furniture purchases of the middling sort (Shammas, 1993; Barry, 1994). Separating middling-sort consumer gentility from elite consumer gentility is an ongoing task: in John Smail's Halifax, professional middling-sort families struggled to balance the claims of thrifty utility and genteel good taste, in so doing forging rank- and income-specific tastes of their own (Hall and Davidoff, 1987: 21–6). Amanda Vickery has, however, pointed out that south Lancashire lesser gentryfolk also conformed, often from economic necessity, to similar standards. A middling-sort income was placed by contemporaries between £50 and £150 p.a., though many prosperous families, particularly those engaged in trade or manufacturing, made much more. Elizabeth Shackleton, mistress of Nethercoats Hall, found London aristocratic high fashion quite as ludicrous as Smail's Halifax lawyers and merchants, who deliberately eschewed York and Harrogate county society, presumably because they disliked it (Corfield, 1991; Vickery, 1993a; Smail, 1993: 93–106).

The domestic architecture and entertainment patterns of prosperous merchants, doctors, lawyers and clergymen suggest that middling-sort families were trying to set themselves apart from other social groups throughout the eighteenth century. New homes in London and the provinces were built in suburbs or some distance from the town with gardens or farms attached, while workshops and counting houses, once part of the household, were housed on separate premises. Communal dining with servants and employees ceased, as did female participation in business affairs, and families aspiring to gentility abandoned community festivals and 'vulgar' popular sports for private domestic entertaining. The lower orders had been cordoned off (Beckett, 1985: 70–8; Smail, 1993: 167–76). Aristocratic and gentry families had been the first to create a domestic sphere for women where responsibility for the household alone, as opposed to business and estate management, lay in female hands. Gone by 1750 were the days when gentlewomen were expected to harvest crops in their husband's absence. Enlightenment ideals of femininity had, however, given women a complementary role to men in the genteel, cultured and increasingly urban society of eighteenth-century

Britain. Women now gave civilised refinement to a sociable and ideally inclusive culture too apt, if dominated by men, to degenerate into crude vulgarity. The Enlightenment was full of intellectual contradictions respecting the role of women: bluestocking authors, novelists, journalists, political hostesses and salon leaders emerged during the eighteenth century alongside a consumer culture that commodified women, and a science of human biology that by 1780 had denied the existence of female sexuality and categorised women in medical terms as passive child bearers and rearers (Klein, 1993; Barker-Benfield, 1987; Laqueur, 1990).

Caroline and Emily Lennox, the heroines of Stella Tillyard's *Aristocrats* (1992), possessed the social confidence and intellectual independence to take what they wished from the culture of the high Enlightenment without feeling constrained by its prescriptions. The fact that their own sisters did not possess the strength of mind to do so highlights the necessity for individualised research before drawing broad conclusions. The literal reconstruction of British urban public space taking place between 1680 and 1780 had created an environment of sociability and *politesse* that, to a certain extent, had broken down older distinctions of rank and status within provincial towns. In the public parks, lending libraries, assembly rooms, theatres, lecture rooms, concert halls, resorts, racecourses and homes of Georgian towns, men and women participated in a process of public display and interaction through which rival claimants to wealth and gentility defined social and cultural space for themselves in an urban melting pot of old and new elite groups. Friction, rather than class conflict, had always characterised urban social and political life, but the urban renaissance was unusual in the extent to which an inclusive ethos of sociability concealed the erection of new barriers between social groups (Borsay, 1989; Barry, 1994). This can be found in Halifax before 1780, where merchants and professionals prevented shopkeepers and artisans from participating in lending library, meeting hall and church organ subscription campaigns by the setting of high minimum contribution limits. The town was unusual for its lack of a dominant gentry presence, with the result that all the social infighting of the urban renaissance took place between the upper middling sort and the lower middling sort. In Birmingham and the West Midlands, trade associations and urban public works projects were by 1780 sites of contest between merchants and manufacturing men on one hand and the old county elites on the other. Though freemasonry might be a cloak for radicalism in Ireland and Scotland, in Birmingham it was a focus for church and king loyalism (Smail, 1993: 226–36; Money, 1977, 1990: 243–68).

Urban corporations, organisations and voluntary societies, be they turnpike trusts or assembly room committees, were the real sites of social and political contest in late eighteenth- and early nineteenth-century Britain

(Morris, 1983, 1990). Volunteer corps too served both to unite and to divide urban elite and would-be elite groups during the French wars. This process took different routes. In Bradford, the Anglican gentry and urban gentry embraced loyalism in 1792 and, in 1794, set up a volunteer corps. Leading Dissenters and Methodists sided in the first instance with the old elite but thereafter broke away, and the socio-political conflicts of the 1790s and 1800s destroyed Bradford's socially harmonious eighteenth-century proto-industrial community (Koditschek, 1990: 70–5). In Manchester, the Anglican urban elite had set up a Church and King Club in 1790 to harass the Manchester Constitutional Society and three separate volunteer corps emerged: Dissenter Whig, Anglican Tory and a populist group led by Joseph Hanson (Bohstedt, 1983: 106–25; Walton, 1987: 135–6). Leeds struck a compromise in a regiment where one battalion was led by Anglicans and the other by Unitarians. Unsuitable persons were excluded from the Newcastle Volunteers by the imposition of a £10 minimum subscription fee, and three Birmingham corps led by the Earl of Dartmouth asserted the identity of the as yet unincorporated town against the county (Cookson, 1997: 238–9). Volunteer units were formed and led in the first instance by the aristocracy and gentry but, over time, landed control over the volunteers could be subverted or supplanted by junior officers. Volunteer commissions were eagerly sought by the middling sort, who regarded them as status symbols and routes of entry to the regular army. The high number of urban corps petitioning the government for top-up funds in 1798 suggests that some units unable to finance themselves in the long term had formed in part to claim a share of social leadership that might later translate into more active and overt political roles (Langford, 1991; Cookson, 1997: 224–32).

The howls of provincial protest that greeted Windham's 1806 proposals to abolish the volunteers bore testimony to their utility as instruments of urban and regional politics: virtually town makers in their own right (Cookson, 1997: 239–42). Ministerialists had long realised that the volunteers could not be subjected to any real central control, for their leaders saw the corps as local, rather than national, institutions embodying English traditions of regional autonomy and self-government. Less is known about the short-lived Reevites, which had been envisaged by Pitt as local associations functioning upon the model of the urban voluntary prosecution associations that collected money by subscription to pay the legal costs of their members in the event of court action. One suspects that they too were 'middle-class' organisations as fissured with socio-economic and cultural divisions as the volunteers (Philp, 1995a: 49–50). The official ethos of loyalism, however, envisaged British society as a unified chain of ranks and orders bound by duty, deference and patriotism in the defence of the realm. Artisans, yeomen, mechanics, merchants, lawyers and bankers were to be led by society's natural leaders, the aristocracy and gentry, to repulse French invaders and subdue domestic treachery. The Pittite press did not contest the appropriation of the term 'middle classes' by the pro-Opposition press during the 1790s and 1800s because any recognition of a divided society, be it into two nations or three classes, was a *de facto* admission that serious conflicts of interest existed in British society. In 1799 George Rose paid tribute to the generosity of the £6m in voluntary contributions to the war received in 1798 alone from members of the royal family to the 'yeomanry, peasantry and domestics' (Rose, 1799: 28). Here was a united society in action. The government had always known that it could exercise little real control over active loyalists and this begs the question what it hoped to achieve through loyalist organisations: unquestioning obedience and vigilante conservatism is not what it got nor, arguably, what it expected. General compliance with its policies was a more realistic expectation (Cookson, 1997: 212). Government journalists instead acknowledged the existence of middling-sort groups while denying them any class-specific rights, interests or virtues. They were assigned a place on the social ladder as 'the link and connection between the higher and lower classes of society' (AJR, 1798: i, #35, 592), and the notion of a distinct 'middle class' was left to the Opposition press during the debates on Pitt's Triple Assessment of 1798 (Wahrman, 1992: 98–107, 1995 Ch. 4).

Whatever the government thought, the reality of social friction in urban communities ensured that the middling sort would claim a share of urban power and authority for themselves. Smail suggests that this process took place in English towns at rates determined by the specific social composition of each urban locality, for the strength and numbers of gentryfolk, professionals and tradesmen varied from town to town. His 'middle-class culture', if not middle-class identity, had taken shape in Halifax by 1780. It involved the adoption of rank-specific and gendered standards of entertainment, public and private architecture, business affairs, cultural patronage and voluntary organisation from which inferiors and superiors were excluded. Cookson (1997: 233–8) describes the volunteers as a middle-class institution and, while this may be true of the officer corps, the motives of the rank and file were more calculating and opportunistic. While all volunteers were determined to defend their localities in the event of invasion, their commitment to vigilante anti-Jacobinism is more suspect. Subscription to the ideal of national self-defence did not preclude volunteer corps from interpreting the terms 'nation', 'defence' and 'patriotism' in their own terms and if, under the mantle of a deceptive conservative loyalism, rivalries of a socio-economic, political and regional nature simmered away, this was normal and healthy in an imagined community of fractured identities. An ostensibly Whig Britain had remained, in many respects, old Tory in its social and political attitudes from 1688 to 1792 and, by the same token, a seemingly Tory Britain remained wedded to old Whig concepts of liberty and good government from 1792 to 1820. It is hardly to be wondered at that volunteers found aspects of both attractive, and this is confirmed by the party affiliations of the 'non-elite' MPs in the House of Commons from 1760 to 1820 (Christie, 1995). No doubt many middling-sort people joined the Friends of Peace, the Hampden Clubs and the Queen Caroline movement, but the extent to which this represented a definite and comprehensive class consciousness remains questionable.

The timing of an urban unit's formation, having taken into account the local conditions under which it took shape, may provide clues as to its ideological identity. In March 1794, when the government called for the first cohort of volunteers to defend the nation against internal and external enemies assumed to be united in spirit and intention, revolutionary France did not present an attractive picture even to popular radicals. Anarchy, atheism and dictatorial government by central executive committees may have been the chief evils that volunteers, particularly on the south coast, sought to keep from Britain's shores, although units formed in areas with a strong radical presence were no doubt also determined to keep the peace in their localities. By 1798, let alone 1803, when many liberals and radicals were losing – or had lost – faith in the revolution, it was easier for volunteer corps of varying political complexions to pledge their hostility to Jacobin principles and practices though they might well be moderates or liberals. Having said this, the determination of the middling sorts to close their ranks to those who did not meet their standards of respectability and gentility strongly suggests that their notions of liberty accorded well with the principles of a 1791 French constitution that divided the nation into active citizens, amongst whom the middling sort belonged, and unenfranchised passive citizens, or the lower orders. As Tim Blanning (1989: 3) has noted: 'If the bourgeoisie had their way, the Revolution would have been closed down by 1791 at the latest'. The intellectual contradictions of nineteenth-century European middle-class liberalism had begun to manifest themselves.

Enclosure and the Proletarianisation of Labour

Britain in 1820, let alone 1785, was still a primarily agricultural country with the majority of its population still employed in the countryside. The living standards of agricultural labourers had changed for the worse since 1760 and more suffering was to come during the 1790s and 1800s. Encouraged by high grain prices during the French wars, landowners would place three million acres of open and common fields under private, as opposed to communal, ownership through the process of enclosure. As small yeomen farmers, cottagers and husbandmen lost their lands and means of independent sustenance to enclosure, they swelled the ranks of a growing wage labour market (Gilboy, 1934, 1936; Flinn, 1974; Kussmaul, 1981; Rule, 1992b: 131–4). The 1808 General Report on Enclosures recognised the magnitude of this loss and recommended that land be set aside at enclosure for yeomen and cottagers. It was silent on the subject of common land-use rights also lost by the poor. Most landowners thought, in common with Frederick Morton Eden, that common land-use rights were near useless to agricultural labourers: 'instead of sticking regularly to such labour, as might enable them to purchase good fuel, they waste their time . . . in picking up a few dry sticks, or in grubbing up, on some bleak moor, a little furze, or heath. Their starved pig or two, together with a few wandering goslings, besides involving them in perpetual altercations without their neighbours, and almost driving and compelling them to become trespassers, are dearly paid for, by the care and time, and bought food, which are necessary to rear them' (Eden, 1797: i, xviii–xix; Young, 1808: 32–4, 167–8; Overton, 1996: 175–82).

The rewards of self-sufficiency were far greater than Eden's remarks suggest. Turbary and grazing rights on the common fields, in addition to gleaning on the open fields, represented a major source of sustenance for rural families. The value of cow ownership has been estimated at £9 p.a., the equivalent of half a male agricultural day labourer's annual salary (Humphries, 1990: 18). Contrary to Eden's claim, the purchase of animal fodder became necessary only after grazing rights were lost and it raised the costs of cow and pig ownership to prohibitive levels. The loss of customary land-use rights also reduced the independent contributions of women and children to the household income, for female agricultural employment had always been less remunerative than its male counterpart, thus encouraging women to work at home after marriage. Before enclosure, women and children could make a significant contribution to the household economy through the exploitation of common land-use rights. After enclosure took place, families relied upon a principal male breadwinner for the bulk of a family income supplemented by the meagre wage earnings of women and children. The gender balance in poor rural households was shifting further in favour of men (Kussmaul, 1981; Snell, 1985: 172–8; Humphries, 1990; Allen, 1994: 117).

Enclosure thus created a rural proletariat increasingly at the mercy of farmers and employers. It also created work in the short and long term, for ditches had to be dug and roads re-routed at enclosure while the larger-scale 'scientific' farming adopted after it took place required more hands.

The new wages received by agricultural labour did not, however, compensate it in real monetary terms for what it had lost (Crafts, 1989; Snell, 1985: 147–58). As farm work was seasonal, families had always turned to other trades during the winter to make ends meet. Carpentry and weaving were common secondary occupations for men, while planting, spinning and sheaf tying were traditional women's work (Rule, 1992b: 94–7). Tasks like bird scaring or sheep tending were left to children. Hand spinning was the first of these traditional employments to be lost to industrialisation during the 1770s and 1780s but was yet to send countryfolk to Blake's dark satanic mills. Mechanisation in agriculture itself did not appear until the very end of the Napoleonic Wars when threshing machines were first used. They would not deprive manual labour of much employment until the 1820s and 1830s (Emsley, 1979a).

The war removed men from both the urban and rural workforce, in the countryside temporarily relieving the problem of rural underemployment, lowering crime rates and absorbing at least one-fifth of the male population (Hay, 1982; Wells, 1988: 333; Crouzet, 1989: 195). Although enclosure ensured that some investment went into agriculture, rural manufacturing in the south suffered from the diversion of capital to ports and the new industrial districts (John, 1967; Hueckel, 1973, 1976; Deane, 1975; Snell, 1985: 23–49, 412–17; Crouzet, 1989). Real living standards did not drop much, thanks to the generosity of the poor law during the French wars, but military service in the army was understandably unpopular for it removed men from their communities, leaving their families dependent upon poor relief. Militia service, though less onerous a burden for families, used up valuable work or leisure time despite the provision of token pay to the militiaman (Emsley, 1979a: 36–40). No arrangements existed in either army or navy until 1796 for remitting pay to the families of active servicemen and, despite the passage of 1792 legislation ordering the payment of a weekly dole from the poor rates to the wives and legitimate children (under 10) of embodied militiamen, militia riots were common. The London crimp house riots of 1794 voiced a widespread resentment against the practice of substitution whereby those selected by ballot for militia service could hire other men to serve in their place, an onerous expense for working men, and militia rioting was common during the 1790s (Wells, 1983; Bohstedt, 1983: 173–81; Emsley, 1979a: 54–5, 1989; Stevenson, 1992: 208–12; Cookson, 1997: 189). In 1797, crowds gathered in many English and Welsh localities to destroy the ballot lists for the new supplementary militia created in 1796. Scotland had no tradition of militia service and sought none: when the volunteers and militia were introduced in 1797–1798, popular resistance was fierce (Meikle, 1912: 150–8; Jones, 1974: 51–3; Logue, 1979: 78–108; Emsley, 1989: 218–20; Fry, 1992: 233–4, 246–8). Ireland sent many regulars into the British army but those who remained in town and country during the French wars found the country's long-established traditions of independent armed self-defence far more attractive than regular militia service. Only Protestants were much interested in the Yeomanry corps (Cookson, 1997: 12–13).

A public culture of militarism, complete with unofficial cults of heroism, private-sector manifestations of patriotism, an urban civic culture in which the volunteer corps played a central role, and a flood of patriotic poems and stage plays produced during the war years, strongly suggests that British society was to some extent militarised during the French wars; but to what extent and in what ways remains largely unknown. Popular respect for a military elite appears from theatre riots, the press and the politics of volunteering to have been strongly qualified by subscription to older and opposing cultural traditions: namely the veneration of commerce over arms in addition to notions of local independence (Russell, 1995; Cookson, 1997: 22–3). As far as ordinary people were concerned, militia service kept men on British soil and was therefore preferable to regular army service. Volunteers, exempted from the army, navy and militia ballot, were more attractive still because military training took up only 12–24 days a year. Many corps, particularly in England, refused point blank to serve outside their localities (Hall, 1992: 3). Prison inmates made up a limited proportion of Britain's armed forces but, with 10% of the male population of military age under arms, hardly the majority. The number of soldiers' wives claiming poor relief during the wars suggests rather that many poor men took the king's shilling willingly to claim the bounty money offered to recruits. Scottish tenant farmers had long found this a welcome source of income in exchange for a younger son. Clan chiefs and landlords, moreover, encouraged the practice by offering tenants improved leases, new holdings or – if persuasion did not suffice – threats of eviction to raise Highland regiments for active service. The government regarded the militia as a source of regular soldiers and encouraged transfers to the army once recruits were habituated to military service. In 1808, the government encouraged volunteer corps to join a reconstituted part-time local militia *en masse* but few units found this option attractive (Emsley, 1979a, 1989: 217–19; Hall, 1992: 4–10; Cookson, 1997).

Military recruitment was less disruptive to local communities than demobilisation, which flooded the domestic workforce and lowered wages everywhere (Hay, 1982). The practice of 'king's freeman', as established from the late seventeenth century onwards, allowed ex-soldiers, sailors and their families to set up in trades without having served a legal apprenticeship. East coast colliers, like many other occupational groups, went on strike in 1815 in protest against the employment of cheap blackleg labour (Snell, 1985: 250; Stevenson, 1989: 78–80). Agricultural underemployment was already noticeable by 1776, when Adam Smith called for the repeal of the Settlement Laws that tied poor relief to established residence in a parish because the laws discouraged families from relocating to other districts. The Settlement and Vagrancy Laws do not, in retrospect, seem to have interfered much with labour mobility but, in 1795, parliament had forbidden the removal of unsettled families from parishes until they became chargeable on the rates. The dearth of adequately paid agricultural employment in many counties nonetheless ensured that poor rates remained high, and the fate of village labourers during the French wars was arguably worse than that which befell their urban counterparts.

Industrialisation has often been blamed for depriving the British people of skilled employment, lowering their wages and worsening their living standards. These assumptions have been hotly contested over the past two decades following the compilation of revised figures suggesting that real wages, if not necessarily living standards, rose from 1770 to 1850 (Feinstein, 1981; Crafts, 1981, 1989; Lindert and Williamson, 1983). A fragile academic consensus has established, for the moment, that wages remained stagnant or declined slightly from 1760 to 1820, after which they rose up to 1850. The role of industrialisation here is complex for it cannot be regarded as a purely urban or 'factory' phenomenon, thanks to modern scholarship that emphasises the symbiotic relationship between the 'modern' and 'traditional' sectors of the British economy. Included in the modern sector are financial services and the new 'industrial' trades: cotton, iron smelting and refining, engineering, heavy chemicals, some transportation and some consumer goods, principally pottery and paper, while agriculture and the old craft trades constitute the 'traditional' economy (Berg, 1994b). As a regional phenomenon, the industrial revolution helped raise all adult male wages in the North, Midlands and lowland Scotland from 1760 to 1800: after that date, the picture is complicated by the marked decline of wages in certain trades, most notably cotton weaving (Gilboy, 1934, 1936; Flinn, 1974; Schwartz, 1990; Botham and Hunt, 1987; Rule, 1992a: 176–86; Mokyr, 1994: 122–6). It is suspected that female and child wages, in general lower than those of men, followed the same trajectory. Wages in most trades, not excepting agricultural labour, rose after 1815 (Lindert, 1994: 368–9). The subjection of women to wage discrimination does not, however, appear to have been systematic (Burnette, 1997).

Cotton production set the standard for all traditional accounts of the industrial revolution because its early mechanisation and rapidly growing share of foreign export earnings presented scholars with an account of fast and dynamic change from 1760 to 1830. Cotton was nonetheless atypical of British manufacturing during the first phase of the industrial revolution and, even here, change was not as rapid or simple as it once seemed (Crafts,

1985: 33–4). James Hargreaves' spinning jenny and Thomas Arkwright's water frame, invented in 1765 and 1769 respectively, were placed into mills during the 1770s and 1780s, but many jennies, built on a six or twelve spindle scale, remained in use amongst hand spinners to produce stronger and higher quality weft threads beyond the capacity of the large factory-based jennies until the Crompton mule (1779), which combined the technologies of the jenny and the water frame, was placed into mule sheds during the 1790s. In the Blackburn mill riots of 1779, only jennies possessing more than 24 spindles were destroyed, for the small machines posed no threat to the livelihoods of workers. Much of the machinery housed in the nineteenth-century factory had in fact been developed in the eighteenth century for domestic or small workshop use but, having said this, hand spinning underwent a swift and terrible decline during the 1780s. The incidence of machine breaking across England during the later eighteenth century nonetheless indicates no overwhelmingly negative response to new 'factory' technology: some workers quite simply accepted the introduction of machines while others did not (Berg, 1987, 1994b: 150–1, 238–9, 250–4). Early textile machinery was both expensive and unreliable with the result that producers, particularly of quality goods, were slow to mechanise. Edmund Cartwright's power mill was invented in 1785 but would not be widely used for cotton weaving until the 1820s although the gig mill, which received its patent in 1797, experienced much faster adoption in the wool trade and became a target of Yorkshire Luddites during the 1810s.

From 1790 to 1820, proto-industrial production remained the norm amongst cotton manufacturers, who often owned one spinning mill employing 50 to 100 operatives, many of them women and children, and relied upon anywhere from 200 to 1000 handloom weavers in outlying districts to produce the cloth. Although cotton weavers enjoyed good wages during the early 1790s, their piece-rates began to drop during the latter half of the decade and, from 1806 to 1815, an adult handloom weaver was earning the same weekly wage at home as an unskilled agricultural labourer at work. The semi-skilled cotton weavers organised themselves quickly into a trade association and regularly struck for better wages in Lancashire throughout the 1800s but their wages fell steadily after 1810, never to recover. By the mid-1820s weavers, who constituted 3–4% of the working population, were facing the same fate as hand spinners of the 1780s (Bythell, 1969: 94–111; Bohstedt, 1983: 132–5; Lindert, 1994: 371–2). The decline of Scottish cotton weaving was slower and more gradual, for power loom technology was not introduced until the 1840s (Murray, 1978: 40–75, 114–16).

Wool production, much slower to mechanise than cotton, remained based in the West Riding of Yorkshire upon small-scale family-firm production and proto-industrial output techniques until the mid-nineteenth century.

Mule spinning was not introduced in wool manufacture until 1816 and power loom weaving would not arrive until the 1860s. When built, the 'company mills' of the West Riding were used by artisan clothiers who then turned to handloom weavers to make the cloth (Berg, 1994a: 134, 1994b: 208–50; Hudson, 1986, 1989; Koditschek, 1990: Ch. 1; Rule, 1981: 65). As Yorkshire rose in importance as a wool producer, East Anglia and the West Country, ancient centres of wool production not blessed with the water power requisite for mill construction, deindustrialised slowly and painfully (Berg, 1994b: Ch. 5). Eden's *State of the Poor* paints a dismal picture of Norwich wool weavers hard hit by the closure of European markets in the 1790s and the longer-term decline of their trade (1797: ii, 476–9). By 1812, many textile workers in the north-west and Midlands would be protesting against the introduction of new machinery and the hiring of unskilled labour to run it but, before looking in any detail at the Luddites, it is necessary to glance at the impact of industrialisation upon other trades.

Industry and Popular Protest

The first industrial revolution was a regional, not a national, phenomenon affecting lowland Scotland, the North, East Midlands, London and South Wales. Modern industry, as we define it, was therefore confined to mining, metalwork and textiles, all of which from 1790 to 1820 experienced the acceleration of trends visible before 1785. Coal mining, based primarily in the north-east, Yorkshire, Staffordshire and Shropshire, grew from 7.09 million tonnes in 1775 to 16.65 million in 1815. This was not used primarily for the firing of steam engines, of which there were perhaps 1000 in 1800, but to fuel domestic fires and a wide range of manufacturing applications needing heat (Flinn, 1984: ii, 26). Most smelting was done by coal in 1700, let alone 1800, when 49% of British steam power was still used in mines and quarries (Von Tunzelman, 1986: 78). By 1800, 25% of Britain's coal was coming from Scotland and South Wales. In all places, mining had acquired steam pumps and lifts by 1785 but remained a dangerous, labour-intensive and skilled trade where the coal was dug from the seams by hand. Increased output and a shortage of manpower during the wars would lead to the increased employment of women and children on mine sites. Mining nonetheless remained a small-scale industry for, as late as 1850, the average British mine employed only 80 men, women and children both above and below ground (John, 1980; Berg, 1994a: 140).

Metal refining had witnessed major technological advances during the eighteenth century although the output of wrought iron, the metal of the industrial revolution, would not begin to grow dramatically until the 1780s. Henry Cort's puddling furnace and rolling mill, patented in 1784, enabled high-quality bar iron to be made from low-grade British pig iron on one production site but, though Cort's work had been carried out under an Admiralty contract, the government funded little industrial research and development either before or during the French wars. Pig iron output rose from 62,000 tonnes in 1780 to 340,000 in 1815 and large-scale operations were the norm by 1800. Abraham Darby employed 1000 at Coalbrookdale (Riden, 1977; Hyde, 1977). A glance at engineering and hardware manufacturing displays more organisational diversity. In 1800, Henry Boulton's Soho foundry, set up five years earlier, employed fewer than 100 persons to make steam engines in a series of specialised workshops employing skilled artisans working with hand tools. Boulton and his partner, James Watt, had begun to break down the manufacturing process into component parts but were far from running an assembly line, while other Birmingham 'iron-mongers' rented shops and tools to craftsmen who were still paid by the piece for finished products. Producers of 'toys' and small metalwares had begun to introduce time-saving devices such as button-stamping and wire-drawing machines by 1800 but, despite this, much of the finishing work was still done by hand (Berg, 1994a: 136–9, 1994b: 203, 266–8).

The term centralised workshop, as opposed to 'factory', is more appropriate for Birmingham metal trades that had grafted economies of scale onto traditional hand craftsmanship. Some sectors of Birmingham manufacturing, most notably the gun trade, still commissioned parts from independent craftsmen, who made stocks, sights and barrels in their own shops, after which the guns were assembled in a central warehouse. Small-arms manufacturing expanded dramatically during the Napoleonic Wars but experienced no major technological advances during that period, and heavy armaments production, like engineering, remained heavily dependent upon craft skills. Despite the fact that the metal and hardware trades suffered badly from the closure of European markets during the French wars, Birmingham metalworkers displayed little interest in popular radicalism and for this the strong 'church and king' identity of the town was responsible (Cookson, 1982: 187; Emsley, 1979a: 30; Hall, 1992: 28–9, 54–7; Berg, 1994b: 258–62).

Sheffield's 6000-odd cutlers and filemakers, in sharp contrast, flocked to the local Society for Constitutional Information. This has been attributed to the survival of independent small workshop production where there were few social distinctions between masters and men (Stevenson, 1989). What made such work 'industrial' was the division of the manufacturing process into distinct phases: in the case of cutlery the forging, sharpening and hafting of blades – all performed by specialists – and the proto-industrial production of goods for a central distributor. By 1820, the vast majority of Sheffield 'little masters' would be working for others rather than themselves and the same could be said for other workshop trades, namely London hatters and watchmakers (Rule, 1992b: 138–50; Berg, 1994a: 139). The 'putting-out' system used by cotton manufacturers was also employed widely in framework knitting and the final stages of iron, steel, brass and copperware production: no fewer than 10,000 rural nailers could be found in the Black Country around Birmingham. Popular radicalism took strong root in Sheffield, a town where three pro-reform newspapers were shut down in succession by local loyalists from 1793 to 1795 and locals were still singing 'God Save Great Thomas Paine' during the 1840s. One reason why the Sheffield SCI presented such a strong front was that it experienced no conflicts between reputable and disreputable radicalism, although other towns in the north were not so fortunate. In Manchester the appearance of the Corresponding Society and the United Englishmen was deeply disturbing to the moderate MCS, and the local radical movement split as a result.

The social environment of early industrial employment may have been more important than low wages to the early politicisation of labour in lowland Scotland, south Wales and the English north-west, for wages in the industrial districts were good: certainly much better than could be found in agriculture or urban unskilled trades (Mokyr, 1993: 94). After 1811, despite the depression of the post-war years, all trades including agricultural labour experienced wage rises. Higher average height statistics and an increasing lifespan for men and women (45–55 years) support the case for improving living standards after 1810, although disclaimers have been made for the period between 1785 and 1815 (Floud, Wachter and Gregory, 1990: Ch. 4; Komlos, 1993; Schofield, 1994; Nicholas and Oxley, 1996; Floud and Harris, 1997; Johnson and Nicholas, 1997). Other biological statistics indicate that death rates were dropping while birth rates and infant life expectancy were rising (Wrigley, 1983: 130–1; Lindert, 1994: 376–7). Consumption patterns indicate, moreover, a rise in the qualities of manufactured goods bought by ordinary people (Rule, 1992b: 8–10, 257–61).

Contemporary skilled labour defined its proper living standard as the ability to maintain a spouse and family without recourse to poor relief and this included the education of children (Rule, 1992a: 107). Urban or 'industrial' environments offered more pay to the ordinary man and woman and, though life in the towns was unhealthier than life in the country, this was nothing new (Thompson, 1968; Perkin, 1969: 130–3; Lindert, 1994: 374–7). Levels of work satisfaction in the emerging 'factory system' are difficult to assess and care must be taken not to romanticise a rural lifestyle idealised by Friedrich Engels and Chartists. Rural employments, though more varied than the monotony of mill work, were equally exhausting and more at the mercy of the weather and seasons. Efficiency and moral control came to be synonymous in nineteenth-century factories but St Monday holidays, strikes and collective bargaining continued to take place throughout the French wars. Centralised workshops allowed employers to monitor quality and prevent the theft of raw materials, a common occurrence in all 'putting out' trades, but did not commit manufacturers to any reform of worker morals (Rule, 1992b: 154–5, 182–6). Robert Owen's New Lanark model community of tidy workers' cottages, launched in 1800, was unusual because it tried to impose middling-sort standards of work and cleanliness upon Glaswegian textile workers (Henriques, 1979: 3–4; Rule, 1992b: 192–7).

It is difficult to see any evidence of radical politicisation in food riots before 1800. The widespread food rioting of 1794–1795 was motivated by general war weariness and the desire for cheap bread. Crowd appeals to a 'moral economy' are difficult to accept as a coherent protest against what by 1790 were century-old capitalist practices in the grain trade. The patterns of food protests did, nevertheless, reflect strongly held notions of community justice, some codified in ancient statutes, ordinances and customary law. Countryfolk were as vehement in their defence of these values as their city cousins and most eighteenth-century food, enclosure and wage riots can be interpreted as attempts to protect popular rights and interests defined in socio-economic terms. The rituals and discipline of rioters, complete with appeals to history and tradition, gave their actions the status of semi-legal demonstrations in the eyes of JPs, who were often sympathetic to rioters' grievances (Stevenson, 1971a: 17; Jones, 1974: 27–30; Booth, 1977: 92, 105; Bohstedt, 1983: 24–6, 203–22; Snell, 1985: 99–100).

'Collective bargaining by riot', a common labour disturbance of the eighteenth century, often took the form of organised strikes. In 1792 a colliers' strike had paralysed the coastal shipping of the entire east coast, for this skilled occupational group, along with miners and weavers, had a reputation for labour militancy. Established trade unions based in London and all major provincial towns were represented by experienced lobbyists capable of petitioning Quarter Sessions meetings, urban corporations and parliament in pursuit of their objectives and who would do so in 1800 to protest against the terms of the 1799 Combination Act. This was introduced by Pitt at the urging of Wilberforce, who as a county MP for Yorkshire had been on the receiving end of manufacturer complaints about the increasing militancy of workers. There is no evidence that the government regarded existing unions as hotbeds of radicalism (Thompson, 1968: 550–1), though they may have been seen as potential engines of sedition, and Pitt told the House of Commons that the legislation was meant to prevent stoppages in the manufacturing trades that might otherwise jeopardise the success of the war against France. He and Wilberforce hoped to prevent the spread of new organised unions into the industrial North and Midlands by giving employers powers of summary jurisdiction to punish strikers, and existing unions mobilised their members to demand the repeal of the 1799 Act or, at the least, modifications to it (Rule, 1993: 113, 127–30).

London millwrights led a campaign against the 1799 Combination Law notable for the impeccable loyalism to crown and constitution displayed in the union petitions to parliament. This, the last successful campaign of the old unions, produced an amended 1800 Act permitting the formation of legal combinations under strictly defined terms. In practice the Combination Laws did not stop new union formation, collective bargaining or wage riots, all of which took place in London and provincial towns throughout the 1800s and 1810s. Artisans and their unions believed that their trades should be regulated by custom and law: by the latter they meant the protectionist legislation of the past that, now in general abeyance, gave skilled craftsmen what the unions called rights (Walton, 1987: 144–5; Randall, 1991: 273–80; Stevenson, 1992: 189–93; Rule, 1993: 115–17). Independence, though cherished by artisans, was an increasing rarity despite the survival of workshop production. In 1800, 1802, 1804 and 1811–1812 metropolitan and provincial unions demanded the enforcement of the 1563 Statute of Artificers that stipulated the employment of men who had undergone full training, as opposed to the cheap unskilled labour increasingly favoured by employers (Dobson, 1980: 48–56; Snell, 1985: 252–8; Prothero, 1979: 51).

Ian Christie has suggested that this defensive 'moral economy' mentality of trade unions militated against the radicalisation of artisan labour. While there is plenty of evidence that artisans joined both trade associations and radical societies during the 1790s, unions were unlikely, at least for labour protest purposes, to espouse a natural rights ideology advocating the perfect equality of men in the employment market. Artisans wanted either the enforcement of the Tudor legislation that defended their status as skilled labour or its replacement by more effective regulations. In 1807, Lancashire cotton weavers applied to parliament for minimum wage legislation and, when their petition was rejected, 60,000 looms came to a halt as the weavers went on strike; by June 1808, manufacturers had accepted new terms (Stevenson, 1989: 78). In 1812, Lancashire weavers, Nottingham frame knitters and West Riding wool croppers began to attack their machines in a series of Luddite demonstrations that took place over the next four years. These protests did nothing to restore the 'moral economy', for the 1812–1813 Commons Select Committee on Apprenticeship recommended the repeal of the Statute of Artificers, in 1813 the powers of JPs to regulate wages were finally abolished, and in 1815 the Assize of Bread disappeared from London (Hilton, 1977: 26–9; Prothero, 1979: 51–61; Bohstedt, 1983: 136–52).

Specific messages were encoded in the machine-breaking of the Luddites which, like all eighteenth-century English rioting, was highly selective in its targets. True Luddites did not damage buildings or other types of private property, confining their attention instead to their chosen equipment: in the case of the knitters and weavers, the stocking frames and looms of employers who refused to comply with Luddite demands for fair pay and working conditions. This discipline, however armed and sinister it seemed to contemporaries, strongly suggests that the Luddite disturbances were labour protests rather than the 'quasi-insurrectionary movement' described by E.P. Thompson (1968: 604). With the repeal in 1806 of legislation that had banned the use of gig mills, their rapid spread along with shearing frames throughout the West Riding and West Country angered shearers and croppers who had been protesting against the construction of the mills since the early 1800s. Here was a clear protest against mechanisation and there was a strong radical political element to Yorkshire Luddism, but Lancashire handlooms and East Midlands stocking frames were neither power driven nor kept on centralised premises. The chief objection to both was the high cost of their rental to domestic outworkers. Machine-breaking in all cases was related to worker frustration with low wages, the introduction of shoddy manufacturing techniques – such as 'cut up' stockings – and the corresponding employment of unskilled labour: workers in all the affected trades had long been fighting a losing battle for proper regulation of wages and work practices. In choosing the mythical folk hero Ned Ludd, King Ludd or General Ludd as their figurehead, Midlands and Northern workers were employing their own brand of radical nostalgia to articulate their dissatisfaction. The employment of 2000 troops to put down the Midlands protestors and, at one stage, 15,000 in Yorkshire, along with the application of the Luddite label to food and other riots during the 1810s, suggests that the messages were not understood by apprehensive magistrates (Hammond and Hammond, 1912; Thompson, 1968: 496–7; Bythell, 1969: 74, 76, 193, 198–9; Thomis, 1970; Emsley, 1979a: 157–9; Royle and Walvin, 1982: 101–6; Rule, 1986: 363–78; Stevenson, 1989: 79–80, 1992: 193–201).

The Combination Laws did not prevent new, or illegal, unions from flourishing in the North and Midlands after 1800, many under the guise of friendly societies. The new unions of the mills were less socially exclusive than their predecessors, needing by definition to encompass most male employees within the workplace, regardless of their social background or skills (Dobson, 1980; Rule, 1996). Women and children were excluded from the union movement despite their mass employment in the mills and, if anything, their employment there only reinforced concepts of patriarchy amongst the lower orders. Skilled labour had been gendered since the Middle Ages and the acceleration of this trend from the late seventeenth century onwards is attributable to changing notions of gender rather than the industrial revolution *per se*. The number of 'respectable' trades for working women to pursue had been declining, if trade directories are to be believed, throughout the eighteenth century, and the casualisation of female labour sent women to work instead in a broad range of menial trades: charring, laundry, hawking and domestic service. In the country, women were increasingly confined to weeding, haymaking, gathering, tying and gleaning. Colquhoun estimated that in 1803 there were 800,000 female domestic servants working in England and Wales and another 500,000 engaged in other occupations (1806: 253; Hill, 1989: 148; Snell, 1985: 56–7, 278–83, 293–4; Kowalski Wallace, 1996: 116–20). Genteel domesticity meant nothing to the poor, who needed the money that female and child labour contributed to the household income, but female guilds would not give way to female unions for skilled female labour, long in decline, was not going to the mills and manufactories of the early industrial revolution.

The food riots of 1800–1801 in Lancashire and Cheshire display evidence of some exposure to Jacobin ideas, a development attributable to the United Societies rather than any lingering or new-found sympathy for revolutionary France. References to trees of liberty, rare in riots of the 1790s can be found in Wigan and Bolton threat letters and handbills of 1800 (Booth, 1977: 104; 1983). Notwithstanding the possible survival of a revolutionary underground in south Lancashire and the West Riding after 1799, by 1815 the socio-economic hardships of war and structural change in the textile trades, rather than Jacobinism, were responsible for the increasing militancy of workers in the north-west. In 1810, a three-month strike paralysed the mills and looms of Lancashire and Cheshire, while 1812 would witness the walk-out of 40,000 cotton workers in Cumberland and Scotland (Walton, 1987; Stevenson, 1992).

Social friction between different occupational groups nonetheless remained evident at the bottom of the social ladder. Industrial towns were melting pots for the mingling of the urban and rural poor from 1780 to 1850, a purpose that the polite provincial towns of the urban renaissance had served for rural and urban elites from 1680 to 1780. The experience of town life did not, however, do more in the first instance than encourage the redefinition of social boundaries along familiar lines of rank and station. The survival of divisions between skilled and unskilled labour can be traced through the residential patterns and kinship networks of nineteenth-century 'working class' families in mining, mill and factory towns, who married and died on the streets where they had been born (O'Gorman, 1998: 342). The industrial revolution, moreover, created new occupational groups such as the highly skilled and paid mule spinners, iron puddlers and engineers who, like the shopkeepers and journalists of the consumer revolution, had to be fitted into the existing social matrix through an ongoing process of social negotiation. This took place in pubs, working men's clubs, unions and factories rather than the assembly halls and lending libraries of the urban renaissance, but nothing resembling a unitary working-class consciousness could emerge in Britain until these new trades had acquired some commonly accepted social station relative to others. While poverty and exploitation were common sufferings encouraging workers to unite and, in their labour protests, adopt a two-nations model of British society pitting rich against poor, older notions of status and hierarchy were slow to change in the lives and beliefs of British workers. When all is said and done, all members of British society found the old cosmology of a great chain more useful and realistic for the practical identification of selves and others than any two- or three-class system.

CHAPTER SIX

Ways and Means

The impact of the French wars on British business, while deemed to have been positive in that Britain emerged in 1815 with the world's strongest economy, emerges from counterfactual speculation with a negative balance sheet. Industrial and commercial development would, it is claimed by J.G. Williamson (1984, 1987), have been more spectacular, had not heavy government borrowing absorbed private-sector capital that might otherwise have been invested in business and manufacturing. Cotton and iron output grew at 7.57% and 4.1% p.a. respectively between 1760 and 1800 and, while both continued to expand during the 1790s and 1800s, fixed capital formation, states Williamson, would have been 6.4% higher, had Britain avoided involvement in the wars against revolutionary and Napoleonic France (Crafts, 1985: 23; Williamson, 1984: 702).

Williamson's thesis has been contested on statistical and analytical grounds by several economic historians and its validity depends on whether or not Britain could afford to fight and industrialise at the same time. In 1793, 6% of Britain's GDP was spent on the war; by 1815, this had risen to over 25%. During the same period the national debt rose from £228m to £876m (O'Brien, 1988, 1989a, 1989b). The fiscal and economic policies of Pittite governments will be treated in the second section of this chapter: suffice it to say here that the French wars were funded by heavy state loans and high taxation, both diverting surplus income and capital away from other uses and pushing up real interest rates until private investment was possibly reduced by government borrowing (Knick Harley, 1993: 221). No economic historian would now say that the French wars were good for the British economy. Although the empire was taking an increasing share of British goods over the eighteenth century, Europe still accounted for 40% of British exports from 1784 to 1820 (Davis, 1979: 88–9; Cain and Hopkins,

1980: 88–9). Overseas trade was not, as was once claimed, a stimulus to industrialisation in itself, for it relied rather upon British demand levels for foreign and colonial goods, but, despite the industrial sector's reliance upon home demand for expansion, periods of slump and stagnation were experienced by all trade and manufacturing sectors at some point during the French wars (Thomas and McCloskey, 1981: 100; Hudson, 1992: 187; Engermann, 1994; Berg, 1994b: 116–17). A post-war depression from 1815 to 1820 would reduce profits even in iron and cotton textiles. The French wars were a traumatic experience for British business, simultaneously hit by the onset of industrialisation and 22 years of overseas market disruption that affected domestic production sectors dependent upon foreign supplies. Opponents of the Williamson thesis point out that Britain, by 1785 already the wealthiest nation in Europe, successfully kept and built upon this lead during the French wars; however, while this is to a certain extent true, it does not entirely answer Williamson (Crouzet, 1989; O'Brien, 1989a, 1989b). In Joel Mokyr's words, 'it seems inescapable that the Industrial Revolution in Britain would have occurred faster and more efficiently if financial constraints had been less stringent' (1993: 109). To what extent those restraints were imposed by war deserves further examination.

Production, Retail and Finance

Arable agriculture was one of the few economic sectors untroubled by war and revolution, experiencing rapid growth and heavy investment from 1793 to 1815. Corn prices kept high by the closure of European markets to British shipping encouraged landowners to enclose in droves. Enclosure bills were introduced in spates following each peak in domestic corn prices: from 1800 to 1815, 800 enclosure acts were passed while agriculture's share of the British economy increased from 33% to 36% from 1801 to 1811 alone. (John, 1967; Yelling, 1977: 211–12; Deane and Cole, 1967: 141–2). Enclosure was accompanied by what was once called the agricultural revolution, by which was meant the widespread adoption of self-fertilising crops, the adoption of new farm implements and the selective breeding of heavier and faster-maturing livestock. Most of these innovations were in fact first introduced to England during the later seventeenth century. While the dating of the agricultural revolution remains contentious, all historians would agree that the enclosure boom of 1793–1815 ensured that agricultural investment would remain a major sector of gross domestic capital formation, amounting to 25% as late as 1815 (Feinstein, 1978: 31, 48–9; Clark, 1993; Overton, 1996: 14–15). Enclosure was expensive, requiring amongst other things the erection of fences, uprooting of trees, clearing of fields and digging of irrigation ditches. Rates of return were nonetheless good and quickly realised for agricultural rents rose by 90% during the French wars (Turner, 1984; Crouzet, 1989: 197–8). The opening of European ports for grain export in 1814 brought the enclosure boom and agricultural prosperity to an end. In 1815, a new Corn Law prohibited the importation of foreign wheat until the domestic price exceeded 80 shillings per quarter, in part to protect the agricultural economy against what the landed interest depicted as total ruin (Horn, 1980a: 72–3).

Enclosure, as Sir John Sinclair asserted to all who would listen, would enable Britain to feed a growing populace without excessive reliance upon foreign wheat (PRO 30/8/178, ff. 137–57). Modern historians now concur that, without enclosure, Britain would not have escaped the Malthusian population trap, for the population grew from 8.25 million in 1785 to 12 million in 1821 (Emsley, 1979a: 129; Wrigley and Schofield, 1989: Ch. 10). This is not to say that the old open-field system was unreceptive to new farming techniques, but agricultural yields in enclosed villages were from 7% to 29% higher than in their open counterparts (Yelling, 1977: 146–292; Turner, 1986: 691; Allen and O'Gràda, 1988; Allen, 1989). Investment in agriculture nevertheless diverted capital from trade and industry (Hueckel, 1981, 1986; Clark, 1993: 229–32). The traditional consumer goods trades – leather, soap, brewing, distilling, glass and paper – experienced moderate growth commensurate with population growth but were subject to high taxation that raised the prices of their products both during and after the wars. Here lies a series of trades that would have grown more in the absence of war, although none could be described as industrial with the exception of paper, thanks to the invention in 1809 of a continuous rolling mill that cut production time for a sheet from three weeks to three minutes. Little is known about the peace or wartime fortunes of many domestic trades but it can be said that the building trades suffered the most as a result of rising house taxes, steep timber prices and the diversion of capital to government loans (Chalklin, 1974: 274–303; Crouzet, 1989: 201–2; Hall, 1992: 89–90; Berg, 1994b: 50–6). Production for the home market in the clearly 'modern' manufacturing sectors of the economy – pottery, cotton textiles and small metalwares – was less affected by rising consumption taxes, but the second and third branches of manufacturing were hard hit by the closure of overseas markets during the 1790s and 1800s.

The only manufacturing sectors to derive direct benefit from the war effort were iron, shipbuilding, woollens and munitions: in the first three, government contracts went primarily to the large firms. Eighteenth-century warfare was manpower rather than equipment intensive and the demand for war materials, based upon a technology of wood and leather, did not stimulate much 'industrial' output in any European country. Food canning was introduced in 1810 to supply the army with tinned meat and soup and the Portsmouth dockyards were reorganised by Henry Maudsley and Marc Brunel, father of Isambard, to produce standardised blocks and pulleys. Here government sponsorship of industrial innovation stopped (Emsley, 1979a: 30–2; Harvey, 1992: 51; Mokyr, 1994: 33). The production of wrought iron increased by 500% from 1785 to 1815, aided by war-imposed interruptions to supplies of high-grade Baltic iron, and production costs per ton dropped from £22 to £14 between 1801 and 1815 (Hyde, 1977: 106). Only 10% of this increased output was taken by government contracts, the rest going to feed metal production for foreign and domestic markets (Crouzet, 1989: 193, 199). The state's demand for military uniforms did not, moreover, prevent a slump in woollen production, which at any rate had been growing at a much slower rate than cotton before 1793. Shipbuilding thrived on government and private-sector contracts but represented a discrete sector of the British economy which, long dependent on supply lines to Baltic hemp and timber, was subject to war-imposed delays in deliveries of its raw materials and wild price fluctuations attendant thereupon. Demand in all these sectors plummeted with the return of peace (Horn, 1980a: 58; Emsley, 1979a: 170; Ville, 1986; Crouzet, 1989).

Iron, cotton and coal were the three fastest growing sectors of the British economy during the French wars but expansion in the first and second was beset with pitfalls. Coal mining remained a purely domestic industry, as did the production of British pig and bar iron. Birmingham metalwares were hard hit by the closure of European markets during the 1790s and 1800s, though India took an increasing share of output and would compensate somewhat for the loss. From 1814 to 1816, metalwares would nonetheless account for only 8% of foreign export earnings, while wool's share would have dropped from 28.5% in 1784–1786 to 18.2% at the end of the war. Cotton was easily the fastest growing sector of British manufacturing. From 1784 to 1786 it represented 6% of Britain's exports, while by 1814 this figure had jumped to 40% (Davis, 1979: 97). Cotton, a fashionable and practical product, was inexpensive enough to be little affected by tariff barriers erected in other countries, something that could not be said for other British goods, but its complete reliance upon foreign raw materials subject to the vissicitudes of wartime shipping produced unpredictable gluts, shortages and price fluctuations (Bythell, 1969: 101–2). Confidence in a speedy return to peacetime prosperity moreover encouraged many manufacturers to overproduce in 1814–1815. When European markets did not reopen for importation as swiftly or completely as had been anticipated, bankruptcies ensued in cotton up to 1820 (Chapman, 1992: 51–6).

Although the acquisition of Dutch and French colonies during the 1790s and, a decade later, the opening of South and Latin American markets compensated British business to a limited extent for its losses in Europe, the search for new buyers and markets was not without perils. The return to war in 1803 resulted in a general scramble to find new trade opportunities outside Europe. Spectacular business losses were experienced by British merchants in Buenos Aires in 1806, followed by an equally costly and unsuccessful effort to break into Rio in 1808–1809; £18m was poured into South America through investment in recently acquired Dutch territories but the establishment of a British commercial presence in South America was a slow and painful process (Crouzet, 1959: ii, 238, 617, 695, 1989: 192–3; Platt, 1972: 3–16; Hall, 1992: 17–18, 97–8). The structure of British overseas retail trade changed considerably in response to the harsher and riskier conditions of business in far flung markets. By 1815, the general wholesale merchant of the eighteenth century would be extinct, having given way to the commission salesmen employed by the new agency houses that would dominate Britain's nineteenth-century trade with Europe and the empire.

These structural changes in British business form part of a more complex tale involving the emergence of specialised financial and retail services told by Stanley Chapman's *Merchant Enterprise in Britain: From the Industrial Revolution to World War I* (1992). Manufacturing, banking and retail had not been discrete economic sectors in 1785 for merchants based in London often underwrote bills of exchange for smaller firms, thus acting as commercial bankers, while a new breed of merchant-manufacturers had by 1785 appeared as owners of Lancashire cotton mills. The extensive involvement of north-western merchants in the Atlantic trade had been responsible for much of Liverpool's development as a rival port to London during the eighteenth century and, possessed of local facilities, merchant-manufacturers had by 1785 begun to displace the wholesale merchants. Merchant-manufacturers did not have to be giants, for smaller firms like William Radcliffe of Stockport could undercut the older houses by selling direct to buyers in Europe (Edwards, 1967: 148–9). Merchant involvement in trade and industry was equally extensive in Scotland and Wales, for the Glasgow tobacco lords had invested heavily in local textile mills, iron works, tanneries, soap works, bottleworks and sugar houses, while the emergence of South Wales iron had been funded largely by merchant capital from London, Bristol and the Midlands (Devine, 1975; John, 1950: 24–6).

By 1815 both wholesale general merchants and merchant-manufacturers would have all but disappeared. War-imposed delays in deliveries of raw materials and finished products exacerbated the international cash flow problems of both in addition to raising domestic operating costs. Under these conditions, merchant-manufacturers found it difficult to keep up both sides of their businesses and were forced to abandon either sales or manufacturing 'sooner or later' (Chapman, 1992: 61). Many general import–export merchants gave up business altogether and retired into parish gentility, where they may have sunk their capital into enclosure and estate improvement or government securities. According to R.G. Wilson: 'The aim of a wealthy merchant was to lead the life of a solid country gentleman, not to spend 15 hours a day running the largest factory in town' (Wilson, 1971: 105–7; Hudson, 1986: 262).

General wholesale merchants and merchant-manufacturers had been the leaders of Britain's export trades but by no means all business had passed through their hands. Small to medium-scale manufacturing firms had sold their wares direct to buyers through the great trade fairs at Hamburg and Frankfurt until the arrival of Napoleon's armies and 'blocus continental' closed these markets to British goods. The deceleration of economic growth rates from 1803 onwards can be blamed in large part upon the Continental System: from 1802 to 1808, the volume of British trade with Europe dropped by half, and was accompanied by declines in the ratios of foreign trade to national product and of exports to industrial output (Crouzet, 1959: 883, 1989: 193; Hall, 1992: 17). The maintenance of British commercial contact with Europe throughout the Napoleonic Wars is less attributable to smuggling, extensive though that was in the Batavian Republic (Schama, 1977: 451–4, 569–76; Crouzet, 1989: 193), than to the establishment of German merchant houses in Britain. Between 1799 and 1806, N.M. Rothschild, H.J. Merck of Hamburg, and Oppenheimer and Lippman of Berlin, turned up in Manchester seeking direct access to English textiles. The emigration of Huguenot and Jewish families to England had been taking place for over a century, having accompanied the emergence of London as the premier trade and money market in Europe and, by 1763, 77% of the firms listed in *Mortimer's Universal Directory* of metropolitan firms had partners of foreign extraction (Neal, 1990: 188–90; Chapman, 1992: 30). From 1799 to 1812 a steady stream of German Ashkenazi Jews came to England in search of British and colonial goods.

This migration of persons and capital to London had been taking place since the outbreak of the revolutionary wars and was not confined to retail: the most important arrivals, from the government's point of view, were the merchants who had begun to diversify into banking and possessed established financial contacts in Europe. Walter Boyd, born a Scot but very much an international capitalist and one-time Paris banker, set up Boyd, Benfield and Co. in 1793 while the Anglo-Dutchman Henry Hope removed from Amsterdam to London at the end of 1794, just ahead of the invading revolutionary armies. Francis Baring was a second-generation

Anglo-Dutch Huguenot wool merchant whose family had settled in Exeter. All three men and N.M. Rothschild, once he moved to London in 1806, were chief contractors for the state loans of the French wars while Baring's and Rothschild's became major merchant banks to boot (Cope, 1983; Neal, 1990: 182–90; Chapman, 1992). The arrival of these bankers and merchants had several important repercussions, most notably the injection of foreign capital into the British economy and the national debt. Not only did the presence of the Continental houses improve financial intermediation between Britain and Europe, a development appreciated by successive governments when it came to making remittance payments to their armies and allies abroad, but the activities of European merchant bankers based in London included the selling of British state securities abroad. In 1806, £14.38m in the Three Per Cent Consols alone were recorded by the Bank of England as owned by overseas investors exempt from British income tax and, in 1813, only £1m of the subsidies Britain gave to its Sixth Coalition allies were said to have been transferred from England (Wright, 1997: 658, 673). The rest came from the payments of Dutch, Austrian, German and Russian investors in the £30m Three Per Cent issue of that year. Larry Neal suggests that Rothschild's succeeded where Boyd, Benfield and Co. had failed a decade earlier: in financing the war against France 'with the resources of the Continent mobilized through the London capital market' (Neal, 1990: 189–90, 182–200, 213–18). A complex web of international banking and brokerage relationships once dominated by Amsterdam, but after 1794 increasingly run from London, made Britain the premier capital market in Europe, while the Royal Navy's command of the sea ensured that the metropolis became the principal European centre for trade with America, the West Indies, Russia, the Baltic and Latin America.

This triumphalist tale was not without its own personal and corporate failures in the City. Banks and stockbrokers dealing in public securities would appear to be the chief beneficiaries of high government borrowing but, even here, bankruptcies were not unknown. During the 1790s Boyd, Benfield and Co. had led the syndicate of City financiers who were the chief contractors of the 1794–1797 state loans, thanks to links with European financial houses that facilitated the remittance of monies to the Austrian government and armed forces; but the firm, having incurred heavy losses on its holdings of government stock, closed early in 1800 (Cope, 1983). It was succeeded by a consortium of brokers led by Nathan and Samuel Goldsmid, Francis Baring and John Julius Angerstein. While Baring's Bank and the Rothschilds flourished through the sale of public and private sector credit, the Goldsmids were less fortunate in their transactions, and both brothers committed suicide during the later 1800s. Samuel's death in 1810 sparked off a panic on the London Stock Exchange and the market crash that ensued denoted the beginning of a major trade slump from which Britain would not recover for another two years (Cope, 1942: 191–200, 203–6). A restructured London stock exchange itself would emerge from the French wars as the undisputed leader of European capital markets (Neal, 1990: 206–18). Despite these disasters, the state never lacked buyers for its loans at home or abroad and, while overseas buyers never owned more than 10% of the national debt, their purchases of British bills and securities on an increasingly international money market constituted a form of investment in British trade and manufacturing that took some of the debt and investment burden off the native business community. Patrick O'Brien (1989b) points out that the increase of the debt carried with it economic benefits: the encouragement of impersonal investment habits; experience, for both individuals and the financial community, in dealing with paper assets; the improvement of financial intermediation and, with them, the evolution of banking and brokerage facilities. Williamson's emphasis upon 'modern' manufacturing and overseas trade as the chief constituents of capital investment may be misplaced, and academic interest is shifting to the City and domestic trade. A.D. Harvey (1992: 25–8), utilising income tax returns, stamp duty records and public works accounts, suggested that domestic trade and manufacturing, protected by the Channel from the ravages of war, experienced healthy growth at the expense of foreign trade and, in particular, Lancashire cottons.

New retail practices were required by British firms to cope with new trade opportunities overseas. By this is meant the rise of the agency houses and sales on commission. The direct purchasing practices of German firms were replicated by the British, who stationed commission agents in Europe and South America to sell goods on behalf of domestic manufacturers. Competition for buyers in South and Latin America was fierce amongst commission agents and, when the East India Company's monopoly expired in 1813, Glasgow, Manchester and Liverpool manufacturers would rush to institute commission sales in South Asia. Profit margins were high in the agency trade and little capital outlay was needed to set up an agency house, for most business was done on credit, for which these firms relied upon the merchant banks. This branch of British finance was not, as the preceding paragraphs might suggest, monopolised entirely by international houses, for many larger London firms of overseas merchants had acted as part-time commercial bankers before the French wars (Ashton, 1959). Those choosing to deal entirely in commercial credit, as opposed to actual commodities, endorsed bills of exchange signed by the agency firms, thereby providing them with the credits to send abroad. The banks did not lend much money for fixed plant or other business development, and British firms, like their European counterparts, were largely self-financing during the eighteenth century (Mokyr, 1993: 108–9). Both Baring's and Rothschild's had started life as textile trading houses but found that more money was to be made in merchant banking: from 1790 to 1806, the gross assets of Francis Baring, reputedly one of the wealthiest men in Britain, grew from £74,000 to £450,000 (Chapman, 1992: 54). Merchant banks would provide the financial support network for the expansion of British trade in the nineteenth century.

The French wars, though cruel to the older branches of British overseas trade, were kinder to British shipping. Napoleon's Continental System might exclude British commerce from Europe but, by the same token, excluded Europe from the wider world, for by 1793 Britain was already pre-eminent in the non-European carrying trade and would acquire a virtual monopoly of worldwide shipping during the Napoleonic Wars. The domestic coasting trade, sailing in the well-protected waters around the British Isles, almost trebled during the war. In 1790, coastal shipping had accounted for 25.9% of all British shipping. By 1824 that figure would have reached 35.9% (Harvey, 1992: 39). Overseas trade also grew: the size of the British merchant marine fleet doubled from 1786 to 1815 to reach 2.6 million tons, a growth rate that would not be surpassed for another quarter century (Ville, 1986: 11–12).

This process was not without cost, for enemy privateers roamed the seas, marine insurance was expensive and the risks of trade were increased in wartime (Fayle, 1948a: 42–3). Although the Admiralty urged the merchant marine to travel in convoy, this mode of transport was slow and did not provide complete protection against enemy attack or mishap. Delays of one to three months in sailing were also common and those unwilling to wait for naval escort sailed alone with predictable results. The London firm of Michael Henley and Son lost five vessels between 1795 and 1797 alone (Ville, 1986: 11–13). In 1798, a Convoy Act forced all but the fastest and most heavily armed merchant vessels to travel in convoys containing anything up to 600 ships. After the Transport Board was set up in 1794, firms could rely on a regular income from government contracts, but this did not entirely compensate them for the strains of wartime commerce and this was reflected in changing ownership patterns. In 1787, only one quarter of 300 vessels on London foreign trade shipping registers possessed one owner, for the sale of shares in English ships was a time-honoured way to spread the risks and costs of overseas trade. By 1815, owners whose primary business lay elsewhere would have disinvested from shipping and the 'modern' shipping firm that owned all its vessels would have emerged (Crowhurst, 1977; Ville, 1986: 3–5, 22).

Neither trade nor manufacturing were heavily taxed, which is just as well in light of their other problems. Merchant and manufacturer interest in the Friends of Peace movement of 1808–1812 is not to be wondered at in light of the sufferings experienced by British commerce. No economic historian disputes that government loans diverted some national income away from fixed capital formation: the question is how much. Conflicting theories of growth and decline complicate the picture: according to some estimates, the economy grew quite quickly during the 1790s and slowed down during the 1800s before recovering during the 1810s. Others claim that economic growth picked up during the 1800s and then faltered during the 1810s. No impressive growth can be seen until the 1820s (Deane and Cole, 1967: 282; Feinstein, 1978: 91; Crafts, 1985: 46–7; Crouzet, 1989: 202). It is not clear how much of a barrier lay between investment markets: those who bought government securities did so from private savings while productive investment in trade and industry was undertaken by business capital. The levels of both remained relatively stable, if low, throughout the French wars, while real interest rates do not appear to have risen dramatically (Mokyr and Savin, 1976: 209; Knick Harley, 1993: 221–3). François Crouzet has also pointed out that the fiscal and monetary policies of the Pitt ministry encouraged private saving and investment while the suspension of cash payments by the Bank of England in 1797 facilitated the grant of commercial credit to business and industry. The 1799 income tax fell lightly on the profits of trade and manufacturing, if not land, and the ability of business to remain self-financing was not severely damaged (Crouzet, 1989: 203–4). Patrick O'Brien, Michael Bordo and Eugene White have argued that the Pitt ministry taxed incomes, and thus consumption, rather than savings and investment: a policy that minimised the impact of public borrowing upon capital investment (O'Brien, 1989b, 1993; Bordo and White, 1991).

British business, despite its sufferings, became more competitive and entrepreneurial over the 1790s and 1800s but the rise of the agency houses, the emergence of merchant banking and the injection of European capital into the British economy must be counterbalanced against the very real disinvestment and non-investment that took place during the period. Although Britain during the nineteenth century would become the 'workshop of the world', it would be unwise to regard this as an inevitable development. All Europe's economies were devastated by the wars and, if Britain fared better than the others by virtue of its island status, overseas empire, diverse manufactures and well-developed commercial and financial infrastructure, there is no doubt that its economy could have grown at a faster pace without the French wars (Crafts, 1977; Landes, 1994: 144–7). Whether or not this would have been good for Britain, all things considered, is a question best left for the social historians to answer.

Wartime Demands and Fiscal Expedients

On 17 February 1792, Pitt promised Britain fifteen years of peace in a budget speech that joined a requiem for the late Adam Smith to a series of tax reductions inaugurated on 31 January. So generous were the tax cuts on leather, candles, carts, wagons, female servants and houses possessing fewer than seven windows that Paine claimed the proposals had been stolen from Part II of the *Rights of Man* before its publication (1996: ii, 519–23). Although this is highly unlikely, for Pitt had been contemplating tax cuts since the previous summer, there was an ideological agenda to his tax reforms. The British constitution, likened by Pitt in his 17 February speech to a vast and complex machine for distributing wealth and ensuring happiness to all sectors of society, would, he claimed, ensure the continued liberty and comfort of Britons in perpetuity. Excise taxes had long constituted the state's chief source of revenue for paying the interest on the public loans that financed its wars and, by introducing tax cuts in a speech that predicted fifteen years of peace for Britain, Pitt was making the point that the British constitution was more protective of liberty, property and prosperity than French liberty. On 9 November 1792 he was contemplating the further reduction of 'Taxes on Leather – Salt . . . Candles – Lowest sort of Hats' – goods consumed by the largest cross-section of the British public – before deciding to suppress domestic sedition and prepare for foreign war. 'It is indeed mortifying', he wrote on 17 November when authorising the recruitment of troops and seamen for the defence of the United Provinces, 'to be exposed to an interruption of a career the most promising that was ever offered to any country.' By this he meant the prospect of peaceful and continued debt reduction while war and revolution reduced France to ruin (PRO 30/8/198, #4, f. 109; Clements MS, Pitt to Dundas; Grenville, 1853: ii, 222–4).

Pitt's expectations of a short war governed the fiscal policies pursued by the British government from 1793 to 1797. Money continued to be set aside for the redemption of the national debt in accordance with plans devised during the 1780s to liquidate the state's accumulated liabilities over a 35-year period (O'Brien, 1989a: 171–6). Pitt, whose commitment to debt reduction was sincere, really did not want war with France or anybody else. Up to 1797, he relied upon loans to fund the government's military expenditures and raised taxes only to cover the additional interest charges on the national debt. Luxury and consumer goods bore the brunt of increased government borrowing up to 1798 and the 'necessaries of life', most notably food, remained exempt from a tax burden that, in theory, fell heaviest upon the rich. In reality, by 1790 only 18% of the government's revenue came from taxes upon land and immobile wealth, for the British people, thanks to a widespread net of indirect taxation imposed on consumers, were three times more heavily taxed per capita than the French (O'Brien, 1988).

During the first two years of the war alone, £36m was raised by loan finance, a level of public borrowing that horrified George Rose, Joint Under-secretary at the Treasury. In September 1795 Rose was writing in the wake of a second consecutive bad harvest and widespread food rioting that the British people would not bear further rises in taxes (W. Suffolk RO, HA T108/44, Rose to Tomline). To make matters worse, a Bank of England concerned about mounting levels of short-term state borrowing was demanding cuts in military spending to keep the state's liabilities in line with existing gold reserves. Government debt fell into two categories: the long-term or irredeemable debt; and the short-term debt, namely the Navy, Ordnance and Exchequer Bills that funded the ministry's day-to-day expenditures. When radical journalists like Cobbett referred to the national debt, they meant the long-term annuities so attractive to private investors. The short-term government bills were similar to the bills of exchange employed by merchants: in essence promissory notes possessing the status of negotiable securities (Cope, 1942: 186–7). The Bank's directors, determined to preserve a safe ratio of bullion to overall levels of private and public sector short-term credit, demanded deflationary action from the Treasury, by which was meant cuts in military spending, to maintain the convertibility of sterling. Such remonstrances were found irksome by a Cabinet still hoping for a swift victory, and when Austria, Britain's last First Coalition ally, was defeated by France in 1796, some other solution to the government's financial problems had to be found (Cooper, 1974; O'Brien, 1989a: 178–80; Ehrman, 1983: 524–8, 617–22).

Either the government or the Bank had to reduce their issues of short-term bills to maintain safe ratios of credit to bullion and Pitt was reluctant to see a contraction of either. In March 1793 the Bank of England had issued a special series of Exchequer Bills to bail out merchants unable to source commercial credit in the wake of the government's return to war. This assistance would be given to the commercial community again in 1797, 1807, 1808 and 1811. In 1793 the Bank had set a limit of £50,000 per firm upon the underwriting of mercantile bills, and any further contraction of private-sector credit by the Bank was frowned upon by Pitt on the grounds that it would raise a chorus of business complaints against the government and possibly reduce tax revenues from manufactured goods. In February 1797, a run on the Bank's gold reserves triggered by news of the French landing at Fishguard prompted Pitt and the Directors to suspend cash payment in gold. Now that sterling was not convertible, both the banks and the government could issue as many short-term bills as they pleased. The chief danger of suspension lay in the removal of a brake to wartime inflation but this did not rise dramatically after 1797, remaining constant at 3.3% throughout the French wars (Emsley, 1979a: 29; O'Brien, 1989a: 242; Neal, 1990: 198–9; Ehrman, 1996: 7–16).

The final failure of the Anglo-French peace talks at Lille during the autumn of 1797 convinced Pitt to abandon loans for a 'new system of finance'. From 1689 to 1783, 80% of Britain's wartime expenditure had been funded by state loans with the result that, when Pitt came to power, 40% of the Exchequer's annual revenue was already earmarked for the service of the perpetual debt. By 1797, that debt stood at £427m and Pitt, who still hoped to pay it off after a peace he saw as two years in the offing, decided that a higher proportion of the government's income had to come from taxes. Two new projects came forward in 1798: the Triple Assessment, which trebled existing taxes on land and a range of luxury goods; and the Sale of the Land Tax, an incentive offered to landowners to contribute to the Consolidated Fund, the sinking fund for the redemption of the national debt that had been set up in 1786 (Fortescue, 1892–1927: iii, 322–3; Ehrman, 1969: 258–69; Mather, 1992, 145–8). This, to which £1m in tax revenue was given every year throughout the French wars, bought existing government stock from the London money market and allowed it to accumulate revenue that, subject to the operation of compound interest, would in time wipe out the long-term debt. Few individuals were interested in the land tax project despite the offer of relief from the payment of the land tax for the next quarter century: the annual yield of this tax, calculated Pitt, was roughly equal to the simple interest that would be earned by lump sum contributions to the sinking fund (PRO 30/8/278, ff. 5–8; PRO 30/58/7, f. 151). Despite Pitt's best efforts to prop up Consols, the fund only worked if the state did not borrow and, by the end of the war, the sinking fund had ceased to perform its function because the government was paying more interest on the money that went into the fund than the fund earned to redeem the debt (Ehrman, 1996: 258–76).

In a series of six finance articles written between November 1797 and July 1798 for Canning's *Anti-Jacobin*, Pitt tried to educate the public in the basic principles of taxation, public credit and debt redemption. Full payment of the Triple Assessment was solicited as a patriotic duty and aid to public credit that would reduce the borrowing requirements of the state by £8m (AJR, 1797: #1, 16–19; #2, 44–6; #3, 85–91; 1798: #12, 391–5; #25, 224–7; #35, 583–94). In 1796 the Treasury had raised £18 in 36 hours for a Loyalty Loan, and Pitt hoped that the British people would come forward once more to support the war effort with voluntary contributions above and beyond the monies they owed the state under the Triple Assessment. Calculations of 1798 indicate that Pitt was still anticipating a swift conclusion to the French wars, to be followed by a generation of high taxation and debt redemption. In spite of his best efforts to convince readers that public credit was as much a pillar of the British constitution as the crown and the church, the Triple Assessment brought in only £1.67m of an anticipated £10m. The Sale of the Land Tax, whose yields were estimated at £3m, produced only £435,885 for the Consolidated Fund in its first two years of operation. Pitt, now baulked of debt-redeeming capital and war-financing revenue, turned his attention next to direct taxation (PRO 30/8/ 197, ff. 51–2; Rose, 1911: 331–3; Mather, 1992: 146; Ehrman, 1996: 259, 271).

The 1799 Property Tax was easily the most unpopular tax of the French wars. Direct taxation was not in itself new for the old Land Tax, traditionally levied in wartime at 4 shillings in the pound, had been collected for a century on the basis of outdated and inaccurate valuations of real estate. The 1799 property tax, imposed on a sliding scale of incomes from £60 upwards, started at 5% and rose to 10% on incomes over £200 p.a. The tax was entirely reliant upon self-assessment until 1803, and so poor were early yields of the tax that the 1801 census, Britain's first, was commissioned to form an accurate estimate of income distribution for tax assessment purposes. In 1803 the Property Tax would be revised by Addington to tax government employees and owners of state securities at source. Addington has been called the 'father of the modern income tax' (Ziegler, 1965: 189–94) because of this innovation but such deductions did not affect the vast majority of British taxpayers. The income tax would produce 80% of the extra revenue raised from taxes after 1798 and 28% of all money raised for the French wars. Despite the Treasury's attempts to impose some central control over the collection of the tax, evasion was widespread and some regions were subject to regular and incompetent under-assessment (O'Brien, 1989a: 181–5).

The income tax, like its predecessor the Land Tax, was administered by amateur country gentlemen. Unlike the Land Tax, assessments of real estate now reflected contemporary market values with the result that the tax fell heaviest upon fixed assets of readily calculable wealth: land, houses, mines and government securities. Equally productive for successive wartime governments were stamp duties levied upon legal documents, such as the marine insurance surtax of 1795, for these too were difficult to evade. Schedule A of the income tax, the profits of land, produced four times the amount returned under Schedule D, the proceeds of trade, industry and the professions. Some sources of income were, and remain, more amenable to creative accounting than others. Trade and industry managed, on the whole, to escape the worst effects of the income tax, although foreign trade suffered more than its domestic counterpart: in Lancashire, Schedule D returns dropped from £2.24m in 1803 to £1.58m in 1812, a set of figures bearing testimony to the sufferings of merchants and manufacturers during the later stages of the Napoleonic Wars (Harvey, 1992: 33).

The Chancellors of the 1800s and 1810s – Addington, Petty, Perceval and Vansittart – did little to modify the policies laid down by Pitt during the 1790s. They inherited more from their master than a set of guidance on loan finance, taxation, debt management and monetary policy. The fiscal policies of 1798–1800 represented a hardening of Pitt's attitudes towards the war and Britain's role in it, incorporating a political economy of the French Revolution that had been taking shape since 1792. From 1787 to 1797, Pitt had assumed that revolutionary France was bound for fiscal and economic ruin in the wake of the social and political upheavals that had devastated its economy. The survival of the first republic into the later 1790s was for Pitt inextricable from its military success as a European imperial power, the subjection of occupied states and sister republicans to command economies providing France with money and war materials. The suspension of allied trade relations with France, written into the 1793 First Coalition Treaties and revived in the 1806–1807 Orders in Council, constituted more than an effort to starve the enemy into submission. They also embodied an official conviction that free commerce, upheld by Britain and its constitution, supported an economic and political order at home and abroad ethically superior to a French republic or empire founded upon conquest and plunder (Rose, 1799: 7, 39).

Ministerialists subscribing to this political economy of the French Revolution were staunch defenders of Pitt's fiscal and monetary policies throughout the French wars, and the Liverpool ministry would retain the sinking fund until 1827 out of deference to his memory despite the fact that the fund had long ceased to redeem any debt. Pitt's fiscal and monetary policies began to acquire sacred status during the 1811 Commons debates on the report of the Bullion Committee. Here divisions between the Christian and classical political economists began to appear. In 1810 a dramatic rise in the price of gold coupled with a sharp fall in the price of the paper pound on European exchanges prompted parliament to commission an enquiry into the monetary policy of the Bank of England. A shortage of small coin had been a chronic problem since 1660, thanks largely to a Bank policy devised in 1717 by which issues of lesser denominations were discouraged to conserve bullion stocks. Silver coinage almost disappeared in the eighteenth century, a situation with which manufacturers, merchants and Thomas Spence coped by producing copper coins and tokens. The switch to paper currency only exacerbated this problem and by 1809 coin was in such short supply that overseers of the poor began to issue their own tokens as money (Pressnell, 1956: 15–24; Fevearyear, 1963: 147–64; Hilton, 1988: 222–5; Emsley, 1979a: 151; O'Brien, 1994: 236–7).

David Ricardo led calls outside parliament for an immediate return to the gold standard in *The High Price of Bullion* (1810) but the all-party Bullion Committee, chaired by the Grenvillite MP Francis Horner, was more cautions in its recommendations. The committee, which included Canning and William Huskisson, agreed that the resumption of cash payments was essential to avert the spectre of runaway inflation. The sixteen resolutions presented by Horner to the House of Commons represented a watered-down version of the committee's conclusions, for its members had hoped for government acquiescence in its demands; Horner therefore spread the blame for the devaluation of sterling, citing foreign exchange fluctuations, the trade slump, state military spending and the Bank's over-issue of paper money. What Horner, Huskisson and Canning actually believed was that the Bank was morally obligated to maintain fixed standards of cash and credit and that, in failing to do so, it was arbitrarily redistributing the nation's wealth and property (Fontana, 1985: 119–23).

Rose and Chancellor Vansittart, as hostile to deflation as Pitt for much the same reasons, defeated Horner's resolutions by denying the relevance of his monetary theory to the realities of money management. In their determination to maintain private-sector confidence both in the government and in the price of sterling, they appealed to evangelical ethics as dictates superseding what they referred to as Horner's sterile theories of political economy. Most MPs, as it transpired, understood neither version of political economy and voted for the government on the grounds that it best understood its monetary policy. Having gambled on swift victory in the Peninsula, the Perceval administration had committed most of its scanty bullion reserves to this theatre and, when they were gone, gold was sought from places as distant as India, China and Mexico. Exchequer Bills were employed by Wellington in lieu of hard cash but, by 1813, these had flooded European money markets and were passing at 25% discount. In 1815, £69.8m in Exchequer Bills, a sum representing half of Britain's annual revenue, would be circulating in Europe. Any resumption of cash payments in 1813 would have required the government to bring its military spending into line with a Bank of England ratio of public credit to gold (Sherwig, 1969: 222–5, 255–8, 263–4; Duffy, 1982; Hall, 1992: 20–1; Harvey, 1992: 36–7, 72; Neal, 1994: 170).

Paper money was, in truth, one of Britain's most powerful weapons of war and would, in the form of the special 'federal paper' created in 1813, finance the launch of the Sixth Coalition (1812–1815) against Napoleon. This experiment, soon abandoned for bullion subsidies and the assumption of allied war debts, nevertheless reflected the strength of the Liverpool ministry's conviction that paper served as an adequate, if short-term, replacement for gold (Sherwig, 1969: 289–90, 301–4). After 1815, the government's continued reliance upon Exchequer Bills was necessitated by a backbench revolt that abolished the income tax in 1816, leaving the ministry to fund a budget of £30m with only £12m in anticipated revenue; 55% of tax revenue now went to debt servicing (O'Brien, 1994: 210). Ministers had believed that peace and the resumption of normal trade relations with Europe would bring a return of steady economic growth. Overseas markets did not, however, open to British commerce as quickly or completely as had been anticipated. In 1815, the national debt stood at £921m and, deprived of the income tax, Vansittart resorted once more to indirect consumption taxes, which did domestic manufacturing no favours and fell heavily upon the poor (O'Brien, 1989a: 184–6).

Overinflation was more of a problem after the war than during it, for the continued issue of Exchequer Bills as a substitute for real money kept commercial interest rates abnormally high. Bullion had always possessed a 'sacred' status amongst Liverpool Tories for it symbolised a free and prosperous economy in addition to a fixed or 'moral' standard of exchange. Despite the government's rejection of the 1810 Bullion Report, all its economic policies from 1815 to 1820 were intended to facilitate the transition from an inflationary wartime economy to its stable peacetime counterpart through a return to gold (Hilton, 1977). By 1818, Liverpool had concluded that the resumption of cash payments could not be put off any longer, both to promote economic recovery and to maintain business confidence in the government. Government finance was nonetheless in a parlous state: in 1819 the budget could be balanced only by the imposition of £3m in new taxes and a £12m raid on Pitt's Sinking Fund. In the same year Ricardo, having recently become an MP, led a Commons select committee on public finance and currency that recommended a return to cash payment no later than 1823. This took place two years earlier than anticipated and, at the same time, import duties were reduced in preparation for a return to freer trade. By 1822 the budget could be balanced without cooking the account books and a new Chancellor could begin to reduce taxes (Hilton, 1977: Ch. 2, 1988: 222–4; O'Brien, 1989a: 186–7).

The Liberal Toryism of the 1820s was as much practical as ideological in focus. Ricardian political economy appealed to the government in part because it justified economic inertia and inaction, but for Christian political economists, Adam Smith's laws of supply and demand were divine moral dictates requiring recognition from the state. For Huskisson, trade was a diplomatic instrument for the promotion of international goodwill and harmony in Europe and the empire, particularly in the colonies, where non-exploitative commerce would encourage western-style economic, political and moral development. The repeal of the Navigation Acts was nonetheless brought about in a slow and halting manner that owed as much to cautious negotiation between vested trade interests as to theoretical conviction. Much of this, including the caution, could be read into the trade and economic policies of the 1780s but, much as Huskisson worshipped Pitt, the dead premier had never possessed his successor's religious convictions nor his intellectual dogmatism (Fay, 1951: 61–6, 71–3; Hilton, 1977: 70, 180–201, 307–14; Mandler, 1990a: 24–6). Political economy had, moreover, come a long way since the 1790s and theories of rent, money and population now accompanied laws of supply and demand as abstract rules by which market trends might be interpreted. Their use by the politicians and statesmen of the 1820s indicates in part a growing awareness that the complexity of Britain's economy and society defied simple explanation and required informed, if not yet professional, analysis and superintendence.

Strategic Aims and Military Objectives

Insofar as the Pitt ministry possessed a grand strategy in 1793, it involved the reduction of France to its 1789 borders, the breakup of the Bourbon maritime empire and the maintenance of Britain's strategic, economic and political position *vis-à-vis* the Low Countries. While these objectives remained consistent over 22 years of war, they shifted in priority of importance in response to Britain's often poor military and diplomatic fortunes. Much British strategy of the French wars was in fact reactive rather than proactive, particularly in Europe. The British army left the Low Countries in 1795, not to return to mainland Europe in force until 1808, when it launched the Peninsular War against Napoleon in Portugal and Spain. Here it would remain until the end of 1813 and the British never played more than a peripheral role in the business of fighting the revolutionary and Napoleonic armies in Europe. The Royal Navy, whose supremacy at sea was never challenged, in contrast fought France almost single handed in a long and gruelling war of blockade against privateers, enemy warships and, in 1808–1809, a Baltic armed neutrality that placed great strains on a navy already overstretched to meet its commitments in Europe and the wider world. When the war was going badly for Britain, as it often did, statesmen and strategists turned their thoughts to India, the Caribbean and South America, but even in overseas theatres, victory was by no means easy or assured. Britain emerged in 1815 with seventeen new colonies but its status as the world's pre-eminent imperial power owed less to the success of

British arms than it did to a Continental System that, by destroying occupied European trade with the colonial world, concentrated that commerce in Britain's hands.

Before embarking upon a survey of the strategic, diplomatic and economic priorities governing the British way of warfare, it is important to understand the material and manpower restraints facing Pitt, Dundas and their successors. The British army, only 39,000 strong in 1793, was held in poor esteem in European military circles, for it had seen no serious action since the early years of the Seven Years War and had been defeated in America. The eighteenth-century British army, best described as an amphibious strike force employed for the taking of various forts, ports and islands, had long been an auxiliary in European campaigns for which Britain preferred to buy German mercenary troops. Its chief duty on the eve of the French Revolution lay overseas in the defence of Britain's colonies where 24,000 of its troops were stationed. The British army of 1793 to 1795 lacked discipline and experienced commanders, performed poorly in the field and was not missed by Britain's allies when it left Europe at the end of 1794. The army was, moreover, plagued with logistical problems of supply, recruitment and transport that would not be solved until the later 1800s. An acute shortage of manpower was already evident by 1794: hence the government's decision to create the volunteer corps for home defence that year, to introduce Quota Acts in 1795 requiring counties to raise men for the army and navy, to create a supplementary militia in 1796 and to establish a provisional cavalry in 1798 (Cookson, 1997: 28–9). These succeeded in creating an adequate defence force for Britain, but no real success against the revolutionary armies would come until the 1801 Egyptian campaign that evicted the remnants of Napoleon's army from Palestine. By the time the army began to perform effectively, the revolutionary wars were over (Mackesy, 1989: 155–6, 1995; Harvey, 1992: 128–9; Hall, 1992: 27–49).

The British army began to come of age in the Peninsular War of 1808–1814. A new drill manual introduced in 1792 had restored order and discipline to the infantry, while a new generation of commanders with battle experience acquired in the colonies, of whom Arthur Wellesley, Duke of Wellington, was most famous, had come forward to replace an older generation of American war veterans and senior generals who had never seen battle. Wellesley never lost a single battle during the Peninsular campaigns, a success attributable to the pursuit of a conservative holding strategy in Portugal until 1812 when Napoleon, distracted by Russia, stemmed the supply of reinforcements to Massena's armies, thus giving Wellington and his Hispano-Portuguese auxiliaries more even odds against the French. By the end of 1813, the French would have been driven from Spain (Mackesy, 1989: 163–4).

By the end of 1814 the British army numbered 187,000 infantry and cavalrymen, supplemented by 26,000 British and foreign artillery and 51,000 foreign and colonial troops. The navy commanded 144,000 seamen and marines while the militia numbered 300,000. The infantry, long drawn from jails, debtor's prisons and Ireland, was referred to by Wellington as 'the scum of the earth' and required careful training and strict discipline to prepare them for active service (cited in Harvey, 1992: 152–3). The navy relied instead upon the recruitment and impressment of merchant seamen, who came from the aristocracy of labour. There were, in addition, half a million part-time volunteer units in Britain. This mobilisation rate of one in ten adult males compares favourably to those of Britain's allies and represents the largest proportion of military-age men in active service hitherto seen in British history (Mackesy, 1989: 152–6; Emsley, 1989: 138–9; Harvey, 1992: 133, n. 44).

Britain entered the war in alliance with Spain and the United Provinces, giving the First Coalition an overwhelming numerical advantage against a revolutionary navy whose 94 battleships were bottled up in French ports by Anglo-Spanish and Anglo-Dutch patrol squadrons from 1793 to 1795. When Spain and the United Provinces surrendered to – and allied themselves with – France in 1795, the scale tipped against Britain, whose 115 capital ships were now pitted against an additional 76 Spanish and 49 Dutch vessels. To compound matters, 40% of Britain's ships were undergoing repairs or refitting at any point in the war, which left the Royal Navy struggling to cover its blockage, convoy and watching briefs in the Channel, North Sea, Atlantic, Caribbean, Indian and South Pacific Oceans. Despite an overhaul of dockyard support services and the continuation of a naval building programme begun during the 1780s, the fleet remained short of frigates, sloops and brigs throughout the war. During the 1800s ships were built of inferior or even unseasoned wood, which rotted quickly (Mackesy, 1989: 151–3; Hall, 1992: 29–32). The permanent shortage of patrol ships was one of the factors determining the maintenance of a distant blockade. Although enemy supply convoys and squadrons occasionally slipped through the net, requiring thereafter to be tracked down and engaged, distant blockade represented a more efficient deployment of precious vessels than the close blockade, only adopted when invasion threatened Britain. Fortunately for the Royal Navy, enemy capital warships seldom emerged from port and, when they did, were successfully defeated at St Vincent (1797), Camperdown (1797) and Trafalgar (1805) (Hall, 1992: 81–6). In 1799 the Royal Navy would carry off the Dutch fleet from Helder, thus ending its threat to maritime security in home waters.

British attacks upon French mainland port installations had been successful during the Seven Years War and, in 1793, Pitt had wanted to launch amphibious expeditions against Brest and Toulon in the hopes of crippling the French North Atlantic and Mediterranean fleets. These plans had been mooted in confidence rather than fear of enemy naval power but, by the end of 1794, when similar plans for the capture or destruction of the Dutch navy were under discussion, the scales of naval power had begun to tilt against Britain (Mori, 1997a). In 1807, the Royal Navy would bombard the Danish fleet in Copenhagen harbour, thus removing one fleet from possible deployment by the French. Odds were furthered evened by the 1808 Spanish rising that denied Napoleon the use of another major fleet. Men-of-war, the floating gun platforms of eighteenth-century navies, were essential for the protection of smaller vessels on blockade, convoy or courier duty. French capital warships were larger and more solidly built than their British counterparts, although the latter were faster and carried more guns: so many that the lower gunports of British warships could not be opened in heavy seas for fear of swamping the vessel. Britain's naval superiority over France lay not in the quality or number of its ships and guns, but in the calibre of its seamen, and one of the government's greatest fears was the seduction of the navy from its duty by popular radicals (Harvey, 1992: 52–4).

'Persons reading Payne's Book in the dockyards', wrote Pitt apprehensively at the end of 1792. Seamen, amongst the most highly skilled workers in Britain, had a reputation for militancy and labour solidarity long predating the outbreak of the French Revolution (PRO 30/8/198, #4, f. 115). They were often reluctant to serve in a navy where they would receive one-quarter of their civilian wages, for the base pay of able-bodied seamen had not changed since the days of Charles II. This grievance drove the sailors of the Channel Fleet to mutiny at a time when a possible French invasion, coupled with an escalation of the navy's coastal, Channel and North Sea convoy duties, were placing severe strains upon the fleet. The Articles of War, the code of naval discipline giving captains autocratic life and death powers at sea, were not seemingly an issue for the sailors in the Channel Fleet, who accepted that harsh standards were necessary in wartime, announced that they would fight if the French put to sea and treated their officers with respect throughout the mutiny. Theirs was a strike for better pay and work conditions. The North Sea fleet contained a higher proportion of Irish seamen (30%) more likely from exposure to the UI to associate institutionalised naval discipline with social injustice: the Nore mutineers' formal demands included the right to cashier officers for misconduct (Wells, 1983: Ch. 6; Gill, 1913; Mainwaring and Dobree, 1935; Stevenson, 1992: 185–7; Ehrman, 1996: 17–32).

The army, which might well have sympathised with the mutineers, was placated by the grant of a pay rise in the spring of 1797. The influence of the UI does not seem to have been strong in the army for, despite the fact

that it was half-comprised of Irishmen, there were no mutinous disturbances in Britain's land forces throughout the French wars. By 1814 the
army was truly British and imperial: indeed, only 20% of its rank and file
men were English and to the Scots, Welsh and Irish under arms could be
added colonial troops raised in Canada, the West Indies and India. The
East India Company had its own army, which remained separate until
1857, but the company's practice of raising native sepoys trained to European standards was adopted by the regular army with some success in the
West Indies. Black slaves, first employed as militiamen in 1793, rose to the
status of regulars in 1795 and, in 1807, were collectively emancipated as a
reward for military service (Buckley, 1977). The navy was international,
containing non-British volunteers or men often impressed from the merchant marines of neutral nations, a practice for which the Royal Navy
made no apologies. The army had always been regarded by the British
government as an auxiliary to the forces of its European allies, but the navy
was central to a strategy of oscillation between the Continent and the
colonies that reflected the realities of a war fought, for the most part,
without active allied assistance in which naval and colonial warfare were
the only, if often ineffective, routes through which to strike at France. This
was no special British way of warfare (Liddell Hart, 1936) but rather a
second-best strategy determined by chance and diplomatic circumstance
guided by a pre-existing need to protect Britain's communication lines to
the wider world. By 1803, however, all British statesmen accepted that their
empire could only be enjoyed in peace and security if the war was won in
Europe (Mackesy, 1989: 159).

By Accident or Design? British Global Warfare, 1793–1801

In June 1793, when the allied armies of the First Coalition were pouring
into France from several directions, Pitt and Dundas devised an ambitious
military strategy requiring the raising of 15,000 fresh troops for rotation
amongst four theatres of war: Flanders, the Mediterranean, the Caribbean
and the East Indies. Pitt, reluctant to go to war throughout 1792, was now
determined to replicate the lightning strike successes of his father during the
Seven Years War (1756–1763). Chatham, however, had come to office a
year after the outbreak of war with France and, with a reliable Prussian ally
in Frederick the Great, could draw battle-hardened British troops from
Germany for service overseas. In 1793, the Duke of Richmond, Master
General of the Ordnance, cautioned the premier against committing raw

recruits to an arduous tour of duty that sent them to three overseas stations in six months. In advising Pitt and the Cabinet to concentrate its resources upon Europe, Richmond fell foul of Home and Colonial Secretary Henry Dundas, whose determination to destroy the French maritime empire and make Britain 'the paramount naval and commercial power in Europe' would squander British manpower and resources on a trio of costly West Indian expeditions during the 1790s (Rylands MS 907, Dundas to Pitt, 29 June 1793, ff. 8–9; Duffy, 1987, 1991).

The British government's intention of taking indemnification for its war costs overseas formed part of a wider punitive project to strip France of all its peripheral territories, be they in Europe or the wider world, for assignation to the safe keeping of Britain and its First Coalition allies. Colonial conquests could, moreover, be returned to France at the peace table if necessary in return for the evacuation of occupied territory in Europe, not that this was a major consideration in 1793. An essentially colonial military strategy governed the thinking of the Pitt ministry throughout the 1790s, extending even to the planning of British operations against France. The Dunkirk expedition of 1793 and the Helder expedition of 1799 were amphibious assault operations intended, with French royalist or Dutch resistance help, to capture and hold bridgeheads for the landing of troops and supplies. Pitt did not, as E.D. Adams claimed in 1904, go to war for the sole purpose of acquiring colonies from France, but the scale of Britain's overseas military operations during the French wars begs the question what role the empire played in British military strategy and official world views. For Vincent Harlow (1940, 1952) the later eighteenth century witnessed a 'swing to the east' away from the Atlantic colonies and the conscious establishment of a second British empire where a spirit of benevolent and vaguely liberal metropolitan custodianship gradually succeeded the spirit of free enterprise that had governed the first empire. Christopher Bayly (1989) dates this shift to the period between 1780 and 1830, denying it a liberal spirit altogether, while Michael Duffy (1998) places it specifically in the 1790s.

Before the 'swing to the east' could take place, the West Indian islands, described by Dundas in 1793 as 'the first objects to make certain', had to lose their status as the jewels in the British and French imperial crowns. St Domingue, now modern Haiti, was split in 1793 between France and Spain. It was also the richest colony in the world. The near loss of Caribbean naval superiority to the French at the end of the American War had demonstrated that the established British colonies of Jamaica, St Kitts and Barbados were vulnerable to enemy attack. The British islands were worth only £4.25m per annum (1784–1786), as opposed to the average £8.25m in sugar, coffee and cotton produced by the French West Indian islands

(1784–1790), and Dundas was intent on the acquisition of St Domingue, Martinique, Guadeloupe and Tobago to give strategic security to the British Caribbean and end the career of France as a colonial re-exports competitor in the European marketplace. Such small and lucrative islands made attractive targets in what was foreseen as a short war, all the more so as French royalist planters hostile to the revolution had appeared in London at the end of 1792 in search of British protection against the reprisals of the National Convention. On 19 February 1793, the Pitt ministry agreed to take and hold St Domingue for future restoration to the Bourbon crown, an arrangement that Dundas, at least, regarded as renegotiable at the peace (Duffy, 1987: 6–16, 27–32, 1998: 186–7).

Dundas has been criticised by many military historians as an unrealistic and overambitious military strategist. The two West Indian expeditions of 1793–1794 and 1795–1796 fell prey to the poor logistical planning and inadequate recruitment, training, supply and transport facilities that plagued the British throughout the first few years of the war. Neither expedition left England on schedule and sent white troops with no natural resistance to tropical disease off to fight in the malaria season. Disease, not battle, was the killer of soldiers and seamen in the Caribbean and 62,000 soldiers met their deaths from yellow fever in the West Indies (Duffy, 1998: 188–90). To compound the manpower problems of the British, French planter assistance was soon lost following the failure of the 1793 St Domingue royalist revolt and when, on 4 February 1794, the National Convention emancipated all slaves in the hopes of raising black manpower for the defence of the French West Indies, the spectre of slave revolt spread to the British islands. The slaves of St Domingue, led by Toussaint l'Ouverture, had risen in 1791 to claim the liberty and equality of their white French brethren, and the appeal of black republicanism, which blended the rhetoric of revolutionary freedom with African traditions of magic and tribal custom, proved irresistible to the slave populations of Martinique and Guadeloupe, not to mention the British islands of Grenada and St Vincent acquired from France in 1763. The 1795 West Indian expedition, intended in part to suppress these risings and the rebellion of Maroon free creoles in Trelawny Town, Jamaica, was meant, as Dundas put it, 'to extirpate disaffection in its seat' (Rylands MS 907, Dundas to Pitt, 30 June 1795, f. 8). British whites, outnumbered six to one by negroes, Amerindians and mixed-race creoles were demanding the protection of their estates and colonial status from the British government in London. Proposals to emancipate British slave troops as a reward for voluntary military service died in Cabinet meetings of 1795, killed in part by planter fears that any concessions to the black population would only exacerbate the revolt. Had the emancipation project been approved, it might well have solved Britain's manpower problems in the Caribbean, but freedom would not be offered to slave troops until 1807, by which date metropolitan thinking about the West Indies had changed (Buckley, 1977; Geggus, 1982; Ehrman, 1983: 359–61, 564–6; Duffy, 1987: Chs. 5–6, 1991).

By 1795, British strategy in the Caribbean was as much defensive as offensive. The British sugar islands, however, escaped the mass slave revolts that engulfed their French neighbours in civil war and devastated their plantations. For this reason, St Domingue was by 1800 of no economic value to France or Britain. The Dutch East Indian empire had taken the place of the French West Indies as the primary object of strategic importance outside Europe. In 1795, when Spain and the United Provinces left the war, the fate of their overseas possessions became a matter of serious concern to Dundas. The possible cession to France of these colonies, most importantly the Cape of Good Hope that guarded the sea route to India, threatened to cut Britain off from its own Asian settlements, and the British army was withdrawn from Europe at the end of the year to take the Cape and Ceylon before they fell into French hands (Duffy, 1998: 191–2). This mentality was defensive rather than offensive and, having realised that war in the Caribbean was an expensive and unprofitable exercise, Dundas abandoned his West Indian imperial ambitions. A final and third expedition of 1796–1797 secured Spanish Trinidad and the Dutch colonies of Demerara, Essequibo and Berbice on the South American mainland for use as bargaining counters at the peace table, while the signature of a 1798 non-aggression pact with l'Ouverture promised to leave St Domingue free from British assault and, more importantly, protect the British islands from the influence of black republicanism. The Pitt ministry pursued a holding strategy in the Caribbean for the rest of the war. As the Second Coalition against France in Europe took shape in 1799, the Cabinet's attention turned back to the Low Countries and Mediterranean, where Napoleon's conquest of Italy and activities in Egypt were arousing concern about the security of India (Ehrman, 1996: 143–5, 609–10).

In 1793 Dundas had sought no more than the eviction of the French *Compagnie des Indes* from its coastal 'factories' at Pondicherry, Chadernagore, Karikal and Mahé. The British government, smarting from the loss of America, had spent the 1780s in a state of acute apprehension about France's supposed designs upon British India and these insecurities were revived upon the appearance of Bonaparte in Egypt. The Royal Navy, having been withdrawn from the Mediterranean in 1796 following the collapse of the First Coalition, returned in 1798 to win the Battle of Aboukir Bay but did not prevent Napoleon from escaping back to France. His plans for India, as such, had gone no further than the possible invasion of Afghanistan, and the fears of Dundas were more indicative of British paranoia about the security of India than of any genuine French threat. Considerable attention would be devoted to the acquisition and defence of Mediterranean bases for the rest of the wars with France and, in 1801, a British expeditionary force of 12,000 men sent from India would expel the French from Egypt (Black, 1994: 92–9; Mackesy, 1957: 154–99, 1995; Duffy, 1998).

The assumption of tax collection and administrative powers by the East India Company (EIC) in 1765 had transformed it from a trading firm into an Indian territorial power, embroiling it in the politics and diplomacy of the subcontinent in a manner little to the liking of successive British governments. The company's military and administrative commitments in Bengal, Bihar, Madras and the Northern Circars had by 1770 become too complex for effective control by its directors and shareholders in London. Pitt's 1784 East India Act placed the EIC under state supervision by setting up a new infrastructure of management that would rule India up to 1857. By leaving the company's business affairs and powers of appointment in the hands of its Court of Directors, the act struck a balance between the EIC's rights as a private trading firm and the duties it owed to the state as a representative of the British crown in India. The crown-appointed Governor General's executive powers over the company's Indian stations in Madras, Bombay and Calcutta were considerably strengthened, while at home a new Board of Control gave the ministry a consultative role in the formulation of company policy. Dundas, the board's first President, did his best during the 1780s to separate the EIC's commercial concerns from its administrative functions but was unable to establish a discrete sphere of metropolitan responsibility for India. He met more success, in conjunction with Governor General Cornwallis (1785–1798), in stabilising and reforming the company's bureaucracy and finances. Pitt's famous Commutation Act of 1784, which lowered the *ad valorem* duty on tea from 200% to 25%, helped boost the EIC's profits and the Treasury's tax revenues, while the 1793 Permanent Settlement introduced in India fixed the company's land tax revenues at predictable, if high, levels (Marshall, 1987: 122–7; Bayly, 1989: 116–20; Lawson, 1993: 128–31; Bowen, 1998).

The EIC could not, under the terms of the 1784 Act, engage in offensive warfare but this it had rarely done in the eighteenth century. The British and French had instead played supporting roles as bankers, mercenaries and arms suppliers to Indian potentates jockeying for power, position and territory against a backdrop of declining Mughal imperial power. By virtue of its financial and military relationships with Indian princes, the EIC had acquired a degree of influence that, in the 1765 Treaty of Allahabad, was translated into formal recognition as territorial power (Marshall, 1993, 1998). Between 1765 and 1799, when the EIC went to war with the French-backed Tipu Sultan of Mysore, the company had fought three wars against its Indian neighbours. The Maratha Confederacy of Muslim powers had long been apprehensive about the growth of EIC power on the subcontinent and, in 1799, would join forces with Tipu to drive the British from India.

By 1800 the British and French companies had long been operating as players in a great game belonging to the history of South Asia rather than the military or diplomatic history of western Europe. Although France could send little practical aid to its ally, neither Tipu nor the Marathas made tame enemies for the adoption of European military tactics had evenly matched the Maratha army with that of the EIC in the wars of 1775–1778 and 1780–1782. Under the leadership of Governor General Richard, Marquis Wellesley, the 90,000-strong company army of sepoys would overpower Tipu in 1799 and destroy the Maratha Confederacy by 1804. Wellesley was determined to make the company dominant on the subcontinent (Ingram, 1981; Duffy, 1998: 197–9, 201). None of this strategy beyond the containment of Tipu, had, however, been planned by Wellesley and the new Governor General arrived in 1798 guided by little more than personal ambition and instructions to contest French intrigues amongst the Indian princes.

The EIC's Indian wars of 1799–1802 were won, much as the Napoleonic Wars would be won in Europe, on the strength of Britain's credit. Up to 1765, the company had been a net importer of specie operating with a negative balance of trade, for Indian buyers were not much interested in English textiles or manufactured goods. The acquisition of the *diwani* tax collection rights from the Mughal crown had, however, changed the company's economic relations with India. When the EIC began to milk its new territories for money, it became a net exporter of specie and the bane of its Indian neighbours, who on paper possessed revenues equalling or surpassing the company's Rs 70m (£7 million in 1793) but lacked the machinery to collect it (Ray, 1998: 516–17, 522). The efficiency of European bureaucracy amazed Indian people and princes alike, for company taxation had bled Bengal dry during the 1770s, exacerbating the effects of a famine that killed one-third of the population. The Permanent Settlement stabilised land tax levels in India and, in so doing, created a new order that extended the protection of British property law to subjects who complied with its terms. Landowners unable to meet the company's tax demands were forced to sell their properties, but this trend concentrated land ownership in the hands of a local elite prepared to accept the mixed blessings of British rule. Most importantly for the purposes of war was the credit the Permanent Settlement gave the company on the Indian money market and, on the strength of the company's revenues, Wellesley could raise Rs 10m (£1m) locally in 1799 to bail out the indebted company stations of Bombay and Madras (Marshall, 1987: 140–59; Ray, 1998: 517).

During his seven years as Governor General, Wellesley would improve the company's financial position through additional annexations of territory. The acquisition of Mysore, the Carnatic and part of Oudh would extend the company's sphere of governance to two-thirds of the Indian subcontinent and raise its annual revenues to Rs 150m (£15m). Further operations against the Dutch East Indies during the Napoleonic Wars would result in the acquisition of Macao and Java for Britain by 1810 (Parkinson, 1954; Ray, 1998: 522). By 1813, when the EIC lost its monopoly on trade to the Far East, it had ceased to rely on commerce as a source of revenue and made the transition from trade to dominion (Lawson, 1993: 137–43). This, nonetheless, had been attributable to defensive warfare for the protection of existing British colonies rather than offensive operations against revolutionary or Napoleonic France. Dundas had great plans for India and the empire but they would not be realised under his leadership, and the extent to which his colonial policy from 1784 to 1805 constituted a conscious and practical strategy of empire-building is a moot point.

From 1780 to 1830, largely under the leadership of Pitt and Dundas, Britain reorganised its management of a vast formal and informal empire. In Bayly's eyes, this 'second empire' was governed by a new ethos of conservative custodial rule based upon a code of professional and paternal imperial service derived from Enlightenment cameralist notions of efficiency, Anglican evangelical fervour and Cannadine's rise of the upper classes (Bayly, 1989: Chs 5–6). This, partnership of *nobleme oblige*, evangelical missionary zeal and Enlightenment conviction that Britain's duty as a world power lay in guiding the commercial, political and moral development of the 'barbarian' cultures and societies under its rule, created a new spirit of overseas imperial mission that, in its policies and practices, was similar to Napoleon's First Empire in Europe. The Bayly thesis is too complex and wide ranging in its implications to receive detailed analysis here but a few points about it can be made from a study of Pittite war policy.

The short war mentality governing the thought of the ministry during the 1790s predisposed both Pitt and Dundas to concentrate upon the acquisition of small and easily acquired colonial outposts of commercial or strategic value, either for retention or for use as bargaining chips at the peace table. This strategy, if anything, favoured the growth of informal empire and most of the seventeen colonies picked up by Britain during the French wars were acquired in defence of trade routes and existing settlements. Although Dundas had plans for India, these did not in themselves produce Britain's 'swing to the east': the catalyst was the surrender of the United Provinces to France in 1795. The naval war from 1794 to 1801 in the eastern seas was not a brilliant success (Parkinson, 1954). By 1803 ministers had realised that the war with France was a contest of endurance and consequently scaled back their colonial operations to concentrate on Europe. So reluctant were ministers to send reinforcements to distant waters that Calcutta merchants suffered terrible losses from French-backed privateering until the appearance of four enemy frigates in 1807 forced the metropolitan government to send troops and ships to the East Indies, in so doing taking the Isles de Bourbon and Mauritius. The War of 1812 was fought, for the most part, by Canadian troops until 1814, when Napoleon's surrender finally freed the British army for overseas service (Hall, 1992: 95, 187–9, 197–8).

Britain's colonies during the 1800s and 1810s were left largely to fend for themselves. The extent to which an anti-Jacobin conservative agenda governed the rule of those colonies outside the West Indies, not to mention the extent to which such a policy was directed from the metropolis, is a moot point. Individual colonial governors might well hate revolutionary France and surround themselves with the panoply of quasi-feudal and regal authority, but this is better seen as a product of general elite insecurity rather than a deliberate policy of conservative imperialism (Bayly, 1989: 134, 160; Colley, 1992). With little in the way of reinforcement forthcoming from home, particularly during the Napoleonic Wars, the willingness of colonial servants to use any tools at their disposal for the reinforcement of their 'proconsular despotisms' is not to be wondered at, nor is the tacit acceptance of such stratagems on the part of a metropolitan government that, in its lack of manpower and resources to control Britain's domestic peripheries, had smiled upon the formation of Reevite associations and volunteer corps. The degree to which imperial pragmatism was driven by a conscious or subconscious ideological agenda is debatable and will be debated for years to come.

Towards a Grand Strategy, 1803–1815

The factories of the *Compagnie des Indes* were formally restored to France at the Peace of Amiens, though no transfer of power was ever to take place for, by late 1802, the Addington ministry was fearful of suspected French designs upon Egypt and instructed the EIC's officials not to restore Pondicherry to France. When Britain went back to war with France in 1803, its colonial and European objectives were better defined than they had been during the 1790s. To a new territorial settlement for western Europe, unveiled to Russia during the Third Coalition negotiations, was the reacquisition of key French and Dutch colonies for retention at the peace. By these were meant the Cape and Ceylon, retaken in 1805–1806, and Tobago, retaken in 1809. The status of the United Provinces as a satellite of France dictated the seizure of the other Dutch colonies upon the outbreak of war, but the French West Indies were left alone until 1809 when Martinique and, in 1810, Guadeloupe were taken in a series of small-scale operations manned by colonial troops. These islands, plus the Dutch colony of Java, would be returned to their original owners in 1815, though in 1805 it was already clear that extra colonies would be held for negotiation purposes by Britain.

The principle governing the selection of colonies for permanent retention was strategic utility rather than economic or territorial expansion. When the war was going badly for Britain in Europe, Dundas would dream of acquiring permanent trade bases in South America (1798–1799) to compensate the country for its European losses. These ambitions were revived in 1805 following the success of an independent attack on Buenos Aires commanded by Sir Home Popham from the Cape of Good Hope (Mackesy, 1984: 84–6, 125–7; Ehrman, 1996: 795–6). To reinforce Popham's position, a supporting expedition of over 11,000 men was sent to Chile and La Plata in the hopes of wresting them from Spain. Britain and its colonies had long been carrying on a semi-legal trade with Spanish South America, a commerce that the seizure of Trinidad in 1797 had been intended to protect, while schemes for New Orleans, mooted as early as 1790, had been geared towards the acquisition of a base for the commercial penetration of North America. Melville's 1805 impeachment for suspected embezzlement in his capacity as Secretary of the Navy would remove him from the government, and the failure of the 1805–1806 Chilean expedition, complete with the loss of Buenos Aires, put an end to British plans for the direct penetration of Spanish America. England's gold, trade and territorial empire were all resented and envied by would-be allies, who interpreted reluctance to fund their troops or lack of interest in east–central Europe as a cunning plan to limit Britain's participation in the land war while wreaking havoc on the maritime empires and treasuries of other powers (Harvey, 1978b; Duffy, 1989: 137, 1998: 193–5). The maintenance of a strong France in Europe was regarded by Austria and Russia as a necessary restraint to the power of Britain, and the British would not be regarded as serious contestants in the Napoleonic Wars until they made a major military commitment to Europe.

This did not, in European eyes, materialise in the Peninsula, regarded by the other powers as a sideshow throughout the war. Britain's gold and willingness to give up colonies for the sake of a lasting peace were, from 1813 to 1815, far more powerful incentives for the formation of the last two allied coalitions than Wellington's activities in Spain and Portugal. Only at the Battle of Waterloo did Europe realise that the British army had come of age. This scepticism is not to be wondered at in the first instance, for Lord Arthur Wellesley's 1808 Spanish expedition had been diverted from Cuba at the last minute to answer the call of a Junta of Seville determined to resist annexation to Napoleon's First Empire. Perceval, soon to be prime minister, was not enthused about the prospect of a Peninsular war nor, for that matter, was Sir John Moore, who soon arrived to take supreme command of the British expeditionary army in Portugal. Moore was, however, killed during the evacuation of Corunna and his successor, Wellesley, believed that Spain was a worthwhile military gamble because it would tie down French troops in south-west Europe and possibly influence the outcome of the war. The Portland government nevertheless remained attracted to the amphibious assault schemes that had served Britain well in the past and would send expeditions to the Caribbean and Low Countries with mixed results. The Antwerp (1808) and Walcheren (1809) expeditions ended in dismal failure.

The Peninsular war was no public relations blessing for the Perceval ministry. While Britain could be presented at home and abroad as an enemy of French tyranny assisting a 'legitimate' government and oppressed people to overthrow the tyranny of Napoleonic rule, the early failure of the British army under Moore and Wellesley to make much headway against the French was highly embarrassing, as was the 1809 Convention of Cintra that evacuated the defeated General Andoche Junot and his men from Portugal aboard British ships. Wellesley, soon to be Viscount Wellington, had been shielded from the scandal by the government despite the fact that he, as supreme commander, was officially responsible for the convention and the blame fell instead upon the head of his second in command, Sir Hew Dalrymple. Wellesley, whose reputation as a successful commander had been made in his brother's Indian wars, was too valuable a hero to be tarnished by the Cintra episode and, as Lord Wellington, would help legitimate the war, the army and the aristocracy in the eyes of the British public (Spence, 1996: 76–85).

Pittites had gone to war in 1804 assuming that Napoleon would, sooner or later, become unpopular in Europe. Although the rejection of Joseph Bonaparte by the Spanish in 1808 seemingly confirmed this thesis, Wellington pursued a cautious and defensive strategy intended to conserve troops until 1812, when the departure of the *Grande Armée* for Russia gave him an opportunity to attack the French with more even odds. Until then, he could do little but defend his Portuguese bridgehead and wrangle with the legitimist governments of Spain. From 1809 to 1812, the Portuguese army, trained to English standards, was integrated into the British armed forces and 45,000 Portuguese regulars would fight alongside the British in the liberation of Spain. The Spanish made more unreliable allies, for their resistance movement was hopelessly divided on ideological and political lines and their leaders were disinclined to trust Wellington: not until 1814 would he be made commander in chief of the Spanish armies in a regional revolt against the central Cortés. In 1810–1811 it had seemed as though Wellington's army would be swept into the sea, for the French had overrun most of Spain and, despite the high costs of guerrilla warfare against the Spanish *partidas*, subdued local resistance to the French presence. Neither Wellington nor his masters in London could do more than wait until Europe rose against Napoleon, but once this took place he was quick to strike. By 1814, the duke would have retaken Spain and invaded southern France.

In 1815 Britain would return almost all its conquests to France and some territory to the Dutch, its government having realised that some rejuvenation of allied maritime and commercial power outside Europe had to be permitted for lasting peace to be achieved. Both the Dutch and French empires had, however, been destroyed by a Continental System that had cut off colonies from Europe. The grant of the once Austrian Netherlands to the Dutch in 1815 with Britain's blessing could not conceal the fact that the Dutch East Indian empire was gone, for the British kept Ceylon, the Cape of Good Hope, Essequibo, Berbice and Demerara and retained its recently acquired trade rights in Spanish and Portuguese South America. In 1793 Britain had set out to destroy a French West Indian empire that, by 1800, had been ruined from within, while the Dutch empire in the East Indies and South America had replaced the French Caribbean in British strategy as much by good fortune as by design. The new colonies Britain had won during the revolutionary and Napoleonic Wars had come from hard choices made from the limited military options available to British statesmen in the conduct of a long, frustrating and often unsuccessful war against France (Duffy, 1998: 203–6).

CHAPTER SEVEN

Pragmatism and Policy

Britain and Europe, 1785–1791

Britain emerged from the Napoleonic Wars in 1815 as a joint architect of the Vienna peace settlement and master of the world's largest empire. This was the last fate anyone would have predicted for it in 1785. Recent defeat at the hands of revolutionary America, aided by a Bourbon France seeking revenge for the humiliations it had suffered during the Seven Years War, had reduced Britain to the ranks of a second-class power saddled with a £242.9m war debt and no allies in Europe. Eight years later, when Britain went to war with revolutionary France, much had been done to revive its international standing and it has been customary to attribute this to the diplomatic and economic policies of the Younger Pitt. When subjected to critical assessment, the successes of Pitt's first decade in office can be attributed as much to fortuitous economic and diplomatic conditions as to prudent and far-sighted policy. Neither the signature of an Anglo-French 'free trade' treaty in 1786, by which England and France agreed to accept each other's exports on a most favoured nations status, nor the establishment of the Consolidated Fund for the redemption of the national debt, in themselves rejuvenated the British economy, though they did much to establish domestic financial and commercial confidence in Pitt. The 1788 Triple Alliance between Britain, Prussia and the United Provinces was the product not of superior British diplomacy during the 1787 Dutch Patriot revolt, but rather of French executive paralysis stemming from the breakdown of relations between crown and nobility coupled with Frederick William II of Prussia's desire to find western European support for his designs upon

Poland (Black, 1990: 223–33, 1994; Murphy, 1982: 432–5; Schama, 1977: 25–75, 79–135; Blanning, 1986: 54–72; Henderson, 1987–8, 1990).

Britain's international recovery during the mid- to later 1780s was primarily attributable to the financial and political problems of France. British diplomats and statesmen rejoiced in the impotence of the Bourbon crown without any sense of what was to come and in fact spent the decade worrying about the suspected designs of France upon what remained of the British empire. Pitt, though not a bellicose statesman by nature, saw Britain and France locked into an inexorable rivalry of military, diplomatic and commercial interests on the Continent and in the colonies, in which occasional truces might be negotiated, but no genuine resolution of differences could take place. The Eden Treaty was one such temporary respite from the longer-term contest, and represented a mutual search for better relations on the part of Pitt and French foreign minister Choiseul. Pitt saw such commercial talks as a low-risk alternative to conventional power politics through which Britain could re-enter the theatre of international relations but was under no illusions as to the identity of France as Britain's natural enemy.

This distinction between conventional diplomacy and its Enlightenment counterpart was not recognised by Pitt's first Foreign Secretary, the Marquis of Carmarthen: from 1790 the Duke of Leeds. Carmarthen, obsessed by the spectre of Bourbon French intrigue with other courts against Britain in Europe, was consequently determined to maintain an assertive international presence from 1783 onwards. His chief interest lay in the creation of a strong anti-Bourbon alliance network headed by Britain, a project that Pitt rejected up to 1788 on the grounds that entangling alliances would commit Britain to military and diplomatic obligations it was in no financial position to honour. Commercial pacts, on the other hand, promoted peace and harmony at low cost without forcing Britain to defend the territories or interests of other states (Gilbert, 1974: 323–49; Black, 1985, 1994: Chs. 2–3; Mori, 1997b: 55–6).

Carmarthen, for whom an associative balance of power was an ideal to be achieved by traditional defensive alliances, never understood Pitt's interest in the trade negotiations with France, Spain, Portugal and Russia launched during the 1780s. Only Portugal and France agreed to Pitt's commercial blandishments but this did not stop him from attempting, in 1787, to launch a series of talks on the possible Europe-wide abolition of the slave trade, another initiative dismissed by Carmarthen as naïve idealism. Since 1784 the Foreign Secretary had been prodding Pitt to authorise action against French subversion in the United Provinces, where the rebel Patriot Party was planning to overthrow the stadtholderate of William V in favour of a return to pure republican government. In 1786, following repeated requests from Carmarthen and Sir James Harris, British ambassador at the Hague, Pitt agreed to subsidise the loyal Dutch Orange Party with Secret Service funds. Neither this, however, nor the British mobilisation of 23 warships during the autumn of 1787, was enough to secure the victory of the Orangists over their foes. Had not a concerned Frederick William sent Prussian troops to quell a Dutch rising deserted by its ally, the French army, the outcome of the Patriot crisis might have been very different (Ehrman, 1969: 520–38).

The Triple Alliance of 1788 was intended by the British to protect western Europe from the threat of French aggression. Had the Patriots deposed the stadtholder successfully, the United Provinces would have fallen into the diplomatic orbit of France, an event that Carmarthen was determined to avert at all costs. France, allied to every major power in Europe, looked superficially strong despite the fact that it had been conducting a defensive and reactive foreign policy since 1763. France nevertheless continued to act as the arbiter of Europe, a role its alliance system was constructed to serve. This defensive diplomatic strategy was not abandoned when France went to the aid of revolutionary America: indeed, French assistance for the Thirteen Colonies had been predicated upon the assumption that no state would come to Britain's aid and this analysis was borne out by the declarations of war against Britain made by Spain and the United Provinces in 1779 and 1780 respectively. In the aftermath of the American war, a strong and influential France was very much feared in British diplomatic circles and this fear of France explains Britain's official response both to the outbreak of the French Revolution and to the possible restoration of the Bourbon monarchy during the 1790s (Cobban, 1954b: 121–8; Ehrman, 1962; Schama, 1977: 64–94; Mori, 1997b: 56–9).

Pitt and Carmarthen were delighted by the 'noble revolt' of 1787, which promised to render the French crown temporarily impotent in the international arena. The British government, determined to exploit this welcome respite from normal diplomacy, devoted its foreign policy during the years from 1788 to 1791 to the construction of what has been called 'Pitt's federative system', a network of alliances through which Carmarthen hoped Britain would replace France as the power broker of Europe (Lord, 1915: 162). This ambition was apparent to French politicians and statesmen who, by 1789, had fallen prey to the same kinds of paranoia that had dominated British views of France during the mid-1780s. On 20 July, the British government was accused by the French foreign ministry of having encouraged the Jacobin Club to participate in the storming of the Bastille (Browning, 1910: ii, 250). Carmarthen's reply not only denied any British involvement in French politics, but declared that Britain was officially neutral to the revolution. In truth, most British ministers were sympathetic to the revolution, if only because the continuation of internal disputes over constitutional reform promised to keep France powerless in Europe and the wider world (Black, 1987, 1994: 361–405).

Carmarthen believed that the paralysis of France and the conclusion of the Triple Alliance gave British diplomats good grounds for 'strutting about Europe with an Air of Consideration unknown to us for some Time' (BL Add 28063, 1790: f. 156). Pitt, on the other hand, was hoping that the recall of Jacques Necker as Comptroller-General in September 1789 would result in the establishment of a 'free constitution' in France and the reopening of abortive 1787 negotiations concerning the abolition of the slave trade (Fortescue, 1892–1927: i, 353). These were not views he was willing to share with French diplomats, particularly royalists. When the Comte d'Artois, the youngest brother of Louis XVI, appeared in London a month later in search of support for the counter-revolution, he was rebuffed by a premier who nevertheless asserted that Britain would not oppose an *ancien régime* restoration of Louis XVI. The leaders of the British government, not excepting George III, had no love for the old French monarchy and the statement was made both to reassure the French crown and to protect Britain from future Bourbon reprisals in the event of a successful counter-revolution (Mori, 1997b: 68–72).

No spectator of the revolution would have predicted in 1789 that Louis XVI would lose his head in 1793, and British uncertainty about the outcome of events in France was a strong incentive for the maintenance of a strict neutrality. During the autumn of 1790, Pitt outlined in a memo three possible political settlements for post-revolutionary France: an *ancien régime* restoration, a constitutional monarchy and an independent American-style republic (FO 72/19, ff. 139–65). The ministry was considering the viability of an alliance with Spain despite its recent and mortifying confrontation with Britain over trade and settlement rights in the Pacific north-west. Upon hearing of the losses suffered by Captain Robert Meares at the hands of the Spanish fleet in 1789, the government had ordered a partial naval mobilisation in the hope of securing a formal apology, an offer of compensation to Meares, and Spain's official acceptance of a British presence on the coast of what is now the Canadian province of British Columbia. Crucial to the success of Pitt's gunboat diplomacy in the Nootka Sound crisis was the non-intervention of a France making the transition from absolutism to constitutional monarchy. In August 1790 a National Assembly intent on wresting control of foreign policy away from the king voted to transform the Bourbon Family Compact into a National Compact. Spain responded by searching for another primary ally in Europe (Norris, 1955; Evans, 1974; Black, 1994: Ch. 5; Mori, 1997b: 86–90).

Carmarthen's chief objective in the diplomacy of the 1780s was to entice Austria away from its 1756 alliance with France. The Habsburg crown, though long dissatisfied with its French connection, was cool towards British offers of friendship throughout the mid-1780s, and the disappearance of France from the ranks of active diplomacy encouraged the British government to attempt a usurpation of its influence in the east, an initiative that would result, in 1791, in the collapse of the Triple Alliance and the return of Britain to isolation. The Triple Alliance was not the tool with which to construct a federative alliance system. Britain operated throughout the eighteenth century as what Jeremy Black has called a 'satiated power', a state with no European territorial ambitions of its own, and this predisposed successive British governments to support the territorial *status quo* in western and central Europe. Prussia, in contrast, was an expanding state whose monarchs sought security in the south and east at the expense of Austria and Poland. Britain was the wrong power to look to for assistance in these enterprises, a fact which became apparent as early as 1788, when Britain and Prussia offered to help resolve two related Russian conflicts in the Baltic and the Balkans: Austria and Russia having declared war upon an Ottoman Porte allied to Gustavus Adolphus of Sweden (Black, 1988; Schroeder, 1994: 59–60).

While the Pitt ministry sought a return to the *status quo* in the north and east, Frederick William hoped for acquisitions of Polish territory as part of any putative peace settlement. No progress was made on the mediation front until 1790, when the British government admitted that modifications to the *status quo* might be made on behalf of the Austrians in Moldavia and Wallachia. Turkish compliance was to be sought by promises of admission to the Triple Alliance. Russia, having been deserted by its Austrian ally, grudgingly accepted an Anglo-Prussian brokered peace. Prospects for its successful conclusion were heightened, at the end of 1790, by a Polish request for admission to the Triple Alliance, in pursuit of which the Poles were prepared to make territorial concessions to Prussia. The acquisition of Thorn and Dantzig had long been sought by Frederick William and the realisation of the project seemingly committed the British government to a new distribution of power in eastern Europe.

Joseph II of Austria had died in 1790 and Leeds, determined to secure Austrian membership in the fast-expanding British alliance network, sent the Earl of Elgin to Italy in November to woo the soon-to-be Leopold II. In March 1791, however, Russia upset all the calculations of Pitt and Leeds by refusing to accept Anglo-Prussian proposals for the evacuation or demilitarisation of

Ochakow, a Crimean fort lying at the junction of the rivers Bug and Dniester. Here lay the origins of the Ochakow crisis which resulted in the resignation of Leeds and the collapse of the Triple Alliance. Pitt, intent in the first instance upon forcing Russia to abandon Ochakow, tried to mobilise the Royal Navy in support of the Prussian army, only to discover that independent backbench MPs were by no means enthusiastic about the prospect of war with Russia. Pitt's majority shrunk to 80 votes, after which the armament was abandoned (Lord, 1915: 178–89; Ehrman, 1969: 542–51, 1983: 3–41; Webb, 1980; Black, 1994: 276–326; Schroeder, 1994: 79–82; Mori, 1997b: 95–8).

Britain's failure to arm its fleet and its consequent withdrawal from eastern European diplomacy over the summer of 1791 amounted to desertions of Prussia and the federative alliance system. Neither the Poles nor the Turks were interested in union with a power that had failed to check the expansion of Russia, while Frederick William, apprehensive that Poland was next on Catherine the Great's list of conquests, abandoned Britain and turned to Austria in search of effective military and diplomatic support. Elgin found himself fobbed off by Leopold and was recalled to London in August 1791. The failure of the Ochakow armament left Britain isolated at a time when European opinion was turning against the French Revolution. The 1791 French constitution had not been finalised without resistance from Louis XVI and the now combined powers of Austria and Prussia, in search of international support for what would become the second partition of Poland, sought western European aid for this project through the famous Pillnitz declaration that promised to restore Louis XVI to all his pre-revolutionary powers. Leeds had resigned the Foreign Office at the end of May, an event that prompted a Cabinet shuffle resulting in the appointment of Pitt's cousin, William Wyndham Grenville, as Foreign Secretary and the movement of Henry Dundas, previously President of the East India Board of Control, to the Home Office. Neither man nor their premier had any desire to interfere in the affairs of Europe for, following the Ochakow débâcle, the government's first priority lay in strengthening its political standing in the House of Commons. No British minister, moreover, saw the outbreak of war against France as likely in the near future. 'These princes', said Grenville, 'are desirous of saying much' but 'are quite determined to do nothing', with which Dundas agreed (Fortescue, 1892–1927: ii, 142–3). Pitt was even more dismissive about the prospect of war. 'Depend upon it,' he told Edmund Burke, 'we shall continue as we are until the day of judgement' (Addington, 1847: i, 72). Britain, having been forced to turn its back upon Europe, would remain inactive on the international scene until the end of 1792, when it once more became an important actor in European politics (Clapham, 1899: 93–9; Madariaga, 1981: 428–31; Ehrman, 1983: 87–8; Black, 1994: 326–8, 367–76).

From Neutrality to War

When war was declared by France on Austria (20 April 1792), the blame was laid by the British government at the doors of the combined German powers. Prussia, Austria and Russia, having agreed in February to embark on the second partition of Poland, had invited the courts of Europe to join their crusade against the French Revolution. The Pitt ministry, while poorly informed about the Polish project, was in no doubt that the counter-revolutionary crusade launched by the eastern powers was a deliberate provocation to prod an unstable and paranoid Girondin French government into war. Pitt and Grenville regretted the commencement of hostilities but saw no reason to abandon Britain's official neutrality. With France's armed forces in disarray and counter-revolutionary revolt breaking out in the west, revolutionary France was not expected to hold out long against what Under-secretary of State James Bland Burges described as 'the best army and the best generals in Europe' (Bath and Wells, 1861: 454; Mori, 1997b: 109–10).

The French government, understandably concerned about the prospect of an international counter-revolution, had sought alliance with England in January, in pursuit of which Talleyrand was instructed to offer Martinique and Guadeloupe to Britain. The Pitt ministry's polite refusal was governed by the belief that a return of Bourbon absolutism would follow the military defeat of revolutionary France. This was not the outcome to the war sought by the British government as Sir James Murray, its military observer stationed with the allied armies, was told by Dundas to make clear to the Prussian high command on 12 September 1792. The British government wanted to see 'the re-establishment of such a government in France as, on one hand, would protect other powers from a renewal of that spirit of restlessness and intrigue which had so often been fatal to the tranquillity of Europe, and, on the other hand, secure to the executive government such a degree of energy and vigour, as might enable it to extirpate those seeds of anarchy and misrule, which had so peculiarly of late characterised the whole transactions of that distracted country' (Fortescue, 1892–1927: ii, 313). British views were not likely to influence the post-revolutionary settlement of France. With the French armies in disarray and Prussian forces only 20 miles from Paris, an allied victory seemed inevitable (Black, 1994: 377–403; Mori, 1997b: 119–20).

The defeat of the Prussian army at Valmy on 20 September marked the beginning of a French military recovery that would be followed by invasions of Nice, Savoy and the Austrian Netherlands. By 13 November the British government was an anxious spectator of events in Europe offering to broker an end to the conflict. This change of heart was attributable to the belief that the successes of French arms might result in what Pitt called 'un nouvel ordre des choses' in Europe (Fortescue, 1892–1927: ii, 344). Over the next three weeks, a series of seemingly interrelated foreign and domestic developments would drive Britain towards war. British popular radicals, who had been quiescent over the summer of 1792, responded with enthusiasm to the success of French arms with bonfires, public dinners, parades and congratulatory addresses to the National Convention. These events, coinciding with the mass arrival of suspicious refugees in flight from the September Massacres, the outbreak of an east coast merchant seamen's strike and incidents of widespread food rioting, had suggested to Pitt as early as 9 November that the revolution was coming to Britain. These developments were not, however, interpreted in an international context until 25 November when the government learned that the French army had forced an entry of the River Scheldt in defiance of international law as laid down in the 1648 Treaty of Munster. The National Convention's 15 November Scheldt decree, described by Grenville as 'a concerted plan to drive us to extremities' (Fortescue, 1892–1927: ii, 344), was regarded in London as one part of an international Jacobin conspiracy involving French military spymasters, British radicals and a Dutch Patriot republican movement brought to new life by the radicalisation of the revolution. Anglo-Dutch solidarity risings in support of the French cause, or so it was believed in London and the Hague, would paralyse the governments of both states and prevent them from taking diplomatic or military action against the revolutionary war effort in Flanders (Murley, 1959: 221–43; Blanning, 1986: 139–50; Black, 1994: 407–32; Ehrman, 1983: 206–63; Mori, 1996).

These fears were not entirely the products of fevered imaginations, if only because the Provisional Executive Council had instructed its London embassy to pursue 'revolutionary diplomacy', by which was meant the conduct of international relations with the British people rather than the British government. French coffee house and tavern diplomats exercised no influence over metropolitan radicals but misled their masters into believing that Britain was ripe for revolution. As a result the French ambassador, the Marquis de Chauvelin, was directed to intimidate the British government into a formal recognition of the first French republic. The Pitt Cabinet, aware that subversionary diplomacy was best countered by a groundswell of support for the old order, gave its blessing to the loyalist movement and, by calling out two-thirds of the English militia in selected maritime counties on 1 December, declared the country in a state of national emergency (Murley, 1959: 120–2; Goodwin, 1979: 247–52).

The public order dimension to the deterioration of Anglo-French relations at the end of 1792 did not drive the Pitt ministry into a conservative counter-revolutionary war against France. On 6 November Grenville admitted that a French republic might take its place among the European powers, while Charles Long, Joint Under-secretary to the Treasury, declared on 18 November that Britain would not fight for the life of Louis XVI (Bath and Wells, 1861: ii, 464–7; Miles, 1866: ii, 253). The British government sought to avoid war with France by two routes over the winter of 1792–1793: an attempt to open a secret channel to the French Foreign Ministry through the envoy extraordinary, Hugues Maret, and repeated offers to broker an armistice between France and the combined powers. Neither Prussia nor Austria, however, wanted to end the war, while Russia, which did express interest in the British peace proposals, insisted on a post-war restoration of the *ancien régime* Bourbon monarchy. On 29 December, Grenville notified the Russian ambassador that the British government sought a peace settlement without outside interference in the political or constitutional future of France. The British government sought to end the war but not necessarily the revolution. Pitt's personal talks with Maret at the beginning of December started promisingly but collapsed when the French insisted that the British government route all its communications through the detested Chauvelin (Cobban, 1968: 192–227; Ehrman, 1983: 239–58; Black, 1994: 415–28).

The ministry maintained from 25 November onwards that it accepted neither the legitimacy of the Scheldt decree nor the French republic and demanded the military evacuation of the Austrian Netherlands as a preliminary to any formal peace negotiation. On 17 November Britain had begun to arm in support of the United Provinces but the government's grounds for war were conventional: the defence of the Low Countries against French aggression. The First Fraternal Decree of 19 November was less of an issue to the British government, although Pitt had mentioned it in his abortive conferences with Maret as 'an insult to neutral nations' (BL Add 34446, ff. 28–30). The British government's insistence on the repeal of the revolutionary decrees constituted a repudiation of the principles they embodied and a demand that France play by the rules of the old diplomatic game. This the Provisional Executive Council refused to do. On 13 December the revolutionary army was instructed to respect Dutch neutrality and move into winter quarters but the French government insisted upon formal recognition of its republican status and principles, central to which was the retention of the decrees. Britain and France had reached stalemate (Ehrman, 1983: 249–55; Duffy, 1989: 129; Black, 1994: 428–54; Schroeder, 1994: 115–16).

Tempting as it is to see the execution of Louis XVI as a natural product of the revolution, this was by no means apparent to contemporaries, nor should it be forgotten that the Convention voted only 387 to 334 to send him to the guillotine. The British government wanted confirmation of the republic's permanence before giving it formal recognition and was reluctant to deal with a government where 'all was provisional and temporary'. The eagerness of the ministry to grasp at Russia's interest in peace indicates that, by 29 December, Pitt and Grenville had given up any hope of negotiating with France. A peace settlement might, however, be imposed on France by a concert of powers, leaving Frenchmen free to settle their internal affairs and constitution. Should any revolutionary government, regardless of principles or personnel, disturb the international peace, a joint European effort could contain its aggression (PR, 1793: xxxiv, 456–9; Mori, 1996).

No European state displayed any interest in British notions of collective security. To make matters worse, the resumption of confidential communications between Britain and Europe starting in December 1792 revealed very different diplomatic and military objectives on the part of other powers. Russia and Spain advocated an *ancien régime* restoration of the Bourbon monarchy in France while Prussia and Austria sought indemnification for their wartime expenditures in Poland and Bavaria. The Bavarian Exchange, though long sought by the Habsburg crown, was anathema to a British government for whom an Austrian Netherlands had been regarded for a century as a barrier to French expansion. The vigour with which Pitt, Grenville and Dundas prepared for war from 20 January onwards was driven by the conviction that Britain's participation in – and leadership of – the war was necessary to prevent the other powers of Europe from pursuing territorial and political projects infinitely more objectionable than the survival of a French republic. Conventional considerations – the containment of France in western Europe and the defence of the Low Countries – thus dominated British thinking on the prospect of war. On 5 February, Grenville sent out a round of dispatches inviting Europe's heads of state to join what would become the First Coalition. The French declaration of war on Britain, made on 1 February, would not reach London until the 9th. On 12 February Britain would declare war upon France and the two nations would be launched on a global conflict that would last for almost a quarter century (Duffy, 1971: 14–21; Mori, 1997b: 144–5).

Talking at Cross Purposes: The First and Second Coalitions

The wartime coalitions of the 1790s were united in little more than name. On 20 January 1793, Pitt had written that Spain and Russia were eager for war and that 'all the little powers only await out giving the signal' (Malmesbury, 1851: ii, 501–2). Although Britain would be the most determined and dauntless enemy of France, constructing and financing six coalitions of powers from 1793 to 1815, successive British governments found it difficult to exercise any real control over their allies and would not work effectively with them until British national interests had been subordinated to the objective of defeating Napoleon and devising a lasting peace settlement for Europe. During the 1790s this was yet to come and the allies of the First and Second Coalitions seldom reached agreement on any of the war's major issues: indemnification, strategy, finance or an ideal post-war political settlement for France.

This inability to agree aims and objectives would not have been so frustrating for the British government had the war been as short as anticipated in 1793: a matter of months, or two years at most. The war aims of Austria and Prussia, fast emerging in 1793 as Britain's principal First Coalition allies, were coloured by the fate of Poland, the partition of which was their chief priority. Up to the end of 1792, the Pitt Cabinet expected Prussia to take its war compensation in renegotiated boundaries for its Rhineland territories – Jülich and Berg – while Austria's indemnification was presumed to be coming from French Flanders. Grenville could do little about Poland and Bavaria but describe Prussia's plans as 'screamingly unjust', but hoped that the First Coalition would redirect Austria's undivided attention to western Europe (Lord, 1915: 348–76, 440–5; Schroeder, 1994: 118–22; Mori, 1997b: 147–56).

This the British government never did and its obsession with the containment of France in the west blinded it to the interests of the eastern powers. British plans for post-war Europe involved the reduction of France to its 1789 borders and the creation of strong buffer states on its peripheries. Prussia's lack of western European territorial ambitions left it with little to gain from the First Coalition except a voice in the conduct of the war, formal allied acceptance of its Polish acquisitions and British subsidy money. By June 1793, with French forces in retreat everywhere, Frederick William was planning to transfer the Prussian army to Poland. The securing of Austria's share was already underway, Francis II having sent only 29,000 of a promised 110,000 men to the French war in 1792, and a disgruntled

Frederick William was determined not to persevere in the French war without financial and military assistance from the coalition.

Prussia's objectives in the west amounted to the repulsion of French advances made in 1792. The Austrians, whose forces were also split between Poland and Flanders, believed that the war would take three to four years to win. Despite the fact that the Austrians soon renounced the Bavarian Exchange, this compliance with Grenville's wishes did not focus the attention of Francis II exclusively upon the French war. Austria did not intend to devote all its resources to the western theatre until its eastern borders were secure, and the British government did not realise that, for Austria, Russia and Prussia, eastern Europe was as legitimate a theatre of revolutionary warfare as Flanders. Austria in particular had other interests in Germany, Italy and Poland which it looked to pursue (Duffy, 1983: 18–19). The disappearance of France from the international arena in 1787 had destabilised an already shaky balance of power in eastern Europe that could only be resolved by the shifting of borders on the parts of Russia, Austria and Prussia. In 1795, an independent Poland completely disappeared and, by 1815, several German states would be casualties of the renegotiation process. The British, whose armed forces were tied down in the war against France, could only watch with dismay, a paralysis appreciated by Russian diplomats for whom the revolutionary wars were a series of conflicts diverting western arms and attention away from the east (Lord, 1915: 326–82; Ehrman, 1983: 264–82; Blanning, 1991: 189–90; Schroeder, 1994: 127–8; Mori, 1997b: 147–8, 210, 230, 215–17).

Russia's interest and involvement in the war up to 1799 was consequently peripheral. Austria and Prussia, aware from the outset that Britain's indemnification would be taken outside Europe, vied for British loans or subsidies. Britain, with its small army, had traditionally hired German mercenaries to do much of its European fighting and was prepared to do so once more. Successive British governments were nevertheless reluctant to pay for *all* the fighting in Europe, although other powers, piqued by the success of British arms in the East and West Indies, believed that financial assistance from Britain was a right. Faced from the autumn of 1793 onwards with Frederick William's threatened withdrawal from the war, in April 1794 Britain and Prussia reached an agreement whereby 50,000 troops would be put at the disposal of the allies in return for a subsidy of £1.3m. The agreement was described thus by Pitt: 'The expense will be comparatively speaking no object, if it produces a real and efficient force at our disposal, in a quarter where it is essential to act with vigour, as part of the general plan for the next campaign.' Without any agreement on war aims, this was unrealistic to expect, as were the ministry's plans to conquer French Flanders and march to Paris in the 1794 campaign season. Neither the money nor the soldiers materialised as expected, which resulted in the complete collapse of relations between Britain and Prussia at the end of 1794 (Fortescue, 1892–1927: ii, 433; Sherwig, 1969: 27–50; Ehrman, 1983: 282–97, 327–78; Mori, 1997b: 163–6, 206–10).

Austria's financial relations with Britain were also acrimonious, if more protracted. From 1795 to 1797, Austria would receive £6.22m in loans to deploy an army of one million men on an offensive front stretching from the Channel to the Alps (Helleiner, 1965; Sherwig, 1969: 365; Schroeder, 1994: 138–42, 144–5, 152–3). The British government, having withdrawn its army from Europe at the end of 1794, was by the autumn of 1795 almost entirely reliant upon the Imperial armies for the continuation of the war in Europe. Not only had the United Provinces been overrun by the French, but Spain and Prussia had in the spring of 1795 sued for peace. The failure of the Imperial grand army to contain, let alone drive back, French forces in the Rhineland and north Italy was intensely exasperating to a ministry whose expectations of a short and successful war had been, as Pitt and Grenville saw it, frustrated by uncooperative allies. The Austrians, busy on two fronts, resented British criticism of their high command and believed that they had been cheated on the interest terms of their 1796 loan, which their government in Vienna refused to ratify and repay. British demands for reimbursement would continue for the next three years despite the departure of Austria from the conflict at Campo Formio in 1797 (Helleiner, 1965: Part II; Sherwig, 1969: 59–62, 89–93, 101–2; Ehrman, 1983: 547–60, 599–602; Mackesy, 1974: 10–14; Schroeder, 1994: 134–5; Mori, 1997b: 213–14, 217–18).

Determined as Pitt was to remove France from the ranks of the great powers, neither Austria nor Prussia, let alone Spain and Russia, were anxious to see Britain gain power, territory and status at the expense of France. This partially explains the lukewarm reception given by the First Coalition to Britain's war plans, particularly the conquest of Flanders, Artois, Alsace-Lorraine, Jura, the Franche Comté, Perpignan and, possibly, parts of Provence for employment as bargaining chips at the peace table, depending upon the relative disposition of allied and enemy forces upon the signature of a final armistice. George III's fellow heads of state did not relish the strengthening of Britain at the expense of France in western Europe in spite of the fact that the French borderlands were intended by Pitt and Grenville for the indemnification of Britain's allies. First Coalition members sought gains elsewhere and Spain was the first state to openly challenge Britain's indemnification plans for the First Coalition, declaring itself uninterested in Perpignan and very much interested in French St Domingue. This brought it into conflict with a British government with designs of its own upon the French half of the island (FO 72/26, ff. 394–8).

Britain's successes at sea only further alienated European powers whose heads of state believed that Britain made war to enrich itself and impoverish its neighbours (Harvey, 1978b; Duffy, 1983: 17–18).

In the heady days of 1793, with the revolutionary armies in retreat everywhere, anything had seemed possible. Pitt's ambitions at the beginning of the war had encompassed both the French West and East Indies but, when the war turned decisively against the allies in the autumn of 1794, his confidence in a clean sweep of the French colonies turned into concern. The government's interest in the French empire had always been driven by defensive considerations because maritime security for Britain was a global issue. When Spain made peace and lost its half of St Domingue in 1795, British attention turned to a Caribbean theatre requiring reinforcement. Dundas had always hoped to cripple the French maritime empire by striking at its richest West Indian possessions: St Domingue, Martinique and Guadeloupe. The 1793–1794 West Indian expedition, intended in conjunction with a French royalist revolt on St Domingue to secure all three, was, however, wiped out by disease, and by 1795 the government was determined to protect the British Caribbean from the spectre of slave revolt. Pitt, tiring of war, was hoping that the 1795–1796 West Indian expedition would acquire enough French and Spanish colonies to employ for bartering purposes at the peace table. At the beginning of 1796, he outlined several diplomatic strategies for Britain to use at any peace conference in which Britain gave up colonies to restore France to its 1792 borders. In the worst-case scenario – the failure of the Austrian army to recover any territory in the Low Countries and Rhineland, coupled with the refusal of France to relinquish it, either voluntarily or in exchange for colonies – Britain would keep everything it had acquired outside Europe, including the colonies of Spain and the United Provinces. Such a peace would not have fulfilled the expectations of 1793 but, as Pitt pointed out to an unhappy George III, 'it would be honourable and probably advantageous' (Stanhope, 1861–2: ii, xxx; Fortescue, 1892–1927: iii, 166; Duffy, 1987, 1991: 134–6; Mori, 1997b: 220–1, 224–5, 228–9).

The abortive Lille peace talks of 1796–1797 offered Britain a peace that, in the eyes of its government, was neither. Sincere though Foreign Minister Charles Delacroix was in his desire for peace, neither he nor the Directorial government of France sought any return to the *status quo*, and expected Britain to surrender all its colonial acquisitions in exchange for an end to the European war. Britain, now left to fight alone, was reduced to the conduct of a defensive war while watching helplessly as the French armies overran Switzerland and southern Italy. By the end of 1797, the government no longer believed in a short war, accepting now that they were engaged in a contest of attrition in which endurance would determine final victory. Pitt unlike Grenville, had no strong ideological commitment to the war and the premier's growing desire for peace was contested fiercely by the Foreign Secretary throughout the later 1790s (Mackesy, 1974: 75–80; Duffy, 1983: 22). Britain was not left to fight alone for long. The annexation of satellite republics to France was also noted with concern by Austria and Prussia: the former determined to preserve its influence in Italy and the Holy Roman Empire, while the latter's new Czar, Paul I, hoped to protect the smaller states of Europe from French bullying and, in so doing, to establish a Russian presence in the Mediterranean (Ehrman, 1983: 588–9, 603–50, 1996: 50–68, 197–257; Mackesy, 1982: Ch. 2; Blanning, 1986: 173–99; Schroeder, 1994: 173–93).

The British government, approached through a Russian offer to resolve the loan dispute with Austria, had realised that the war must be won in Europe with land armies for which it would have to pay. Money was not the impediment preventing the negotiation of a Second Coalition, for Pitt was willing to subsidise Prussia's army despite its perfidious conduct in 1794. Frederick William, who was unwilling to go to war, declined the alliance overtures of 1798–1799. Austria, regarded throughout the eighteenth century as Britain's natural ally, was now seen in London as a faithless power no longer sharing an interest in the recovery or defence of the Low Countries against France. Prussia, on the other hand, was known to fight if paid and its engagement in the war was guaranteed to arouse Austrian jealousy, which the Pitt ministry was determined to use constructively in the Second Coalition. An angry and suspicious Austria funded indirectly by Britain through Russia was bound to fight hard for territorial gains of its own in Germany and Italy, expelling the French from regions of little interest to the British (Mackesy, 1982: 18–19; Sherwig, 1969: 114–19; Schroeder, 1987, 1994; Duffy, 1989: 132–3; Ehrman, 1996: 197–202).

Russia was now regarded as Britain's best alliance partner and, at the end of 1795, Grenville had begun to woo it with offers of subsidies for the use of its ships and troops. Catherine the Great had been reluctant to commit any military resources to western Europe. Her successor, Paul, promised £1m for an army of 50,000 to re-establish the House of Orange in the United Provinces, signed an alliance with Britain on 29 December 1798 in return for recognition of Russia's interests and growing power in the Near East. Napoleon's Egyptian adventure had produced some interesting results, not least the drawing of Turkey and Sweden, at Russia's request, into the Second Coalition. By 1798, Pitt and Grenville had concluded that Britain was powerless to intervene in eastern Europe and that Russia, a state with no western European ambitions, made a potentially better ally than Austria, over which it could exercise more military and diplomatic influence than Britain by virtue of shared interests in east–central Europe, the Balkans and Near East. This explains Austria's real – and Prussia's would-be – subordinate status in the Second Coalition. Although Austria made a better ally at a distance in 1799–1800 than it had in direct partnership with Britain from 1793 to 1797, British disgust with the poor quality of leadership and military discipline displayed by the Russian army in 1799, in addition to Paul's abrupt withdrawal of his troops from western Europe on 23 October, resulted in a reversion to Austria as Britain's primary ally in 1800 (Sherwig, 1969: 123–6, 128–35; Mackesy, 1982: 52–5; Schroeder, 1994: 179–93, 198).

France had declared war on Austria on 12 March 1799. By August a largely Austrian allied army had retaken most of Italy and driven the French from much of Switzerland. Britain's contribution to the war, apart from loans and subsidies for Austria and Russia, was the Helder expedition, an invasion of Holland which, with Dutch Orangist assistance and Russian reinforcement, was intended to expel the French and re-establish an independent United Provinces (Schama, 1977: 389–96). The Anglo-Russian strategy of 1799 involved the liberation of Italy, Switzerland, the United Provinces, Netherlands and left bank of the Rhine, aided by indigenous resistance movements seeking freedom from French rule. Risings in the Netherlands, Luxembourg, Switzerland and southern Italy taking place in 1798–1799 indicated that the French fraternity and republicanism were no longer popular while discontent seethed in the Rhineland and United Provinces (Godechot, 1972: Chs. XV–XVI; Schama, 1977: 321–84; Blanning, 1983: 302–4).

New peace plans were drawn up by Grenville from 1797 to 1799 to reflect changes in the relative fortunes of the combatants. France, to be reduced once more to its pre-war borders, was permitted to keep a maritime West Indian empire whose wealth had been destroyed by slave revolt. Britain's indemnification and maritime security was to come now from the French East Indian stations, Dutch Ceylon and the Cape of Good Hope. The buffer state mentality was still in force. Belgium was to be joined to an independent United Provinces and a similar merger was contemplated for Genoa and Piedmont. The co-operation of the Dutch Orangists was instrumental in Grenville's eyes to the success of the plan and Pittite governments would rely increasingly upon European resistance movements in the future (FO 65/45, Grenville to Whitworth, 19 Nov. 1799; Rose, 1904a: 51–61; Sherwig, 1962: 284–93; Duffy, 1989: 132). Although the British succeeded in carrying off most of the Dutch fleet, they were repulsed from their Helder bridgehead and the army was evacuated on 18 October. The military fortunes of the Second Coalition began to decline at the Second Battle of Zürich (25–30 September). The allied armies never recovered the initiative, and by the time Britain and Austria signed their alliance treaty on 30 June 1800, a new First Consul returned from Egypt had inflicted a crushing defeat on the Austrians at Marengo. By stalling for time, postponed a final peace until February 1801, hoping in the interval to rally their forces. The peace of Luneville left Britain once more without allies and the 1 October armistice, followed by the Treaty of Amiens on 25 March 1802, ended eight years of war between Britain and France. All of the West Indian conquests, Malta, recent gains in Egypt, the Cape of Good Hope and Ceylon, taken from the Dutch in 1795, were returned to their original owners. Many in Britain felt that too much had been sacrificed at Amiens but there had been few choices for Britain to make at the peace table. Britain had won the war at sea but France was the master of western Europe (Rodger, 1964: 154–7, 204–7; Duffy, 1987: 324–5, 377–9; Schroeder, 1994: 226–8; Ehrman, 1996: 363–411).

The British Government and the Bourbon Restoration

On 19 February 1793 the British government had concluded a pact with royalist rebel planters stipulating that St Domingue be taken and held in trust for the French crown until the peace. Nine months later Britain would send the first of several amphibious expeditions to the aid of French insurgents in Brittany and Poitou demanding the restoration of the Bourbon monarchy. In April 1794 the Émigré Corps Act would enable Frenchmen to serve in special units of the British army and, early in 1795, the Pitt administration would, through an agent in neutral Switzerland, begin to fund the White Terror in the south of France. None of this, however, represented any real commitment on the part of Pitt and his colleagues to an *ancien régime* Bourbon restoration. Everything about British diplomacy from 1787 to 1792 indicates that the British government had no desire to see a return of the French Bourbons to the international arena. As Pitt put it in 1791, the introduction of representative government in France would make it 'a much less objectionable neighbour' (PH, xxviii, 321). Attached as Pitt and Grenville were to constitutional monarchy in theory and practice, the conservatism of Artois and his elder brother Provence made them unattractive candidates for the French crown and British ministers would have settled for a 'secure and lasting peace' with any stable French republic (Cobban, 1954b: 44–5; Duffy, 1983: 15, 1989: 134–6; Mori, 1997a, 1997b: 154–5).

The failure of such a republican government to emerge in France between 1793 and 1795 was the principal reason for the British government's interest in the French counter-revolution. Royalist rebels in the Vendée were early recipients of British arms and money sent via the Channel Islands, but the brothers of Louis XVI were kept at arm's length in spite of repeated requests from the *chouans* for a Bourbon prince to lead them. Artois and Provence, trenchant enemies of French constitutional reform, registered equally vehement objections to any losses of Caribbean and French mainland territory, regarded by the princes as the sacred patrimony of the French crown. Mauritius and the Isles de Bourbon were offered to the British by the princes in 1793 as rewards for the re-establishment of the Bourbon monarchy in France but these were not the gains that Pitt and Dundas wanted from France (Hutt, 1983: i, 105–7).

The surrender of Toulon to Admiral Lord Hood on 28 August 1793 forced the Pitt ministry to declare itself a supporter of a Bourbon restoration. The governors of Toulon were, in fact, republican opponents of the National Convention whose surrender in the name of Louis XVII, a child of eight languishing in a Paris prison, had been driven by a desire to propitiate Hood and his masters. These hopes were not misplaced. A ministry hoping to use the south of France as a base for future royalist military operations intended to run the city, in the first instance, in consultation with its existing republican institutions and personnel, but to reintroduce it slowly to the provincial government of the Bourbons. By this was not meant an *ancien régime* restoration, for a blueprint of a constitutional monarchy built on a foundation of pre-revolutionary legal and political institutions had emerged from Pitt's and Grenville's deliberations on the fate of Toulon. The exercise was futile because Toulon was lost to republican forces on 19 December, but the model survived as an ideal in British minds (PRO, 30/8/334, ff. 183–202; Kelly, 1982; Ehrman, 1983: 303–26; Duffy, 1983: 15–16; Mori, 1997a).

The counter-revolution was always a secondary priority for a British government reluctant to accept any long-term diplomatic responsibility for imposing a political settlement upon France (Duffy, 1989: 135–6). French royalists were subsidised throughout the 1790s in the hope that they would distract the republic's military attention away from other theatres. This was an objective the royalists, split into *pur* and *constitutionnel* camps, rarely achieved and their inability to agree on the political shape of a future Bourbon restoration was deeply frustrating to the British, who hoped to unite the French behind the standard of a reformed monarchy. The Quiberon expedition of 1795, in which *émigrés* and *chouans* supplied by the British were supposed to draw French troops away from an Austrian offensive in the east, was a military catastrophe resulting in the brutal suppression of the Vendée royalists. After the British army was evacuated from Europe, their compatriots in the south of France acquired increasing importance as the sole route through which direct blows could be struck against mainland France. In October 1794, William Wickham was sent to the Berne embassy under diplomatic cover to liaise with *constitutionnel* royalists who, with right-wing republican deputies in the Convention, were purportedly plotting to overthrow the Thermidorean regime and replace it with a constitutional monarchy. The conspiracy proved to be hoax, although agreement between the two groups was real and Wickham's links to the counter-revolution were strengthened through contact with royalist terrorists in Jura and the Franche Comté (Mitchell, 1965: 44–52; Sparrow, 1990: 367–70; Mori, 1997b: 218–20).

When the Directory began to take shape during the spring of 1795, *constitutionnels* and *modères* republicans began to plan in earnest for a restoration of the monarchy. The Constitution of the Year III placed executive power in the hands of five elected Directors responsible to a bicameral legislature whose lower house, the Council of 500, was to be infiltrated by the conspirators and their associates standing for election on an anti-war platform. This constitutional structure would remain unchanged except for the addition of a king at its head. The project appealed to a British government growing weary of the war and, when the young Louis XVII died in June, Grenville sent an ambassador to make Provence see the necessity for clemency and royal restraint in the event of a restoration. Lord Macartney found this uphill work but the success of the scheme depended upon French voters rather than Provence. No one anticipated that a Law of Two Thirds requiring the return of old *conventionnels* to the Council of 500 would accompany the ratification of the 1795 Constitution by the outgoing Convention on 22 and 30 August (Fryer, 1965: 44–8; Ehrman, 1983: 567–87). The royalist *journée* of 13 *vendémiaire* was a frustrated response to the Law of Two Thirds but did not prevent royalist candidates from standing for election on 12 October. The results were by no means disheartening for the British. Three Directors had been victims of persecution for their moderate views under Robespierre's 'Reign of Terror' and both councils were dominated by moderate to right-wing republicans. The Constitution of the Year III, with its Declaration of the Rights and Duties of Man, two-tier electoral system and high property suffrage, was a conservative republican settlement devised by men determined to restore social and political stability to France. On 8 December Pitt announced in the Commons that his government was willing to make peace with the republic (Mitchell, 1965: 51–74; Godechot, 1972: 279–86; Duffy, 1983: 23–4; Ehrman, 1983: 368–73, 567–87; Mori, 1997b: 225, 228–9).

Wickham's covert intrigues did not end with the failure of the *vendémiaire* plot. The *constitutionnels*, though forbidden on pain of death from openly advocating a restoration, continued to put up right-wing candidates for the conciliar elections, a strategy that soon produced results. In 1797, they helped the French right win a spectacular victory in general elections that returned only 13 *conventionnels* to the Directory's councils (Fryer, 1965: Chs. 6–7; Mitchell, 1965: 140–74; Sparrow, 1990: 367–73, 1993; Hants RO, 38M49/1/1/67, 38M49/1/79/1; Fortescue, 1892–1927: iv, 117–19). Between 28 March 1795 and 12 January 1802 Wickham had received the staggering sum of £187,494 9s. 2d. in secret service funds at the rate of £30,000 per month to fund the *constitutionnels* and White Terror in the south of France. James Talbot, who headed the Swabian agency responsible for infiltrating the Paris police, got the scarcely less impressive sum of £114,500 (PRO HD 1/1, fo. 1). A French government aware of Wickham's activities demanded his expulsion from Switzerland following the royalist– *modère fructidor* coup that annulled 49 elections and removed 177 deputies from the lower house of the Directory. The gradual rise of the right in both Directorial councils had by late 1796 already produced a strong disposition for peace but, when Lord Malmesbury arrived at Lille in October for a preliminary round of peace talks, he discovered that neither the Directors nor the legislature shared Britain's views on colonial indemnification and European security. The second round of Lille negotiations, taking place during the autumn of 1797, ended in failure and Pitt concluded that Europe 'must for some time longer be left to its fate' (Fortescue, 1892–1927: iv, 354–5; Godechot, 1972: 287–91; Schroeder, 1994: 157–9; Ehrman, 1996: 62, 219–31, 250–1). Following Wickham's expulsion from Switzerland the British government continued to fund espionage abroad with the assistance of the London merchant banks up to and beyond 1815 (Hutt, 1962, 1986; Sparrow, 1998).

Pitt did not object to the Directory as a form of government in 1795 because its constitutional infrastructure seemed to herald a secure and stable future for France. Grenville, who insisted on a restoration of property and religion, if not the *ancien régime* monarchy, always regarded the French Revolution as a social revolution and, by 1798, was convinced that no lasting peace could be achieved in Europe 'till the principle itself be attacked and subdued in its citadel at Paris' (Fortescue, 1892–1927: vi, 46–7). Pitt preferred to see the revolution as a series of power struggles that had, for a brief period in 1793–1794, degenerated into totalitarian anarchy and saw danger in the policies, rather than the principles, of successive French governments. He had no objections to the establishment of Napoleon as the president of an American-style republic, and so great was Pitt's respect for 'mixed or moderate' systems of government that, were this to take place, 'no man can pretend that there would be any Thing in the Form or essential Principles of such a Government, which would make Treaty with It unsafe. – The only Questions would be whether there was any Prospect that the Government would stand; and secondly whether, if it should be overturned, there was an evident Probability; that the Party overturning it would break a Peace once concluded' (Canning MS 30, Pitt to Canning, 3 Dec. 1799). For Pitt the abstract principles supposedly embodied in any state were, for practical purposes, meaningless because the real measure of a government's worth lay in the practical ability of its formal and informal institutions to represent and reconcile the desires of major interest groups within the national community. Had any French republican government of the 1790s seemed stable and prepared to honour a peace treaty, Pitt would have accepted it (Mori, 1997b: 281–3).

Pitt and Grenville had nevertheless hoped that underground French royalist resistance would facilitate the prosecution of the 1799 military campaign. Royalism, forced underground after *fructidor*, remained alive in the south and west by taking the form of secret terrorism. From August to October 1799 it flared into guerrilla warfare and open revolt in Normandy, Anjou, Brittany and the Midi. The Comte de Provence and future Louis XVIII, from the security of the Duke of Brunswick's Blankenburg estates, had kindled the risings through a royalist underground of spy networks but had not changed the reactionary views that made the British so reluctant to recognise his claim to the French throne. Having distanced himself from the *constitutionnels* in 1797, Provence would go on in 1814 to reject the first constitution he was offered by Talleyrand because it contained no reference to the divine right of Bourbon kings. The British had no choice but to accept Napoleon, the Consulate and a French-dictated peace settlement. Ministers, notwithstanding their suspicions of Napoleon's military ambitions, may have breathed a sigh of relief. A restoration was not a viable option until the Bourbons and their supporters recognised some of the grievances that had produced the 1789 revolution (Sparrow, 1993).

From the Peace of Amiens to the Battle of Waterloo, 1801–1815

On 18 May 1803, Britain declared war on France, thereby initiating the second round of a military conflict that would culminate in the defeat and banishment of Napoleon to St. Helena, the restoration of Louis XVIII and the inauguration of the congress diplomacy that would keep the peace in Europe until 1854. None of this could have been predicted in 1803. The peace of Luneville–Amiens and the status it gave France as the master of western Europe was accepted by all states and, in the case of the German principalities, welcomed as a counterweight to Austria. Prussia and Bavaria gladly became junior diplomatic partners of France while Austria and Russia were content with their status in Europe. Grenville and Dundas were horrified by the loss of 'everything except Ceylon and Trinidad; even Malta – and what is worse, if possible, more than that – even the Cape of Good Hope' (Fortescue, 1892–1927: vii, 49–51, 56–8). When Napoleon made himself emperor, refused to withdraw French troops from the United Provinces and barred British commerce from French Europe, the Addington ministry prepared for war (Addington, 1847: ii, 257–60). Had Napoleon's imperialism taken a less flamboyant form, it might well have been accepted by Europe, but the peacetime invasion and annexation of Piedmont was a warning of what might come heeded by Britain and Russia (Duffy, 1987: 388–9; Schroeder, 1994: 211–16, 227–30, 232–3, 242–5).

Britain, whose isolationist tendencies always emerged when its diplomatic and military prospects were bleak, had been, claims Paul Schroeder, prepared in 1801 to leave western Europe to Napoleon provided that its access to continental markets was secure. Britain nevertheless had a choice about launching the second round of the contest against France and, despite losing its allies again within two years, remained committed to the conflict to the bitter end. Neither Pitt nor his followers believed that Napoleonic France was stable and, once Napoleon's designs upon Italy and the Low Countries became apparent, London observers felt that external pressure in the form of war would eventually bring about his downfall. The diplomacy and military strategy of 1798 were consequently revived: Britain would seek a primary Russian alliance to make Austria and Prussia fight and, if necessary, endure a long and gruelling contest with a France that, unable so soon to sustain again the strains of total war, would suffer near complete economic and political collapse. Pitt's political economy of the French Revolution was alive and well.

The Third Coalition of 1805–1806 thus represented an attempt to make the Second Coalition work rather than a sea change in British attitudes to war and peace. In a memo Pitt drafted for the Russian ambassador on 19 January 1805, a new post-war peace settlement promised to redraw the map of Europe by enlarging upon Grenville's 1798–1799 plans. Nothing was said about Poland or Germany east of the Rhine except to stipulate the return of Hanover to George III, but smaller states were now earmarked for absorption by their larger neighbours in Italy, the Low Countries and Rhineland to create a stronger buffer against French expansion. France was to return to either its 1789 or 1792 border and to evacuate the Low Countries, left bank of the Rhine and Italy for the strengthening of the United Provinces, Prussia and Austria in these respective regions (Rose, 1904a, 1919; Webster, 1919: 389–94, 1931: 57–63; Ziegler, 1965: 198–9; Ingram,

1981: 103–16; Duffy, 1989: 133; Schroeder, 1994: 244–68, 273–6; Ehrman, 1996: 726–45).

The war plans of 1804–1805 thus looked to the past rather than the future. The British government still assumed that it could use the armies of other states to enforce its ideas about peace upon Europe. While Britain and Russia initially agreed not to take any territorial indemnification for themselves, the Cape was soon stipulated as a necessary acquisition, and both powers admitted that they could not prevent the other from making conquests outside Europe. In May 1804, Adam Czartoryski, Russia's foreign affairs minister, admitted that whatever other powers did in Europe, 'England would still pursue her own mode of warfare' (Rose, 1904b: 11). Amphibious expeditions were once more mooted for the Low Countries and both states agreed to raise troops for Mediterranean service. Malta nevertheless remained a bone of contention, for Russia was determined, if possible, to see its evacuation by England while the British, having failed to evacuate the island as stipulated at Amiens, were equally intent on keeping it (Schroeder, 1994: 262–5; Sherwig, 1969: 148–61; Rose, 1904b; Hall, 1992: 113–17).

Having spent most of 1804 hammering out their treaty of alliance, Britain and Russia signed it on 11 April 1805. Austria, tempted by Italian territory, joined the Third Coalition on 6 November 1804 but Prussia, having been offered Hanover by Napoleon, declined. Although the coalition allies were officially pledged to liberate Europe, to restore 'the repose, security and independence of the several states of Europe, the balance of power, the preservation of publick right, and faith, and of all social order', the Napoleonic Wars were no ideological conflict (Rose, 1904b: 37). Napoleon was, quite simply, a dictator. All the planning of the allies was in vain for the new war was over in four months. Prussia and Saxony were then recruited to form the Fourth Coalition (1806–7). Russia, knocked out of the war at the Battle of Friedland, made peace at Tilsit in July 1807, losing Poland in the process. Russia, unlike Austria and Prussia, signed a negotiated peace with Napoleon, as opposed to the *diktats* – complete with alliance treaties – forced upon Austria and Prussia at Pressburg and Jena. After the collapse of the Fourth Coalition, Britain would be diplomatically cut off from most of Europe until 1812. Russia would exploit its French alliance for the next five years, employing it as security for expansionist projects in the Baltic and Crimea, and had no desire to revive its British alliance.

On 16 May 1806, the All Talents ministry issued an Order in Council forbidding British trade with French Europe, an interdict that would in 1807 be extended to neutrals and lead to war with America in 1812. Napoleon's Continental System, promulgated and modified in a series of decrees from 1806 to 1812, was intended to subordinate occupied Europe to French economic control: the primary economic instrument with which Napoleon tried to construct an empire. Trade with Britain's colonies was never banned and Napoleon's real intention was arguably the regulation – rather than elimination – of European trade with Britain by France (Schroeder, 1994: 383–95; Fayle, 1948b: 80–1; Crouzet, 1959: 282–3). In 1810, following steep increases in the continental price of tropical goods, the Trianon Decree introduced a system of licences for colonial commerce with Britain available only to French merchants. By 1812, Napoleon was prepared to introduce a similar system of licensed shipping for British trade to any part of the First Empire (Crouzet, 1959: 606–12, 1989). Successive Pittite governments left without allies and, consequently, any real strategy in Europe, clung to the Orders in Council as a commercial and ideological weapon despite their domestic unpopularity (Emsley, 1979a: 130–46; Christie, 1982: 270–315; Schroeder, 1994: 383–8). In 1809 Austria appealed to Britain for money to mobilise its armies and rejoin the war, but George Canning, then Foreign Secretary, stipulated that no regular subsidy would go to Austria until fighting with France was underway. Britain's century-old friendship with Austria was well and truly dead and Canning felt that, until Europe would accept dictation from Britain about war and peace, 'everything should remain as unsettled as possible'. As he put it: 'Whenever the true balance of the world comes to be negotiated, we are the natural mediators of them all, and it is only through us alone that they can look for secure and effective tranquillity' (Canning MS, 48: Canning to Gower, 2 Oct. 1807). Until that time should come, Europe would have to endure Napoleon.

When nationalist resistance to 'King' Joseph Bonaparte broke out on 2 May 1808, a British government already pledged to defend neighbouring Portugal against a seemingly imminent French invasion acquired a new ally. War in the Peninsula, where British and Portuguese troops fought with the help of a Spanish guerrilla resistance movement inspired by genuine popular hostility to France, was complicated by the presence in its ranks of equally strong hatred of the Spanish *ancien régime*: in declaring for Ferdinand, Prince of Asturia, held prisoner by Napoleon in France, Spanish liberals and moderates could mount legitimate opposition to the old Bourbons and their policies. This complicated British dealings with the Spanish authorities, as did Spanish jealousy of Britain's colonies, commerce and designs upon South America. The evacuation of the Portuguese royal family to Brazil by the Royal Navy in 1807 had opened the colony to British economic infiltration, a development regarded with apprehension by the Portuguese and downright hostility by the Spanish. Having retaken the Dutch South American colonies in 1803–1804, successive British governments encouraged their use as bases for mercantile expansion in South America and flirted with nationalist movements in Spain's own colonies. This made for tense Anglo-Spanish and Anglo-Portuguese relations, for both Iberian governments suspected, quite rightly, that the British were conspiring to destroy their overseas empires. In 1810, when Venezuela and Mexico declared their independence from a Spain then in imminent danger of surrender to France, British offers to mediate between the mother country and its colonies only strengthened Spanish apprehensions about Britain's diplomatic and commercial activities in Latin and South America (Kaufman, 1951: Chs. 2–3; Mackesy, 1957: 265–71, 289–96; Bartlett, 1966: 75–80; Sherwig, 1969: 191–2, 221–2; Schroeder, 1994: 431–3; Duffy, 1998: 193).

Although the Perceval administration sought no mainland colonial gains from Spain or Portugal, it tried to gain trade concessions through the 1810 mediation offer. By 1805, even Melville was aware that Europe was jealous of the British empire and the statesmen of the later 1800s were never allowed to forget it. Britain's remaining colonial expeditions, as its diplomats explained to their host courts, were intended either to defend existing colonies or to acquire bargaining counters to be used at the peace. By 1807 this was largely true, all the important enemy colonies earmarked for permanent post-war retention having been retaken at the beginning of the war: namely the Cape, Ceylon, Surinam, Essequibo, Berbice, French Tobago and St Lucia. Curacao would be captured in 1807, French Cayenne and Martinique in 1809 and Guadeloupe and Java in 1810 but, of these five colonies, only Java would be retained by Britain at the peace. One Dundas imperial project of the 1790s was revived by the Perceval ministry and this, the capture of New Orleans, would end in failure in 1815 (Hall, 1992: 184–90; Duffy, 1998: 193–4).

By 1803, the once French town was American, having been sold to the United States in the Louisiana Purchase Treaty for $15m. The war of 1812, in the context of which the New Orleans expedition arose, had broken out ostensibly over American resentment of the 1807 Orders in Council and the continued impressment, in contravention of the 1794 Jay Treaty, of American merchant seamen into the Royal Navy. The rights of neutral shipping and the high-handedness of the British navy were, however, pretexts for a war involving a much more complex set of American–Canadian issues: trade and settlement rights in the disputed border territory south of the St Lawrence river, aboriginal–white relations in the Great Lakes region, American ambitions to occupy the entire North American continent, and the resentment of one-time American colonists, now Canadians, who had been expelled from the United States for their loyalty to Britain during the War of Independence. The objectionable Orders in Council were repealed 12 days after the United States declared war on Britain, but this did not difuse tensions between the combatants. Most of the fighting in the war of

1812 was done by Canadians and their aboriginal allies, for Britain could spare few troops for its colonies until the war in Europe was over, and neither side won a decisive victory: the 1814 Treaty of Ghent re-established a *status quo* peace (Schroeder, 1994: 435–9, 574–5; P. Marshall, 1998).

Russia, jealous of Britain's naval and commercial power, offered repeatedly and unsuccessfully to broker a settlement with the United States. Russia had, however, done very well out of its alliance with Napoleon, having briefly resurrected the Baltic League of Armed Neutrality (1808–1809) and acquired Finland and Aaland from Sweden (1809). It was also contesting the possession of Moldavia and Wallachia with Turkey, in the pursuit of which it demanded Anglo-Spanish diplomatic assistance as the high price of an alliance in 1811. The Perceval ministry refused and Russia, unable to find allies, was invaded by Napoleon in 1812 (Sherwig, 1969: 275–93; Schroeder, 1994: 449). The decimation of his army as it retreated from Moscow was the signal that other states had been waiting for to renegotiate their relationship with France. In Prussia and the United Provinces, liberation movements began to gather steam at the end of 1812 having, in the case of the Dutch Orangists, long been promised British arms and money. The King of Prussia and his Chancellor, Karl von Hardenberg, had since the summer of 1811 been playing a double game of appeasing Napoleon whilst harbouring a radical anti-French army conspiracy led by General Scharnhorst. This involved the expansion of the Prussian army, the creation of a volunteer militia and popular revolt against France on the Spanish model. When the Prussian army took matters into its own hands, raising the standard of revolt at the end of 1812, Frederick William III finally threw in his lot with the rebels, signing an alliance with Russia at Breslau, calling upon the German people to rise and, on 19 March 1813, declaring war on France (Schama, 1977; Schroeder, 1994: 450–7).

Britain's participation in shaping the future of Europe was by no means assured from its war record as France's most determined and long-serving enemy. Metternich wanted to keep Napoleon and his empire as a counterweight to British power while Prussia was willing to ally with Russia but wary of Britain and desirous of keeping Hanover. Castlereagh, who had become Foreign Secretary when the Liverpool ministry took office in April 1812, was, however, prepared to be flexible and brought a shrewd realism to Pittite views of war, revolution, indemnification and security. During the autumn of 1812, he re-established relations with Russia, relying on it once more to attract or intimidate Prussia and, more importantly, Austria into alliance with Britain. Metternich, who saw the future of Europe lying in the hands of France and Russia, would offer to mediate between the two on three occasions from December 1812 to June 1813 and only joined Prussia and Russia at Reichenbach after Napoleon had turned them all down.

Castlereagh, realising that Russia and Prussia would not admit Britain to their councils without generous grants of money, offered both a consolidated subsidy of £2m and both accepted. Austria was promised financial assistance after it declared war on France, which it did on 11 August (Webster, 1931: 148–55; Sherwig, 1969: 294–302; Schroeder, 1994: 457–9).

British diplomats, finally readmitted to Europe in force, were now prepared to fund the entire war effort against Napoleon and £26.25m in subsidies would be given to the allies between 1813 and 1815. This represented £3.25m more than Britain's entire subsidy bill from 1803 to 1812. British frustration at allied demands for cash throughout the 1790s and 1800s stemmed from the fact that their demands simply could not be met until the income tax became functional and Britain's financial services base had expanded enough to provide the necessary foreign exchange facilities (Roach, 1983; Duffy, 1989: 138–9, 142). By 1812 Castlereagh was aware that Albion would not be trusted until it shed its perfidious reputation by acting as the paymaster of Europe, renouncing its claims to French colonies and taking an active part in the resettlement of Germany and Poland. Liverpool and the Cabinet were consequently asked to moderate their demands for French and Dutch colonies, cough up cash on demand for would-be allies and accept a high degree of British involvement in the Polish and Saxon settlements of 1815. None of these requests were popular in London and parliament had to be misled about the extent of British involvement in the settlement of Naples and Saxony (Webster, 1919: 146, 178, 219–20, 1931: 488–9; Duffy, 1989: 145).

Castlereagh had long hoped that Europe would rise against Napoleon and was delighted by the appearance of liberation movements in 1813 (Castlereagh, 1848–53: ix, 20–3, 39–44). Although the British refused to give any direct assistance to the Bourbons and kept them at arm's length until 1815, the Liverpool ministry longed in private for a restoration of the monarchy in France. In 1805 Pitt had defined this as a desirable but dispensable war aim for the Third Coalition and his successors agreed (Webster, 1919: 394). Much to the horror of Metternich, every other 'legitimist' movement from the Dutch Orangists to the Swiss federalists and Sicilian monarchists received some kind of British encouragement in 1814. Prussia was left to Alexander I of Russia, who wished to liberate Germany. The reconciliation of Britain and Austria was attributable largely to the Treaty of Reid, by which Metternich guaranteed the independence and borders of Bavaria a day before concluding Austria's 9 October 1812 subsidy and alliance treaty with Britain. This self-sacrificing diplomacy, bearing in mind that Bavaria had long been coveted by the Habsburg crown, convinced Castlereagh that Austria was more committed to long-term European peace than Alexander, whose liberal populist rhetoric masked a determination to redraw the map of Germany without consulting anyone else. In the spring of 1814, Lord William Bentinck, Britain's envoy to Sicily and chief *agent provocateur* in Italy, would be told to forsake his liberal constitutionalist friends on the mainland and co-operate with the Austrians in the restoration of peace to Italy (Castlereagh, 1848–53: ix, 20–3, 39–44; Webster, 1921: 16–19, 94–6, 1931: 258–60; Bartlett, 1966: 114–20; Schroeder, 1994: 475–6, 490, 510–11). In the 9 March 1814 Treaty of Chaumont that bound the four allies together for another year of war, Britain agreed to fund all the powers for another year, surrender most of France's captured colonies and join a European collective security network. This moderation, more than anything else, convinced the eastern powers that Britain was serious about peace.

The British had been determined since 1805 to give no aid to the Bourbons unless public opinion welcomed their return to France. Castlereagh, having convinced Metternich and Alexander to accept Louis XVIII as an alternative to Napoleon, who had ruled himself out by refusing to accept any allied peace terms, allowed Alexander and Talleyrand to carry out a restoration without British assistance (Webster, 1919: 126–8; Duffy, 1989: 144). When Napoleon returned to power during the 100 Days a British government that gave 35,000 stands of arms to royalists in the west and south of France, admitted that no second Bourbon restoration could take place if the French people resisted the allied invasion (Webster, 1931: 443–52, 514–15). The Cabinet, by no means sure that the king would keep his throne after the allied armies left France, urged Castlereagh to impose a harsh second peace upon France in the event of a 'Jacobin or revolutionary system' succeeding Louis (Webster, 1919: 339–40, 351–3). Castlereagh and Metternich were nonetheless determined to recruit France as an ally against Russia and on 3 January 1815, the French returned to European diplomacy in alliance with Austria and Britain (Emsley, 1979a: 161–6, 169–76; Schroeder, 1994: 485–502, 505–8). Both men therefore strove to prevent the imposition of too punitive a second peace following the 100 Days and, though France was saddled with allied occupation and a 700 million franc war indemnity, it escaped more lightly than the smaller powers had wished. The British devoted much effort to reducing the indemnity for the sake of future peace (Webster, 1921: 251–5, 260–73, 276–86, 1925: 83–5; Schroeder, 1994: 521–2, 529–31, 551–7).

The broad outlines of the final peace settlement exemplified the new ideas of Liverpool and Castlereagh towards Europe. Much of the treaty enacted the peace envisaged by Pitt in 1805: an independent United Netherlands had been created in the Low Countries, Austria had acquired land in northern Italy to check French expansion to the south; Prussia and the one-time United Provinces had been strengthened on the Rhine; and Hanover was preserved as an independent German state with links to Holland and

Britain. British attitudes to Europe had nevertheless changed: all colonies but Tobago, St Lucia and the Seychelles were restored to France, the Ionian Islands taken in 1809 to strengthen Britain's position in the Mediterranean had been offered to Austria, and Castlereagh had embroiled Britain in the resettlement of east–central Europe (Webster, 1919: 1, 1931: 387–90; Mackesy, 1957: 351–5; Duffy, 1989: 138, 143–5). From 1813 to 1815, Britain had also given very generous financial assistance to its allies with no strings attached: no longer were diplomats tying financial aid to specific diplomatic or military projects. Last but not least, France was no longer regarded as an inveterate enemy, but rather as a potential ally in the containment of Russia.

Having said this, Russia did not replace France as Britain's natural enemy nor was Austria resuscitated as a natural ally. British concepts of a balanced Europe throughout the eighteenth century had been based on two assumptions: that Britain's role lay in containing France while a self-sustaining balance of great powers kept the rest of Europe in check. The creation of intermediate states such as the United Netherlands and the Kingdom of Sardinia–Piedmont, towards which the British government had been moving since 1797, marked a move away from the assumption that some other major power would act as a buffer against French expansion outside Britain's immediate sphere of influence. Not only did Britain accept responsibility for the defence and independence of such states, but no attempts were made to turn the United Netherlands or, for that matter, post-war Spain into satellites or dependents, despite the fact that both states possessed imperial and commercial interests opposed to those of Britain (Schroeder, 1994: 538–75).

Although the Congress System of diplomacy set up at Vienna endured for less than a decade, the general peace it negotiated for Europe survived much longer. Most of the older claims about the Congress of Vienna – that it represented a restoration of the old order; that it ignored popular demands for freedom and natural rights; that it arbitrarily redrew the map of Europe – have been discredited. As Schroeder argues (1994: 575–82), the Vienna Congress represented a genuine attempt on the part of all its participants to seek a permanent, forward-looking solution to Europe's problems. Eighteenth-century concepts of balance, according to which self-adjusting ratios of military strength and diplomatic influence were in some mysterious fashion to prevent the outbreak of war, were jettisoned in favour of an equilibrium based upon the co-existence of great power strength and small power independence. Although many of the annexations and alienations of territory by which these dispositions were established did not endure, particularly in the case of Poland, the United Netherlands and Lombardy–Venetia, potential conflict in all the trouble spots of Europe was contained much longer by the Vienna system than by any of its predecessors or successors. The congress confronted every major dispute in contemporary European politics, hammered out new rules and procedures for establishing co-operation and resolving differences, did listen to so-called liberal and nationalist pleas for natural rights – which invariably meant special privileges – and, where possible, tried to reconcile them with political and strategic realities.

The Congress of Vienna did not restore the *status quo ante bellum*: rather it created a new system of states in which greater, lesser and intermediate states possessed rights guaranteed by treaty under international law and whose sovereignty lay in the states as legally defined rather than in the legitimacy of their dynastic rulers. Britain has always emerged from the Congress of Vienna with a positive reputation: it sought nothing for itself in Europe; it gave away colonies to other states for the sake of peace; it promoted free trade and the abolition of the slave trade; it extended a hand of friendship to France and it acted as an objective mediator in disputes between other states (Sked, 1979). All of this can be upheld, although it should be recalled that all this statesmanship was largely the product of one man's efforts and leadership. Whatever Castlereagh had learned from two decades of war, his thinking was out of step with Cabinet and domestic public opinion, which bayed for the imposition of a punitive peace on France and wanted nothing to do with Europe (Webster, 1925: 21). Britain's eighteenth-century national cultural identity, in place by 1789, had defined the nation in conscious opposition to Europe and, particularly, France. The vast majority of Britons saw themselves as a people apart and their government, in accepting a role for Britain at Vienna as a policeman of Europe, was adopting a role the majority of its citizens would not come to see as their nation's duty for much of the next century.

BIBLIOGRAPHY

Printed Primary Sources

All texts published in London unless otherwise stated. Every attempt has been made to cite from collected works and modern editions. Only works that have been cited or referred to in the text have been listed here.

Addington, H. (1847). *The Life and Correspondence of the Right Honourable Henry Addington*, ed. G. Pellew. 3 vols.

Bath and Wells [Eden], Bishop of, (1861). *Journal and Correspondence of William Lord Auckland*. 3 vols.

Bentham, J. (1982) [1789]. *Introduction to the Morals and Principles of Legislation*, eds. J.H. Burns and H.L.A. Hart.

Bentham, J. (1818). *The Church of England and its Catechism Examined: preceded by Strictures on the Exclusionary System, as pursued in the National Society's Schools: interspersed with parallel views of the English and Scottish Established and Non-Established Churches.*

Bentham, J. (1823). *Not Paul, but Jesus.*

Bentham, J. (1838). *Works*, ed. J. Bowring. 11 vols.

Bowles, J. (1800). *Reflections at the Conclusion of the War: being a sequel to Reflections on the Political and Moral State of Society at the Close of the Eighteenth Century.*

Brougham, H. (1871–2). *The Life and Times of Henry, Lord Brougham.* New York.

Browning, O. (ed.) (1910). *Despatches from Paris, 1784–1790.* 2 vols.

Burke, E. (1958–78). *The Correspondence of Edmund Burke*, ed. W. Copeland, 10 vols.

Burke, E. (1981–97). *The Writings and Speeches of Edmund Burke*, ed. P. Langford. 9 vols, Oxford.

Burke, J. (1803). *A Genealogical and Heraldic History of the Peerage, Baronetage and Knightage.*

Cartwright, J. (1826). *The Life and Correspondence of Major John Cartwright*, ed. F.D. Cartwright. 2 vols.

Castlereagh, R.S. (1848–53). *The Memoirs and Correspondence of Viscount Castlereagh, Second Marquess of Londonderry*, ed. C. Vane. 12 vols.

Claeys, G. (ed.) (1992). *Political Writings of the 1790s.* 8 vols.

Clifford, R. (1798a). *Memoirs, illustrating the History of Jacobinism, written in French . . . and Translated into English.* 4 vols.

Clifford, R. (1798b). *Application of Barruel's Memoirs of Jacobinism to the Secret Societies of Ireland and Great Britain, by the Translator of that Work.*

Cobbett, W. (1795). *A Bone to Gnaw, for the Democrats: containing, 1st. Observations on a Patriotic Pamphlet, entitled, 'Proceedings of the United Irishmen'; 2dly. Democratic Principles Exemplified by Example: 3dly. Democratic Memoires, or, An Account of Some Recent Feats Performed by the Frenchified Citizens of the United States of America.* Philadelphia.

Cobbett, W. (1804–20). *The Parliamentary Debates from the Year 1803 to the Present Time: Forming a Continuation of the Work entitled 'The Parliamentary History of England from the Earliest Period to the Year 1803'.* 36 vols.

Cobbett, W. (1815). *An Account of the Rise, Progress, Extent, and Present State of the Funds and of the Paper-Money of Great Britain; and Also of the Situation of that Country as to its Debt and other Expenses; its Navigation, Commerce, and Manufactures; its Taxes, Population, and Paupers; drawn from Authentic Documents, and Brought Down to the End of the Year 1814,* 2 vols.

Cobbett, W. (1930) [1821–8]. *Rural Rides, in the Southern, Western and Eastern Counties of England, Together with Tours in Scotland and in the Northern and Midland Counties of England, and Letters from Ireland,* eds. G.D.H. and M. Cole. 3 vols.

Cobbett, W. (1947). *The Autobiography of William Cobbett: The Progress of a Plough-Boy to a Seat in Parliament,* ed. W. Reitzel.

Coleridge, S.T. (1817). *Biographia literaria, or Biographical sketches of my literary life and opinions.*

Coleridge, S.T. (1956–71). *The Collected Letters of Samuel Taylor Coleridge,* ed. E.L. Griggs. 6 vols, Oxford.

Coleridge, S.T. (1971–). *The Collected Works of S.T. Coleridge,* eds. K. Coburn and B. Weisner.

Colquhoun, P. (1806). *A Treatise on Indigence: exhibiting a General View of the National Resources for Productive Labour; with Propositions for Ameliorating the Condition of the Poor . . .*

Cusac Smith, W. (1791). *Rights of citizens: being an enquiry into some of the consequences of social union, and an examination of Mr. Paine's principles touching government.*

Eaton, D.I. (1794–5). *Politics for the People; or, A Salmagundy for Swine.* 2 vols.

Eden, F.M. (1797). *The State of the Poor.* 3 vols.

Elliot, G. (1874). *The Life and Letters of Sir Gilbert Elliot,* ed. Countess of Minto. 3 vols.

Fortescue, J.B. (1892–1927). See Historical Manuscripts Commission.

Fox, C.J. (1853–7). *The Memorials and Correspondence of Charles James Fox,* ed. J. Russell. 4 vols.

George III (1962–70). *The Later Correspondence of George III,* ed. A. Aspinall. 5 vols, Cambridge.

Godwin, W. (1946). *An Enquiry Concerning Political Justice,* eds. F.E.L. Priestley. 3 vols.

Godwin, W. (1992). *Collected Novels and Memoirs of William Godwin,* ed. M. Philp.

Granville, Castilia, Countess of [Gower] (1916). *Private Correspondence of Lord Granville Leveson Gower, 1781–1821.* 2 vols.

Grenville (1853). *Memoirs of the Court and Cabinets of George the Third. From original family documents,* ed. Duke of Buckingham and Chandos. 4 vols.

Grey, Lt. General (1861). *Some Account of the Life and Opinions of Charles, 2nd Earl Grey.*

Hall, C. (1805). *The Effects of Civilization on the People in European States. With: Observations on the Principal Conclusion in Mr. Malthus's Essay on Population.* New York.

Hardy, T. (1817). *Memoir of Thomas Hardy, Founder of and Secretary to, The London Corresponding Society, for diffusing Useful Political Knowledge among the People of Great Britain and Ireland, and for Promoting Parliamentary Reform.*

Historical Manuscripts Commission (1892–1927). *The Manuscripts of J.B. Fortescue preserved at Dropmore*, eds. W. Fitzpatrick and F. Bickley. 10 vols.

Historical Manuscripts Commission (1894). *The Manuscripts of Lord Kenyon*, ed. W. Sharpe.

Hutton, J. (ed.) (1885). *Selections from the Correspondence of James Bland Burges, Bart.*

Jones, W. (1793). *A Letter Addressed to Jno. Bull, Esquire, from His Second Cousin Thos. Bull, author of the 1st and 2nd Letters to His Brother John.*

Keith, R.M. (1849). *The Memoirs and Correspondence of Sir Robert Murray Keith*, ed. Mrs. Gillespie Smith. 2 vols.

Klingberg, F.J. (ed.) (1944). *The Warning Drum. The British Home Front faces Napoleon; Broadsides of 1803.*

London Corresponding Society (1983). *The Papers of the London Corresponding Society, 1792–1799*, ed. M. Thale. Cambridge.

Mackintosh, J. (1791). *Vindiciae Gallicae: a Defence of the French Revolution and its English Admirers against the Accusations of the Right Hon. Edmund Burke: including some Strictures on the Late Production of Mons. de Calonne.*

Mackintosh, J. (1836). *Memoirs of the Life of the Right Honourable Sir James Mackintosh*, ed. R.J. Mackintosh.

Malmesbury, 3rd Earl (ed.) (1851). *The Diaries and Correspondence of James Harris, Earl of Malmesbury*, 3 vols.

Malthus, T.R. (1796). *The Crisis. A View of the Present Interesting State of Great Britain, by a Friend to the Constitution.*

Malthus, T.R. (1992). *An Essay on the Principle of Population*, ed. D. Winch. Cambridge.

Miles, C.P. (1866). *The Correspondence of William Augustus Miles on the French Revolution 1789–1817.* 3 vols.

More, H. (1835). *Memoirs of the Life and Correspondence of Mrs. Hannah More*, ed. W. Roberts. 4 vols.

Nares, R. (1792). *Principles of Government deduced from Reason, Supported by English experience, and Opposed to French Errors.*

Ogilvie, W. (1781). *An Essay on the right of Property in Land, with respect to its foundation in the law of nature: its present establishment by the municipal laws of Europe; and the regulations by which it might be rendered more beneficial to the lower ranks of mankind.*

Owen, R. (1813). *A New View of Society.*

Paine, T. (1996) [1894–6]. *The Writings of Thomas Paine*, ed. M.D. Conway. 6 vols.

Paley, W. (1792). *Reasons for contentment addressed to the mechanics, journeymen and day labourers of Great Britain.*

Paley, W. (1793a). *Equality, as consistent with the British Constitution, In a Dialogue between a Master-Manufacturer and One of His Workmen.*

Paley, W. (1793b). *The Best Use of Bad Times, or, Friendly Hints to Manufacturers and Mechanics, on Their Present Distresses.*

Paley, W. (1819). *The Works of William Paley*, ed. A. Chalmers. 5 vols.

Perceval, S. (1800). *Observations intended to point out the Application of a Prophecy in the eleventh Chapter of the Book of Daniel to the French Power.*

Pitt, W. (1797). *The Speech of the Right Honourable William Pitt, in the House of Commons, on Friday November 10th. 1797, on Sir John Sinclair's proposed amendment to the Address of the Lords, relative to the Negotiation at Lisle, as laid before the House, by His Majesty's Command.*

Place, F. (1972). *Autobiography of Francis Place*, ed. M. Thale.

Playfair, W. (1785). *The Commercial and Political Atlas, Representing, by means of Stained Copper-Plate Charts, the Progress of the Commerce, Revenues, Expenditure, and Debts of England.*

Playfair, W. (1795). *The History of Jacobinism, its crimes, cruelties and perfidies.* 2 vols.

Playfair, W. (1796). *For the Use of the Enemies of England, A Real Statement of the Finances and Resources of Great Britain.*

Playfair, W. (1805). *An Inquiry into the Permanent Causes of the Decline and Fall of Powerful and Wealthy Nations.*

Price, R. (1789). *A Discourse on the Love of Our Country.*

Reeves, J. (1793). *Association Papers.*

Reeves, J. (1795). *Thoughts on English Government.*

Ricardo, D. (1951–3). *The Works and Correspondence of David Ricardo*, eds. P. Sraffa and M.H. Dobb. 11 vols, Cambridge.

Rogers, S. (1859). *Recollections.*

Rose, G. (1799). *A Brief Examination into the Increase of the Revenue, Commerce, and Manufactures of Great Britain, from 1792 to 1799.*

Rose, G. (1860). *Diaries and Correspondence of George Rose*, ed. L.V. Harcourt. 2 vols.

Rose, J.H. (1904b). *Select Dispatches from the British Foreign Office Archives relating to the Formation of the Third Coalition against France, 1804–1805.*

Rose, J.H. (1912). *Pitt and Napoleon: Essays and Letters.*

Smith, A. (1976). *The Works and Correspondence of Adam Smith*, eds. D.D. Raphael and A.L. Macfie, 6 vols, Oxford.

Society for Bettering the Condition and Increasing the Comforts of the Poor (1797–1817). *Reports*, 8 vols.

Spence, T. (1982). *The Political Works of Thomas Spence*, ed. H.T. Dickinson. Newcastle upon Tyne.

Stanhope, P.H. (1861–2). *Life of the Right Honourable William Pitt.* 4 vols.

Stewart, D. (1854–60). *Collected works of Dugald Stewart*, ed. W. Hamilton. 11 vols, Edinburgh.

Thelwall, J. (1995). *The Politics of English Jacobinism: The Writings of John Thelwall*, ed. G. Claeys.

Tomline, G.P. (1821). *Memoirs of the life of the Right Honourable William Pitt.* 2 vols.

Vane, C. (1961). *Wellington at War, 1794–1815; a Selection of his Wartime Letters.*

Volney, C.F. (1819). *The Ruins; or a Survey of the Revolutions of Empires.*

Wade, J. (1820). *The Black Book; or, Corruption Unmasked!*

Walpole, S. (1874). *The Life of the Right Honourable Spencer Perceval.* 2 vols.

Ward, R. Plumer (1850). *Memoirs of the Political and Literary Life of Robert Plumer Ward*, ed. E. Phipps. 2 vols.

Wilberforce, R.I. and S. (1838). *The Life of William Wilberforce.* 5 vols.

Windham, W. (1912). *The Windham Papers*, ed. Mrs H. Baring. 2 vols.

Wollstonecraft, M. (1793). *A Vindication of the Rights of Woman.*
Wordsworth, W. (1985a). *The Two-Part Prelude William Wordsworth,* ed. J. Wordsworth. Cambridge.
Wordsworth, W. (1985b). *The Fourteen-Book Prelude,* ed. W.J.B. Owen. Ithaca, NY.
Wyvill, C. (1794–1802). *Political Papers, chiefly respecting the Attempt of the County of York . . . to effect a Reformation of the Parliament of Great Britain.* 6 vols, York.
Yates, R. (1815). *The Church in Danger: A Statement of the Cause, and of the Probable Means of Averting that Danger.*
Yates, R. (1817). *The Basis of National Welfare: considered in reference chiefly to the Property of Britain, and Safety of the Church of England.*
Young, A. (1793). *The Example of France; a Warning to Britain.*
Young, A. (1800). *The Question of Scarcity plainly stated and Remedies Considered.*
Young, A. (1808). *General Report on Enclosures.*

Secondary Source Bibliography

All texts published in London unless otherwise stated.

Accworth, A.W. (1925). *Financial Reconstruction in England, 1815–22.*
Adams, E.D. (1904). *The Influence of Grenville on Pitt's Foreign Policy, 1787–1798.* Washington, DC.
Aers, D., Cook, J. and Punter, D. (eds) (1981). *Romanticism and Ideology: Studies in English Writing, 1765–1830.*
Allen, R.C. (1989). 'Enclosure, farming methods and the growth of productivity in the South Midlands'. *Research in Economic History,* Supplement 5, Part A: 69–88.
Allen, R.C. (1994). 'Agriculture during the industrial revolution', in Floud and McCloskey (eds), i, 96–122.
Allen, R.C. and O'Gràda, C. (1988). 'On the road again with Arthur Young: English, French and Irish agriculture during the industrial revolution'. *Journal of Economic History* 48: 93–116.
Anderson, B. (1983). *Imagined Communities: Reflections on the Origins and Spread of Nationalism.*
Andrew, D.T. (1989). *Philanthropy and Police: London Charity in the Eighteenth Century.* Princeton, NJ.
Andrew, D.T. (1996). 'Popular culture and public debate: London, 1780'. *Historical Journal* 39: 405–23.
Andrew, D.T. (1997). ' "Adultery à-la-mode": privilege, the law and attitudes to adultery, 1770–1809'. *History* 82: 5–23.
Anstey, R. (1975). *The Atlantic Slave Trade and British Abolition, 1760–1810.*
Ashton, T.S. (1959). *An Economic History of England. The Eighteenth Century.*
Aspinall, A. (1949). *Politics and the Press, 1780–1850.*
Atherton, H.M. (1982). 'The British defend their constitution in political cartoons and literature'. *Studies in Eighteenth Century Culture* 11: 8–31.
Ayling, S. (1988). *Edmund Burke: His Life and Opinions.*
Aylmer, G. (1980). 'From office holding to civil service: the genesis of modern bureaucracy'. *Transactions of the Royal Historical Society* 5 30: 91–108.

Bahmueller, C.F. (1981). *The National Charity Company. Jeremy Bentham's Silent Revolution*. Berkeley, CA.

Barker-Benfield, G.J. (1987). *The Culture of Sensibility: Sex and Society in Eighteenth Century Britain*. Chicago.

Barnes, D.G. (1939). *George III and William Pitt, 1783–1806*. Stanford, CA.

Barnes, D.G. (1965). *A History of the English Corn Laws, from 1660 to 1846*. New York.

Barnett, D.C. (1967). 'Allotments and the problem of rural poverty, 1780–1840', in E.L. Jones and G. Mingay (eds), 162–83.

Barry, J. (1994). 'Bourgeois collectivism? urban associations and the middling sort', in J. Barry and C. Brooks (eds), *The Middling Sort of People: Culture, Society and Politics in England, 1550–1800*. 84–112.

Bartlett, C.J. (1966). *Castlereagh*.

Bartlett, T. (1992). *The Fall and Rise of the Irish Nation: the Catholic Question, 1690–1830*. Savage Md.

Baugh, D.A. (1988). 'Great Britain's blue water policy, 1688–1815'. *International History Review* 10: 1–58.

Bayly, C.A. (1989). *Imperial Meridian: the British Empire and the World, 1780–1830*.

Bebbington, D.W. (1989). *Evangelicalism in Modern Britain from the 1730s to the 1980s*.

Beckett, J.V. (1981). *Coal and Tobacco: The Lowthers and the Economic Development of Cumberland, 1660–1760*. Cambridge.

Beckett, J.V. (1985). *The Aristocracy in England, 1660–1914*. Oxford.

Beckett, J.V. (1987). 'Stability in politics and society, 1680–1750', in C. Jones (ed.), *Britain in the First Age of Party*, 1–18.

Beedell, A.V. (1993). 'John Reeves' prosecution for seditious libel 1795–6: a study in political cynicism'. *Historical Journal* 36: 799–824.

Beer, J. (1977). 'The "Revolutionary Youth" of Wordsworth and Coleridge: another view'. *Critical Quarterly* 18: 49–67.

Belchem, J. (1978). 'Henry Hunt and the evolution of the mass platform'. *English Historical Review* 93: 739–73.

Belchem, J. (1981). 'Republicanism, constitutionalism and the radical platform in early nineteenth-century England'. *Social History* 6: 1–32.

Belchem, J. (1985). *'Orator' Hunt: Henry Hunt and English Working Class Radicalism*. Oxford.

Belchem, J. (1990). *Industrialisation and the Working Class: the English Experience, 1750–1900*. Aldershot.

Benjamin, K.W. (1990). 'The United Irishmen and the great naval mutiny of 1797'. *Eire-Ireland* 25/3: 7–18.

Berg, M. (1987). 'Women's work, mechanisation and the early phases of industrialisation in England', in Joyce (ed.) 64–94.

Berg, M. (1994a). 'Factories, workshops and industrial organisation', in Floud and McCloskey (eds) i, 123–50.

Berg, M. (1994b). *The Age of Manufactures, 1700–1820: Industry, Innovation and Work in Britain*, 2nd edn. Harlow.

Best, G.F.A. (1964). *Temporal Pillars Queen Anne's Bounty, the Ecclesiastical Commissioners, and the Church of England*. Cambridge.

Black, E.C. (1963). *The Association: British Extraparliamentary Political Organisation, 1769–1793*. Cambridge.

Black, J. (1985). 'The Marquis of Carmarthen and relations with France, 1784–1787'. *Francia* 12: 283–302.

Black, J. (1987). 'Anglo-French relations in the age of the French Revolution, 1787–1793'. *Francia* 15: 405–32.

Black, J. (1988). 'Britain's foreign alliances in the eighteenth century'. *Albion* 20: 573–602.

Black, J. (1990). *A System of Ambition: British Foreign Policy, 1660–1793*. Harlow.

Black, J. (1994). *British Foreign Policy in an Age of Revolutions, 1783–1793*. Cambridge.

Black, J. and Woodfine, P. (eds) (1988). *The British Navy and the Use of Naval Power in the Eighteenth Century*. Leicester.

Blackstock, A. (1993). 'The social and political implications of the raising of the yeomanry in Ulster, 1796–8', in Dickson, Keogh and Whelan (eds), 234–43.

Blanning, T.C.W. (1983). *The French Revolution in Germany: Occupation and Resistance in the Rhineland, 1792–1801*. Oxford.

Blanning, T.C.W. (1986). *The Origins of the French Revolutionary Wars*. Harlow.

Blanning, T.C.W. (1989). *The French Revolution: Aristocrats vs. Bourgeoisie?*

Blanning, T.C.W. (1991). 'The French Revolution in Europe', in Lucas (ed.), *Rewriting the French Revolution*, 183–206.

Blanning, T.C.W. (1996). *The French Revolutionary Wars, 1787–1802*.

Blaug, M. (1963). 'The myth of the old poor law and the making of the new'. *Journal of Economic History* 23: 151–84.

Blaug, M. (1964). 'The Poor Law Report re-examined'. *Journal of Economic History* 24: 229–45.

Bohstedt, J. (1982). *Speenhamland County. Poverty and the Poor Laws in Berkshire, 1782–1834*. New York.

Bohstedt, J. (1983). *Riots and Community Politics in England and Wales, 1790–1820*. Cambridge, MA.

Bohstedt, J. (1988). 'Gender, household and community politics: women in English riots, 1790–1810'. *Past and Present* 77: 84–107.

Bolt, C. and Drescher, S. (eds) (1980). *Anti-Slavery, Religion and Reform: Essays in Memory of Roger Anstey*. Folkestone.

Booth, A. (1977). 'Food riots in north-west England, 1790–1801'. *Past and Present* 120: 88–122.

Booth, A. (1983). 'Popular loyalism and public violence in the north-west of England, 1790–1800'. *Social History* 8: 295–313.

Booth, A. (1989). 'English popular loyalism and the French Revolution'. *Bulletin of the Society for the Study of Labour History* 54: 26–31.

Bordo, M.D. and White, E.N. (1991). 'A tale of two currencies: British and French finance during the Napoleonic Wars'. *Journal of Economic History* 51: 303–16.

Borsay, P. (1989). *The English Urban Renaissance, 1680–1780*. Oxford.

Bossy, J. (1975). *The English Catholic Community, 1570–1850*.

Botham, F.W. and Hunt, E.H. (1987). 'Wages in Britain during the industrial revolution'. *Economic History Review* 40: 380–99.

Bowen, H.V. (1996). *Elites, Enterprise and the Making of the British Overseas Empire, 1688–1775*.

Bowen, H.V. (1998). 'British India: the Metropolitan context, 1765–1813', in Marshall (ed.) 530–51.

Boyce, D.G. (1982). *Nationalism in Ireland*. Dublin.

Boyer, G.R. (1990). *An Economic History of the English Poor Law, 1750–1850*. Cambridge.

Bradley, I. (1974). 'The Politics of Godliness: Evangelicals in Parliament, 1784–1832'. Unpublished Oxford D. Phil thesis.

Bradley, I. (1976). *The Call to Seriousness: The Evangelical Impact on the Victorians*. New York.

Bradley, J.E. (1975–6). 'Whigs and non-conformists: slumbering radicalism in eighteenth century politics, 1739–1789'. *Eighteenth Century Studies* 9: 1–27.

Bradley, J.E. (1989). 'The Anglican pulpit, the social order and the resurgence of Toryism during the American Revolution'. *Albion* 21: 361–88.

Bradley, J.E. (1990). *Religion, Revolution and English Radicalism: Nonconformity in British Politics and Society*. Cambridge.

Breihan, J.R. (1983). 'William Pitt and the Commission on Fees, 1785–1801'. *Historical Journal* 27: 59–81.

Brewer, J. (1989). *The Sinews of Power: War, Money and the English State, 1688–1783*.

Briggs, A. (1956). 'Middle-class consciousness in English politics, 1780–1846'. *Past and Present* 1: 65–74.

Briggs, A. (1959). *The Age of Improvement. England, 1783–1867*.

Briggs, A. (1967). 'The language of class in early nineteenth century Britain', in A. Briggs and J. Saville (eds), *Essays in Labour History in Memory of G.D.H. Cole*, 43–73.

Brims, J. (1989). 'The covenanting tradition and Scottish radicalism in the 1790's', in T.M. Brotherstone (ed.), *Covenant, Charter and Party: Traditions of Revolt and Protest in Modern Scottish History*. Aberdeen, 50–62.

Brims, J. (1990). 'From reformers to Jacobins: the Scottish Association of the Friends of the People', in T.M. Devine (ed.), *Conflict and Stability in Scottish Society, 1700–1850*. Edinburgh, 31–49.

Brims, J. (1993). 'Scottish radicalism and the United Irishmen', in Dickson, Keogh and Whelan (eds), 151–66.

Brock, W.R. (1941). *Lord Liverpool and Liberal Toryism, 1820 to 1827*. Cambridge.

Brooks, C. (1994). 'Apprenticeship, social mobility and the middling sort, 1550–1800', in Barry and Brooks (eds), 52–83.

Brown, D.J. (1998). 'The government of Scotland under Henry Dundas and William Pitt'. *History* 83: 265–79.

Brown, F.C. (1961). *Fathers of the Victorians: The Age of Wilberforce*. Cambridge.

Brown, P. (1967). *The Chathamites: a Study in the Relationship between Personalities and Ideas in the Second Half of the Eighteenth Century*.

Brown, P.A. (1918). *The French Revolution in English History*.

Browning, R. (1983). *Political and Constitutional Ideas of the Court Whigs*. Baton Rouge. LA.

Browning, R. (1984). 'The origin of Burke's ideas revisited'. *Eighteenth Century Studies* 18: 57–71.

Buckley, R.N. (1977). *Slaves in Red Coats: The British West India Regiments, 1795–1815.* New Haven, CT.

Burnette, J. (1997). 'An investigation of the female–male wage gap during the industrial revolution in Britain'. *Economic History Review* 50: 257–81.

Burrow, J.W. (1988). *Whigs and Liberals: Continuity and Change in English Political Thought.* Oxford.

Butler, M. (1975). *Jane Austen and the War of Ideas.* Oxford.

Butler, M. (1981). *Romantics, Rebels and Reactionaries: English Literature and its Background, 1760–1830.* Oxford.

Byatt, A.S. (1989). *Unruly Times: Wordsworth and Coleridge in Their Time.*

Bythell, D. (1969). *The Handloom Weavers. A Study of the English Cotton Industry during the Industrial Revolution.* Cambridge.

Cain, P. and Hopkins, A.G. (1980). 'The political economy of British expansion overseas, 1750–1914'. *Economic History Review*, 2nd series, 23: 463–90.

Cain, P. and Hopkins, A.G. (1986). 'Gentlemanly capitalism and British expansion overseas. I. The old colonial system, 1688–1850'. *Economic History Review*, 2nd series, 40: 1–26.

Cain, P. and Hopkins, A.G. (1993). *British Imperialism: Innovation and Expansion, 1688–1914.* Harlow.

Calhoun, C. (1982). *The Question of Class Struggle: The Social Foundations of Popular Radicalism during the Industrial Revolution.* Cambridge.

Cannadine, D. (1994). *Aspects of Aristocracy.* New Haven, CT.

Cannadine, D. (1999). *The Rise and Fall of Class in Britain.* New York.

Cannon, J. (1972). *Parliamentary Reform from 1660 to 1832.*

Cannon, J. (ed.) (1981). *The Whig Ascendancy: Colloquies on Hanoverian England.* Cambridge.

Cannon, J. (1982). *Aristocratic Century. The Peerage of Eighteenth Century England.*

Caretta, V. (1990). *George III and the Satirists from Hogarth to Byron.* Athens, GA.

Carnall, G. (1960). *Robert Southey and His Age: The Development of a Conservative Mind.* Oxford.

Chalklin, C.W. (1974). *The Provincial Towns of Georgian England: A Study of the Building Process, 1740–1820.* Kingston and Montreal.

Chambers, J.D. (1952–3). 'Enclosure and labour supply in the Industrial Revolution'. *Economic History Review* 5: 319–413.

Chambers, J.D. and Mingay, G.E. (eds) (1966). *The Agricultural Revolution, 1750–1880.*

Chandler, J.K. (1984). *Wordsworth's Second Nature: a Study of the Poetry and Politics.* Chicago.

Chapman, S.D. (1984). *The Rise of Merchant Banking.*

Chapman, S.D. (1992). *Merchant Enterprise in Britain: From the Industrial Revolution to World War I.* Cambridge.

Chard II (1975–6). 'Joseph Johnson: father of the book trade'. *Bulletin of the New York Public Library* 79: 51–82.

Charlesworth, A. (1982). *An Atlas of Rural Protest in Britain, 1549–1900.*

Chase, M. (1988). *The People's Farm: English Radial Agrarianism, 1775–1840*. Oxford.

Chitnis, A. (1976). *The Scottish Enlightenment: a Social History.*

Chitnis, A. (1986). *The Scottish Enlightenment and Early Victorian England.*

Christie, I.R. (1962). *Wilkes, Wyvill and Reform: the Parliamentary Reform Movement in British Politics, 1760–1785.*

Christie, I.R. (1970). *Myth and Reality in Eighteenth Century British Politics, and Other Papers.*

Christie, I.R. (1982). *Wars and Revolutions, England, 1760–1815.*

Christie, I.R. (1984). *Stress and Stability: Reflections on the British Avoidance of Revolution.* Oxford.

Christie, I.R. (1991). 'Conservatism and stability in British society', in Philp (ed.), 169–87.

Christie, I.R. (1995). *British Non-Elite MPs, 1715–1820*. Oxford.

Claeys, G. (1981). 'Four letters between Thomas Spence and Charles Hall'. *Notes and Queries* August: 317–21.

Claeys, G. (1987). *Machinery, Money and the Millennium: from Moral Economy to Socialism, 1815–1860*. Oxford.

Claeys, G. (1989). *Thomas Paine: Social and Political Thought*. Boston, MA.

Claeys, G. (1990). 'The French Revolution debate and British political thought'. *History of Political Thought* 11: 59–80.

Claeys, G. (1994). 'The origins of the rights of labor: republicanism, commerce and the construction of modern social theory in Britain, 1796–1805'. *Journal of Modern History* 66: 249–90.

Clapham, J.H. (1899). *The Causes of the War of 1792*. Cambridge.

Clapham, J.H. (1945). *The Bank of England: A History*. 2 vols. Cambridge.

Clark, A. (1990). 'Queen Caroline and the sexual politics of popular culture in London, 1820'. *Representations* 31: 47–68.

Clark, G. (1993). 'Agriculture and the Industrial Revolution, 1700–1850', in Mokyr (ed.), 227–66.

Clark, J.C.D. (1980). 'A general theory of party, opposition and government, 1688–1832'. *Historical Journal* 23: 295–325.

Clark, J.C.D. (1985). *English Society, 1688–1832*. Cambridge.

Clark, S. and Donnelly, J.S. (eds) (1983). *Irish Peasants, Violence and Political Unrest, 1780–1914*. Madison, WI.

Clive, J. (1957). *Scotch Reviewers: The Edinburgh Review, 1802–1815.*

Coats, A.W. (1960–1). 'Economic thought and poor law policy in the eighteenth century'. *Economic History Review*, 2nd series, 13: 39–51.

Coats, A.W. (1972). 'Contrary moralities: plebs, paternalists and political economists'. *Past and Present* 54: 130–3.

Cobban, A. (1954a) [1929]. *Edmund Burke and the Revolt against the Eighteenth Century; a Study of the Political and Social Thinking of Burke, Wordsworth, Coleridge, and Southey.*

Cobban, A. (1954b). *Ambassadors and Secret Agents: The Diplomacy of the First Earl of Malmesbury at the Hague.*

Cobban, A. (1968). 'British Secret Service in France, 1784–1792', in A. Cobban (ed.), *Aspects of the French Revolution*, 192–224.

Colley, L. (1982). *In Defiance of Oligarchy: the Tory Party 1714–60*. Cambridge.

Colley, L. (1984). 'The Apotheosis of George III: Loyalty, royalty and the British nation, 1760–1820'. *Past and Present* 102: 96–129.

Colley, L. (1986). 'Whose nation?: class and political consciousness in eighteenth century Britain'. *Past and Present* 113: 97–117.

Colley, L. (1992). *Britons, Forging the Nation, 1707–1837*. Cambridge, MA.

Colley, L. (1994). 'The reach of the state, the appeal of the nation: mass arming and political culture in the Napoleonic Wars', in L. Stone (ed.), *An Imperial State at War: Britain from 1689 to 1815*, 165–84.

Collini, S., Burrow, J. and Winch, D. (eds) (1983). *That Noble Science of Politics: a Study in Nineteenth-Century Intellectual History*. Cambridge.

Cone, C.B. (1968). *The English Jacobins; Reformers in Late Eighteenth Century England*. New York.

Cookson, J.E. (1975). *Lord Liverpool's Administration, 1815–1822*. Edinburgh.

Cookson, J.E. (1982). *The Friends of Peace: Anti-War Liberalism in England, 1793–1815*. Cambridge.

Cookson, J.E. (1983). 'Political arithmetic and war in Britain, 1793–1815'. *War & Society*, 1: 37–53.

Cookson, J.E. (1989). 'The English volunteer movement of the French wars, 1793–1815'. *Historical Journal* 32: 867–92.

Cookson, J.E. (1997). *The British Armed Nation, 1793–1815*. Oxford.

Cooper, R.A. (1974). 'William Pitt, taxation and the needs of war'. *Journal of British Studies* 12: 94–103.

Cope, S.R. (1942). 'The Goldsmids and the development of the London money market during the Napoleonic Wars'. *Economica*, New Series, 9: 180–206.

Cope, S.R. (1983). *Walter Boyd, A Merchant Banker in the Age of Napoleon*.

Corfield, P.J. (1991). 'Class by number and name in eighteenth century Britain', in P.J. Corfield (ed.), *Language, History and Class*. Oxford, 101–30.

Corfield, P.J. (1995). *Power and the Professions in Britain, 1700–1850*.

Corfield, P. and Evans, C. (eds) (1996). *Youth and Revolution in the 1790s: The Letters of William Pattison, Thomas Amyot and Henry Crabbe Robinson*. Gloucester.

Courteney, C.B. (1974). 'Edmund Burke and the Enlightenment', in A. Whiteman, J.S. Bromley and P.G.M. Dickson (eds), *Statesmen, Scholars and Merchants: Essays in Eighteenth Century History Presented to Dame Lucy Sutherland*. Oxford, 304–22.

Crafts, N.F.R. (1977). 'The Industrial Revolution in England and France: some thoughts on the question "Why was England first?"'. *Economic History Review* 30: 421–41.

Crafts, N.F.R. (1981). 'The eighteenth century: a survey', in Floud and McCloskey, 1–16.

Crafts, N.F.R. (1985). *British Economic Growth during the Industrial Revolution*. New York.

Crafts, N.F.R. (1989). 'Real wages, inequality and economic growth in Britain, 1750–1850: a review of recent research', in Scholliers (ed.).

Crafts, N.F.R. and Harley, C.K. (1992). 'Output growth and the British industrial revolution: a restatement of the Crafts-Harley view'. *Economic History Review* 45: 703–30.

Cremasci, S. and Daval, M. (1996). 'Malthus and Ricardo on economic methodology'. *History of Political Economy* 28: 475–511.

Crimmins, J.E. (1990). *Secular Utilitarianism: Social Science and the Critique of Religion in the Thought of Jeremy Bentham*. Oxford.

Crimmins, J.E. (1994). 'Bentham's political radicalism re-examined'. *Journal of the History of Ideas* 55: 259–81.

Crossley, C. and Small, I. (eds) (1989). *The French Revolution and British Culture*. Oxford.

Crouzet, F. (1959). *L'Economie britannique et le blocus continental, 1806–13*. 2 vols, Paris.

Crouzet, F. (1964). 'Wars, blockade and economic change in Europe, 1792–1815'. *Journal of Economic History* 24: 567–88.

Crouzet, F. (1989). 'The impact of the French wars on the British economy', in Dickinson (ed.), 189–210.

Crouzet, F. (1990). *Comparative Studies in Franco-British Economic History*. Cambridge.

Crowhurst, P. (1977). *The Defence of British Trade, 1689–1815*. Folkestone.

Cullen, L.M. (1980). 'The cultural basis of modern Irish nationalism', in R. Mitchison (ed.), *The Roots of Nationalism: Studies in Northern Europe*, 91–106.

Cullen, L.M. (1990). 'The political structures of the Defenders', in Gough and Dickson (eds), 117–38.

Cullen, L.M. (1993). 'The internal politics of the United Irishmen', in Dickson, Keogh and Whelan (eds), 176–96.

Cunliffe, J. (1990). 'The neglected background of radical liberalism'. *History of Political Thought* 11: 467–90.

Cunliffe, J. (1994). 'Charles Hall: exploitation, commercial society and political economy'. *History of Political Thought* 15: 535–53.

Cunningham, H. (1981). 'The language of patriotism, 1750–1914'. *History Workshop Journal* 12: 8–33.

Curtin, N.J. (1985). 'The transformation of the Society of the United Irishmen into a mass revolutionary organisation, 1794–6'. *Irish Historical Studies* 24: 463–92.

Curtin, N.J. (1993). 'The United Irish organisation in Ulster', in Dickson, Keogh and Whelan (eds), 209–21.

Curtin, N.J. (1994). *The United Irishmen: Popular Politics in Ulster and Dublin, 1791–1798*. Oxford.

Dann, O. and Dinwiddy, J. (eds) (1988). *Nationalism in the Age of the French Revolution*.

Darnton, R. (1996 edn.). *The Forbidden Best Sellers of Pre-Revolutionary France*. New York.

Davies, G. (1919). 'The Whigs and the Peninsular War, 1808–14'. *Transactions of the Royal Historical Society* 2: 113–31.

Davis, H.W.C. (1929). *The Age of Grey and Peel*. Oxford.

Davis, R. (1979). *The Industrial Revolution and British Overseas Trade*. Leicester.

Deane, P. (1975). 'War and industrialisation', in J.M. Winter (ed.), *War and Economic Development: Essays in Memory of David Joslin*. Cambridge, 91–102.

Deane, P. and Cole, W.A. (1975). *British Economic Growth, 1688–1959*. Cambridge.

Deane, S. (1988). *The French Revolution and the Enlightenment in England, 1789–1832*. Cambridge, MA.

Derry, J. (1963). *The Regency Crisis and the Whigs, 1788–1789*. Cambridge.

Derry, J. (1981). 'Governing temperament under Pitt and Liverpool', in Cannon (ed.), 125–45.

Derry, J. (1989). 'The Opposition Whigs and the French Revolution, 1789–1815', in Dickinson (ed.), 39–60.

Deutsch, P. (1996). 'Moral trespass in Georgian London: gaming, gender and electoral politics in the age of George III'. *Historical Journal* 39: 639–56.

Devine, T.M. (1975). *The Tobacco Lords: a Study of the Tobacco Merchants of Glasgow and Their Trading Activities, c.1740–90*. Edinburgh.

Dickinson, H.T. (1977). *Liberty and Property: Political Ideology in Eighteenth-Century Britain*.

Dickinson, H.T. (1985). *British Radicalism and the French Revolution, 1789–1815*. Oxford.

Dickinson, H.T. (1986). *Caricatures and the Constitution, 1760–1832*.

Dickinson, H.T. (1989). 'Popular conservatism and militant loyalism in Britain 1789–1815', in H.T. Dickinson (ed.), *Britain and the French Revolution, 1789–1815*, 103–26.

Dickinson, H.T. (1990). 'Radicals and reformers in the age of Wilkes and Wyvill', in J. Black (ed.), *British Politics and Society from Walpole to Pitt*. Basingstoke, 123–46.

Dickinson, H.T. (1992a). 'Britain and the ideological crusade against the French Revolution', in L. Domergue and G. Lamoigne (eds), *Actes du Colloque Internationale*, Toulouse, 153–74.

Dickinson, H.T. (1992b). 'The French Revolution and counter-revolution in Britain', in H.C. Schroeder and H.D. Metzger (eds), *Aspekte der Französichen Revolution*, Darmstadt, 231–63.

Dickson, D., Keogh, D. and Whelan, K. (eds) (1993). *The United Irishmen: Republicanism, Radicalism, and Rebellion*. Dublin.

Dickson, P.G.M. (1967). *The Financial Revolution in England: a Study in the Development of Public Credit, 1688–1756*.

Dinwiddy, J.R. (1968). 'The use of the Crown's powers of deportation under the Aliens Act'. *Bulletin of the Institute of Historical Research* 41: 193–211.

Dinwiddy, J.R. (1970). 'Charles James Fox and the people'. *History* 55: 342–59.

Dinwiddy, J.R. (1971). *Christopher Wyvill and Reform, 1790–1820. Borthwick Papers* 39. York.

Dinwiddy, J.R. (1974a). 'The "Black Lamp" in Yorkshire 1801–2'. *Past and Present* 64: 113–23.

Dinwiddy, J.R. (1974b). 'Utility and natural law in Burke's thought: a reconsideration'. *Studies in Burke and His Time* 16: 105–28.

Dinwiddy, J.R. (1975). 'Bentham's transition to political radicalism, 1809–10'. *Journal of the History of Ideas* 35: 683–700.

Dinwiddy, J.R. (1976). 'Charles Hall, early English socialist'. *International Review of Social History* 21: 256–76.

Dinwiddy, J.R. (1978). 'Burke and the Utilitarians: a rejoinder'. *Studies in Burke and His Time* 19: 119–26.

Dinwiddy, J.R. (1979). 'Luddism and politics in the northern counties'. *Social History* 4: 33–63.

Dinwiddy, J.R. (1980). 'Sir Francis Burdett and Burdettite radicalism'. *History* 65: 17–31.

Dinwiddy, J.R. (1986). *From Luddism to the First Reform Bill: Reform in England, 1810–1832*. Oxford.

Dinwiddy, J.R. (1989). 'English Radicals and the French Revolution, 1800–1850', in Furet and Ozouf (eds), 447–66.

Dinwiddy, J.R. (1990). 'Conceptions of revolution in the English radicalism of the 1790s', in Hellmuth (ed.), 535–60.

Dinwiddy, J.R. (1991). 'Interpretations of Anti-Jacobinism', in Philp (ed.), 38–49.

Ditchfield, G.M. (1981). 'The House of Lords and parliamentary reform in the 1780s'. *Bulletin of the Institute of Historical Research* 54: 207–25.

Ditchfield, G.M. (1985). 'Parliament, the Quakers and the Tithe Question, 1750–1835'. *Parliamentary History* 4: 87–114.

Dobson, C.R. (1980). *Masters and Journeymen: a Pre-history of Industrial Relations, 1717–1800*.

Donnelly, F.K. and Baxter, J. (1974). 'The revolutionary "underground" in the West Riding: myth or reality?'. *Past and Present* 64: 124–35.

Dozier, R.R. (1983). *For King, Constitution and Country: the English Loyalists and the French Revolution*. Lexington, KY.

Drayton, R. (1998). 'Knowledge and Empire', in P.J. Marshall (ed.), 231–52.

Duffy, I.P.H. (1982). 'The discount policy of the Bank of England during the suspension of cash payments, 1797–1821'. *Economic History Review* 35: 67–82.

Duffy, M. (1971). 'British War Policy: the Austrian Alliance, 1793–1801'. Oxford University D.Phil thesis.

Duffy, M. (1983). 'British foreign policy in the war against revolutionary France', in C. Jones (ed.), 11–26.

Duffy, M. (1986). 'Pitt, Grenville and the control of British foreign policy in the 1790s', in J. Black (ed.), *Knights Errant and True Englishmen: British Foreign Policy, 1660–1800*. Edinburgh, 151–72.

Duffy, M. (1987). *Soldiers, Sugar and Seapower: The British Expeditions to the West Indies and the War against Revolutionary France*. Oxford.

Duffy, M. (1989). 'British diplomacy and the French wars, 1789–1815', in Dickinson (ed.), 127–46.

Duffy, M. (1991). 'War, revolution and the crisis of the British empire', in Philp (ed.), 118–45.

Duffy, M. (1996). 'William Pitt and the origins of the Loyal Association Movement'. *Historical Journal* 39: 943–62.

Duffy, M. (1998). 'World wide war, 1793–1815', in P.J. Marshall (ed.), 184–207.

Dyck, I. (1992). *William Cobbett and Rural Popular Culture*. Cambridge.

Earle, P. (1987). *The Making of the English Middle Class: Business, Society and Family Life in London, 1680–1730*.

Eastwood, D. (1989a). 'Amplifying the province of the legislature: the flow of information and the English state in the early nineteenth century'. *Bulletin of the Institute of Historical Research* 62: 276–94.

Eastwood, D. (1989b). 'Robert Southey and the intellectual origins of romantic conservatism'. *English Historical Review* 104: 308–31.

Eastwood, D. (1991). 'Patriotism and the English State in the 1790s', in Philp (ed.), 146–68.

Eastwood, D. (1992). 'Robert Southey and the meanings of patriotism'. *Journal of British Studies* 31: 265–87.

Eastwood, D. (1994a). *Governing Rural England: Tradition and Transformation in Local Government, 1780–1840*. Oxford.

Eastwood, D. (1994b). 'John Reeves and the contested idea of the constitution'. *British Journal of Eighteenth Century Studies* 16: 197–212.

Eastwood, D. (1995). 'E.P. Thompson, Britain and the French Revolution'. *History Workshop Journal* 39: 79–88.

Eastwood, D. (1997). *Government and Community in the English Provinces, 1700–1870*.

Edwards, M.M. (1967). *The Growth of the British Cotton Trade, 1780–1815*. Manchester.

Ehrman, J. (1962). *The British Government and Commercial Negotiations with Europe, 1783–1793*. Cambridge.

Ehrman, J. (1969). *The Younger Pitt: the Years of Acclaim*.

Ehrman, J. (1983). *The Younger Pitt: the Reluctant Transition*.

Ehrman, J. (1996). *The Younger Pitt: the Consuming Struggle*.

Elliott, M. (1977). 'The "Despard conspiracy" reconsidered'. *Past and Present* 75: 46–61.

Elliott, M. (1978). 'The origins and transformation of early Irish republicanism'. *International Review of Social History* 23: 405–28.

Elliott, M. (1982). *Partners in Revolution: the United Irishmen and France*. New Haven, CT.

Elliott, M. (1983). 'French subversion in Britain during the French Revolution', in C. Jones (ed.), 40–52.

Elliott, M. (1985). 'The UI as diplomat', in P.J. Corish (ed.), *Radicals, Rebels and Establishments*, 69–81.

Emsley, C. (1978). 'The "London insurrection" of 1792: fact, fiction or fantasy?' *Journal of British Studies* 17: 66–86.

Emsley, C. (1979a). *British Society and the French Wars, 1793–1815*.

Emsley, C. (1979b). 'The Home Office and its official sources of information and investigation, 1791–1801'. *English Historical Review* 94: 532–61.

Emsley, C. (1981). 'An aspect of Pitt's Terror: prosecutions for sedition during the 1790s'. *Social History* 6: 155–84.

Emsley, C. (1985). 'Repression, terror and the rule of law in England during the decade of the French Revolution'. *English Historical Review* 100: 801–26.

Emsley, C. (1989). 'The social impact of the French wars, 1789–1815', in Dickinson (ed.), 211–28.

Emsley, C. (1991). 'Revolution, war and the nation state: the British and French experiences, 1789–1801', in Philp (ed.), 99–117.

Engermann, S. (1994). 'Mercantilism and overseas trade, 1700–1800', in Floud and McCloskey (eds), i, 182–204.

Epstein, J. (1988). 'Radical dining, toasting and symbolic expression in early nineteenth century Lancashire'. *Albion* 20: 271–91.

Epstein, J. (1989). 'Understanding the cap of liberty: symbolic practice and social conflict in early nineteenth century England'. *Past and Present* 122: 75–118.

Epstein, J. (1994). *Radical Expression: Political Language, Ritual, and Symbol in England, 1790–1850.* Oxford.

Erdman, D.V. (1991 edn.). *Blake. Prophet against Empire: a Poet's Interpretation of the History of His Own Times.* New York.

Evans, E.J. (1976). *The Contentious Tithe: the Tithe Problem and English Agriculture, 1750–1850.* Leicester.

Evans, H.V. (1974). 'The Nootka Sound controversy in Anglo-French diplomacy'. *Journal of Modern History* 46: 609–40.

Fay, C.R. (1951). *Huskisson and His Age.*

Fayle, C.E. (1948a). 'Shipowning and marine insurance', in Parkinson (ed.), 25–48.

Fayle, C.E. (1948b). 'The employment of British shipping', in Parkinson (ed.), 72–86.

Feiling, K. (1924). *The Second Tory Party, 1714–1832.*

Feinstein, C. (1978). 'Capital formation in Great Britain', in P. Mathias and M.M. Postan (eds), vii, 28–96.

Feinstein, C. (1981). 'Capital accumulation and the industrial revolution', in Floud and McCloskey (eds), i, 128–42.

Fevearyear, A. (1963). *The Pound Sterling. A History of English Money.*

Fitzpatrick, M. (1990). 'Heretical religion and radical political ideas in late eighteenth century England', in Hellmuth (ed.), 339–72.

Flinn, M.W. (1974). 'Trends in real wages, 1750–1850'. *Economic History Review* 27: 395–411.

Flinn, M.W. (1984). *History of the British Coal Industry.* 2 vols. Oxford.

Floud, R.C. and Harris, B. (1997). 'Health, height and welfare: Britain, 1700–1980', in Floud and Steckel (eds), 91–126.

Floud, R.C. and McCloskey, D.N. (eds) (1983). *The Economic History of Britain since 1700.* 3 vols, Cambridge.

Floud, R.C. and McCloskey, D.N. (eds) (1994). *The Economic History of Britain since 1700,* 2nd edn. 3 vols, Cambridge.

Floud, R.C. and Steckel, R.H. (eds) (1997). *Health and Welfare during Industrialization.* Chicago.

Floud, R.C., Wachter, K. and Gregory, A. (1990). *Height, Health and History. Nutritional Standards in the United Kingdom, 1750–1980.* Cambridge.

Fontana, B. (1985). *Rethinking the Politics of Commercial Society: the Edinburgh Review, 1802–1832.* Cambridge.

Foord, A.S. (1964). *His Majesty's Opposition, 1740–1830.* Oxford.

Forbes, D. (1970). 'Sceptical Whiggism, commerce and liberty', in A. Skinner and T. Wilson (eds), *Essays on Adam Smith,* 179–201.

Forbes, D. (1976). *Hume's Philosophical Politics.* Oxford.

Ford, C.H. (1996). *Hannah More: a Critical Biography.* New York.

Frey, L. and Frey, M. (1993). ' "The reign of the charlatans is over": the French revolutionary attack on diplomatic practice'. *Journal of Modern History* 53: 706–44.

Fry, M. (1992). *The Dundas Despotism.* Edinburgh.

Fryer, W.R. (1965). *Republic or Restoration in France? 1794–7.* Manchester.

Fulcher, J. (1996). 'The English people and their constitution after Waterloo: parliamentary reform, 1815–1817', in Vernon (ed.), 52–82.

Furet, F. and Ozouf, M. (eds) (1989). *The French Revolution and the Creation of Modern Political Culture, iii: The Transformation of Political Culture.* Oxford.

Gahan, D. (1995). *The People's Rising: Wexford 1798.* Dublin.

Garrett, C. (1975). *Respectable Folly: Millenarians and the French Revolution in France and England.* Baltimore, MD.

Garvin, T. (1982). 'Defenders, Ribbonmen and others: underground political networks in pre-famine Ireland'. *Past and Present* 96: 133–53.

Gascoigne, J. (1989). *Cambridge in the Age of the Enlightenment: Science, Religion and Politics from the Restoration to the French Revolution.* Cambridge.

Gash, N. (1978). 'After Waterloo'. *Transactions of the Royal Historical Society* 28: 145–58.

Gash, N. (1986). *Pillars of Government and other Essays on State and Society, c.1770–1880.*

Gates, D. (1997). *The Napoleonic Wars, 1803–1815.*

Gattrell, V.A.C. (1982). 'Incorporation and the pursuit of liberal hegemony in Manchester, 1790–1839', in D. Fraser (ed.), *Municipal Reform and the Industrial City.* Leicester, 16–55.

Gattrell, V.A.C. (1994). *The Hanging Tree: Execution and the English People, 1770–1868.* Oxford.

Geggus, D. (1982). *Slavery, War and Revolution: the British Occupation of St. Domingue, 1793–1798.* Oxford.

George, D.R. (1959). *English Political Caricature: a Study of Opinion and Propaganda.* 2 vols, Oxford.

Gilbert, A.D. (1976). *Religion and Society in Industrial England: Church, Chapel, and Social Change, 1740–1914.*

Gilbert, A.D. (1979). 'Methodism, dissent and political stability in early industrial England'. *Journal of Religious History* 10: 381–99.

Gilbert, A.D. (1993). 'Religion and political stability in early industrial England', in O'Brien and Quinault (eds), 79–99.

Gilbert, F. (1977). 'The new diplomacy of the eighteenth century', in F. Gilbert (ed.), *History, Choice and Commitment.* Cambridge, MA, 323–49.

Gilboy, E.W. (1934). *Wages in Eighteenth Century England.* Cambridge, MA.

Gilboy, E.W. (1936). 'The cost of living and real wages in eighteenth-century England'. *Review of Economics and Statistics* 18: 134–43.

Gill, C. (1913). *The Naval Mutinies of 1797.* Manchester.

Gilmartin, K. (1996). *Print Politics: the Press and Radical Opposition in the Early Nineteenth Century.* Cambridge.

Ginter, D.E. (1966). 'The Loyalist Association movement of 1792–3 and British public opinion'. *Historical Journal* 9: 179–90.

Girouard, M. (1981). *The Return to Camelot: Chivalry and the English Gentleman.*

Glover, R. (1963). *Peninsular Preparation: the Reform of the British Army, 1795–1809.* Cambridge.

Godechot, J. (1972 trans.). *The Counter Revolution. Doctrine and Action, 1789–1804.*

Goodwin, A. (1979). *The Friends of Liberty: the English Democratic Movement in the Age of the French Revolution.* Cambridge, MA.

Gordon, B. (1976). *Political Economy in Parliament, 1819–23*.

Gosden, P.H.J.H. (1961). *Friendly Societies in England, 1815–75*. Manchester.

Gosden, P.H.J.H. (1973). *Self Help*.

Gough, H. and Dickson, D. (eds) (1990). *Ireland and the French Revolution*. Dublin.

Gray, D. (1963). *Spencer Perceval: the Evangelical Prime Minister, 1762–1812*. Manchester.

Green, D. (1985). *Great Cobbett*. Oxford.

Gunn, J.A.W. (1983). *Beyond Liberty and Property: the Process of Self-Recognition in Eighteenth Century Political Thought*. Montreal and Kingston.

Haakonson, K. (ed.) (1996). *Enlightenment and Religion: Rational Dissent in Eighteenth Century Britain*. Cambridge.

Habermas, J. (1989). *The Structural Transformation of the Public Sphere: an Inquiry into a Category of Bourgeois Society*. Cambridge, MA.

Halevy, E. (1949). *The History of the English People in the Nineteenth Century*. 2nd revised edn.

Halevy, E. (1972) [1928]. *The Growth of Philosophic Radicalism*.

Hall, C. and Davidoff, L. (1987). *Family Fortunes: Men and Women of the English Middle Class, 1780–1850*.

Hall, C.D. (1992). *British Strategy in the Napoleonic Wars, 1803–15*. Manchester.

Hammond, J.B. and Hammond L. (1911). *The Village Labourer*.

Hammond, J.B. and Hammond L. (1912). *The Skilled Labourer*.

Hammond, J.B. and Hammond L. (1917). *The Town Labourer*.

Hampsher-Monk, I. (1978). 'Civic humanism and parliamentary reform: the case of the Society of the Friends of the People'. *Journal of British Studies* 18: 70–89.

Hampsher-Monk, I. (1991). 'John Thelwall and the eighteenth-century radical response to political economy'. *Historical Journal* 34: 1–20.

Hancock, D. (1994). ' "Domestic bubbling": eighteenth century London merchants and individual investment in the Funds'. *Economic History Review* 67: 679–702.

Hancock, D. (1995). *Citizens of the World: London Merchants and the Integration of the British Atlantic Community, 1735–1785*. Cambridge.

Hargreaves, E.L. (1930). *The National Debt*.

Harling, P. (1996a). 'Leigh Hunt's *Examiner* and the language of patriotism'. *English Historical Review* 111: 1159–1181.

Harling, P. (1996b). *The Waning of Old Corruption: The Politics of Economical Reform in Britain, 1779–1846*. Oxford.

Harling, P. (1996c). 'The Duke of York Affair (1809) and the complexities of wartime patriotism'. *Historical Journal* 39: 963–84.

Harlow, V.T. (1940). 'The new imperial system, 1783–1815', in J. Holland Rose *et al.* (eds), *The Cambridge History of the British Empire*, ii, 129–87.

Harlow, V.T. (1952). *The Founding of the Second British Empire, 1763–93*. 2 vols.

Harrison, M. (1988). *Crowds and History: Mass Phenomena in English Towns, 1790–1850*. Cambridge.

Harvey, A.D. (1972). 'The Ministry of All the Talents: the Whigs in office. February 1806 to March 1807'. *Historical Journal* 15: 619–48.

Harvey, A.D. (1978a). *Britain in the Early Nineteenth Century*.

Harvey, A.D. (1978b). 'European attitudes towards Britain during the French Revolutionary and Napoleonic Era'. *History* 63: 356–65.

Harvey, A.D. (1992). *Collision of Empires: Britain in Three World Wars, 1793–1945.*

Hay, D. (1975). 'Property, authority and the criminal law', in Hay *et al.*, *Albion's Fatal Tree: Crime and Society in Eighteenth Century England.* New York.

Hay, D. (1982). 'War, dearth and theft in the eighteenth century'. *Past and Present* 95: 117–60.

Hayter, T. (1978). *The Army and the Crowd in Mid-Georgian England.*

Heal, F. and Holmes. C. (1994). *The Gentry in England and Wales, 1500–1700.*

Heavner, E.K. (1996). 'Malthus and the secularisation of political ideology'. *History of Political Thought* 17: 408–30.

Helleiner, K.F. (1965). *The Imperial Loans. A Study in Financial and Diplomatic History.* Oxford.

Hellmuth, E. (ed.) (1990). *The Transformation of Political Culture: England and Germany in the Late Eighteenth-Century.* Oxford.

Hempton, D. (1980). 'Evangelicals and eschatology'. *Journal of Ecclesiastical History* 31: 179–84.

Hempton, D. (1984). *Methodism and Politics in British Society, 1750–1850.*

Hempton, D. (1996). *The Religion of the People: Methodism and Popular Religion, c.1750–1900.*

Henderson, W.O. (1987–8). 'The Anglo-French commercial treaty of 1786'. *Economic History Review* 10: 104–12.

Henderson, W.O. (1990). 'The exchange of products of the soil and industrial goods in the Anglo-French commercial treaty of 1786'. *Journal of European Economic History* 19: 377–41.

Henriques, U.R.Q. (1961). *Religious Toleration in England, 1787–1833.*

Henriques, U.R.Q. (1979). *Before the Welfare State: Social Administration in Early Industrial Britain.*

Hill, B. (1989). *Women, Work and Sexual Politics in Eighteenth Century Britain.* Oxford.

Hilton, B. (1977). *Cash, Corn and Commerce: The Economic Policies of the Tory Governments, 1815–30.* Oxford.

Hilton, B. (1988). *The Age of Atonement: The Influence of Evangelicalism upon Social and Economic Thought.* Oxford.

Hobsbawm, E. (1964). *Labouring Men: Studies in the History of Labour.*

Hole, R. (1983). 'British counter-revolutionary propaganda in the 1790s', in C. Jones (ed.), 59–63.

Hole, R. (1989). *Pulpits, Politics and Public Order in England, 1760–1832.* Cambridge.

Hole, R. (1991). 'English sermons and tracts as media of debate on the French Revolution, 1789–1799', in Philp (ed.), 18–37.

Holmes, G. (1981). 'The growth of political stability in England', in Cannon (ed.), 1–22.

Holmes, G. (1986). *Politics, Religion and Society in England, 1679–1742.*

Hone, J.A. (1974). 'William Hone, publisher and bookseller: an approach to early nineteenth century London radicalism'. *Historical Studies* 16: 55–70.

Hone, J.A. (1982). *For the Cause of Truth: Radicalism in London, 1796–1821.* Oxford.

Hont, I. and Ignatieff, M. (eds) (1983). *Wealth and Virtue: the Shaping of Political Economy in the Scottish Enlightenment.* Cambridge.

233

Horn, P. (1980a). *The Rural World, 1780–1850: Social Change in the English Countryside*.

Horn, P. (1980b). *History of the French Invasion of Fishguard in 1797*. Fishguard.

Horne, T. (1991). *Property Rights and Poverty: Political Argument in Britain, 1605–1834*. Chapel Hill, NC.

Hope-Jones, A. (1939). *Income Tax in the Napoleonic Wars*. Cambridge.

Howell, D.W. (1986). *Patriarchs and Parasites: the Gentry of South West Wales in the Eighteenth Century*. Cardiff.

Hudson, P. (1986). *The Genesis of Industrial Capital: a Study of the West Riding Wool Textile Industry, c.1750–1850*. Cambridge.

Hudson, P. (ed.) (1989). *Regions and Industries: a Perspective on the Industrial Revolution in Britain*. Cambridge.

Hudson, P. (1992). *The Industrial Revolution*.

Hueckel, G. (1973). 'War and the British economy, 1793–1815: a general equilibrium analysis'. *Explorations in Economic History* 10: 365–96.

Hueckel, G. (1976). 'English farming profits during the Napoleonic wars'. *Explorations in Economic History* 13: 331–45.

Hueckel, G. (1986). 'Relative prices and supply response in English agriculture during the Napoleonic wars'. *Economic History Review* 29: 401–14.

Humphries, J. (1990). 'Enclosures, common rights and women: the proletarianization of families in the late eighteenth and early nineteenth centuries'. *Journal of Economic History* 50: 17–42.

Hunt, M. (1995). *The Middling Sort: Commerce, Gender and the Family in England 1660–1750*. Berkeley, CA.

Hutt, M. (1962). 'Spies in France, 1793–1808'. *History Today* 12: 158–67.

Hutt, M. (1983). *Chaouannerie and Counter-Revolution: Puisaye, the Princes and the British Government in the 1790s*. 2 vols, Cambridge.

Hutt, M. (1986). 'The 1790s and the myth of "Perfidious Albion"'. *Franco-British Studies* 2: 3–15.

Hyde, C.K. (1977). *Technological Change and the British Iron Industry, 1700–1870*. Princeton, NJ.

Ingram, E. (1981). *Commitment to Empire: Prophecies of the Great Game in Asia*. Oxford.

Innes, J. (1990). 'Politics and morals: the reformation of manners movement in later eighteenth century England', in Hellmuth (ed.), 57–118.

Jackson, M.V. (1989). *Engines of Instruction, Mischief and Magic: Children's Literature from Its Beginnings to 1939*. Aldershot.

Jackson, R.J. (1985). 'Growth and deceleration in English agriculture, 1660–1790'. *Economic History Review* 38: 333–51.

Jacob, M. (1991). *Living the Enlightenment: Freemasonry and Politics in Eighteenth Century Europe*. Oxford.

James, P. (1979). *Population Malthus. His Life and Times*.

Jenkins, P. (1983). *The Making of a Ruling Class: the Glamorgan Gentry, 1640–1790*. Cambridge.

Jewson, C.B. (1975). *The Jacobin City: a Portrait of Norwich in its Response to the French Revolution, 1788–1802*.

John, A.H. (1950). *The Industrial Development of South Wales*. Cardiff.

John, A.H. (1967). 'Farming in wartime, 1793–1815', in E.L. Jones and G. Mingay (eds), 22–46.

John, A.V. (1980). *By the Sweat of Their Brow: Women Workers at Victorian Coal Mines.*

Johnson, D. (1974). *Regency Revolution: the Case of Arthur Thistlewood.* Salisbury.

Johnson, P. and Nicholas, S. (1997). 'Health and welfare of women in the United Kingdom, 1785–1920', in Floud and Steckel (eds), 201–49.

Jones, C. (ed.) (1983). *Britain and Revolutionary France: Conflict, Subversion and Propaganda.* Exeter.

Jones, C.B. (1993). *Radical Sensibility: Literature and Ideas in the 1790s.*

Jones, D.J.V. (1974). *Before Rebecca: Popular Protests in Wales, 1793–1835.*

Jones, E.L. (1967). 'Industrial capital and landed investment: the Arkwrights in Hertfordshire, 1809–43', in Jones and Mingay (eds), *Land, Labour and Population in the Industrial Revolution: Essays Presented to J.D. Chambers*, 48–71.

Jones, M.G. (1952). *Hannah More.* Cambridge.

Jones, P.M. (1999). 'Living the Enlightenment and the French Revolution: James Watt, Matthew Boulton and their sons'. *Historical Journal* 42: 157–82.

Jordan, G. and Rogers, N. (1989). 'Admirals as heroes: patriotism and liberty in Hanoverian England'. *Journal of British Studies* 28: 201–24.

Joyce, P. (ed.) (1987). *Historical Meanings of Work.* Cambridge.

Jupp, P. (1985). *Lord Grenville, 1759–1834.* Oxford.

Kaufman, W.W. (1951). *British Policy and the Independence of Latin America, 1804–28.* New Haven, CT.

Kelly, G. (1976). *The English Jacobin Novel, 1780–1850.* Oxford.

Kelly, G. (1992). *Revolutionary Feminism: the Mind and Career of Mary Wollstonecraft.*

Kelly, J. (1992). *Prelude to Union: Anglo-Irish Politics in the 1780s.* Cork.

Kelly, P. (1982). 'Strategy and counter-revolution: the journal of Sir Gilbert Elliot, 1–21 September 1793'. *English Historical Review* 98: 328–48.

Kinross, J. (1974). *Fishguard Fiasco: an Account of the Last Invasion of Britain.*

Klein, L. (1993). 'Gender, conversation and the public spheres', in J. Still and M. Worton (eds), *Textuality and Sexuality.* 100–15.

Knick Harley, C. (1993). 'Reassessing the Industrial Revolution: a macro view', in Mokyr (ed.), 171–226.

Knox, T.M. (1977). 'Thomas Spence: the trumpet of jubilee'. *Past and Present* 76: 75–98.

Koditschek, T. (1990). *Class Formation and Urban Industrial Society: Bradford, 1750–1850.* Cambridge.

Komlos, J. (1993). 'The secular trend in the biological standard of living in the United Kingdom, 1730–1860'. *Economic History Review* 46: 115–44.

Kowalski Wallace, B. (1996). *Consuming Subjects: Women, Shopping and Business in the Eighteenth Century.* New York.

Kramnick, I. (1970). 'Scepticism in English political thought: from Temple to Burke'. *Studies in Burke and His Time* 1: 1627–60.

Kramnick, I. (1977). *The Rage of Edmund Burke: Portrait of an Ambivalent Conservative.* New York.

Kramnick, I. (1982). 'Republican Revisionism revisited'. *American Historical Review* 87: 629–64.

Kussmaul, A. (1981). *Servants in Husbandry in Early Modern England*. Cambridge.

Lacy, M.J. de (1971). *The Cloth Industry in the West of England from 1640 to 1880*. Oxford.

Landau, N. (1990). 'The regulation of immigration: economic structures and definitions of the poor in eighteenth century England'. *Historical Journal* 33: 541–72.

Landau, N. (1991). 'The eighteenth century context of the Laws of Settlement'. *Continuity and Change* 6: 417–39.

Landes, D. (1994). 'The fable of the dead horse; or, the Industrial Revolution revisited', in Mokyr (ed.), 132–70.

Langford, P. (1980). 'Old Whigs, Old Tories and the American Revolution'. *Journal of Imperial and Commonwealth History* 8: 106–30.

Langford, P. (1988). 'Property and "virtual representation" in eighteenth century England'. *Historical Journal* 31: 83–115.

Langford, P. (1991). *Public Life and the Propertied Englishman, 1688–1798*. Oxford.

Langton, J. and Morris, R.J. (eds) (1986). *Atlas of Industrializing Britain, 1780–1914*.

Laprade, W.T. (1909). *England and the French Revolution, 1789–1798*. Baltimore, Md.

Laqueur, T. (1974). 'The Queen Caroline affair: politics as art in the reign of George III'. *Journal of Modern History* 54: 417–66.

Laqueur, T. (1976). *Religion and Respectability: Sunday Schools and Working Class Culture, 1780–1850*. New Haven.

Laqueur, T. (1990). *Making Sex: Mind and the Body from the Greeks to Freud*. Cambridge, MA.

Lawson, P. (1993). *The East India Company: a History*.

Liddell Hart, J. (1932). *The British Way in Warfare*.

Lindert, P.H. and Williamson, J.G. (1983). 'English workers' living standards during the Industrial Revolution: a new look'. *Economic History Review* 36: 1–25.

Lindert, P.H. (1994). 'Unequal living standards', in Floud and McCloskey (eds), i, 357–86.

Linebaugh, P. (1993). 'A little jubilee? the literacy of Robert Wedderburn in 1817', in Rule and Malcolmson (eds), 174–220.

Lobban, M. (1990). 'From seditious libel to unlawful assembly: Peterloo and the changing face of political crime, c.1770–1820'. *Oxford Journal of Legal Studies* 10: 307–52.

Logue, K. (1979). *Popular Disturbances in Scotland, 1789–1815*. Edinburgh.

Lord, R.H. (1915). *The Second Partition of Poland*. Cambridge, MA.

Lovegrove, D. (1983). 'English evangelical dissent and the European conflict, 1789–1815'. *Studies in Church History* 20: 263–76.

Lovegrove, D. (1988). *Established Church, Sectarian People: Itinerancy and the Transformation of English Dissent, 1780–1830*. Cambridge.

Lucas, C. (ed.) (1991). *Rewriting the French Revolution*. Oxford.

Maccoby, S. (1955). *The English Radical Tradition, 1763–1914*.

Mackesy, P. (1957). *The War in the Mediterranean, 1803–1810*.

Mackesy, P. (1974). *Statesmen at War: the Strategy of Overthrow, 1798–1801*.

Mackesy, P. (1982). *War without Victory: the Downfall of Pitt*. Oxford.

Mackesy, P. (1989). 'Strategic problems of the British war effort', in Dickinson (ed.), 147–64.

Mackesy, P. (1995). *British Victory in Egypt 1801: The End of Napoleon's Conquest.*

Macpherson, C.B. (1980). *Burke.* Oxford.

Madariaga, I. (1981). *Russia in the Age of Catherine the Great.* New Haven, Ct.

Mainwaring, G.E. and Dobree, B. (1935). *The Floating Republic; an Account of the Mutinies at Spithead and the Nore in 1797.*

Mandler, P. (1990a). *Aristocratic Government in the Age of Reform: Whigs and Liberals, 1830–1852.* Oxford.

Mandler, P. (1990b). 'Tories and paupers: Christian political economy and the making of the new Poor Law'. *Historical Journal* 33: 81–104.

Marshall, D. (1926). *The English Poor in the Eighteenth Century: a Study in Social and Economic History.*

Marshall, J.D. (1968). *The Old Poor Law, 1795–1834.*

Marshall, P. (1998). 'British North America, 1760–1815', in P.J. Marshall (ed.), 372–93.

Marshall, P.H. (1984). *William Godwin.* New Haven, CT.

Marshall, P.J. (1987). *Bengal: The British Bridgehead. Eastern India, 1740–1828.* Cambridge.

Marshall, P.J. (1993). 'British expansion in India in the eighteenth century: a historical revision', in P.J. Marshall (ed.), *Trade and Conquest: Studies on the Rise of British Dominance in India.* Aldershot, 28–43.

Marshall, P.J. (ed.) (1998). *The Oxford History of the British Empire: The Eighteenth Century.* Oxford.

Mason, H.T. and Doyle, W. (eds) (1989). *The Impact of the French Revolution on European Consciousness.* Gloucester.

Mather, F.C. (1992). *High Church Prophet: Bishop Samuel Horsley and the Caroline Tradition in the Later Georgian Church.* Oxford.

Mathias, P. and Postan, M.M. (eds) (1978). *The Cambridge Economic History of Europe. vii. The Industrial Economies: Capital, Labour and Enterprise.* Cambridge.

Matthias, P. and O'Brien, P.K. (1976). 'Taxation in Britain and France: a comparison of the social and economic incidence of taxation collected for the central governments'. *Journal of European Economic History* 5: 601–50.

McBride, I. (1993). 'William Drennan and the dissenting tradition', in Dickson, Keogh and Whelan (eds), 49–61.

McCahill, M. (1981). 'Peerage creations and the changing character of British nobility'. *English Historical Review* 96: 259–84.

McCahill, M. (1982). 'The House of Lords and the collapse of Henry Addington's administration'. *Parliamentary History* 6: 69–94.

McCalman, I. (1984). 'Unrespectable radicalism: infidels and pornography in early nineteenth century London'. *Past and Present* 104: 74–110.

McCalman, I. (1988). *Radical Underworld: Prophets, Revolutionaries and Pornographers in London, 1795–1840.* Oxford.

McDowell, R.B. (1940). 'The personnel of the Dublin Society of United Irishmen'. *Irish Historical Studies* 2: 12–53.

McDowell, R.B. (1979). *Ireland in the Age of Imperialism and Revolution, 1760–1801.* Oxford.

McDowell, R.B. (1986). 'The age of the United Irishmen: revolution and the union', in T.W. Moody and W.E. Vaughan (eds), *A New History of Ireland, iv. Eighteenth Century Ireland, 1691–1800.* Oxford, 339–73.

McFarland, E.W. (1994). *Ireland and Scotland in the Age of Revolution: Planting the Green Bough.* Edinburgh.

McKendrick, N., Brewer, J. and Plumb, J. (1980). *The Birth of a Consumer Society: the Commercialization of Eighteenth-Century England.* Bloomington, IN.

McKenzie, L.A. (1986). 'The French Revolution and English parliamentary reform: James Mackintosh and the *Vindiciae Gallicae'. Eighteenth Century Studies* 16: 264–82.

Medd, P. (1968). *Romilly: a Life of Sir Samuel Romilly, Lawyer and Reformer.*

Mee, J. (1992). *Dangerous Enthusiasm: William Blake and the Culture of Radicalism in the 1790s.* Oxford.

Meikle, H. (1912). *Scotland and the French Revolution.*

Miles, D. (1987). *Francis Place: the Life of a Remarkable Radical.* Sussex.

Miles, M. (1986). 'A haven for the privileged: recruitment into the profession of attorney in England, 1709–1792'. *Social History* 11: 197–210.

Miller, N.C. (1968). 'John Cartwright and radical parliamentary reform 1809–1819'. *English Historical Review* 83: 705–28.

Minchinton, W.E. (1953). 'Agricultural returns and the government during the Napoleonic Wars', *Agricultural History Review* 1: 29–43.

Mingay, G.E. (1963). *English Landed Society in the Eighteenth Century.*

Mingay, G.E. (1976). *The Gentry: the Rise and Fall of a Ruling Class.*

Mingay, G.E. (ed.) (1989). *The Unquiet Countryside.*

Mitch, D. (1993). 'The role of human capital in the first Industrial Revolution', in Mokyr (ed.), 267–307.

Mitchell, A. (1961). 'The Association Movement of 1792–1793'. *Historical Journal* 4: 56–77.

Mitchell, A. (1967). *The Whigs in Opposition, 1815–1830.* Oxford.

Mitchell, H. (1965). *The Underground War against Revolutionary France: the Missions of William Wickham, 1794–1800.* Oxford.

Mitchell, L.G. (1971). *Charles James Fox and the Disintegration of the Whig Party, 1782–1794.* Oxford.

Mitchell, L.G. (1980). *Holland House.*

Mitchell, L.G. (1992). *Charles James Fox.* Oxford.

Mokyr, J. (1987). 'Has the Industrial Revolution been crowded out? Some reflections on Crafts and Williamson'. *Explorations in Economic History* 24: 293–319.

Mokyr, J. (1993). 'Editor's introduction: the New Economic History and the Industrial Revolution', in J. Mokyr (ed.), *The British Industrial Revolution: An Economic Perspective.* Boulder, CO, 1–115.

Mokyr, J. (1994). 'Technological change, 1700–1830', in Floud and McCloskey (eds), 12–43.

Mokyr, J. and Savin, N.E. (1976). 'Stagflation in historical perspective: the Napoleonic wars revisited'. *Research in Economic History* 1: 198–259.

Money, J. (1977). *Experience and Identity: Birmingham and the West Midlands, 1760–1800*. Montreal and Kingston.

Money, J. (1990). 'Freemasonry and the fabric of loyalism in Hanoverian England', in Hellmuth (ed.), 235–71.

Montluzin, E.L. (1988). *The Anti-Jacobins: the Early Contributors to the Anti-Jacobin Review*. Basingstoke.

Mori, J. (1996). 'Responses to revolution: the November crisis of 1792'. *Bulletin of the Institute of Historical Research* 69: 284–305.

Mori, J. (1997a). 'The British government and the Bourbon restoration: the occupation of Toulon, 1793'. *Historical Journal* 40: 699–720.

Mori, J. (1997b). *William Pitt and the French Revolution, 1785–1795*. Edinburgh.

Mori, J. (1998). 'The political theory of William Pitt, 1759–1806'. *History* 83: 234–48.

Morley, A. (1993). 'William Blake and the Great Eastcheap orthodoxy', in Rule and Malcolmson (eds), 139–73.

Morris, M. (1998). *The British Monarchy and the French Revolution*. New Haven, CT.

Morris, R.J. (1983). 'Voluntary societies and British urban elites, 1780–1850'. *Historical Journal* 26: 95–118.

Morris, R.J. (1990). 'Clubs, societies and associations', in F.M.L. Thompson (ed.), iii, 395–444.

Morrow, J. (1990). *Coleridge's Political Thought: Poverty, Morality and the Limits of Traditional Discourse*. Basingstoke.

Morton, R.G. (1967). 'The rise of the yeomanry', *Irish Sword* 8: 58–64.

Murley, J.T. (1959). 'The Origin and Outbreak of the Anglo-French War of 1793'. Unpublished Oxford D.Phil. dissertation.

Murphy, O.T. (1982). *Charles Gravier, Comte de Vergennes: French Diplomacy in the Age of Revolution, 1719–1787*. Albany, NY.

Murray, N. (1978). *The Scottish Handloom Weavers, 1790–1850. A Social History*. Edinburgh.

Murray, N.U. (1975). 'The Influence of the French Revolution on the Church of England and its Rivals, 1789–1802'. Unpublished Oxford D.Phil. dissertation.

Natrass, L. (1995). *William Cobbett and the Politics of Style*. Cambridge.

Neal, L. (1990). *The Rise of Financial Capitalism: International Capital Markets in the Age of Reason*. Cambridge.

Neal, L. (1991). 'A tale of two revolutions: international capital flows, 1789–1819'. *Bulletin of Economic Research* 43: 57–92.

Neal, L. (1994). 'The finance of business during the industrial revolution', in Floud and McCloskey (eds), i, 151–81.

Neeson, J.M. (1993). *Commoners, Common Right, Enclosure and Social Change in England 1700–1820*. Cambridge.

Nelson, R.R. (1969). *The Home Office, 1782–1801*. Durham, NC.

Neuman, M. (1982). *The Speenhamland County: Poverty and the Poor Law in Berkshire, 1795–1834*. New York.

Newlyn, L. (1986). *Coleridge, Wordsworth and the Language of Allusion*. Oxford.

Newman, G. (1975). 'Anti-French propaganda and British liberal nationalism in the early nineteenth century: suggestions towards a general interpretation'. *Victorian Studies* 18: 385–418.

Newman, G. (1987). *The Rise of English Nationalism: a Cultural History, 1720–1830.* New York.

Nicholas, S. and Oxley, D. (1996). 'Living standards of women in England and Wales 1785–1815: new evidence from Newgate prison records'. *Economic History Review* 49: 591–9.

Nicholson, E. (1996). 'Consumers and spectators: the public of the political print in eighteenth century England'. *History* 81: 5–21.

Norris, J. (1963). *Shelburne and Reform.*

Norris, J.M. (1955). 'The policy of the British Cabinet in the Nootka Crisis'. *English Historical Review* 70: 562–80.

Obelkevitch, J. (1976). *Religion and Rural Society: South Lindsay, 1825–75.* Oxford.

Obelkevitch, J. (1990). 'Religion', in F.M.L. Thompson (ed.), iii, 311–56.

O'Brien, P.K. (1988). 'The political economy of British taxation, 1660–1815'. *Economic History Review* 41: 1–32.

O'Brien, P.K. (1989a). 'Public finance in the wars with France 1793–1815', in Dickinson (ed.), 165–88.

O'Brien, P.K. (1989b). 'The impact of the revolutionary and Napoleonic wars upon the long term growth of the British economy'. *Review of the Fernand Braudel Centre* 12: 335–83.

O'Brien, P.K. (1994). 'Mercantilism and overseas trade, 1700–1800', in Floud and McCloskey (eds), i, 205–41.

O'Brien, P.K. (1996). 'Path dependency: of why Britain became an industrialised and urbanised nation long before France'. *Economic History Review* 49: 213–49.

O'Brien, P.K. and Quinault, R. (eds) (1993). *The Industrial Revolution and British Society.* Cambridge.

O'Gorman, F. (1967). *The Whig Party and the French Revolution.*

O'Gorman, F. (1973). *Edmund Burke: His Political Philosophy.*

O'Gorman, F. (1982). *The Emergence of the British Two Party System, 1760–1832.*

O'Gorman, F. (1989a). 'Pitt and the "Tory" reaction to the French Revolution 1789–1815', in Dickinson (ed.), 21–38.

O'Gorman, F. (1989b). *Voters, Patrons and Parties: the Unreformed Electorate of Hanoverian England, 1734–1783.* Oxford.

O'Gorman, F. (1998). *The Long Eighteenth Century. British Political and Social History, 1688–1832.*

Oldfield, J.R. (1995). *Popular Politics and British Anti-Slavery: the Mobilization of Public Opinion against the Slave Trade, 1787–1807.* Manchester.

Oliver, W.H. (1978). *Prophets and Millenialists.* Oxford.

Overton, M. (1996). *Agricultural Revolution in England: the Transformation of the Agrarian Economy, 1500–1850.* Cambridge.

Pakenham, T. (1969). *The Year of Liberty: the History of the Great Irish Rebellion of 1798.*

Palmer, R.R. (1959). *The Age of the Democratic Revolution: a Political History of Europe and America, 1760–1800.* Princeton, NJ.

Palmer, R.R. (1971). *The World of the French Revolution.* New York.

Palmer, S.H. (1988). *Police and Protest in England and Ireland, 1780–1850.* Cambridge.

Parkinson, C.N. (ed.) (1948). *The Trade Winds: a Study of British Overseas Trade during the French Wars, 1793–1815*.

Parkinson, C.N. (1954). *War in the Eastern Seas, 1793–1815*.

Parsinnen, T.M. (1972). 'The Revolutionary Party in London, 1816–1820'. *Bulletin of the Institute of Historical Research* 48: 266–82.

Parsinnen, T.M. (1973a). 'Association, convention and anti-parliament in British radical politics, 1771–1848'. *English Historical Review* 83: 504–33.

Parsinnen, T.M. (1973b). 'Thomas Spence on the origins of English land nationalisation'. *Journal of the History of Ideas* 34: 135–41.

Pedersen, S. (1986). 'Hannah More meets Simple Simon: tracts, chapbooks and popular culture in late eighteenth-century England'. *Journal of British Studies* 25: 84–113.

Pendleton, G.T. (1976). 'English conservative propaganda during the French Revolution, 1789–1802'. Unpublished Emory University PhD dissertation.

Perkin, H. (1969). *The Origins of Modern English Society*.

Peters, M. (1993–4). 'The myth of William Pitt, Earl of Chatham, great imperialist'. *Journal of Imperial and Commonwealth History* 21–2: 31–74, 393–431.

Peters, M. (1998). *The Elder Pitt*. Harlow.

Philp, M. (1986). *Godwin's Political Justice*. Ithaca, NY.

Philp, M. (1991). 'The fragmented ideology of reform', in M. Philp (ed.), *The French Revolution and British Popular Politics*. Cambridge, 50–76.

Philp, M. (1995a). 'Thompson, Godwin and the French Revolution'. *History Workshop Journal* 39: 39–101.

Philp, M. (1995b). 'Vulgar conservatism, 1792–3'. *English Historical Review* 110: 42–69.

Philpin, C.H.E. (ed.) (1987). *Nationalism and Popular Protest in Ireland*. Cambridge.

Platt, D.C.M. (1972). *Latin America and British Trade, 1806–1914*.

Pocock, J.G.A. (1960). 'Burke and the ancient constitution – a problem in the history of ideas'. *Historical Journal* 3: 125–43.

Pocock, J.G.A. (1971). *Politics, Language and Time: Essays on Political Thought and History*.

Pocock, J.G.A. (1975). *The Machiavellian Moment: Florentine Political Thought and the Atlantic Republican Tradition*. Princeton, NJ.

Pocock, J.G.A. (1982). 'The political economy of Burke's analysis of the French Revolution'. *Historical Journal* 25: 331–49.

Pocock, J.G.A. (1985). *Virtue, Commerce and History: Essays on Political Thought and History, Chiefly in the Eighteenth Century*. Cambridge.

Pocock, J.G.A. (1989). 'Edmund Burke and the redefinition of enthusiasm: the context as counter-revolution', in Furet and Ozouf (eds), 19–43.

Pollard, S. (1978). 'Labour in Great Britain', in Mathias and Postan (eds), vii, 97–179.

Porter, R. and Teich, M. (eds) (1981). *The Enlightenment in National Context*. Cambridge.

Porter, R. and Teich, M. (eds) (1988). *Romanticism in National Context*. Cambridge.

Porter, R. (1990). 'Science, provincial culture and public opinion in Enlightenment England', in P. Borsay (ed.), *The Eighteenth Century Town: a Reader in English Urban History*, 243–67.

Poynter, J.R. (1969). *Society and Pauperism: English Ideas on Poor Relief, 1795–1834*.

Pressnell, L.M. (1956). *County Banking in the Industrial Revolution*. Oxford.

Price, R. (1961). 'Eighteenth-century price riots and public policy in England'. *International Review of Social History* 6: 277–92.

Prochaska, F.K. (1973). 'English state trials in the 1790s: a case study'. *Journal of British Studies* 13: 63–72.

Prothero, I. (1979). *Artisans and Politics in Early Nineteenth Century London: John Gast and His Times*. Folkestone.

Pullen, J.M. (1981). 'Malthus's theological ideas and their influence on his principle of population'. *History of Political Economy* 13: 39–54.

Radcliffe, E. (1993). 'Revolutionary writing, moral philosophy and universal benevolence in the eighteenth century'. *Journal of the History of Ideas* 54: 221–40.

Randall, A. (1991). *Before the Luddites: Custom, Community and Machinery in the English Woollen Industry, 1776–1809*. Cambridge.

Randall, J. (1985). *The Origins of Modern Feminism*.

Rapp, D. (1974). 'Social mobility in the eighteenth century: the Whitbreads of Bedfordshire, 1720–1815'. *Economic History Review* 27: 380–411.

Rapp, D. (1982). 'The left wing Whigs: Whitbread, the Mountain and Reform, 1809–1815'. *Journal of British Studies* 21: 34–66.

Rattenbury, A. (1981). 'Methodism and the Tatterdamilions', in E. and S. Yeo (eds), *Popular Culture and Class Conflict, 1590–1914: Explorations in the History of Labour and Leisure*. Brighton, 28–61.

Ray, R.K. (1998). 'Indian society and the establishment of British supremacy, 1765–1818', in P.J. Marshall (ed.), 508–29.

Raybould, T.J. (1973). *The Economic Emergence of the Black Country: A Study of the Dudley Estate*.

Riden, P. (1977). 'The output of the British iron industry before 1870'. *Economic History Review* 30: 442–59.

Rigby, B. (1989a). 'The French Revolution and English literary radicals: the case of the *Analytical Review*', in Mason and Doyle (eds), 91–103.

Rigby, B. (1989b). 'Radical spectators of the Revolution: the case of the *Analytical Review*', in Crossley and Small (eds), 63–83.

Roach, E.E. (1983). 'Anglo-Russian relations from Austerlitz to Tilsit'. *International History Review* 5: 181–200.

Robbins, C. (1959). *The Eighteenth Century Commonwealthman: Studies in the Transmission, Development and Circumstances of English Liberal Thought from the Restoration of Charles II to the War with the Thirteen Colonies*. Cambridge, MA.

Roberts, M. (1939). *The Whig Party, 1807–1812*.

Roberts, M.J.D. (1983). 'The Society for the Suppression of Vice and its early critics, 1802–1812'. *Historical Journal* 26: 160–74.

Robertson, J. (1983a). 'The Scottish Enlightenment at the limits of the civic tradition', in Hont and Ignatieff (eds), 137–78.

Robertson, J. (1983b). 'Scottish political economy beyond the civic tradition: government and economic development in the *Wealth of Nations*'. *History of Political Thought* 4: 451–82.

Robertson-Scott, I. (1989). '"Things As They Are": the literary response to the French Revolution 1789–1815', in Dickinson (ed.), 229–50.

Rodger, A.B. (1964). *The War of the Second Coalition, 1798–1801*. Oxford.

Rodger, N.A.M. (1986). *The Wooden World: an Anatomy of the Georgian Navy*.

Roe, N.M. (1988). *Wordsworth and Coleridge: the Radical Years*. Oxford.

Roebuck, P. (1981). *Yorkshire Baronets, 1640–1760*.

Rogers, N. (1979). 'Money, land and lineage: the big bourgeoisie of Hanoverian London'. *Social History* 4: 437–54.

Rogers, N. and Hay, D. (1997). *Eighteenth-Century English Society: Shuttles and Swords*. Oxford.

Rose, J.B. (1960). 'The Priestley riots of 1791'. *Past and Present* 18: 68–88.

Rose, J.H. (1904a). 'Pitt's plans for the settlement of Europe', in J.H. Rose (ed.), *Napoleonic Studies*. 41–84.

Rose, J.H. (1911). *William Pitt and the Great War*.

Rose, J.H. (1919). 'The struggle with revolutionary France, 1792–1802', in Ward and Gooch (eds), i, 216–308.

Rosen, F. (1992). *Bentham, Byron and Greece. Constitutionalism, Nationalism and Early Liberal Political Thought*. Oxford.

Rostow, R.R. (1960). *The Stages of Economic Growth*. Cambridge.

Royle, E. and Walvin, J. (1982). *English Radicals and Reformers, 1760–1848*. Brighton.

Rubinstein, W.D. (1983). 'The end of "Old Corruption" in Britain, 1780–1860'. *Past and Present* 101: 55–86.

Rude, G. (1964). *The Crowd in History: a Study of Popular Disturbances in France and England, 1730–1848*. New York.

Rule, J.G. (1981). *The Experience of Labour in Eighteenth Century Industry*.

Rule, J.G. (1986). *The Labouring Classes in Early Industrial England, 1750–1850*. Harlow.

Rule, J.G. (1988). *British Trade Unionism, 1750–1850: the Formative Years*.

Rule, J.G. (1992a). *Albion's People: English Society, 1714–1815*. Harlow.

Rule, J.G. (1992b). *The Vital Century: England's Developing Economy, 1714–1815*. Harlow.

Rule, J.G. (1993). 'Trade unions, the government and the French Revolution, 1789–1801', in J.G. Rule and R. Malcolmson (eds), *Protest and Survival: the Historical Experience: Essays for E.P. Thompson*, 112–38.

Rupp, G. (1986). *Religion in England, 1688–1791*. Oxford.

Russell, G. (1995). *The Theatres of War: Performance, Politics and Society, 1793–1815*. Oxford.

Sabel, C. and Zeitlin, J. (1985). 'Historical alternatives to mass production: possibilities, markets and technology in nineteenth century industrialisation'. *Past and Present* 108: 133–76.

Sack, J.J. (1979). *The Grenvillites, 1801–29: Party Politics and Factionalism in the Age of Pitt and Liverpool*. Chicago.

Sack, J.J. (1980). 'The House of Lords and parliamentary patronage in Great Britain, 1802–1832'. *Historical Journal* 23: 913–37.

Sack, J.J. (1987). 'The memory of Burke and the memory of Pitt: English conservatism confronts its past'. *Historical Journal* 30: 623–40.

Sack, J.J. (1993). *From Jacobite to Conservative: Reaction and Orthodoxy in Britain, 1760–1832*. Cambridge.

Schama, S. (1977). *Patriots and Liberators: Revolution in the Netherlands, 1780–1813*.

Schenk, H.G. (1966). *The Mind of the European Romantics: an Essay in Cultural History*.

Schofield, P. (1986). 'English conservative thought in response to the French Revolution'. *Historical Journal* 29: 601–22.

Schofield, P. (1992). 'British politicians and French arms: the ideological war of 1793–1795'. *History* 72: 183–201.

Schofield, R.S. (1994). 'British population change, 1700–1831', in Floud and McCloskey (eds), i, 60–95.

Scholliers, P. (ed.) (1989). *Real Wages in Nineteenth and Twentieth Century Europe*. New York.

Schroeder, P. (1987). 'The collapse of the Second Coalition'. *Journal of Modern History* 59: 244–90.

Schroeder, P. (1992). 'Did the Vienna Settlement rest on a balance of power?'. *American Historical Review* 97: 683–706, 733–5.

Schroeder, P. (1994). *The Transformation of European Politics, 1763–1848*. Oxford.

Schwartz, L.D. (1990). 'Trends in real wages: an answer to Botham and Hunt'. *Economic History Review* 43: 90–8.

Seed, J. (1990). 'Gentlemen dissenters: the social and political meanings of rational dissent in the 1770s and 1780s'. *Historical Journal* 23: 299–325.

Seed, J. (1992). 'From "middling sort" to middle class in late eighteenth and early nineteenth century Britain', in M.L. Bush (ed.), *Social Orders and Social Classes in Europe since 1500*, 114–35.

Semmel, B. (1973). *The Methodist Revolution*.

Senior, H. (1966). *Orangism in Ireland and Britain*. Dublin.

Shammas, C. (1990). *The Pre-Industrial Consumer in England and America*. Oxford.

Sherwig, J.M. (1962). 'Lord Grenville's plan for a Concert of Europe, 1797–99'. *Journal of Modern History* 34: 284–93.

Sherwig, J.M. (1969). *Guineas and Gunpowder. British Foreign Aid in the Wars with France, 1793–1815.* Cambridge, MA.

Shoemaker, R.B. (1998). *Gender in English Society, 1650–1850*. Harlow.

Siberling, N.J. (1919). 'British financial expertise, 1790–1830'. *Review of Economics and Statistics* 1: 282–97.

Siberling, N.J. (1923–4). 'Financial and monetary policy of Great Britain during the Napoleonic Wars'. *Quarterly Journal of Economics* 38: 214–33, 397–439.

Sked, A. (1979). *Europe's Balance of Power, 1815–1848*.

Slack, P. (1990). *The English Poor Law 1531–1782*.

Smail, J. (1993). *The Origins of Middle Class Culture: Halifax, Yorkshire, 1660–1780*. Ithaca, NY.

Smith, E.A. (1975). *Whig Principles and Party Politics, Earl Fitzwilliam and the Whig Party, 1748–1833*. Manchester.

Smith, E.A. (1992). *Lord Grey, 1764–1845*. Oxford.

Smith, O. (1984). *The Politics of Language, 1791–1819*. Oxford.

Smyth, J. (1990). 'Popular politicisation, Defenderism and the Catholic Question', in Gough and Dickson (eds), 109–16.

Snell, K.D.M. (1985). *Annals of the Labouring Poor: Social Change and Agrarian England 1600–1900*. Cambridge.

Soloway, R.A. (1969). *Prelates and People; Ecclesiastical Social Thought in England, 1783–1852*.

Sparrow, E. (1990). 'The Alien Office, 1792–1801'. *Historical Journal* 33: 361–84.

Sparrow, E. (1993). 'The Swiss and Swabian Agencies'. *Historical Journal* 35: 861–84.

Sparrow, E. (1998). 'Secret Service under Pitt's administrations, 1792–1806'. *History* 83: 280–94.

Spence, P. (1996). *The Birth of Romantic Radicalism: War, Popular Politics and English Radical Reformism, 1800–1815*. Aldershot.

Stafford, W.O. (1982). 'Religion and the doctrine of Nationalism in England at the time of the French Revolution and Napoleonic Wars'. *Studies in Church History* 18: 381–95.

Stafford, W.O. (1997). 'Narratives of women: English feminists of the 1790s'. *History* 82: 24–43.

Stanhope, G. and Gooch, G.P. (1914). *The Life of Charles, 3rd Earl Stanhope*.

Stanhope, J. (1962). *The Cato Street Conspiracy*.

Stanlis, P. (1958). *Edmund Burke and the Natural Law*.

Stern, W. (1964). 'The Bread Crisis in Britain, 1795–6'. *Economica* 31: 168–87.

Stevenson, J. (1971a). 'Disturbances and Public Order in London, 1790–1821'. Unpublished Oxford University D.Phil. thesis.

Stevenson, J. (1971b). 'The London Crimp Riots of 1794'. *International Review of Social History* 16: 140–58.

Stevenson, J. (1975). 'Food riots in England', in J. Stevenson and R. Quinault (eds), *Popular Protest and Public Order: Six Studies in British History, 1790–1820*, 33–74.

Stevenson, J. (1989). 'Popular radicalism and popular protest, 1789–1815', in Dickinson (ed.), 61–82.

Stevenson, J. (1992, 2nd ed.). *Popular Disturbances in England, 1700–1832*.

Stone, L. and Stone, J.F. (1984). *An Open Elite? England, 1540–1880*. Oxford.

Stone, L. and Stone, J.F. (1987). *The Past and the Present Revisited*.

Stone, L. (ed.) (1994). *An Imperial State at War: Britain from 1689 to 1815*.

Stuart-Jones, E.H. (1947). *The Last Invasion of Britain*. Cardiff.

Thale, M. (1989). 'London debating societies in the 1790s'. *Historical Journal* 32: 57–86.

Thomas, R.P. and McCloskey, D.N. (1981). 'Overseas trade and empire, 1700–1860', in Floud and McCloskey (eds), i, 87–102.

Thomis, M.I. (1970). *The Luddites: Machine Breaking in Regency England*.

Thomis, M.I. and Holt, P. (1977). *Threats of Revolution in Britain, 1789–1848*.

Thompson, E.P. (1968 edn.). *The Making of the English Working Class*. Harmondsworth.

Thompson, E.P. (1992). *Customs in Common*.

Thompson, F.M.L. (1966). 'The social distribution of landed property in England since the sixteenth century'. *Economic History Review* 19: 505–17.

Thompson, F.M.L. (ed.) (1990). *The Cambridge Social History of Britain, 1750–1950*. 3 vols, Cambridge.

Thompson, N. (1984). *The People's Science: the Popular Political Economy of Exploitation and Crisis, 1816–34*. Cambridge.

Thorn, R.G. (1986). *The House of Commons, 1790–1820*. 5 vols.

Trumbach, R. (1991). 'Sex, gender and sexual identity in modern culture: male sodomy and female prostitution in Enlightenment London'. *Journal of the History of Sexuality* 2: 186–203.

Turley, D. (1991). *The Culture of British Anti-Slavery, 1780–1860*.

Turner, K.S.H. (1993). 'The Politics of Narrative Singularity in British Travel Writing. 1750–1800'. Unpublished Oxford University D.Phil. thesis.

Turner, M. (1984). *Enclosure in Britain, 1750–1830*.

Turner, M. (ed.) (1986). *Malthus and His Times*. Basingstoke.

Turner, M.J. (1997). 'The limits of abolition: government, Saints and the "African Question", c.1780–1820'. *English Historical Review* 122: 319–57.

Urdank, A. (1990). *Religion and Society in a Cotswold Vale*. Berkeley. CA.

Valenze, D. (1978). 'Prophecy and popular literature in eighteenth-century England'. *Journal of Ecclesiastical History* 29: 75–92.

Veitch, G.S. (1913). *The Genesis of Parliamentary Reform*.

Vernon, J. (1993). *Politics and the People: a Study in English Political Culture, c.1815–1867*. Cambridge.

Vernon, J. (ed.) (1996). *Re-Reading the Constitution: New Narratives in the Political History of England's Long Nineteenth Century*. Cambridge.

Vickery, A. (1993a). 'Women and the world of goods: a Lancashire consumer and her possessions, 1751–81', in J. Brewer and R. Porter (eds), *Consumption and the World of Goods*, 274–301.

Vickery, A. (1993b). 'From golden age to separate spheres: the categories and chronology of English women's history'. *Historical Journal* 36: 194–209.

Ville, S.P. (1986). *English Shipowning during the Industrial Revolution: Michael Henley and Son. London Shipowners, 1770–1830*. Manchester.

Vincent, D. (1989). *Literacy and Popular Culture: England, 1750–1914*. Cambridge.

Vincent, E. (1993). '"The Real Grounds of the Present War": John Bowles and the French Revolutionary Wars 1792–1802'. *History* 78: 393–420.

Vincent, E. (1994). 'The responses of Scottish churchmen to the French Revolution, 1789–1802'. *Scottish Historical Review* 73: 191–215.

Vincent, E. (1998). *The War of Ideas: British Attitudes to the Wars against Revolutionary France, 1792–1802*. Aldershot.

Virgin, P. (1989). *The Church in an Age of Negligence: Ecclesiastical Structure and the Problem of Church Reform, 1700–1840*. Cambridge.

Von Tunzelman, G.N. (1978). *Steam Power and British Industrialisation to 1860*. Oxford.

Von Tunzelman, G.N. (1986). 'Coal and steam power', in J. Langton and R.J. Morris (eds), *An Atlas of Industrialising Britain, 1780–1914*.

Wahrman, D. (1992). 'Virtual representation: parliamentary reporting and languages of class in the 1790s'. *Past and Present* 136: 83–113.

Wahrman, D. (1995). *Imagining the Middle Class: the Political Representation of Class in Britain, c.1780–1840*. Cambridge.

246

Wahrman, D. (1996). 'Public opinion, violence and the limits of constitutional politics', in Vernon (ed.), 83–122.

Walsh, J.D. (1965). 'Methodism at the end of the eighteenth-century', in R. Davis and G. Rupp (eds), *A History of the Methodist Church in Great Britain*, i, 278–308.

Walsh, J.D. (1972). 'Methodism and the mob in the eighteenth century', in G.J. Cuming and D. Baker (eds), *Popular Belief and Practice: Papers Read at the Ninth Summer Meeting and the Tenth Winter Meeting of the Ecclesiastical History Society*. Cambridge, 213–27.

Walsh, J.M. (1995). *Edmund Burke and International Relations*. Basingstoke.

Walton, J.K. (1987). *Lancashire: A Social History, 1558–1939*. Manchester.

Walvin, J. (1986). *England, Slaves and Freedom*. Basingstoke.

Ward, A.W. and Gooch, G.P. (eds) (1919). *The Cambridge History of British Foreign Policy, 1783–1914*, i. Cambridge.

Ward, W.R. (1972). *Religion and Society in England, 1790–1850*.

Wardroper, J. (1973). *Kings, Lords and Wicked Libellers; Satire and Protest, 1760–1837*.

Waterman, A.M.C. (1991). *Revolution, Economics and Religion: Christian Political Economy, 1798–1833*. Cambridge.

Watson, G. (1976). 'The revolutionary youth of Wordsworth and Coleridge'. *Critical Quarterly* 18: 49–66.

Watts, M.R. (1978–95). *The Dissenters*. 2 vols, Oxford.

Webb, P.C.L. (1977). 'The rebuilding and repair of the Fleet 1783–1793'. *Bulletin of the Institute of Historical Research* 50: 194–209.

Webb, P.C.L. (1983). 'Seapower in the Ochakow affair of 1791'. *International History Review* 2: 13–33.

Webb, P.C.L. (1988). 'Construction, repair and maintenance in the battle fleet of the Royal Navy, 1793–1815', in Black and Woodfine (eds), 207–20.

Webb, S. and Webb, B. (1910). *English Poor Law Policy, 1689–1835*.

Webster, C.K. (1919). *The Congress of Vienna, 1814–1815*.

Webster, C.K. (1921). *British Diplomacy, 1813–1815. Select Documents Dealing with the Reconstruction of Europe*.

Webster, C.K. (1925). *The Foreign Policy of Castlereagh, 1815–1822*.

Webster, C.K. (1931). *The Foreign Policy of Castlereagh, 1812–1815. Britain and the Reconstruction of Europe*.

Wells, R. (1982). 'The militia mutinies of 1795', in J. Rule (ed.), *Outside the Law: Studies in Crime and Order, 1650–1850*. Exeter, 35–64.

Wells, R. (1983). *Insurrection: The British Experience, 1795–1803*. Gloucester.

Wells, R. (1988). *Wretched Faces. Famine in Wartime Britain, 1750–1801*. Gloucester.

Wells, R. (1991). 'English society and revolutionary politics in the 1790s: the case for insurrection', in Philp (ed.), 188–226.

Werkmeister, L. (1963). *The London Daily Press, 1772–1792*. Madison, WI.

Western, J.R. (1956). 'The Volunteer Movement as an anti-revolutionary force, 1793–1802'. *English Historical Review* 71: 603–14.

Western, J.R. (1965). *The English Militia in the Eighteenth Century*.

Wharam, A. (1992). *The Treason Trials, 1794*. Leicester.

Whelan, K. (1993). 'The United Irishmen, the Enlightenment and popular culture', in Dickson, Keogh and Whelan (eds), 269–96.

Whelan, K. (1996). *The Tree of Liberty: Radicalism, Catholicism and the Construction of Irish Identity, 1760–1830*. Cork.

Whetstone, A. (1981). *Scottish County Government in the Eighteenth and Nineteenth Centuries*. Edinburgh.

Wilkinson, D. (1997). ' "How did they pass the Union?": Secret Service expenditure in Ireland, 1799–1804'. *History* 82: 223–51.

Williams, G.A. (1969). *Artisans and Sans-Culottes: Popular Movements in England and France during the French Revolution*. New York.

Williamson, J.G. (1984). 'Why was British growth so slow during the industrial revolution?'. *Journal of Economic History* 44: 687–712.

Williamson, J.G. (1987). 'Debating the British Industrial Revolution'. *Explorations in Economic History* 24: 269–92.

Willis, R. (1972). 'Fox, Grenville and the recovery of the Opposition'. *Journal of British Studies* 11: 24–43.

Willis, R. (1977). 'William Pitt's resignation in 1801: re-examination and document'. *Journal of British Studies* 44: 239–77.

Wilson, R.G. (1971). *Gentlemen Merchants: the Merchant Community in Leeds, 1700–1830*. Manchester.

Winch, D. (1983a). 'Science and the legislator: Adam Smith and after'. *Economic Journal* 93: 501–20.

Winch, D. (1983b). 'The system of the North: Dugald Stewart and his pupils', in Collini, Burrow and Winch (eds), 23–61.

Winch, D. (1983c). 'Higher maxims: happiness versus wealth in Malthus and Ricardo', in Collini, Burrow and Winch (eds), 63–89.

Winch, D. (1992). 'Adam Smith: Scottish moral philosopher as political economist'. *Historical Journal* 35: 91–113.

Winch, D. (1996). *Riches and Poverty: an Intellectual History of Political Economy in Britain, 1750–1834*. Cambridge.

Wood, M. (1991). 'Thomas Spence and modes of subversion'. *Enlightenment and Dissent* 10: 51–77.

Wood, M. (1994). *Radical Satire and Print Culture, 1790–1822*. Oxford.

Worrall, D. (1992). *Radical Culture: Discourse, Resistance and Surveillance, 1790–1822*. Detroit.

Wright, J.F. (1997). 'The contribution of overseas savings to the funded national debt of Great Britain, 1750–1815'. *Economic History Review* 50: 657–74.

Wrigley, E.A. (1983). 'The growth of population in eighteenth century England: a conundrum resolved'. *Past and Present* 98: 121–58.

Wrigley, E.A. (1988). 'Malthus on the prospects for the labouring poor'. *Historical Journal* 31: 813–29.

Wrigley, E.A. and Schofield, R.S. (1989 edn.). *The Population History of England, 1541–1871*. Cambridge.

Yelling, J.A. (1977). *Common Fields and Enclosure in England, 1450–1850*.

Ziegler, P. (1965). *Addington: a Life of Henry Addington, First Viscount Sidmouth*.

INDEX

249